Holding Faith

Cynthia L. Rigby

Holding Faith

A Practical Introduction to Christian Doctrine

Abingdon Press
Nashville

HOLDING FAITH:
A PRACTICAL INTRODUCTION TO CHRISTIAN DOCTRINE

This book is printed on acid-free paper.

Library of Congress Cataloging-in-Publication Data has been requested.

978-1-4267-5814-0

Sources Frequently Cited

Karl Barth, *Church Dogmatics*, 13 vols. (Edinburgh: T&T Clark, 1975–2009).

John Calvin, *Institutes of the Christian Religion*, 2 vols., ed. John T. McNeill (Philadelphia: Westminster, 1960).

Glory to God (Louisville: Westminster John Knox Press, 2013).

18 19 20 21 22 23 24 25 26 27—10 9 8 7 6 5 4 3 2 1
MANUFACTURED IN THE UNITED STATES OF AMERICA

For my parents, Charles and Ethel Rigby,
who taught me faith would hold.

Let us hold fast to the confession of our hope without wavering, for the one who has promised is faithful.

—Hebrews 10:23 (NRSV)

Faith . . . is a new capacity, which, in whatever freedom we previously lived or thought we lived, we did not even remotely know.

—Karl Barth, *Church Dogmatics* IV/2, 244

Contents

Preface

Welcome to *Holding Faith: A Practical Introduction to Christian Doctrine.* My hope, as the author of this book, is to in some way companion with you on your faith journey. I'm imagining that you have this book in hand because you desire to know something more about the major *doctrines* (or teachings) of the Christian faith. I am betting you also want to explore the "so what?" of them—that is, why they matter to our lives and to the life of the world. This is my passion: to enter into the treasure trove of the Christian faith and revel in what we have inherited, sorting through it all with curiosity, honesty, and integrity. While some of what we discover there has obvious application to our lives, other pieces must be tinkered with before their value can be discovered. While some of what is there knocks us out with its beauty and life-giving energy, other findings seem to distort what is true, honorable, just, pure, pleasing, commendable, excellent, and worthy of praise.[1] There are times, therefore, when exploration of Christian doctrine leads us to grieve and even repent of the ways Christianity has done harm.

Perhaps you are a pastor, youth pastor, or church leader and are responsible for teaching others. You might already be well-read in theology and know a great deal about what Christian doctrines look like. You might be aiming less at learning the theological basics and are coming to this book with the hope that it will help you explore how the historic doctrines of the church are connected to what is going on, concretely, in the life of the twenty-first-century church and world. Or you might be coming to this book as a student of theology who is enrolled in a course in a college or at a seminary. In that case, my hope is that this book will help you gain a basic grasp of major Christian doctrines as well as explore why and how they matter to our lives of faith. Finally, perhaps you self-identify not as a Christian believer but as a seeker who wants to learn if Christianity has anything to offer. If this is the case, I'm hoping this book can also serve you—both by (1) helping you appreciate the value of certain pieces in the treasure trove of the faith by showing you what life they bring to the world and (2) by honestly naming the ways in which the teachings of Christianity have fallen short and even, at times, done harm. The aim here is always to talk about Christian doctrines in ways that promote abundant life.

I write this book as someone who has been teaching theology for over twenty years. I teach seminary students, laity, pastors, Christian educators, and anyone else who is interested. I teach theology in a lot of different contexts: in classrooms and lecture halls; in church sanctuaries, fellowship halls, and Sunday school rooms; at conference and retreat centers; online and on location. Sometimes I am given under an hour to consider, with a class, why the Trinity matters in real life; sometimes I am asked to pack as much of my regular, twelve-week introductory theology course into a one-week intensive class, or even into a single intensive weekend, as I possibly can. Other times I have the luxury of spending several sessions on a theological theme, such as "Living into God's Amazing Grace," "Being a Christian in a Crazybusy World," "What Difference Does It Make to Believe in God?" or "Confronting (the) Cross." The one commonality in all these teaching and learning occasions is that people keep showing up and wanting more. Students, pastors, educators, and laypersons; men and women; people of all ages, life circumstances, and educational levels. People keep on coming, and they want to learn—and to share—as much as they can. Why do they come, and why do they want to press as much theological study into the limits of whatever space and time is available? I think the answer to this is clear. It is because they hope and believe theology matters both to their lives and to the life of the world.

I am aware that the assertion that people keep showing up for theological reflection flies in the face of current cultural and ecclesial rhetoric, which highlights the demise of the mainline churches[2] and the so-called secularization—or at least "dechristianization"[3]—of our culture. At the moment I am not interested in offering an analysis of or making a case against any of these phenomena. I am simply making the anecdotal observation that, whatever the statistics and changing realities regarding the role of institutionalized religion in American society, people are consistently interested in thinking about theology. I am convinced the reason for this is because they haven't given up the hope that, in one way or another, theology matters.

If you are reading this book, you likely believe theology matters. Perhaps you want to deepen in relation to what you already know. Perhaps you want to know more about how, for example, the Christian confession that God is Trinity plays out in real life. Or maybe for you the jury is still out on whether or not theology matters, and you are looking at these pages with the hope that it does, wanting to be convinced. It might be that you come from a background (whether conservative or liberal) where you were told that theology matters, but your ideas for *why* and *how* it matters are shifting. Or maybe you have until recently had the mind-set that theology does not really matter much at all, but you are beginning to think there might be more to it all than you have always presumed. I have students in my theology classes who have come from each and all of these places, and I have stopped at some of them myself as I've journeyed with theology. Regardless of where you are coming from, I hope this book offers you something meaningful.

I understand this book to be an ongoing, collaborative, effort. This might seem in one sense an odd thing to say, given that I am the one who is doing all the "talking" by way of the words written in this text. What I mean is that I approach the writing of this book as an extension of teaching my introductory theology class at Austin Presbyterian Theological Seminary. Along these lines, my philosophy of teaching inevitably floods the tone of the prose and the flow of the content I choose to present. If the ideas presented here invite you as a reader to reflect theologically, I give a great deal of credit to the hundreds of students over the years whom I have had the privilege of teaching. They tell me I helped them become theologians; they have certainly helped me become a better one. In each year's new classroom of students, there are always different circumstances that drive different emphases. This means that my ongoing interaction with my students continues to shape the ideas presented in this book.

It is my students first and foremost, then, whom I need to thank for helping me shape what is worthwhile in this volume. For its flaws I take complete responsibility. I am indebted also to the many pastors who have invited me to spend weekends with their church communities, teaching and preaching, learning always more about how local churches both nurture those who come through their doors and reach beyond their walls to participate in the work of the Spirit in the broader community. I thank Austin Presbyterian Theological Seminary, the institution I have proudly served since 1995, for encouraging me to be the theologian I've always wanted to be: a theologian who cares about the "so what?" of Christian doctrines for everybody. I am particularly indebted to President Theodore J. Wardlaw and Academic Dean David H. Jensen, as well as to our supportive board of trustees. In particular, I appreciate the encouragement of Austin Seminary Trustee Judge David Peeples, who read the proposal and first chapters and offered constructive suggestions. I also owe a debt of gratitude to my student researchers and ministerial colleagues, Rev. Amanda Mackay and Ms. Pamela Jarvis. Amanda helped me with the early research. Pam walked with me through every word and every footnote, editing, suggesting, rewriting, and inspiring along the way. I am blessed to have her as a colleague and friend.

I am grateful, also, for the work and vision of Abingdon Press. I thank Kathy Armistead, former editor at Abingdon, for believing I have something to offer and soliciting this book. I thank David Teel for his patience, ongoing encouragement, theological prowess, passion for movies, and editorial skills. My conversations with him have fed this book as it has taken shape over the years.

Finally, I am grateful for my immediate family for their love and support. For Bill Greenway, my spouse, friend, and theological colleague, who challenges me always to love the world as God so loves it. For my children, Xander and Jessica, who surprise and delight me every day with theological insights and questions that have never before occurred to me.

For my brothers, Scott and Mark Rigby, who challenge me never to assume I have arrived at what it means to "hold faith," but continuously to think critically and expansively about the faith in which we were raised.

I dedicate this book to my parents, the Rev. Charles and Ethel Rigby, who nurtured me in the Christian faith and have journeyed with me through the decades, as my theological understandings have changed and deepened. And I write it with the hope that Xander, Jessica, and all the children of this world will continue exploring how theology matters.

Introduction
Transforming Theology

One time, years ago, I was introduced to a church group as a "relevant theologian." The pastor who introduced me kind of chuckled to himself, adding: "Now there's an oxymoron, if I've ever heard one—a theologian who is *relevant*!" Everyone in the room laughed, and I laughed along with them as I rose to speak. Except that I felt a twist in the pit of my stomach. I was glad the pastor and the people were so honest, but I was disturbed by the way theologians were being caricaturized. I had to admit to myself, however, that there must be something true about the depiction if the mere mention of a theologian being "relevant" sends two hundred people into peals of laughter. This out-of-touch, head-in-the-clouds reputation is something we theologians need to change, and not only so we can do a better job of marketing Christian doctrine. We need to work on how we are perceived because such stereotypes are antithetical to the very core of what we claim to believe—that words about God do not sit at a distance from where people live and breathe precisely because the Word became flesh.[1] If theologians talk about God, and God is present and active in our lives, then we'd better be talking about things that are relevant, or we are not talking about God at all.

Why is theology in general, and the discussion of Christian doctrines in particular, often thought of as "irrelevant"? I'd like to highlight three possible answers to this question, which I seek to address in the course of this book. First, I think theology and its related doctrines are sometimes thought to be irrelevant because they are not well enough explained or understood. Second, I think theology and doctrines are seen as irrelevant because they are associated with a kind of closed-mindedness and certainty that is unable effectively to engage others in an increasingly diverse and global world. Third and finally, I think theology and doctrines are seen as irrelevant because—in our crazy-busy, polarized culture—it is hard for us to make the time and space fully to explore them. The introduction will close with some reflection on how it is faith itself that motivates us to take the time and make the effort, because faith by its very nature seeks to know better what has touched and formed us.

Learning What Doctrines Are About

First, sometimes Christian doctrines are thought to be irrelevant because they are not well enough explained or understood. Theological discourse has its own technical language that, when it is not known, can seem to serve as a barrier to those who are trying to gain access to what it is about. Here are just a handful of some of the technical things theologians commonly emphasize: God created "out of nothing" (*ex nihilo*); human beings fell and are "totally depraved"; Jesus Christ is "of the same substance" (*homoousios*) as the Father; we are saved "by grace alone" (*sola gratia*) but are still "at the same time both righteous and sinners" (*simul justus et peccator*); we live between the "now and the not yet," waiting for God's Kingdom to come "on earth as it is in heaven." Why do theologians put things in these certain ways, and what does all this stuff actually mean to the way we live *today*?

There have been many occasions when I have had the privilege of "opening up" a technical theological concept for a roomful of people who suddenly seem to grow in their awareness that theological truths are not enigmas to be deciphered by trained theologians, but gifts for us all. It is gratifying to see the light dawn on people's faces when concepts they had always wondered about suddenly start to "click" into relevance. But it is hard to answer the question that inevitably follows: "So…if that's what it means, why didn't someone just tell me earlier?" I want to figure out how we might more clearly and consistently explore and convey the relevance of Christian doctrines to our day-to-day lives. This is, in large degree, the stated purpose of this book: to get at the question of *why Christian doctrines matter* to our everyday lives of faith. Often enough, what seems to trigger the "ah-ha!" response of those I teach is not my dumbing down doctrine, but rather my unpacking the meaning of theological terms they have never before understood. The problem most often has nothing to do with the complexity of the theological concepts coming against the limits of their capacity to understand. The problem is simpler than that: people have never been taught the meaning of the terms themselves.

In my view, the solution to the obfuscation of Christian doctrines is not to reduce them to already-known language that can be readily understood. This common approach too often fails to communicate because what is distinctively meaningful about the terms in question can get lost in the process. One example of the problems caused by moving away from distinctively theological language is seen in a translation of Scripture that does not use the theological term *grace*, instead substituting words and concepts that are more readily understood, including "wonderful kindness" and the idea that we are treated "better than we deserve."[2] But there is something about grace that is different than "wonderful kindness"—isn't there? In banning the theological term *grace* in favor of using language that is more immediately accessible, an important "so what?" of Christian doctrine is lost.[3]

Rather than changing the language, therefore, I will in this book try to do something I really work at in my teaching. That is, I will offer clear explanations of certain key technical terms, believing that as soon as readers know the basic meaning of a term, their feeling of being excluded or intimidated from what it is all about will dissipate. After all, the content of Christian doctrine is not the exclusive property of trained theologians, so why should they be the only ones who know how to access it? Some knowledge of technical terms will equip anyone who gains it to enter into the meaning-full worlds into which theological words invite us.

Theological terms, once unpacked, serve as portals through which anyone who looks can see theological landscapes wide open to exploration, discovery, and challenge. It might be appropriate to be intimidated by God, but it is never appropriate to be intimidated by words *about* God!

Let me try another way of making the case for why we might even *want* theology to sound technical, at least part of the time. Here's an analogy I hope will be useful: When I go to the doctor, I expect and want that person to know more than I know. I don't want doctors to talk over my head too much, of course. But I do like it if they say some things that are not obvious to me; things I have to ask questions about in order to understand. If they told me they didn't bother learning any technical stuff in medical school because they didn't think their patients would want to hear it, I would surely leave their office and go find another doctor. Maybe we should feel the same way about theological teachers and pastors. They should say "God is love," but be able also to say *why* we believe that, when called upon to do so, explaining how Christian doctrines help deepen our understanding.

Those trained in theology, then, should be able to explain technical theological language in ways that help others have access. But they should also be able to speak coherently, in ordinary language, about what it is they know. Theologians, like all people of faith, should be "always prepared to give anyone who asks an account of the hope" that is in them.[4] This instruction, offered to Timothy by the Apostle Paul, suggests that one way to keep theology relevant is to remember it is not for a closed club, but for the sake of the world. Because theology is for everyone, transformative theological ideas need to be explained in a language that can be understood and put into action also by those who are not theologically trained.

The complicating factor in all this is that we are all called to be theologians, whereas we are not all called to be doctors. Maybe on some level we recognize this, and this is why we are impressed when medical doctors use language that is above our pay scale, but slightly offended when trained theologians appear to be leaving us out of the discourse with their technical language. Not all patients are doctors, but every seeking person of faith is, in fact, a theologian—a person who talks about God. The word *theology* means, in fact, "words about God" (*theos* = "God" and *logos* = "words"). So, there are theologians who are trained in the technical language of the field, just as there are doctors, lawyers, and other professionals who are trained in the technical language of their fields. But there are also theologians who have not received advanced training and do not know the technical language. This does not mean they cannot understand theological language, but only that they may want to put some extra effort and attention into attending to the concepts the "doctors of the church" might in certain ways better understand, in order to discern the relevance of doctrine for our lives and the life of the world.

When doctrines are either not well explained or not well understood, the idea that theology is "irrelevant" is a kind of easy way out of the quagmire—it takes much less effort to declare theology "irrelevant" and walk away than it does to invest in deciphering it. Yet so many are willing to make a significant investment in sorting it all out, hoping that the search for understanding will be worth the investment. My experience has been that it is.

We begin by asking: "What is the content of theology?" and "Why does theology matter?" These are questions that need to be worked on in tandem with each other. It is because theology has substance that it finds meaning in the world. It is because theology proves itself to have real-life implications that it "pushes" people of faith to explore its substance. The philosopher Immanuel Kant once said, "Thoughts without content are empty; intuitions without concepts are blind."[5] Along the same lines, theological doctrines that don't meet us in our experiences are worthless to us, and spiritual experiences that have no grounding in teachings passed on through ages might be pleasant in and of themselves, but they don't connect concretely enough to real communities, histories, and ways of thinking to be able to influence them.

The suspicion that theologians have empty thoughts in the sense that they are obsessed with matters that are irrelevant to real life is a common one. For instance, you may have heard tell of the classic theological question: "How many angels can dance on the head of a pin?" This question is sometimes invoked to disparage theologians whose ideas do not appear to be generating products of measurable (and, preferably, immediate) value. It originated as a means of highlighting the obscurity of questions ostensibly explored by European theologians during the scholastic period, such as Bishop Anselm of Canterbury and Saint Thomas Aquinas.[6] Why would these great intellectuals, people of faith who had so much to do and think about, spend time on such a seemingly irrelevant question? Going back to the development of the question itself helps us gain some clarity on this, while at the same time illustrating that even the most obscure-sounding theological claim has relevance to our lives once we work it a bit. Here goes: As it turns out, the popular formulation of the "pin" question doesn't seem to be exactly how the scholastics asked it—the question as we know it was formed by those who mocked them. What we know about the scholastics is that they did ponder the character of angels as a way of getting at the difference between corporeal beings (including us) and spiritual beings (i.e., God) so that they could better articulate how we and God are related to each other. In a nutshell, they were trying to figure out what it means and why it matters to make the theological claim that God is immaterial (that is, a spiritual rather than a physical being). They suspected that thinking about angels would be a helpful step toward understanding the mystery of God because angels, like God, are spiritual beings. When our answer to the question "how many angels can dance on the head of a pin?" is "an infinite number," they argued, we are correctly recognizing that spiritual beings do not take up any actual space, even when they are present somewhere. Thinking about the angels on the head of a pin helps us understand, they thought, how we can say God is everywhere without saying God takes up all the space. Corporeal beings have to take up space to be somewhere; God can be everywhere without taking up space.

How does this relate to us, and our relationship to God? We can say God is completely present in and to creation without thinking there is no space left for creation. We can know that the fact God is with us everywhere we go[7] compromises not one bit on the space needed for us to be present, with our physical bodies. We can be reassured that God's presence is always whole and entire even as it never pushes us aside.

The point of raising this complicated question here is to show that even theological questions and explorations that are seemingly esoteric and abstract often have on-the-ground relevance that can begin to be discovered and discerned if we take the time to consider their origination and/or motivation. Once we have seen this, we can then pick up on what seemed to be at stake for our forebears and to run with it in our context, in relation to the issues we face in our twenty-first-century, globally connected lives. It would be silly not to start with the great contributions of those who have gone before us, but it would be irresponsible and just plain lazy of us not to take the theological baton extended by our forebears and run our hearts and minds out with it. We are the current generation of theologians. So, let's appreciate what we have inherited, and then imagine what we can build from there!

Let me qualify this, lest I be misunderstood: Grabbing hold of the baton held by our forebears does not require us to believe all theological ideas are equally profound, relevant, or life-giving. Faithful theological work includes discerning when God-talk is irrelevant and when it is, in fact, destructive. Also, grabbing hold of the baton might for some of us be less about receiving something offered by a willing teammate and more about wrenching it out of their hands and running in a new direction. As we will see in chapter 6, for example, female theologians have in the last fifty years challenged the presumed correlation between "sin" and "pride" to include the sin of "self-deprecation."

My hope, however, is that we can concede there have been real and necessary changes without assuming that anything we don't understand, or anything that seems silly or outdated, has no relevance to our lives or to the life of the world. Sometimes, we're too quick to write off ideas and doctrines when we cannot immediately see the so-called takeaway. In this book, we will do our best to give doctrines the benefit of the doubt. This doesn't mean we will find all of them equally relevant, but it does mean we will give them a fair hearing. As Jacob wrestled with God, we will wrestle with some of the strange claims of Christian traditions, looking for what they have to offer us. My hope is that, like Jacob, we will walk away with the blessing, even if we walk away also with a limp.[8]

Resisting Arrogance; Remembering Mystery

A second reason why we write theology off as irrelevant is because we associate it with a kind of certainty that cuts off conversation, rather than entering into healthy and productive dialogue. One of my favorite *Peanuts* comic strips, along these lines, features Snoopy sitting atop his doghouse, typing. Charlie Brown comes along and says, "I hear you're writing a book on theology. I hope you have a good title." "I have the perfect title," Snoopy replies, as he types: "*Has It Ever Occurred to You That You Might Be Wrong?*"[9]

I used to keep a copy of this comic on my office door alongside another that someone gave me. I've never been able to trace its origination. In the foreground stands a man who has apparently just been asked by a woman (silhouetted in the background) why he is talking so loudly. "You want to know why I'm speaking so loudly?" he yells back. "I'll tell you why I am talking so loudly! Because I'm *wrong*—that's why!" he says.

Both of these comics make us laugh, I think, because they bring to light what on some level we already know—that being right isn't everything. When we leverage our "rightness" at the expense of being in conversation, the cost is too high. When we assert it even when we are wrong in an attempt to override our fear and vulnerability, something of who we are is certainly lost. We might laugh because we have been in the presence of know-it-all religious people or loud-mouthed colleagues who mildly bully everyone around them with their "rightness." Or we might laugh because we see something of ourselves in these characters and they make us appropriately uncomfortable, challenging us to change.

A mentor, Bob, once asked me a question that shapes how I think about "rightness" in relation to talking about God. He asked me, "Would you rather be *boring* or *wrong*?"

If we wanted to be right at all costs, we wouldn't worry too much about being interesting. We might articulate things slowly and carefully, taking no risks. If being right were our only goal, whether theology and church are boring or not would be a matter of little concern. What we would care about is accuracy, watching our step, keeping the rules, demonstrating our piety—whatever got us to "right."

Except, of course, that the Gospel calls us not to be bound to rules but to live in freedom. And Jesus's message isn't that we should err on the side of safety but that we should take risks. We should risk vulnerability (as he emptied himself for us[10]), risk upsetting the status quo (as he overturned the money changers in the synagogue[11]), risk including outsiders as well as insiders (as he did by inviting fishermen to be disciples; by eating with tax collectors and sinners; by accepting the Canaanite woman as having "great faith"[12]). We should risk, even, looking foolish for the sake of obeying the will of God (as when Jesus decided to feed five thousand–plus people with five loaves and two fish[13]).

Of course, what Bob had (intentionally) laid out for me was a false dichotomy. One doesn't have to choose between being right and being interesting. Because God is our subject matter, as theologians, and because our subject matter is both beautiful and good, and because beauty and goodness are *interesting,* to be boring is, actually, *not* right—not right at all! This is glorious news, to those of us who care about theological language being beautiful, interesting, and compelling as well as accurate, true, and right.

It seems to me that God calls us first and foremost to focus not on being "right," but on being faithful disciples. I think along these lines of Peter, who gives Jesus a "right" answer but nonetheless completely misses what Jesus is calling him to do and to be. "You are the Christ, the Son of the living God," Peter says, and Jesus responds by telling him he has given the answer that is "right"[14]—specifically, Jesus says that Peter is blessed, that the "Father who is in heaven" has revealed this to Peter, and that Peter will be the "rock" upon which the church is built.[15] But in the story that follows, just a few verses later, the same Peter who gave the perfect answer cannot imagine that the one he calls Christ would be called to go the way of suffering. Peter argues with Jesus about what will come to pass, and Jesus rebukes him, saying, "Get behind me, Satan!"[16] Peter may have given the right answer, but it turns out he has no idea what he is talking about.

The story of Peter reminds us that whatever we do know that is right about God pales in comparison to the reality of who God is. If we say, for example, "God is love," we are saying something that is true. But we have only the vaguest idea of what this love is all about, if we compare our understanding to the actuality of God's love, which is greater than any human language can convey, greater than any human understanding can fathom. We will consider, in the first chapter, how it is that we can speak of God given the fact that God is infinite and we are finite. If God is primarily mysterious, why bother saying anything at all? And how do we decide what it is we should say, if the possibilities for what can be said are endless? How do we know when something being said about God is wrong?

Many spiritual-but-not-religious people in American culture, fed up with religious people who talk too often as though they are right, are testing less traditional ways of participating in the mystery that is beyond us all. These might include the "Nones"—the "religiously nonaffiliated" who do not identify with any particular Christian denomination. It might also include the "Dones"—those who have declared that "enough is enough," leaving their church communities for being too judgmental or too hypocritical even as they profess that they are still Christians. It includes people who are curious, in doubt, and/or skeptical; people who associate the overabundance of certainty they often find in churches with standing in the way of their spiritual journeys. To them, Christian doctrine is irrelevant when it seems more focused on giving right answers than on exploring open questions.

My hope is that book will help change the perception that theology is irrelevant by being genuinely open to learning from uncertainties as well as certainties. Because this is a book about what Christians believe and why what Christians believe matters, it assumes most of its readers are people of faith. But it doesn't require readers to think of themselves as having great faith in order to gain from it. What it does hope for is that the people who read it are curious about what it is they believe, and why they believe it. It also invites readers to think about what teachings of the Christian faith they do not believe, and why they don't believe them.

Along these lines, this book welcomes into its pages and ideas the hearts and minds of those who are curious enough to be skeptical of certain claims made by the Christian faith, and skeptical in ways that lead to further pursuit of what matters rather than to "shutting down" in relation to matters of faith. I think, for example, of biblical figures such as Nicodemus and Thomas, both of whom are skeptical of seemingly bizarre ideas like being "born again" or bodily resurrection. But their skepticism, at least insofar as it drives their curiosity, leads them to pursue opportunities to investigate further.

This emphasis on curiosity as both closely related to faith and including enough wiggle room for good doses of healthy skepticism leaves open the possibility that this book will be of interest not only to those who self-identify as "Christian," but also to spiritual seekers such as the "Nones."[17] Is there a way of saying Nones also have a kind of faith—insofar as they are driven by curiosity about what really matters, about whether there really is something worth believing, and about what this something would be? What do we make, for example, of Eric Weiner, a religious journalist and author of *Man Seeks God,*[18] who has gone on record saying he is "hoping someday to believe in God," asking for "a new approach to religion that is "highly interactive and absolutely intuitive"?[19] I hope this book will have something valuable to say not only to professing Christian believers, but to Weiner and to everyone who is curious about exploring what it is they believe, do not believe, and/or want to believe.

I imagine Anselm was saying something important about curiosity when he insisted Christians be people of *fides quarens intellectum* ("faith seeking understanding").[20] It would be boring to have faith and never push on it, to never pursue understanding of it. Similarly, Weiner, nine centuries later, imagines a faith that is "highly interactive and intuitive."[21] Weiner suggests what he is hoping for, today, is a "new approach to religion" that works to connect us to the metaphysical the way an iPad connects us to the web. He is tired, it seems, of religions that claim to be exhaustive; religions in which "God does not laugh"; religions that seem to barricade rather than open us to the bigness of what really matters.

Interestingly, some of the greatest writers in theological history (those who could never have imagined iPads!) would have joined Weiner in critiquing religion that seems to shut down, rather than to open up, curiosity and inquiry. "If you understood, it would not be God," Saint Augustine said, back in the fifth century CE, pushing us neither to confine ourselves comfortably to nor to wield around definitively any given thought, doctrine, or saying about God.[22] "God is that than which nothing greater can be conceived," wrote Anselm, eight centuries after Augustine.[23] When we remember that what we are trying to talk about or participate in is always greater than our words or efforts, we can be candid about our skepticism, we can keep feeding our curiosity, we can deign to imagine, play in, and contribute to the coming of God's Kingdom on earth as it is in heaven—all without risk of creating idols of own making. While the worlds of our imaginations will ultimately come up against limits, the world God imagines and desires for us is bounded only by God's own determination. Whatever God has in store, we are promised, is always more than the best we can ask or imagine.[24]

Making Time to Reflect

A third reason why theology and its related doctrines have gained a reputation for being irrelevant is simply because there is little encouragement, at least in the context of our overextended American culture, to take the time to figure out what it is all about. There is a crisis in *thinking* in the US: people are either too busy or too tired to do it. Edward Hallowell, in his best-selling book *CrazyBusy,* suggests we need to make time to think if we are going to make changes in our lives or in the life of the world.[25] And even making *time* isn't enough, with the world teeming around you. According to one *New York Times* article, we also have to find *space* for quiet, in a culture committed to noise.[26] Making the time to read about and ponder Christian doctrines is difficult, but there is no other way, really, to begin grasping their substance, so we can then move on to exploring their impact and relevance. Deepening understanding inevitably takes at least some invested time and effort.

Remember how Winnie-the-Pooh used to go to his "Thoughtful Spot" in order to think in "the most thoughtful way he could think"?[27] It was right between his house and Piglet's, and there were even times when the two met there to ponder difficult questions together. Do you have a thoughtful spot in your world? A place where you can go to think, to pray, to read, to ponder the practical significance of Christian doctrine? It seems to me that, with the portability of computers and reading devices, it should be relatively easy to find a place to think—it might even be the public space of a coffee shop! More difficult, perhaps, is making the effort on a day or in a week when it seems we have absolutely nothing extra to give.

There are voices all around us that try to temper our concern about not having the space and time to think by assuring us thinking is overrated—*doing* is where it's at. I certainly agree that there is such a thing as too much thinking and too little doing. I remember, as a kid, my dad would sometimes tell my brothers and me "to quit our navel gazing and get to work." He was good at snapping us out of whatever unproductive reveries we were engaged in. And my mom sometimes advised me to "Don't think; just do"—usually she said this when I was overthinking things, exhausted, and just needing to get my homework done so I could go to bed. Unquestionably, my parents were onto something. Developing the capacity to *do* is a great life skill to have in your bag of tricks, when you really need to crank it out.

The problem comes when not-thinking and just-doing becomes a way of life. One of my favorite T-shirts says on the front: "Liberal Arts Educated." And on the back of it: "Will Think for Food." What makes this so funny is the idea that anyone could get *paid* (in food or in any other way) for thinking. We don't pay for thinking, pondering, or treasuring. We pay for *doing*. Culturally, we have moved away from valuing a liberal arts education *for its own sake*.[28] The faster we can get from the thinking to the doing, the better.

When I think of biblical models of thinkers, Mary—the mother of Jesus—immediately comes to mind. She always seems to be "pondering." Sometimes I imagine her, lying on the floor of that barn with her new baby, fighting away the urge to ask Joseph to send those shepherds away so they can have a little time and space for just the three of them—a new family. But then she hears them talk about seeing the angels, and she remembers. And so, in the midst of this hectic scene, in the midst of their crazy story, Mary has the wherewithal to be amazed: to remember, treasure, and ponder, once again. Some have chalked this up to maternal sentimentalism—*you know how new mothers are.* Except that she's still at it twelve years later, long after Jesus's onesies have been passed on to a younger child.

At another point in the story, Mary and her family have traveled to Jerusalem for the Passover. On their way home, Jesus goes missing. Joseph and Mary assume he is traveling with friends and relatives. When they don't see him for a day, they start looking, finally winding up all the way back in Jerusalem, where they find Jesus—after *three days*—sitting and talking in the temple with the teachers.

Mary scolds Jesus for being inconsiderate. "Child, why have you treated us like this?" she asks. "Look, your father and I have been searching for you in great anxiety." Notice that, for a change, it is not Mary doing the pondering. Rather, it is *Jesus* who has been pondering—studying Torah with the scribes. Like mother, like son, I suppose. And I think Jesus is possibly reminding his mother of their shared habit when he shoots back, at his parents, the following questions: "Why were you searching for me?" and "Did you not know that I must be in my Father's house?" I imagine the conversation might have gone further: *Mom, you have been pondering the words of the angel Gabriel since the day I was conceived. You were amazed at the story shared by the shepherds at the time of my birth, and you've always puzzled over the prophecies of Simeon and Anna. Mom, you've always reminded me to seek to do the will of God. Where else could I possibly have been but here? How could you not have figured this out sooner?* And Mary treasures the ponderings of her son and is reminded again of who he is, and who she is. "Let it be unto me as you have said" (she probably repeats, under her breath, after counting to ten!). "Behold, I am the Lord's servant."[29]

You might be reading this on the cusp of another wave of busyness. It might be an especially hectic time at work. Maybe you are a parent during a too-packed spring in which you will feel lucky simply to survive all the play rehearsals, soccer practices, and standardized tests you've got to get your kids through. Or maybe it is late fall, and you are gearing up for the slew of holiday preparations that always seem to overtake everything else. Or perhaps you are a pastor, with too many people needing too much of your attention all in the same week. "Just keep swimming," we remember Dory telling us in *Finding Nemo*.[30] Just keep moving, and all will be well, the wisdom goes.

In contrast to Dory's advice, the suggestion here is not that we just "keep swimming," but that we pause to reflect on who we are in relation to the God who has entered into life with us and called us "blessed."[31] How do we make the time, and where do we make the space, to ponder this? We might need to stop our swimming, now and again. We need to recognize that we are constantly in danger of getting so caught up in the frenzy of doing that we forget to think. And if we don't think, what we do might be done energetically, but it will never serve what matters most.

Mary and Joseph search frantically for their lost twelve-year-old son, Jesus. But Jesus isn't impressed in the least by their exhausted, emergency-driven, uncentered efforts. *Why were you searching for me?* he asks. *Didn't you know where I would be?*

I wonder if Jesus asks us the same questions. As with Mary and Joseph, we are, perhaps, seeking to find him. My guess is that anyone reading this book wants to make a difference in the world. Many of us want to live what it means to be Christian, or at least to check in on what it means. Maybe we want to make sure our church stays faithful, relevant, and appealing. And so we get a little hyper about it all, and move faster, and consult with neighbors and relatives about what it is they have seen and what they think it will take. We, like Mary and Joseph, are frantically trying to find Jesus in new places and in new ways.

But didn't you know where I would be? Jesus asks us, a bit surprised that we have gotten so far off track. *I really thought you would know.*

Perhaps we should stop "doing," for a moment. Perhaps we should pause, find a thoughtful spot, and think. Consider the doctrines of the faith and what they have to offer; think about them in the midst of the panic about declining church numbers, or concern about church disagreements, or new solutions to the worship wars. Recognize that Christ has entered all the way into the depth of creaturely brokenness, even unto death on the cross. We *do* know where he is—don't we? He is in this world—his Father's house—studying and conversing. He has already joined with us in pondering the great mystery that is our faith.

You who are reading this book have already decided to put aside some time and energy for reflection: for thinking and for pondering, for figuring out what doctrines are *about*. As I write this, I wish we could see you face-to-face to wish you all the best in this endeavor! I sincerely hope that at least some of what you find here provides a service to you both in terms of offering some basic information about doctrines, and also in terms of suggesting how these doctrines impact our daily lives and our particular ministries. You will find that I include some exercises, reflection questions, and discussion starters here and there that I hope will help the relevance of particular doctrines click with you. Most of these have been tried and tested in my classes at Austin Seminary, and/or with church groups. The point of all of these is to remember, in the very structure of this book, that theology is not off in the proverbial ivory tower, but on-the-ground.

Our Starting Point: Faith Holds Christ

As we begin, a few words about faith are in order. This is because, if we believe theology matters, we are likely beginning the theological enterprise with a certain modicum of faith. Now, let me say from the outset that this faith can certainly include doubt. I have suggested that a seed of faith can be found even in skepticism—at very least in that version of skepticism that seeks to wonder and pays homage to mystery, and possibly even in skepticism that fights hard against belief.[32] Jesus suggests we don't need a lot of faith to begin seeking, to begin following, to begin acting. He said, specifically, that even if we had only a mustard-size seed's worth of faith, we could move mountains.[33] Apparently, a little bit of faith goes a long way toward contributing to the healing of a world that often seems impossibly broken.[34] Just a little faith can "hold" us in place as participants contributing to the mending of the world.

Some of the claims of theology do look like they need to be swallowed with more than just a spoonful of faith, I'll admit. Consider the Virgin Birth, the Second Coming, the resurrection of the body, the forgiveness of sins... these are all elements of the Apostles' Creed[35] most of us find to be difficult, if not impossible, to fathom. A dose of faith is necessary to get us started at imagining what these statements could possibly mean, and how they might actually matter. A little faith is even a necessary precursor to doubting some of the strange claims of the Christian faith, it seems to me. In order to doubt, we have to believe enough in what the Bible and the creeds say to bother wrestling with it at all, even to wind up rejecting it. A little faith lends itself to spiritual seeking, which ideally leads to greater understanding.

But what is it that we are to put our faith *in,* exactly? Surely, it is not the case that we should put our faith in *doctrines* (meaning "teachings of the church"). The purpose of doctrines is to direct us to the proper locus of our trust, by assisting us in helping to see the big picture of Scripture (more about this role of doctrine in chapter 2). Neither should we put our trust in the text of Scripture itself. All of Scripture is "profitable" for "equipping" us,[36] but it is not *in* Scripture that we put our trust. It is not our faith *in Scripture* that holds us, but our faith *in God* that does.[37] "Have faith in God,"[38] Jesus tells his disciples in the Gospel of Mark. "You believe in God, believe also in me," he says in the Gospel of John. Holding faith, Jesus suggests, is about laying claim to the hope that what God has promised will come to fruition. This includes Jesus's own promises—to the disciples, and to us—that he has actually not abandoned us, even when the circumstances of our lives and this world seem to indicate otherwise.

"Don't be troubled," he says. "I won't leave you as orphans."[39] "When I go to prepare a place for you, I will return and take you to be with me so that where I am you will be too."[40] Faith that holds refuses to give up on promises like this, even when it is colored by doubts or skepticism.

I love the biblical story of the man who holds tightly to faith, desperate for his son's healing. "If you can do anything, help us! Show us compassion!" he says to Jesus. "*If* you can do anything?" Jesus exclaims. "All things are possible for the one who has faith." "I have faith," said the man, immediately, "help my lack of faith!"[41] This father's faith is interlocked with doubt, but he refuses to let go of it because he wants so badly for his son to be healed. It is this doubt-riddled faith that drives him to seek understanding; that leads him to seek Jesus; that strengthens him not to be bogged down by his skepticism, but to force out an affirmative, if honest, answer to Jesus's question.

Martin Luther argued, back in the sixteenth century, that what faith holds on to most directly is not even God's promises, but Jesus Christ himself. "Faith takes hold of Christ and has Him present, enclosing Him as the ring encloses the gem,"[42] Luther says. Faith unites us to the Christ in whom we participate, the Christ who makes us righteous, the Christ who is present to us and who shares with us everything he has. He is the content to which our faith clings; the one in whom we live and move and have our being; the Savior of the world and also of each and every one.

Moving Forward on the Journey: We Hold Faith

Our faith holds Christ, but we also hold faith. One of the million-dollar questions in theology is: Do we have the capacity, in and of ourselves, to generate faith? Theologians through the ages have generally agreed that human beings cannot achieve faith on their own. The big debate is whether or not they contribute anything at all. Thomas Aquinas thought that human beings were capable of making their way toward God; that God had instilled every human creature with this capacity. Calvin held that human beings had enough capacity that they could turn in the right direction, but (following his interpretation of Romans 1) he thought that soon thereafter they were liable to create idols rather than to worship the one true God. Wesley thought faith was out of range for human beings apart from God's doing; at the same time, he thought human beings (assisted by prevenient grace) do have a part to play: they choose whether to accept, or to reject, God's extended gift.

The theologian with whom I resonate most, on this, is Karl Barth. Barth lived from 1886 to 1968 and is part of the Reformed tradition, following John Calvin. Barth observed that human beings who believe they have the capacity to contribute something of their own to God's work of salvation were apt to mistake their own agendas for the will of God. His idea was that even our faith is a gift of God. He describes faith, in fact, as a kind of surplus grace, explaining that "grace is so truly grace, and so truly free as grace, that it is capable of this (doubly undeserved) superfluity."[43]

The faith we hold is the faith that holds Christ, and the faith that holds Christ is surplus grace. It is a faith that will never let us go because it is an overflow of the unconditional love of God.

It is with the confidence that God's got us—even when we doubt or are skeptical—that we forge ahead.

Part One

Speaking of God

Chapter One

How Can We Speak of God?

The Doctrine of Revelation

The Magnitude of God

The first and enduring challenge of theology is that our subject matter—God—is greater than any of us can comprehend. In other words, no matter how big we think about God, God is bigger than that. If we box God in, in the way we think about God, God is bigger than that. But if we proudly boast that we believe in a God who is outside the box—God is bigger than that, still! The Bible testifies it is *what God does*, as well as *who God is*, that is beyond our best understandings. Paul puts this beautifully when he marvels that God is able to do "far beyond all that we could ask or imagine."[1] This doesn't mean that we don't know anything about God, or that we can never say for sure what God is up to. But it does mean that there is always more that we *don't* know—even about the things we do know about! When we say God loves us, for example, we can say this with confidence even while realizing God's love is "wider, deeper, and higher"[2] than we will ever completely understand, no matter how much we manage to grow into it.

The more we learn about God, then, the more we come to gain insight into God's unknowability. One of the scenes in literature that reminds me of this is in C. S. Lewis's story of Narnia, when the resurrected Aslan (the Christ figure, depicted as a lion) wakes up the girl Lucy (his disciple) by touching his tongue to her nose. "Aslan," Lucy exclaims, "you're bigger." Aslan explains to Lucy that he has always been that size, but that her perception of his magnitude will grow with every year she does.[3]

This idea that the more we know, the more we realize we don't know is of course applicable to more than just the field of theology. I have friends who are scientists who almost seem to take joy in what they *don't* know, reveling in their awareness that the cosmos seems to be composed of an infinite number of universes or that separated molecular particles appear to relate to one another even when they have been separated by miles.[4] Our son has a T-shirt with a picture of a sweep of stars and planets on it, an arrow pointing to one small spark with the message "You are here." This shirt's message is clever because it highlights our relative ignorance by invoking our knowledge not of what we know but of what we do not know.[5] In other words, it admits we do not know everything even as it brags about knowing that we do not know everything.

Despite our awareness of our relative ignorance, however, we in twenty-first-century American culture continue to place a high value on gaining mastery of subjects, developing skill sets we can use in order to produce and contribute. For this reason, the idea that God will seem even *less* manageable the more we study, reflect, and contemplate can seem a bit pointless, when it comes to engaging the task of theology.

I have a story that reminds me of this. The first day I was in college, I sat down in the cafeteria next to a fellow student who was clearly younger than me. As I recall, he boasted that he was part of a special program sponsored by a high-powered university that was studying how high-IQ teenagers would do in college if they went to college early. I tried not to be intimidated, at my ripe old age of eighteen, with this peer who was fifteen. "What do you want to major in?" he asked me.

"I want to study psychology," I said. "I'm really interested in knowing how human beings work."

"Why in the world would you want to study psychology?" he asked. "I wouldn't want to do that.... It would be impossible to learn everything there is to know. Human beings are just too complicated," he added.

"Well, what do *you* want to study?" I asked him.

"I want to study *bacteria,*" he answered. "Bacteria is something I can master," he explained. "I'm going to learn everything there is to know about bacteria."

It wouldn't surprise me to find that this fellow college student is, today, one of the world's leading experts on bacteria. And, if he is, I am betting he would now laugh at his old assertion that he could eventually come to know everything there is to know about it. Surely, any biologist would argue that the world of bacteria is greater than any of us can see; that it is a mysterious world whose boundaries keep expanding with every bit of information we gain. If this is true of the world of bacteria—a person of faith would have to ask—how much more true must it be of the universe of God in which bacteria occupy only one small sphere?

The Drive to Know and the Risk of Knowledge

One answer to why we should continue seeking to know that which appears to be beyond us, commonly found in popular culture, is that we have a much greater capacity to know things than we are aware. Often, statistics are given about what percentage of our brains we actually use. For years we were told that we use about 10 percent of our brain power.[6] This is a popular fiction, of course, but what would happen—articles, movies, and books ask us—if we used the full 100 percent? We would be able to do anything! We would be able to know everything! We would be able to change the world! Or would we?

This idea that we can know more, and thereby improve our lives, is certainly not new. Human beings since the time of Eve and Adam have been driven by curiosity. We want to know things. And we want, at best, to improve things by applying what we know to what we do. Coupled with our conviction that it is always possible to know more is a great deal of anxiety about whether we will use our knowledge for good or for ill. We are anxious for good reason—when we take a hard look at history, it is unclear whether knowledge is more often capaciously shared in the interest of the good or leveraged harmfully to gain power, wealth, or prestige.

This tension between *reaching to embrace knowledge* and *fearing what knowing too much might lead to* has been explored in many popular films and television shows in the United States over the last three decades. In the next several paragraphs I will survey how a few of these have reflected on what American culture thinks human beings can know and not know, and when knowledge is useful and when it is dangerous. Understanding how our culture thinks about *epistemology*, or how we come to know, will help us make better sense of how we approach the knowledge of God.[7]

The downside both of knowing too much while also not knowing enough is well depicted in the 2014 film *Lucy*. In this film, the protagonist gains in her capacity to use brainpower to the point of her self-dissolving into a kind of cosmic oneness. In contrast to many others in history (not to mention other characters in the movie), she uses her increasing knowledge only to identify the good and promote it; only to isolate what is wrong and fight against it. Tellingly, the story of the movie argues that harboring an ever-increasing capacity for knowledge is unsustainable. There is only so much human creatures can bear. Only so much knowledge, only so much awareness of suffering, only so much perception of beauty. Knowing too much, too fast, will likely destroy us.[8]

A 1997 movie titled *The Fifth Element* had earlier played on this theme. In it, a knowledge-absorbing being named LeeLoo becomes so distraught by the history of violence in this world, so overwhelmed by the magnitude of its beauty, that she begins to get incapacitating headaches. Even she—an alien unrestrained by many of the limitations of human creatures—cannot sustain such an expansive capacity for knowledge, especially knowledge of life and death.[9]

There are scores of science-fiction stories, movies, and television shows leading up to the era of being concerned with what will happen if we gain *too* much knowledge that play with this theme of how we need to respect the vastness of what we are exploring, taking into account our limited capacities to absorb it all. Science fiction of the 1950s and 1960s aimed, along these lines: (1) to recognize the limits of human knowledge; (2) to encourage humans to participate in knowledge bases bigger than themselves; and (3) to reassure humans that there are safeguards to the risks of pursuing knowledge that is beyond human capacities. Sometimes science fiction stories of this era created certain rules that set perimeters in which explorations and pursuit of knowledge can more safely thrive.[10] The science-fiction writer Isaac Asimov, for example, in 1950 created "The Three Laws of Robotics" intended to protect human beings even when they create technologies that can potentially outdo them.[11] Another strategy for encouraging humans to continue their pursuits emphasizes that humans are not the only ones who are limited—artificial intelligences have their failings too. In *2001: A Space Odyssey* (1968), audiences are simultaneously both reassured and disturbed by the discovery that the sentient computer Hal does not necessarily have better answers than do the human space explorers. Sometimes, as it turns out, Hal is just plain wrong and—even worse—murderous.[12] The reassuring message of the movie is that perhaps there is some place for us humans, after all.

From the 1970s to the 1990s there seems to have been less emphasis on trying to outmaneuver the admitted limits of human knowledge and more on seeking to experience what cannot be cognitively understood. Classic movies suggesting we allow ourselves to be vulnerable to the beauty and wisdom of what and whom we *don't* know include *Close Encounters of the Third Kind* (1977),[13] *E.T.* (1982),[14] and *Contact* (1997).[15] Luke Skywalker, in *Star Wars: Episode IV* (1977), destroys the Death Star by making the needed shot without looking into his targeting computer. In order to do this, he leans into mystery he has experienced: mystery he has been trained to respect, engage, and—even—submit to.[16] His actions are shaped not only by what he knows, but also by what he knows he doesn't completely understand. He allows himself to trust "the Force."[17] But he doesn't trust blindly. He and the mentors with whom he is in relationship have had enough experience of the Force and enough training in its ways that Luke knows how to use it, even if he doesn't understand it. Jean Luc Picard, in the television series *Star Trek: The Next Generation* (1987–1994), presses on with his space explorations even though he recognizes there are myriad unknowns he and his crew will be called upon to navigate. He audaciously makes decisions and orders his staff to "make it so" even while knowing perfectly well he is operating with knowledge that falls far short of the total picture. He nonetheless believes his limited knowledge is worth something. (Often it is worth more, even, than the omnipotent, omniscient knowledge of a regular guest character on the series, Q). Picard seems to trust that the cosmos, for all its ambiguities, will honor his efforts as long as he follows the "prime directive,"[18] respecting the knowledge and experience of others.

If I were to go further in analyzing our cultural context and how it both reflects and shapes our understanding of how we should relate to that which we do not know, I might mention that I see a range of possible strategies in the movies I watch with our kids. The Harry Potter series, for example, clearly emphasizes, as Star Wars and Star Trek do, taking the risk of participating in mysteries beyond our understanding. The series shows that avoiding that which cannot be understood is, actually, stupid—consider the mockery made of Harry's uncle, aunt, and cousin Dudley, when they try to ignore the fact that Harry has magical powers.[19] But then there is also the animated movie *Monsters vs. Aliens*,[20] which includes a satirical scene in which General Warren Monger greets the alien spaceship by optimistically playing (on his portable electric piano) the five-note sequence that worked to establish relationship between human beings and their alien visitors in *Close Encounters of the Third Kind*. The aliens in *Monsters* respond by attacking, which just goes to show you: you can't always trust what you don't know. But sometimes you can, the movie insists. Sometimes you have to trust the mysterious, good monsters to help you conquer the evil aliens.

The last few paragraphs have reflected on how recent movies have played with themes of knowledge and mystery as a way into considering how we, in American culture, relate to what we do not fully understand, and perhaps will never understand. Maybe you have been reflecting, as you have read the last few pages, on which movies you like best or which characters you most resonate with. Perhaps you identify with certain characters more than others—maybe you would align yourself more with the skeptical but curious Jodie Foster character (Ellie) from the earlier part of *Contact*; or maybe you are wired more like the little boy Elliott, from *E.T.*—a character who has no hesitation investing his entire self in that which he cannot understand. Before we move to more explicit discussion of how we can speak about the God who is greater than any and all words, it might be helpful to pause, for a few moments, and reflect on how we tend to think about relating to that which cannot be understood, more generally. I have included some suggested reflection questions in the box below, if you would like to engage them.

YOU MIGHT WANT TO ASK YOURSELF . . .

- Do you tend to *resist* things that are mysterious, finding ways to ignore them or work around them (maybe like a nicer Uncle Vernon, in *Harry Potter*, or Elliott's mom, for most of *E.T.*)? If you do, is it because you find them to be inconvenient, silly, scary, too awesome to think they could possibly have anything to do with you, and/or too risky? Or is it for some other reason you can name? - OR -

- Do you tend to *accept* that some things are mysterious but try to respect them from a distance, recognizing your helplessness in relationship to that which is beyond your understanding (maybe more like the earlier Hans Solo, from *Star Wars*, who recognizes the Force and its implications but tries to keep from getting too involved)? - OR -

- Do you tend to look for ways to *plunge into* mysteries, even when you are aware you will never completely understand them (like the kids in *E.T.*, Ellie [at least eventually!] in *Contact*, or Luke Skywalker in *Star Wars*)? If so, how do you go about doing so? Through listening to music, doing some kind of art, talking with your friends, doing yoga, attending different kinds of worship services?

Although theology takes into account all of these responses to mystery, it is especially invested in the third—the actual plunging into the mysteries. Jesus's hope, clearly, is that we will participate in that which is greater than ourselves. This is why he is always encouraging people to follow him,[21] to sin no more,[22] to drink living water,[23] to be born again,[24] to show hospitality to those who cannot repay it,[25] or to share the good news.[26] This is why he invites Peter to the transfiguration,[27] and tells Mary she has chosen "what is better" when she takes a break from her chores to listen to his teaching,[28] and instructs the disciples to "abide" in him as branches abide in a vine.[29] Jesus knows and teaches that knowledge of God is not primarily something that is acquired in exchange for our hard work, or sacrifice, or good intentions. It is, rather, something that is experienced when we risk recognizing that we are in relationship with the God who is beyond our knowledge. It is then, and only then, that we know the very God who at the same time remains beyond our capacity to know.

I realize this way of thinking might sound like a mere word game after a while and for this reason might become frustrating for those who are genuinely interested in knowing God. What kind of sense does it make to talk of being in relationship to One who will remain ever mysterious? What would it actually look like to move from here to there? On what basis would we go about actively taking such a risk? Why would we not assume that the chasm between ourselves and the unknowable God is too great to be crossed, focusing our attention on what *can* be known, instead? In short, on what basis *can* we know the unknowable God?

The simple, though not simplistic, answer to this is: because the one who is unknowable has shared God's own self with us.

How We Know the Unknowable

As mentioned in the introduction, Augustine famously reminds us that we can never gain exhaustive knowledge. "If you understood," he says, "it would not be God."[30] But he at the same time also testifies that the God who is beyond our understanding ceaselessly pursues relationship with us. The story of Augustine's own coming to faith, found in his *Confessions*,[31] describes in many beautiful, compelling, and (at times) even exasperating ways how he comes to the awareness that the God whose power and majesty is beyond all comprehension meets every individual one of us with love and concern. "O thou Omnipotent Good," he exclaims, "thou carest for every one of us as if thou didst care for him [or her] only, and so for all as if they were but one."[32] Augustine knows the unknowable God not because he somehow musters the wherewithal for such knowing, but because this God in some way reaches out and claims him.

Augustine would remind us that, if we in all humility confess only that we *cannot* know God, we have been inattentive to the most wondrous fact of all—that the God who is unknowable has chosen to know us. Christians, of course, center this claim in God's self-revelation in Jesus Christ. But sometimes we inadvertently talk about Jesus as though he somehow corrects some sort of problem in God. As we will reiterate when we discuss the Trinity and the incarnation in later chapters, Jesus does not compensate for God's otherwise aloof and seemingly unloving character, nor does he bridge any sort of gap or chasm between us and God. Rather, Jesus reveals who God is, was, and always will be. And who this God is can be seen not only in the central event of Jesus Christ, but wherever and however God has acted in creaturely history—in God's creation of the world, in God's calling of Israel, in God's enlivening the church by the power of the Holy Spirit.

Who God is and what God does may be "beyond anything we could ask or imagine" in the sense that we can never know, understand, or explain everything about God.[33] But because God is self-revealed, there are many, many *true* things we *can* say about God. Again, we can say things that can be trusted—and even that we can build our lives upon—about who God is and what God does. We can share, preach, teach, and live these things even though our understandings and testimony can never exhaust who God is and what God does.

One of the first and foremost things we can say about the God who reaches out to us is that this God has not left us behind. God is not, as the song says, "watching us... from a distance."[34] On the contrary, the divine self-disclosure itself testifies to God's unmitigated and often unnerving presence with us. As the psalmist who wrote Psalm 139 marvels, in prayer to God: "If I went up to heaven, you would be there. If I went down to the grave, you would be there too! If I could fly on the wings of dawn, stopping to rest only on the far side of the ocean—even there your hand would guide me; even there your strong hand would hold me tight!"[35] What amazes the psalmist is not only that God is in all places at once, and therefore cannot be escaped. What amazes her[36] is that this God who is all-in-all is radically present with us in our particular lives and circumstances. "You knit me together while I was still in my mother's womb," she says. "On your scroll every day was written that was being formed for me."[37] The God who is everywhere present is not present *in general* or *as an observer only.* The God who is everywhere present is the hands-on fashioner of each and every person, invested in each and every one of our days.[38] The psalmist clearly believes this reality is awesome:[39] "That kind of knowledge is too much for me," she says, "it's so high above me that I can't fathom it."[40]

Notice that the psalmist *knows* she cannot get her mind wholly around the mystery that the God who is all-in-all knows and cares for every detail about us. Like Lucy encountering the resurrected Aslan, her knowing of the God who knows her includes a deepening awareness of God's magnitude. And the deepening awareness of God's magnitude somehow and in turn seems to remind her that God has called *her* by name—her, as a particular individual. This flies in the face of what we might associate with emphasis on the divine mystery. Why would a God who is all-powerful care about every sparrow that falls to the ground?[41] Why would a God who is "mighty in power" insist that "not one is missing";[42] that *every* knee bow and *every* tongue confess?[43] Why would a God who is surrounded by a crowd of admirers stop and search for a single hemorrhaging woman, asking, "Who touched me?"[44] As Marilynne Robinson has recently put it, reveling in Calvin's take on precisely this mystery, "It is as if we were to propose... that that great energy only exists to make possible our miraculously delicate participation in it."[45]

These testimonies to how the Almighty God reaches out to particular and beloved ones—offered by a range of people of faith including Augustine, the psalmists, the Gospel writers, Paul, Calvin, and Robinson—all press us to recognize that the magnificent, mysterious God who will never be fully known or managed by us also insists on meddling with us: loving us, claiming us, and trying to influence how we think of our own value and the value of our days.

It should be noticed that the path to knowing the unknowable I am recommending here does not lean first and foremost on offering proofs of God's existence or defenses of God's character, as worthy as such enterprises can be, when engaged from the vantage point of faith.[46] I am also not suggesting that seekers of faith should master the right balance of spiritual practices, or achieve perfect sincerity, or learn to let go of their fears, as if any of these things were a requirement for knowing the God who has met us as we are. From the vantage point of grace, the only thing recipients can really *do* is realize they cannot do anything at all to achieve it. And even that insight itself, we would do well to conclude, is a gift of God.

Admitting our incapacity to gain what matters most may be, for many of us, somewhat aggravating. This is entirely understandable, given the nature of the water we swim in in twenty-first-century American culture. We have been shaped, after all, in a context that tells us we *can* "make it so"—even when it seems unrealistic to think we can do so.[47] Spock is always telling Captain Kirk, for example, that the "statistical likelihood" the crew members of the USS *Enterprise* will succeed in its current mission is something less than 5 percent.[48] But then they always do, despite the odds. The little engine says, "I think I can, I think I can, I think I can." Her wherewithal pays off and she is able to pull the heavy load all the way up the mountain.[49] Like this engine-that-can once she really puts her mind to it, we too are often told we can overpower our own limitations if we concentrate hard enough on doing so.

So why shouldn't we, hearing that finding our way to God is impossible, simply pull ourselves up by our bootstraps and vow to make the impossible happen, anyway? Even if we aren't sure we can make it to the top of the mountain, we likely reason, we might as well give it our best shot. I once saw a coffee mug that recommended, along these lines, a kind of spiritually modified version of our just-do-it mind-set. "Do your best," it read. "God will take care of the rest." Hard to argue with this statement, because it seems so very reasonable and balanced.

Taking such a reasonable and balanced approach might actually get in the way of our perceiving God's own self-revelation. This is because revelation comes our way not in drips and drabs made manifest by our own best efforts, but as a pure, whole, and often unwieldy gift. Divine revelation is an offering, by God, of God's own self for us. Knowing God is not like doing a science project, where you test and hypothesize and examine results. It is not like writing a book, where you are working to put together sentences until you craft paragraphs and then pages that seem coherent and true. Rather, it is more like receiving someone who wants to share life with us. As Jesus put it, "Look! I'm standing at the door and knocking. If any hear my voice and open the door, I will come in to be with them, and will have dinner with them, and they will have dinner with me."[50]

This is all well and good, of course, for those who in one way or another hear God knocking. But what about those of us who have not had that experience and who remain skeptical that such experience is possible or, even, desirable? In the next section I suggest that, even though we cannot acquire knowledge of God by way of our own efforts—whether through good works, scientific inquiry, or artistic pursuits—God presents God's own self to all kinds of people, on all kinds of spiritual journeys, and in many kinds of ways.

The Journey to Intimate Knowledge

If you are someone who appreciates the mystery of God but who is really skeptical that you want or even can in some way find your way into the experience of it, you are in very good company. Even in Scripture—a place where you might expect most of the cast of characters to be consciously walking with God—there are numerous examples of people who at first either resist mystery or sometimes blithely accept it, but with no expectation that they themselves could ever participate in it. Consider Moses, who at first holds God's call at arm's length but winds up leading the nation of Israel out of Egypt and into the Promised Land.[51] Or the psalmist who asks God, "What are human beings that you think about them?"[52] Or Mary, who at first inquires of the angel Gabriel, "How will this happen?"[53] And then there is Jonah, whose resistance is so extreme it takes the form of sin.[54] And Nicodemus, who keeps showing up even when he can't quite take the plunge.[55] And Martha, who accepts and makes provision for others to participate in mystery, but who sometimes needs to stop managing everything long enough to participate herself.[56]

Theology, as a discipline, benefits when it takes into account all of these sorts of personality types and journey-places. Some approaches cater to those who, like Ellie in *Contact*, need a little more rational, empirical explanation before they can move toward participation in that which cannot be entirely understood. Thus, one approach to theology focuses on *apologetics,* or making a case for proposed beliefs.[57] Other approaches, trying to challenge those who have accepted mystery to step more deeply into a concrete relationship with it, focus more on *testimony,* or telling the story of the personal and profound difference beliefs make to our lives of faith. This is the approach the woman takes when she goes back to the townspeople and speaks words about her encounter with Jesus at the well.[58] She doesn't try to prove he is Messiah—she simply tells the story of their encounter, and how it is affecting her. This testimony is, finally, what leads the townspeople to travel to the well. At first they believe because of the testimony of the woman, but then they believe because they have heard Jesus's teachings for themselves.[59]

Similarly, Paul in his travels described in Acts 17 is eager for those he encounters to experience God for themselves. As Jesus did before him, Paul frames the message of the Gospel in whatever ways best communicate it to particular people in particular contexts. He knows that different people have different kinds of relationships to that which is mysterious, and he is willing to employ a full range of approaches in speaking about God with them.

Several days after he arrives in Athens, following a series of debates he has had "in the synagogue... with... Jews and the devout persons,"[60] Paul is invited to speak at the Aereopagus, a place that serves as a hub for public exchange, debate, and judicial proceedings. Clearly, Paul has already gained the respect and interest of the community leaders, who now want to hear more of what he has to say. Following his own dictum that Christians are to be "all things to all people,"[61] Paul tries to engage them in ways they will appreciate, showing them respect as he uses both apologetics and testimony to convey the good news. "I see you are religious in every way," he says to them, "you even have an altar to an unknown God."[62] It's interesting, though, that finally Paul does not develop any kind of proof for the fact that this God is actually known.[63] Rather, he simply asserts it as true. "What therefore you worship as unknown," he says, "this I proclaim to you." He continues by making two important points: First, he explains that the approach the Athenians are taking will not get them to the God who is unknown. God cannot be accessed, he says, by way of shrines, idols, or any human efforts or creations. Paul's second point, however, is that there *is* a way for the unknown God to be known. That way comes from God, not from human capacities. Paul makes the startling claim that God is "not far from each one of us," insisting that God's presence has been made known by way of the resurrection of "the man whom God has appointed."[64]

Among other things, Paul is a very good advertiser. He notices there is something his immediate constituency (the community of Athenians) desires, and he notes how they are trying to get it (by creating idols). He recognizes and affirms their desire, but then names what they, perhaps, are already aware of: their methods are ineffectual; they cannot get what they want in the way they are going after it (Paul suggests, in fact, that their altar "to an unknown God" is proof that they recognize their failure to know God as they want to). But Paul shows them that they *can* get what it is they are seeking. Interestingly, it is not exactly by employing another way of getting it, but by recognizing it has already been made available. *Yeah... there's an app for that,* we might imagine Paul claiming in our day and age.[65] *But,* he might quickly add, *it is not an app made by human hands. It is a gift of God. And it is as intuitive and interactive as it is possible to get.*

"God is not far from any of us," Paul insists.[66] This is because this God who created all things also created each of us who exist in this world. God gives us our "life," our "breath," and "all things."[67]

Paul is here telling the Athenians—and us—a great deal about the character of revelation. He emphasizes that revelation is accomplished by God, and not by us. He explains that revelation means that the God we thought is unknowable is knowable, grounded in the person of Jesus Christ. And he clearly thinks, as he testifies to the Athenians, that the kind of knowledge of God that brings life is the kind that somehow includes *participation* on the part of the knower. Paul is suggesting that "God is not far from each of us" and neither are we far from "the one in whom we live and move and have our being."[68] The model of knowing for which Paul is advocating—even as he develops his arguments before the Athenians—is not as much about gaining information as it is about being affected *by* the content of what is being known, and known better and better. For those who speak French or Spanish, it is the "knowing" associated with *connaître* or *conocer* more than with the "knowing" conveyed by *savoir* or *saber.* It is a knowing that is not about gathering data as much as it is about entering into relationship. It is a knowing of a subject matter that is, in fact, itself a Subject.

"Participating" in the God Who Is Near to Us

Following Paul's speech to the Athenians, we are told that "some scoffed"[69] and "some... came to believe."[70] Two people who joined Paul are indicated by name: Dionysius the Areopagite and Damaris.[71] While we don't know the specifics of their conversion, it is likely safe to say they in some way came to recognize their participation in the God Paul identifies as the one in whom "we live, move, and exist."[72] A question for those of us who want to know God is: How do we—with Dionysius and Damaris—go about participating in this God Paul says is near to us? Paul suggests we need to set aside our own idols, recognizing the limits of our spiritual efforts and even repenting of our ignorance.[73] This is hard for us to do, especially in a culture that encourages us to override any limitation.

Referencing again the can-do emphasis in American culture, we historically seem to name as heroes those who press the boundaries of their own limits. Think of Jack Bauer, the star of the Fox TV series *24*, who not only saves the world in twenty-four hours, but does it without ever dozing off, or eating a snack, or using a bathroom. In 2014, sales of Red Bull energy continued their rapid increase, selling 5.6 billion cans in 170 countries. It is no wonder that *Forbes* magazine named it as one of the "world's most valuable brands."[74] There's little question, I think, that we imagine Red Bull makes us a bit more like Jack Bauer. More able to push through our limits; more able to do the things we think we can get done.

Finding ways to conquer limits might be useful for accomplishing many things, but it is not a helpful strategy for knowing God. Just as problematic, however, is attempting to master our finitude by dramatically declaring that we know nothing of value. This is because *thinking we have the capacity to figure it all out* and *deciding to forego figuring anything out* suffer the same malady—each strategy refuses to acknowledge the fact and implications of finitude, the first by resisting its limits and the second by resisting its possibilities. In short, neither being a know-it-all nor throwing up one's hands in a gesture of triumphant helplessness is really being very honest about the creaturely condition in which we find ourselves. And neither does anything to advance depth of relationship. We cannot know everything, and may not be able to know anything, completely, by way of our own doing. But the story of revelation does not end there. We actually know, and can relay, a great deal of what is true, not because we have the capacity to transcend our creaturely limits but because God has entered into these limits and shown us how beautifully they equip us to participate in the things that matter most.

Tip #1 for Speaking about the Infinite God: Appreciate Analogies

Once we have recognized not only the greatness of God but also our own incapacity (in and of ourselves) to know God, we might find ourselves back to wondering how we can say anything about God at all. How can we who are limited honestly believe we can understand and articulate something meaningful about the Reality that is beyond all understanding? If God is mystery, shouldn't we leave well enough alone?

Many of us feel—and maybe a lot of the time!—as though it takes everything we've got just to muddle through another day in the office, get Sunday's sermon written, make time to return that phone call, get the kids shuttled around to all their after-school activities, or pass that big test at the end of the week. We have enough trouble negotiating our complicated, over-packed lives, so full they are of work to do, fun things to try, responsibilities to fulfill, daily needs to attend to, and people with whom to build relationships. Our life in the here and now is plenty enough to manage, it seems, without setting out to say something about a God we need to work to see and strain to hear, especially if what we finally see and hear is only a fraction of what there is to know.[75]

Recognizing the limits of even the best language we have for God, some people of faith find there is much we can learn about God by setting words to the side altogether. How does being silent before God create a context in which God can be experienced? Traditions emphasizing these approaches are commonly known as *apophatic* or following the *via negativa*—coming to know God by way of what cannot, rather than what can, be said.

This book is funded by the conviction that words about who God is and what God is up to can facilitate knowledge of and relationship to God. As such, it participates more in what are known as *kataphatic* (active way) traditions than in *apophatic* ones. To say that the words we exchange when we participate in a Bible study, the words we share in when we engage in worship, and even the words we might hear when we go to a good movie help us understand and know God better is not to forget, of course, that any and all words about God are limited. But it is to celebrate the fact that words, though they can never tell us *everything*, can often tell us *something* of value.

Theologians have always, of course, tried to speak in ways that honor the magnitude of God while at the same time clearly conveying particular, concrete truths about who God is and what God is up to in the world. The writer of the Gospel of John, crafting his prologue to his account of Jesus's life, formulated a poetic way of bearing witness that must have seemed, to some, to be oxymoronic. What could it possibly mean, they surely wondered, to say "the Word became flesh"?[76] The Word (or *logos*) was thought to be not concrete and specific flesh, but the organizing principle of the universe. And this person who dwelt among us in the flesh—how could he, possibly, be the Word? Exactly, Paul argues. And he goes on, in the same vein, to talk about the resurrection of the dead. Again, a mixing of something mysterious with something all too concrete.

The leaders of the earliest church councils, similarly, looked for ways to articulate, concretely, the teachings of the church without compromising on the divine mystery. "One *ousia* in three *hypostases*," they said, for example, in 362 CE—describing the character of God as triune.[77] When asked what they meant by this, given that *ousia* and *hypostasis* were commonly understood to be synonyms, they said: "what mattered was not the language used but the meaning underlying it."[78] The words, they were acknowledging, conveyed something. But they did not exhaust everything there is to know about the triune God.

Most notably, perhaps, Thomas Aquinas back in the twelfth century sought to give us the means to balance these concerns by articulating how all our language for God is *analogical.* It is not *univocal*, he argued, meaning that our words do not exhaust the reality they are meaning to reference. And it is also not *equivocal,* he said, reminding us that it is *not* the case our words have *no* relationship to what they are meaning to reference. Our theological language reflects the fact that we know *something* true, but not *everything,* about the mystery that is God.

An example might help show the importance of this. Let's take the statement "God is love." Thomas would remind us that this statement is not univocal, because whatever "God is love" actually means, the phrase itself is only a fraction of what God's love is all about. But neither is the statement equivocal, precisely because "God is love" tells us something true and, even, transformative. It is an amazing and humbling thing that we can say things that are true about the God who will not be defined by any words or lack of words, but only by God's very own self.

A related way to understanding the analogical character of our language for God is to remember what we learned in English class: analogies are both like and not like that to which they refer. "Mama always said life was like a box of chocolates," Forrest Gump famously says.[79] "You never know what you're going to get." But life is also, of course and in many ways, *not* like a box of chocolates. To acknowledge both the "is" and the "is not" of any particular analogy for God is, then, neither to reduce God to riddles nor to try to slip away from saying anything real or concrete about who God is and what God is like. Rather than subtracting from our knowledge, our hope is that acknowledging both that "God is love" and that "God is *not* love" adds something *to* our knowledge of the God we truly know as loving. It reminds us, again, that whatever "God is love" references is beyond anything we could even begin to articulate. The same is true for other analogies: God *is* ruler, king, and the all-knowing One, for example, but at the same time *is not* ruler, king, and the all-knowing One, at least in the sense we—with our limited understanding—might understand these titles. The bottom line is that we actually know more, and not less, about God when we risk remembering both the "is" and "is not" of every analogy we use.

Let me illustrate the relevance of what I am saying, here, by considering an analogy for God that has been particularly meaningful to most Christian believers over the centuries: the analogy that God is our "Father." Jesus prayed to the Father, teaching us to do likewise. Some have argued that the language of fatherhood is so important to how we understand God that Father should be thought of more univocally than analogically (to quote Thomas, as mentioned above).[80] But forgetting the analogical character of the Fatherhood of God actually diminishes its capacity to draw us into the mystery of the divine fatherliness because it confines us to human understandings of what it means to be a father. Theologians as wide-ranging as Calvin (sixteenth century) and Elizabeth A. Johnson (twenty-first century) agree that any time we think we have captured God in any one term or idea we have committed the sin of idolatry. Calvin reminds us, in his commentary on Isaiah, that we can use the analogy of mother as well as father for God because "by no [one] metaphor . . . can [God's] incomparable goodness be described."[81] Johnson points out that using analogies for God in addition to father helps us have a fuller sense of what God's fatherliness is all about.[82]

Karl Barth reminds us that the God who is our kind, nurturing, protective Father is at the same time *not* father in the sense that God's fatherliness could never be determined or confined by earthly notions of fatherliness.[83] In other words, it is not as though we assess God's qualifications or the shape of God's fatherliness the way we might ascertain (for example) that a human person is a father because he has a child he cares for and provides for. The claim of faith, rather, is that it is God's fatherliness that sheds light on human fatherliness, and not the other way around. As Barth suggests, when considering what *can* be said rightly of God, it is best to work "from above to below," rather than "from below to above."[84] When we call God "Father," for example, we should consider what who God is tells us about the character of fatherhood, rather than what various versions of human fatherhood tell us about God. The words we use for God, he explains, are then premised in our faith in God, rather than derived from any likeness we surmise exists between ourselves and God.

Tip #2 for Speaking about the Infinite God: Talk about What Matters

A second tip for speaking about the infinite God is to focus less on how much we can say and more on testifying to *how what we know matters.* Madeline L'Engle tells the story, along these lines, that a woman came up to her after a lecture and said, "I read *A Wrinkle in Time* when I was eight or nine. I didn't understand it, but I knew what it was about." L'Engle goes on to comment that, once we know "what it's about," we will "have the courage to go wherever we are asked to go, even if we fear that the road might take us through danger and pain."[85] This, of course, is a pretty tall order. The implication is that what analogical language draws us into is something of value that cannot be ignored and that even transforms us.

This short account of L'Engle has helped me think more productively about what it is we are doing when we seek to ascertain and articulate God's revelation. Recognizing our limits, we know we can never understand it in any exhaustive sense. But, surprisingly enough, we *can* know what it's about. I don't understand God's love—it is so very great—but I know it is *about* my being claimed by God, my being held by God, and me having the capacity, therefore, to reach out and enter into mutual relationship to others.

As we move in the chapters that follow into consideration of doctrines such as the Trinity, salvation, and Christian hope, it will be helpful to keep L'Engle's distinction in mind. We will never *understand* (for example) the three-in-one and one-in-three, but we *can* know, and discuss, and teach *what it is about* and how it matters to our lives. And once we start doing that, we will be well positioned to understand God's revelation less as information to be gathered and disseminated and more as a means to being met, made, blessed, and sent by God.

Tip #3 for Speaking about the Infinite God: Say Something about Everything

Once we realize it is impossible fully to understand the things that matter most, we might be tempted to think we shouldn't even try. We might decide—as did that audacious fellow student I met on my first day of college—that since understanding God or even fellow human beings is a losing game, we may as well focus our attention on things at which we can at least appear to be "expert."

Whether it be saying everything about bacteria or about the emergence of jazz in early twentieth-century American culture; whether it be saying everything about the way the protons and electrons of an atom continue to interact with one another even when separated from a mile of distance or saying everything about the number of ways it is possible successfully to boil an egg; many of us are vastly knowledgeable about *something.* A doctor may know everything about neurology but not dare to say words about gynecology; a professor in seminary might brilliantly interpret New Testament Greek but laugh at the prospect of teaching a Christian education class; and a chef may be expert at making pastries but be considered unqualified to grill the steaks at a fancy restaurant.

In her book *Living by Fiction*, Annie Dillard points out, along these lines, that most of what we have to say to one another is about "artifacts"—that is, specific things that have already been made by human beings that can be created, managed, examined, known, and mastered.[86] Dillard seems to include, in her understanding of artifacts, not only physical objects we make and use, or make and admire. She includes, also, the systems we develop that frame what is beyond our scope—perhaps the periodic table, the color wheel, or, even, a birdwatchers' guide. What is lacking in our world and our lives is not intriguing discussions of artifacts. What is lacking, she says, are those who are courageous enough to say something immediate about existence itself. "Who will interpret the raw universe?" she asks. "We have a shortage of metaphysicians."[87] This is a problem, Dillard thinks, because "if we confine our interpretive investigations to strictly bounded aspects of culture... we miss learning what we most want to know."[88]

But what is it that we most want to know? Influenced by Dillard, I have come to think about it this way: what we want to know most, I believe, is not everything about something, but something about everything. We want someone to say something that makes sense of the cosmos, of creation, of God, of love, of suffering, of existence. We are impressed with those who know everything there is to know about the periodic table, but we also want someone to risk saying *something* meaningful about the raw universe, even while acknowledging it will never be possible to say *everything* about it. The question is: Who among us is willing to risk speaking about what matters most?

Theology is committed to knowing and saying something about everything. It is in the business of articulating what matters most to our lives, and the life of this world. As such, it is a discipline that risks engaging in conversations outside of its presumed expertise. The perimeters of the theological enterprise are delimited not by what theologians can most ably navigate, nor even by the specific callings of God to engage particular needs of the world. Bill Placher, reveling in the wide expanse of possibilities for theological discourse as they are reflected in the writings of Barth, writes: "From a Christian perspective one can engage in conversation with anybody about anything—from Mozart to Nietzsche to Pure Land Buddhism."[89] This, again, is not because Christians are expert in all subjects but because they are free to discover and articulate whatever something about everything is life-giving for all.

The key, of course, is knowing what to look for and being able to discern it. How do we discern God's Word in this world so packed with both beauty and discordance? How do we go about exploring all that is around us in ways that get lost in the wonder of it all while still making judgments about meaning, value, and truth? Why is it so hard to get to what matters most, and how are we going to surmount these obstacles in our quest to discover and articulate the right words to say about God?

To Whom Is God Disclosed? General and Special Revelation

Calvin gives us a couple of categories that can help us frame our search for meaning in relation to God's self-revelation. In brief, he distinguishes between *general* and *special* revelation. By *general revelation*, he is referring to how God is self-revealed equally and to everyone in the world shared by all of us—in nature, in our philosophies, and in the way we conceive and develop governmental, ethical, and social systems. By *special revelation*, Calvin is referencing how God reveals Godself to particular individuals in particular ways not common to everyone. God's self-disclosure to the Israelites, for example, is a story of God selecting one particular nation to be God's people. God chose to love Israel, the biblical witness attests, not because of any virtue or merit of their own, but just because God wanted to.[90] God brought the father of Israel, Abram (later to be called "Abraham") outside to see the stars, telling him: "so shall your descendants be."[91] Special revelation, in this case, names the fact that Abraham was called by name, in the context of a particular event not experienced in general and by everyone.

When we consider how the doctrine of special revelation hits the ground in relation to our day-to-day lives, we will likely raise concerns about the sense in which it seems to endorse exclusivity even as we give thanks for the ways in which it affirms God's self-disclosure as personal and intimate. There is no question that, historically, this doctrine has been used to advance the idea that some are "in" and some are "out," in relation to God's favor.[92] It is strongly linked to the controversial doctrines of *election* and *predestination*—the idea that God selects whom God wills without rhyme or reason. At the extreme, it is linked even to the problematic idea of *double predestination*—that God elects some to salvation and others to reprobation or damnation.[93]

But it at the same time reminds us that the God who reveals Godself to us does so as the one who knows and loves *us*—as particular, cherished ones. What the doctrine of special revelation shows us is that God's self-disclosure is not geared toward showcasing *God* in isolation from the world. God's self-revelation is for the purpose of showing that God knows *us.* Christians confess that God meets us, incarnationally, in the person of Jesus Christ. "The Word made flesh"[94] is, indeed, the central instance of special revelation in the Christian faith. But special revelation extends even more broadly than the incarnation to all the ways God meets us personally and particularly; to all the ways God demonstrates God knows us and holds us dear. The Bible is full of particular stories of particular people being called in particular ways both to know they belong to God and to act accordingly: among them are Moses, Jonah, Rahab, Samuel, Esther, the psalmists, Mary (Jesus's mother), Peter, Mary (Martha's sister), the man born blind, Paul, and Lydia. The Christian conviction that God continues calling particular people in particular ways reminds us, then, that the content of God's self-disclosure is not only about *who God is*, but also about *who we are.*

The Startling "So What?" of Special Revelation

This last point is an important takeaway of the doctrine of revelation. To recap it in a different way: at first, we may have thought the most startling thing about revelation is that it gives us ways to know the God who is unknowable. As if this isn't remarkable enough, it is also the case that God's self-revelation gives us ways to know ourselves; to see ourselves in a new way; to see ourselves as God sees us. We are God's people; we are God's children; we are heirs to God's promises; we are beloved.

This is the kind of knowledge that does more than boggle our minds. It, in fact, changes everything because it undoes and remakes us from our very core.[95] It is knowledge that is, arguably, nothing less than redemptive. Why is this? Because when we see ourselves as God sees us—as chosen, holy, and beloved—we carry ourselves in this world differently.[96] When we see ourselves as God sees us, we seek to discern and articulate what matters most as those who are reminded that *we* matter, because God has entered into relationship with us. When we are reminded of our identity as God's children, we gain confidence that we can say something about everything, because we in a very real way have learned something that has changed everything for us. To know God, in fact, is to know something that makes a difference to everything.

But how, concretely speaking, do we go about receiving special revelation? Quite maddening, for some, is the answer commonly given by Calvin and others. That is: there is nothing at all we can do to uncover or discover knowledge of God; it simply comes to us as a gift. We will immediately ask a follow-up question, in light of this: If God is solely responsible for doing the revealing, and there is nothing whatsoever we can do, why is it so hard (and for some more than others) to know the presence, character, and work of God? Is God lying down on the job? Or are we just not paying enough attention?

When I was in seminary I had a professor named Diogenes Allen who used to encourage us students to pay attention. "Be enough of a person that God can find," he would tell us. I don't think he believed we could find our way to God ourselves. But I do think he was giving us some down-to-earth advice about how we could give the Holy Spirit a bit of a leg up in conveying what it is God has to say. I thought about Dr. Allen's exhortation quite a bit, in the years I was working on my MDiv.[97] And I started noticing, in Scripture, stories of people who hear God speaking, but only when they pause long enough to hear. My favorite is the story of Elijah.[98] Running away from Queen Jezebel, he is ministered to by angels sent by God. Forty days and nights of this, and finally he arrives at his self-determined destination. He sits down in a cave to rest. And it is then—and only then—that he hears the voice of God calling him to the mouth of the cave. To cut a long and very interesting story short, what God tells Elijah is very different from what Elijah imagines God will tell him. While Elijah apparently expects God to be fully understanding about his running away from Jezebel, and very proud of him for being the "only one left in Israel" who has not bowed down to the false god, Ba'al, God instead listens to Elijah's story and then replies, simply, "Go back the way you came."[99] The point that bears notice in this rich and somewhat humorous story is that, though Elijah has no say in shaping the content of what God tells him, he actually does seem to contribute to when and where he hears God's words.

This story seems to jibe with contemporary accounts of spiritual journeys. So often seminary students and pastors, recalling how they came to discern their call to ministry, include reference to the number of times they believe God tried to tell them what God had in mind when they just kept pressing forward with their lives, determined to resist listening. Only once they found themselves in their version of Elijah's "cave" were they able to hear God's direction for their lives. To illustrate this with a contemporary example: the well-known poet Christian Wiman testifies that there were three events in his life that created the space he needed to listen for God. First, he lost, for a time, his capacity to write poetry. Second, he fell in love. Third, he was diagnosed with a rare, incurable blood cancer.[100] Wiman refuses in any way to romanticize his illness, which he views only as dreadful. It is not that he has found "equanimity" in relation to the cancer, he explains, when asked about the nature of his encounter with God. It is that God speaks to him from out of the "abyss" itself.[101] The unknowable God, it would seem, has the propensity to reach out and be known to us in the many different kinds of spaces we create or experience in our lives—spaces characterized by rest or wonder; study or contemplation; suffering or challenge.

Scripture as the Space for Knowing

One way to understand the place of the Bible, in Christian faith, is that it creates for us a rich space in and through which we can encounter the revelation of God. This is not to say that Scripture is the only place we can encounter God. As Barth reminds us—God can be seen wherever and however God chooses to self-disclose. What is the case, however, is that Christians throughout history have claimed that Scripture is a place where God is found. In the next chapter we will continue exploring revelation by way of considering how Scripture helps create a space in which we can know and speak of God.

Chapter Two

Where Do We Find the Right Words to Say?

The Doctrine of Scripture

In the last chapter, we focused on the character of what we can know and say about God. We discovered that we can say things about God that are true, even though we can never exhaust who God is or what God is like. This does not mean, however, that *whatever* we say about God is true. Sometimes I think of it this way: while there are an infinite number of points on a line, this does not mean every point that exists or can be imagined is on the line. In addition, some things said about God are more meaningful than other things, even when everything said is painstakingly accurate. "God is with us," for example, often carries more weight than "God is immutable," particularly if what is being said is being said to a person who is suffering.

Our goal in speaking of God, then, should not be to make statements that are only technically correct. Rather, we should also aim to articulate truths about God that can impact lives and transform the life of the world. Remembering this, we will in this chapter continue reflecting on the doctrine of revelation by considering *where we should go* to gather words about God and *how we should go about discerning* among them. What *norms and sources* do we engage to find the words that best convey who God is and what God is doing in our world?

"Authority": A Recommended Exercise

Before we move any further into the discussion, it might be helpful to pause and reflect on how you, the reader, are already negotiating among various sources as you seek to know what is most meaningful and true. Do you privilege one source over others, in making your assessments? The exercise that follows is designed to draw you into reflecting on how you are already navigating multiple truth claims coming from various sources. My thought is that, if you have an awareness of how you are already working with the sources, this will help you reflect, in a more grounded way, on what you might want to do differently and/or which approaches you might want to claim as your own methodological brand.

Let me offer one further word of guidance related to the instructions given for the exercise. It has to do with the word *authority*, a word that receives mixed reviews in our day and age, when claims to authority are rightly questioned. The reason I use this word is because it is a term people of faith have traditionally applied to Scripture, as a way of identifying the important role the Bible has in helping us discern words about God. More will be said about this as the chapter proceeds, but for now I'm asking that, if you are willing, you engage the exercise with whatever understanding of authority is operative for you. Getting at how you think about authority is, in fact, itself a goal of the exercise—so it is important that the term not be overly defined in advance of it.

That said, here is the exercise. Thanks for giving it a try, if you can, and I hope you enjoy it!

AUTHORITY EXERCISE (VERSION 1)

Rank the following statements according to how much authority you believe them to have (on a scale of 1–5, "1" being most authoritative and "5" being least authoritative):

a. ______ "In life and in death we belong to God."

b. ______ "By the way of Mount Seir it takes eleven days to reach Kadesh-Barnea from Horeb."

c. ______ "One contrary cannot be the cause of another. But evil is the contrary to good. Therefore, good cannot be the cause of evil."

d. ______ "I have accepted Jesus Christ as my Lord and Savior."

e. ______ "The earth revolves around the sun once every 365.25 days."

How did you do? Which of the five did you rank the highest, and which the lowest? What criteria came into play, as you made your determinations? Is there anything that surprised you about your own process for thinking through the ranking? What understanding of authority—if any at all—was operative for you?

It might also be worthwhile to consider whether you at any point wished for more information about where each of the statements you ranked came from. Think about whether it would have made a difference to you, for example, if the exercise had asked you to rank a different list of items, looking like this, instead:

AUTHORITY EXERCISE (VERSION 2)

Rank the following statements according to how much authority you believe them to have (on a scale of 1–5, "1" being most authoritative and "5" being least authoritative):

a. ______ Presbyterian Church (USA), Brief Statement of Faith[1]

b. ______ Deuteronomy 1:2

c. ______ Thomas Aquinas, *Summa Theologica*

d. ______ a good friend of yours

e. ______ Dr. Saturna Galexa, well-respected astronomer[2]

Would knowing where the statements came from have changed your ranking in any way? Why or why not? And what if the exercise were to evaluate among *categories* of sources, like this:

AUTHORITY EXERCISE (VERSION 3)

Rank the following statements according to how much authority you believe them to have (on a scale of 1–5, "1" being most authoritative and "5" being least authoritative):

a. ______ tradition

b. ______ Bible

c. ______ logic (reason)

d. ______ experience (personal testimony)

e. ______ logic (scientific fact)

If you think the order of your selections may have been different if you had begun with versions 2 or 3 of the exercise, you are not alone. People who have done this exercise in live classrooms and churches frequently comment that they would have ranked the Bible first had they been handed version 3 of the exercise but that they were distracted by the statement about traveling to Kadesh-Barnea in version 1. Others say they would have given more credence to the experiential statement about accepting Jesus if they had known it was coming from a good friend (as in version 2). And a far greater number of people in the last five years, compared with those who did the exercise twenty years ago, select the astronomical statement as having the most authority. "It is the least subjective," they often say, "and therefore can be embraced by the greatest number of people. That's what gives it its authority."

Interestingly, I have had a handful of people choose the Kadesh-Barnea statement (version 1, choice b) over the years, telling me they did so precisely because they did know it was in the Bible. One man insisted he would rank it the same as one of the most beloved and oft-quoted verses in the Bible—John 3:16. For this person of faith, the *source* of the Kadesh-Barnea statement, even more than the *content* of the statement itself, holds the greatest sway in determining how much authority the Bible has. Though I myself would privilege John 3:16 over Deuteronomy 1:2, I admire this man for following through with what he held to be the implications of subscribing to biblical authority. He reminds me that, if I am going to say the Bible is God's Word and then privilege some verses over others, I am going to need to explain how to hold together my claims with my practice! I can also recall a couple of memorable moments that occurred in the context of discussing the logic statements included on the exercise. First, I once had a trained scientist in class who ranked the "365.25 days" astronomy question last because she said it was *imprecise*: 365.25 days is only an *approximation,* she posited, visibly frustrated because others in the room were referencing the statement as though it were a measurable *fact.* Much to my surprise, this same scientist said she had ranked the Kadesh-Barnea statement highest, explaining that she did this because it seemed to proffer very accurate and useful information for anyone traveling, by foot, from Kadesh-Barnea to Horeb. She thought the statement was actually more accurate than the 365.25 statement because it was only offering an approximate travel time (eleven days). Significantly, reasonably accurate approximations had more authority, for this scientist, than slightly[3] inaccurate statements presented as fact.

One further anecdote, thinking of past reflections on the exercises: it is of great interest to me, as someone who values philosophical and theological thinking, that the good/evil logic statement made by Thomas Aquinas is inevitably ranked the lowest of all. Additionally, associating the statement with Thomas (in the context of a group discussion) does not seem to lead participants to give the statement a second look, or to make adjustments to the ranking. I'm not sure of the reason for this. Maybe the statement seems nonsensical to them, regardless of who said it. Or perhaps they aren't very familiar with Thomas, and therefore have no reason to be impressed that *he* is the one who said it. Or maybe it is the case that this type of statement itself represents a way of thinking that is so alien to the ordinary way we process things it is easier to dismiss it as outdated and irrelevant than to gain the skills needed fully to evaluate it.

As you have likely surmised in the reading of the last few paragraphs, what can make this exercise truly worthwhile is not simply doing it, but reflecting on what values came into play in the assigning of your rankings. Such reflection can help any and all of us think not only about what claims we want to make about where we learn our words about God, but also about what truthfully does come into play, in the shaping of our understandings. Knowing ourselves, what questions we have, what conflicts we are managing, and how we honestly operate can better position us to consider alternate approaches, to strengthen our own positions, or at least to have broader ways of imagining how we might pursue what is most meaningful.

With the insights we have gleaned from taking and reflecting on this exercise, let us turn now to deeper consideration of how we navigate these various sources as we discern what words to say about God. Along the way we will also consider what it might look like, practically speaking, to join people of faith in claiming that the Bible has privileged status in relation to all other sources.

The Bible Tells Me So?

Many Christians will quickly respond to the question "Where do I go to learn what is true about God?" with what they have been taught is the definitive answer: "the Bible!" The Bible, indeed, is always front and center when it comes to discerning what should be said about God. Sometimes Christian believers (particularly Protestant Christians) even proudly identify themselves as "People of the Book."[4] While the Bible is the central source many Christians consult in seeking to know God, it is not the only source. We also learn about God from our communities—from our churches and our families, from our friends and our teachers. These communities have, of course, been influenced by their reading of and interpretations of Scripture. But—both for better *and* for worse—the reading and study of the Bible is never done in a vacuum. Interpreting communities are continuously shaped by the traditions they themselves are shaping—that is, the traditions of the church—including its creeds, confessions, catechisms, and other statements of faith passed down through the ages.

In addition to learning about God in the context of communities and their traditions, we might also learn of God by meditating on the natural world—standing in wonder (as Psalm 145, for example, puts it) of all God has made. Or we might utilize our reason as we *wonder about* certain things, working to assess what words do and what words do not make sense to say of God. Reason might lead us to marvel, for example, at how knowledge can deepen our appreciation of mystery. Or it might help us recognize that some of the most nonsensical words might nevertheless be the most meaningful. Reason can also help us eliminate from our discourse words that are untrue about God, words that are often misleading or cause harm.

Finally, a source that virtually always comes into play when we choose what words to say about God is our own experience. Who and what we have encountered as we have made our way through our lives affects how we read the biblical text, how we interpret the traditions valued by our communities, and how we go about deciding what is reasonable and what is not. Our experiences also supply us with a constant stream of readily accessible data we can draw from in thinking about God, and God's involvement in the world.

People of faith have always spent a good deal of time arguing about how the Bible, reason, tradition, and experience should be prioritized, and whether and how they mutually influence one another. The Roman Catholic Church, for example, emphasizes that the Bible was shaped by the traditions of the church, both in the content of its message and in the process of its canonization, when church leaders developed criteria for assessing which biblical books should be included, and which should not. Those who value reason often hold that we should be open to the data and insights of all disciplines when formulating theological claims.[5] Liberationist scholars, including feminist, womanist, black, and Latin American liberation theologians, have emphasized that our experiences—both the context in which we have been formed and the stories that have shaped us—can never be laid to the side when we are interpreting other sources. Inevitably they affect which figures we identify with when we read Scripture, for example, and whether we resonate with particular creeds and confessions or find them meaningless.

Many Protestant Christians, trying to take all of these sources into account, argue that the Bible is the *norming norm*, that is, that it should have a "higher status" than the other sources, even though those sources are always in play as we seek to know and speak about God. The United Methodist Church, following the lead of John Wesley, often helps people of faith conceptualize how multiple norms and sources come into play by using the image of a quadrilateral—with each of the four sides representing Bible, reason, tradition, and experience, respectively. (Since Methodists emphasize that the Bible has greater authority than the other three, the side representing it is often depicted as longer.)[6]

In the remainder of this chapter we will consider how we negotiate among these various and often mutually affecting sources for speaking of God. In the language of theologians, this means we will be thinking not only of what sources we draw from in formulating our words about God, but also what norms come into play in negotiating between and among them. As was the case in the last chapter when we considered the character of our theological language, it will be helpful for us to consider not only the kind and quality of the sources and our norms for navigating them, but also what our own capacities and incapacities are as we read, explore, and discover. We might want to ask ourselves how prepared we are—intellectually, emotionally, and spiritually—to explore and interpret the content of the Bible, the confessions of our traditions, the philosophical logic that shapes the way we think about the relationship between God and the world, and the stories of our own experiences as they relate to who we understand God to be.

Most of us probably feel as though we are not ready in relation to at least some of these areas of inquiry, especially if we are in earnest about discerning what it is that God has to say to us. We might be heartened by the realization that feeling inadequate or unnerved, in the face of what it is we are doing, might not be so problematic—as long as we continue to "hold faith," that is, and not give up! I once had a pastor friend tell me that the only time he ever worried, just before he preached, was when he wasn't worried at all. That was a sure sign, he said, that he wasn't taking the charge to learn and speak about God seriously enough.

When it comes to speaking words about God, remembering that we can never gain mastery of the subject matter might be the most important preparation of all. As we discussed in chapter 1, recognizing our creaturely limits reminds us that knowledge of God comes not as a result of our own efforts, but rather in the form of a gift. When we keep that in mind, we are then able freely to pursue knowledge of God because we believe—even when we have difficulty believing—that this God has already reached out and laid claim to us. (This last statement is, of course, an unabashed statement of faith—an affirmation of the very doctrine of revelation we considered in chapter 1.)

As we hold on to faith and dive into negotiating the many norms and sources for doing theology, it will be helpful to return to the distinction between general and special revelation raised at the end of chapter 1. These two overarching categories have been used by theologians including Thomas and Calvin to give people of faith a way to begin reflecting on the character of the sources from which we draw, and how able we are, in and of ourselves, to benefit from them. How and what do we learn from God by way of general revelation, and how able are we to receive what is extended to us? How and what do we learn from God by way of special revelation, and is there anything at all we can do to facilitate our receipt of it, if it is truly and only a gift?

General Revelation: Right before Our Eyes (but Tough to See!)

Calvin's favorite biblical passage about general revelation was Romans 1:18-32. Let me give you a sense for how he interprets this passage. In the opening of his letter to the Roman church, Paul is describing a problem with the human condition: we are unable to see, he explains, what is right before our eyes. "What can be known about God," Paul insists, is evident in "the things God has made."[7] But instead of coming to know the one true God by way of creation, Paul laments, human beings crafted for themselves idols resembling elements of the created order.[8] We humans gave up worshipping the immortal God and instead began worshipping that which is created. According to Calvin, this idolatrous behavior is indicative of our incapacity as well as our depravity—in and of ourselves, we simply cannot make our way to God. In and of our own strength, we are unable to see what is right before our eyes and available to us.[9] That is why, Calvin thinks, we need special revelation. Not because there is anything wrong with general revelation (through which everything about God has been made clear), but because there is something damaged in us that keeps us from seeing.

Wait a minute, some of us might be thinking, reading Romans 1 over Calvin's shoulder. While it looks pretty clear that humans did commit the sin of idolatry, on what basis does Calvin conclude all human beings will *necessarily* commit the same sin? Perhaps, you might say, there is a more positive way of reading this passage. Maybe it can serve as a warning to us, we might suggest, so that we who witness revelation will not follow in the way of "fools" (see verse 22), but will rather be led to pursue the God before whom there are no other gods.[10]

If you read Romans 1:18-32 more as a warning about the limits of human capabilities than as a devastating diagnosis, you are in good company. Calvin, as we have seen, emphasizes humanity's utter incapacity to access general revelation. Thomas (12th c), however, thinks differently, teaching that human strides toward knowing God can certainly be made by way of general revelation. Pascal (17th c) treats self-reflection as a form of general revelation, referring to the "infinite abyss" that we might, however unsuccessfully, try to satisfy with other things.[11] John Wesley (18th c) believes God extends prevenient grace to all people, as is evidenced in the fact that all have "some tendency toward life, some degree of salvation, the beginning of a deliverance from a blind, unfeeling heart, quite insensible of God and the things of God."[12] C. S. Lewis (20th c) comments, following this same trajectory, that "if I find in myself a desire which no experience in this world can satisfy, the most probable explanation is that I was made for another world."[13] It is not surprising that Lewis, consistent with this statement, thought that helping people recognize their dissatisfaction could turn them toward belief.

Calvin, again, resisted any suggestion that dissatisfaction, or the ordered beauty of nature, or some innate sense of what is right and what is wrong could effectively lead us to faith. Apart from God's intervention in our lives, he would say, dissatisfaction will likely lead to rampant consumerism or gluttony, the beauty of nature to the creation of art that distracts us from the Creator of all, and moral sensibility to devising religious systems of our own making that are antithetical to "true religion" (as he and other sixteenth-century Reformers called it)[14] given to us by God. As the Israelites worshipped a golden calf instead of the one true God, so we in our sinfulness replace the God who stands right before us with gods of our own making. In the words of Paul Tillich, a twentieth-century theologian, our "ultimate concern" is not what it should be, or even what we claim it is.[15] Like Jesus's friend Martha, we are "worried and distracted by many things" rather than attending to what matters most.[16] It would be hard to find a person of faith who would disagree with this assessment, in our day. Nearly every sermon I've heard, lately, mentions this idea. The goal of every spiritual practice is to center our lives in that which is meaningful rather than that which is empty. And there might not be a one of us who hasn't asked, at least from time to time, why living in cognizant relationship to God is so difficult, if it is, indeed, what we were made for.[17]

Calvin has an answer to this, though it is, again, not the answer that every Christian thinker might give. He thinks all of us are, as a consequence of the Fall, *totally depraved.* By this he means not that we are worthless or beyond repair, but that we are incapable, by virtue of our own will or wherewithal, of overriding the dullness that is symptomatic of our sin in order to perceive the God who is self-revealed all around us. Theological ethicist Paul Lehmann explains, along these lines, that "total depravity...simply expresses the fact that whatever it takes to overcome the ethical predicament of humanity does not lie within the powers of humanity. Human renewal is not intrinsic to human capacity; it comes to humanity as a gift."[18] Whenever this gift of renewal is received, Lehmann thinks (agreeing with Calvin), it has come by way of special revelation.

Special Revelation: Refuses to Let Us Go

Special revelation, when understood to name God's gracious but persistent pursuit of us, is generally identified with specific acts of God intentionally breaking through our dullness to sharpen our perception of what really is. What is tricky about describing special revelation is that we have neither the right nor the capacity to delimit the form it might take. Put another way, what this means is that God speaks to us in any way God chooses to speak. "God may speak to us through Russian Communism, through a flute concerto, through a blossoming shrub or through a dead dog,"[19] Barth famously asserts. Now, it is very important to note that this does not mean that God *does*, necessarily, speak to us through a flute concerto, a shrub, or a dead dog. What Barth is saying, rather, is that however and wherever God is saying something to us—regardless of how expected the vehicle of that speaking—we would do well to pay attention.

The Bible is full of stories of God reaching out to heal the perception of those who have not yet seen, so they can know who God is and witness what God is up to in the world, understanding who they are and what their relationship is to God's work. The ways God reaches out are varied and, in many cases, surprising (and even bizarre!). God promises Abraham and Sarah that they will become parents of many descendants by taking Abraham out and showing him that sky full of stars.[20] God charges Moses with an impossible mission by commanding him from out of a burning bush.[21] God lets Joseph know his eleven brothers will one day bow down to him by speaking through a dream in which each of the brothers is represented by a bundle of wheat.[22] God corrects Balaam by causing a donkey to talk.[23] God calls Mary through a visitation by the angel Gabriel, telling her she is blessed to be the bearer of the Messiah.[24] There are whispers outside of caves, and tablets brought down from mountains, and stars that shine over stables, and angels that sing glorious choruses for lowly shepherds; there are visions, and callings in the night, and descending doves and wrong-flowing water and consuming fire and pillars of salt and dew-resistant fleeces—all ways in which God says: I am here, you are in relationship to me; I am up to something, here's how you are a part of it.[25]

Our God, the one who stays in relationship to us as God did for our forebears, is an active participant in the life of the world. Because this is true, we can understand God to be a God of history. Our story unfolds as a grander narrative in which God participates alongside us rather than dispassionately watching from outside. African American systematic theologians are among those who persistently remind us that God acts in history. James Evans writes, in *We Have Been Believers,* "Revelation is inseparable from the historic struggle of black people for liberation. . . . The history of revelation and the history of liberation are the same history," incomplete insofar as human history is yet unfolding.[26] That our God acts in and shapes this unfolding history is an aspect of our covenantal relationship with God, a part of the promise God has made never to abandon us. That our God is a God of history describes one way God is with us and for us. The stories remind us of the innumerable ways this participation has manifested itself.

The book that contains all of these stories is itself considered to be a vehicle of special revelation. This is not only because it recounts specific stories about God's claim on particular communities and particular people, but because people of faith have consistently testified that they, through hearing these stories, have come to perceive their own place in the narrative of salvation. Through the story of God's fearsome love for Israel, we experience God's relentless love for us. Through lamenting and praising with the psalmists, we see that doubt, honesty, and wonder are all and together true aspects of faith. Through listening into Jesus's encounters with others, we encounter him for ourselves. Through reading the Epistles—Paul's letters to particular churches—we, too, are instructed, affirmed, and challenged to live our lives as disciples of Christ.

How does it happen, exactly, that we are drawn to hearing God speaking to us, in particular, by way of the biblical witness? Harkening back to Calvin, again, it is not by virtue of our own energies or strategies, as they are applied to biblical study. It is not that special revelation is contained, somehow, in the words of the Bible if we can only figure out how to unlock them. The key to hearing God speak is not reading the Bible with a certain interpretive method, or learning Hebrew and Greek (the languages in which it was written), or praying beforehand, or being more deeply sincere or humble. While all of these might be worthy goals for us to embrace freely and joyfully for their own sakes, they should never be undertaken as means to the end of knowing God. It should never in any way be suggested that we need to do a certain amount of grunt work if we are to reap the benefit or earn the reward of perceiving God. To proceed in such a way would be to focus again on ourselves and our own achievements, rather than to revel in God's bounteous gifts. And even if Calvin is only halfway right in what he says about total depravity, proceeding as though perception of God is something to be accomplished will likely lead us only to frustration; to wondering why it is that we haven't been successful in accomplishing *our* goal of knowing God better, given how hard *we* have worked.

To illustrate this point: In the context of teaching a workshop on the subject of Reading the Bible Theologically, I once asked a roomful of people about their Bible-reading practices. After a couple of people gave sincere but kind of typical answers (e.g., "I was in the 'Read the Bible through the Year' program last year";[27] "I try to get up early every morning and have my devotions, otherwise my day just doesn't go as well"), I was taken aback by a woman who suddenly blurted out, much to the shock of the entire group: "I *hate* reading the Bible!" She looked kind of surprised, herself, that she had said it. And after she spoke the group immediately went silent, waiting to see how I would respond. Fortunately, the woman seemed to re-center herself before I attempted to answer, explaining to us that she had been reading the Bible diligently every single day for years, using a popular method of study recommended by her pastor. But all her reading and study had yet to pay off, she told me. She did not know God any better, and now she dreaded her devotional time and was at a loss to know what to do.

My advice to her was, believe it or not, to *stop* reading the Bible for a year. I suggested this because I suspected she was associating her reading so much with her own efforts and failure that she needed a break in order to approach her reading in a way that allowed the Holy Spirit to work. The advice I gave probably surprised some participants in the workshop even more than did the woman's initial outburst! Still, I thought I saw flickers of empathy in the eyes of some others sitting around the circle. Maybe they wouldn't say they *hated* Bible reading. But they might say there were lots of times when they found it boring and even more times when reading the Bible didn't actually seem to make a difference to their day, even when they were hoping it would.

This woman reminded me, just a bit, of the rich young ruler who comes to Jesus having "kept every one of the commandments since the day he was born."[28] He wants to know what else he needs to do to inherit eternal life. Isn't it interesting that keeping all the rules, as he understood them, wasn't enough to make him feel confident and secure in his faith? It is no accident, then, that Jesus tries to get him to let go of the letter of the law and live more in the spirit of it. He tells the wealthy young man to sell his stuff, give away that money, and follow Jesus's path.[29] In this effort, Jesus is trying to free the young man up from tallying his own spiritual credentials so he can engage, instead, that which matters most.

The woman I met in the workshop, unlike the rich young ruler, seemed relieved to be told she needed to let go of her self-imposed program for spiritual advancement. Maybe she had made the comment already suspecting her habitual Bible reading had in some sense become her god, rather than helping her better to know God. It is probably true of most of us—right alongside of her—that we have at times felt dis-ease in relation to what we imagined were the most faithful spiritual practices. When this happens, it may help to remember that revelation is not a product of our own effort. Of course, there is a certain letting go of power associated with following through on our realization of this—a relinquishing the rich young ruler resisted. What we would all do well to remember is that faith is not about subjecting ourselves to certain rules or spiritual strategies, but only to the God we are hoping to hear. "Be still, and know that I am God!"[30] the psalmist wrote, exhorting us to pause and recognize God's presence even in the midst of the world's turmoil. But perhaps we have to pause and be still, even, in relation to the turmoil we create for ourselves—even if this turmoil has taken the form of the very best spiritual practices.

This brings us full circle, again, to special revelation. What God has to say comes to us as it comes to us, and there is no guarantee it will come to us through reading the Bible in a particular way, or with particular fervor, any more than there is any bar on how or from where it will come. That said, Christians have through the last two millennia consistently testified that the Holy Spirit speaks to them through the stories and teachings in the biblical text, "revealing to their minds" and "sealing upon their hearts" the "knowledge of God's benevolence toward us" as it is "founded upon the truth of the freely-given promise in Christ."[31] The Bible has a special place in the life of Christians because Christianity recognizes people have been changed when they read the words printed on its pages, when they listen to passages read and preached in worship and in Sunday school, and when they study and discuss the texts in Bible studies. Christians have confirmed, both in individual testimony and in communal statements of faith, that the Spirit has ministered to them as they have engaged the biblical text, helping them to perceive their own identity in relationship to God. As Calvin puts it, "The highest proof of Scripture derives in general from the fact that God in person speaks in it."[32] According to this line of reasoning, it is not that we can make a case for biblical authority first, and only then move on to reading the Bible and being affected by it because we are already convinced it is worthwhile. Rather, it is in the reading of it that we become convinced of its efficacy, and only then because God has spoken, through it, to us.

Looking through the "Glasses" of Scripture and Seeing What's There

Something that is often missed, by those who agree with Calvin that knowledge of God cannot be gained apart from special revelation, is that special revelation, once it is received, allows us to discern God's presence and work by way of general revelation. In other words, once we recognize God "calling us by name"[33] in particular ways (through the biblical witness, for example), we can look out at the beauty of a sunset (for example) and do more than wonder about the awesome intelligence that created it. Having received special revelation, we can look at that sunset and know even better the God to whom we have already been introduced. "I will sing to the Lord as long as I live," exclaims the psalmist,[34] following verses that extol God's creation of, presence in, and working through the earth and the waters, the wind and the grass, the darkness and the sunrise, the animals and the people. The psalmist, again, is able to look at everything around her and move from wondering at creation to knowing the Creator.

Pushing this point even further, when special revelation serves as a lens through which the natural world is interpreted, it leads us to stand in awe not only of who God is, but also of who we are in relationship to this God who has created such beautiful things. "What are human beings that you think about them; what are human beings that you pay attention to them?" the psalmist asks.[35] Notice something very important here, that is: the psalmist is able to ask this question only because he has experienced God's particular claim on him, as a particular person. Special revelation leads him to marvel, all the more, that this God who claims him is the God of the "heavens... the moon and the stars." And it is by way of marveling at God's majestic work that the psalmist is brought to a deeper appreciation that he is known and cared for by God. So, it is not only that special revelation facilitates our perceiving God via the natural world; it is also the case that the capaciousness of nature leads us to construe God's particular claim on us as all the more miraculous.

How, again, might we understand the role of the Bible in relation to all this? The famed metaphor used by Calvin for that familiar book we pull off our shelves, fish out of our backpacks, or find on our bedside tables is "spectacles." Calvin describes the Bible as the eyeglasses through which we look in order to be able to see who God is and what God is up to in the world. Putting together some of the ideas we have been discussing, in the last few pages: God is self-revealed to us when we look through the *spectacles of Scripture*[36] and the Holy Spirit enables us to perceive what is true and real. Our "bleary-eyed" incapacity is corrected, Calvin explains, and we are able to see clearly.[37] With our eyeglasses in place, we do not turn away from God to create idols. Rather, we are drawn to stand in awe of the majesty of God and the glorious inclusion of ourselves.

Giving the Spirit a "Leg Up": Three Suggestions

While revelation is initiated and accomplished by God, this does not mean we are merely passive recipients of it. On the contrary, we may live intentionally as people of faith seeking understanding while still honoring God as sovereign actor. Because the character of God's power is not to lord over others, but to include them, it is possible to envision revelation as an event that is at once both all God's and also ours. This idea correlates, theologically speaking, to the Christian conviction that our "life is hidden with Christ in God."[38] Because, in and through Jesus Christ, we are included in God's life and work, our active participation is part and parcel of God's saving story without any loss of distinction between us and God. We will discuss the details and relevance of this when we come to the doctrines of incarnation and Trinity. For now, however, our task is to think through what it would look like to partner with God in relation to our reading of Scripture. How is it that we can position ourselves to participate in the revelation being gifted to us by way of this central source of our faith?

I have three suggestions I believe might help us engage God's self-revelation, as it comes to us by way of Scripture. Allow me to list them, and then to consider them in a little more detail as a way of moving toward making a practical plan for how, exactly, we might go about reading and interpreting Scripture in ways that are faithful.

First, if we are to be "people God can find" by way of the biblical witness, it will serve us well to think broadly about the genres and purposes of various biblical texts. We will benefit from considering figurative, as well as literal, meanings.

Second, and returning to some of the reflection done at the opening of this chapter, it will be fruitful to make some considered decisions about how we engage multiple sources, as we seek to hear what God is saying to us. If we hold that Scripture is the norming norm for all other sources that come into play, we will seek to consider, as we read it, how it might challenge the wisdom we have derived from our experiences, the conclusions we have drawn from our reasoning, and the value we assign to our traditions.

Third and finally, when we read something in Scripture that seems completely incoherent or just plain wrong, keeping Christ at the center of our readings will make it possible to name real problems while at the same time honoring Scripture's authority.

Thinking Expansively about Biblical Meanings

I have found there is often an association made between reading the Bible literally and valuing its authority. I want to be clear: I reject this association. To allow only for literal readings of the biblical texts is to limit the ways God can speak to us through the words of the Bible. If, through engaging Scripture, we are seeking to know the God who is always greater than any of our knowledge,[39] we will practice thinking expansively about the range of genres, histories, contexts, audiences, and writers that the Bible engages in conveying its stories and wisdom.

For some of us, the idea that the Bible should be read other than literally might seem somewhat threatening. We might be worried that, once we move away from the straightforward meaning of the words, there is a danger we will impose on the text meanings that are not really there. This is a valid concern that should be kept in mind. Interestingly, however, history seems to reveal that those who subscribe to literal readings of the Bible are at least as guilty of leveraging Scripture to promote their own agendas as those who do not.[40] Further, I suggest that thinking more expansively about the meanings of the biblical witness does not mean interpretation will inevitably become a free-for-all. As we will discuss further, attending to how we order the sources from which we draw as well as to the interpretive keys that lie at the center of our readings, will help us guard against imposing our own agendas in ways that inhibit us from hearing what the Bible genuinely has to say.

For others of us, the suggestion that we can read the Bible more expansively while still honoring its authority will be something of a relief. For one thing, many of us find it quite boring to be confined to only literal readings in our quest to know God better. We may feel guilty about this, especially if we have come to the text with the hope and expectation that we will be transformed by its message. It might be helpful to know that some of the most influential theological thinkers in the history of the church were disappointed by the quality of the biblical writing, especially when they were comparing it with other great literature of their day. This was true, for example, of Augustine, who was encouraged by the preaching of his mentor, Ambrose, to overlook the simple prose of the Scriptures in order to gain from its message.

I remember being shocked to discover, when I was in college, that the idea that the Bible is literally without error is fairly new. A book that helped me think through this, and that I highly recommend, is George Marsden's *Fundamentalism and American Culture*.[41] In it, Marsden explains how the idea that everything in the Bible is empirically true and could therefore in principle be tested by methods of scientific inquiry developed in the nineteenth century, following the scientific revolution of the Enlightenment period. In the course of this era, science continued advancing by leaps and bounds and all other disciplines were highly affected. Historical research, for example, became more focused on the importance of making only warranted claims.[42] Debates about how the limits of applying the so-called empirical method to nonscientific fields were lively then, and continue today. Historians often point out that historical events, unlike science experiments, are unique—they cannot be duplicated, because conditions inevitably vary. Many theologians are concerned, similarly, that attempts to align incarnation or resurrection with measurable facts may actually compromise on their truth. That said, modern theologians or historians are not apt to deny that empirical facts must be noted and taken into account as they engage the work of their disciplines. The question is: When does scientific method further understanding, and when does it impede it?

The problem with reading all passages of Scripture as though they are composed of literal facts is that it misses out on much of what the Bible has to offer, since not all passages were meant to be read and interpreted literally. Clearly, the Bible is full of literary genres and styles, including: poetry (e.g., Song of Solomon), instruction (e.g., Deuteronomy, Jesus's teachings, the Epistles), historical biography (e.g., 1 Samuel 8–15), parables (e.g., as told by Nathan in 2 Samuel 12 and as told by Jesus throughout the Synoptic[43] Gospels), songs (e.g., Psalms), prophecy (e.g., Daniel, Revelation), advice for wholeness (e.g., Proverbs), drama (e.g., prelude to Job), lament (e.g., Ecclesiastes), and—most controversially, perhaps—myth (e.g., Genesis 1–3). Each of these should be enjoyed and studied in the form it takes, otherwise something will be lost. We would not, of course, engage a performance of *Romeo and Juliet* in the same way we would engage a lecture on addressing global warming. One is not necessarily more important or true than the other, but each invites us to explore matters that are meaningful in very different ways. Why would we, then, read the story of creation in Genesis in the same mode in which we read a biology textbook? Why would we read the prophecy of John in Revelation as though it is a blueprint of the future, assuming our goal should be to map it with verifiable events in history so we might in that way master its code? Such approaches to biblical study run the risk of valuing literalism and fact-finding to the point of missing out on what is really there.

Genesis is a story that tells us far more than the blow-by-blow process for how the earth was created, for example. It bears witness to the creative, playful power of God; the goodness of all that was made; the created harmony between humanity and God, humanity and nature, and men and woman that was God's creative intention, but that somehow was lost. The Genesis creation myth (with *myth* naming the genre of the story without compromising in any way on its truth) names sin for what it is: an aberration that is contrary to what God made, intends, or desires. Sin is a problem, it says. A big problem. And this is the problem the story of salvation addresses. Any question about whether *God* literally *made Eve out of Adam's rib* pales into comparison with the truth that *God made Eve out of Adam's rib*, meaning that she is—and we all are, in relation to one another—bone of bone, flesh of flesh. This matters, simply put, because it says something about everything. When I know you are bone of my bone and flesh of my flesh—I will love you as I love myself. I will treat you justly, doing you no harm. When each one of us knows they share bones and flesh with every other, violence will cease. Bodies will be valued, and fed, and protected. The wholeness and harmony that is God's creative intention will be restored.

This truth of the creation story can never be diminished (and might even be enhanced!) by whatever is true in evolution. Genesis 1–3 tells the story of the truth that lies at the heart of all existence, all relationships, all the cosmos. It is a truth about God's power, God's goodness, God's creativity, God's generosity. It is a truth about the goodness of creation, a truth that insists brokenness is *not* okay, but a terribly big problem. Genesis 1–3 sets our sights on redemption, not only because Eve and Adam fell but because their fallen nature is an aberration in a story where what God made is called good, good, good, good, good, and, finally, "very good."[44]

Whatever literal meaning the Bible's creation stories have might be compared to a thimbleful of sea water in relation to the ocean of truth of which they are a part. And to read them, interpret them, and make them our own is to participate in this truth. It is to participate in this truth, again, with no fear of learning whatever can be learned from the biological sciences, open to gaining a clearer perception of God in the interplay of multiple sources.

One of the advantages of reading the Bible expansively rather than literally is, then, that doing so helps us see where and who we are in relation to what we are reading. It invites us to identify with biblical characters or—when we don't resonate with who they are or what they are up to—to ask "wondering" questions about them.[45] "Wondering" questions tend to push off face-value statements in the biblical text, going on to engage them with imagination and even empathy. We might notice Sarah being left behind on the day, for example, when Abraham and Isaac climb Mount Moriah.[46] We might go on actively to wonder, for example, what she might have been thinking or doing.

Or we might wonder about Abraham. The texts of Genesis tell us a lot about him: he hears God, he obeys God, he is willing to jeopardize even God's promise for the sake of his relationship with God. We can rehearse these points and throw up our hands at the mystery of how Abraham was able to do these things, and how God was able to command such a horrific act. But to think expansively about the story would mean not only rehearsing the facts about it, or even only throwing up our hands in the face of the mysteries of it, but working hard at wondering about it—at asking questions about how Abraham must have been feeling; at how, really, he could have managed to be obedient to such a command. Sometimes, even, the question about this story takes the form of wondering whether God actually did require Isaac to be killed, or whether it was the authors of the story who somehow interpreted what happened in this way.

The thinker who first helped me think expansively, rather than only literally, about the biblical text is Søren Kierkegaard. Kierkegaard is masterful at asking wonder questions in relation to Bible stories—both the beautiful ones and the difficult ones. His "wonderings" demonstrate that he has moved deeper than the face value of texts, stepping into the stories, teachings, and quandaries of the biblical witness in ways that show how affected he is by them.

There is no text, it seems, that affects Kierkegaard more than Genesis 22. When he tries to put himself in the sandals of Abraham, Kierkegaard has great difficulty. But he doesn't pull back from the text and label Abraham's behavior a "mystery," concluding there is no place for him to enter in and try to understand. On the contrary, his curious befuddlement leads him to pursue connection with Abraham all the more diligently. "Who can be an Abraham?" he wonders, asking the question again and again as he seeks to fathom how Abraham can possibly hear God, and obey.[47] I imagine Kierkegaard sitting at his desk and pouring over the story, examining it from all angles. Some of his imaginings are published, midrash-style, at the opening of his stunning but disturbing work *Fear and Trembling.* Trying to get not only into the mind and heart of Abraham, but also at the dynamics between God, Abraham, and Isaac, Kierkegaard paints four different scenarios: In the first, Kierkegaard imagines Abraham pretending to be a psychopath who has orchestrated the journey to sacrifice Isaac himself. He misrepresents himself, Kierkegaard suggests, so Isaac will not lose faith in the God who commanded his murder. In the second midrash, Kierkegaard imagines Abraham doing what God asks, but forever afterward living a joyless life as a person who has lost his faith. In the third, Abraham goes to Mount Moriah alone and asks God's forgiveness for having even considered sacrificing Isaac. (This rendition of the story moves the furthest away from a literal reading of Genesis 22; perhaps Kierkegaard has in mind, here, that Abraham's confession is represented by the ram being caught in the underbush.) Finally, in the fourth scenario Kierkegaard imagines Isaac becoming contemptuous of Abraham because Abraham falters, in his despair, while raising the knife to kill him. The hypothesis is that perhaps Abraham isn't as unquestioning in his obedience as he appears in a straightforward reading of the text.

When I was in college and reading these scenarios that were written by Kierkegaard, I experienced a range of conflicting reactions. Frankly, I was on the one hand panicked at how he seemed to be playing fast and loose with the biblical text. I mean—really!—how far can you take a wondering approach like this before becoming unfaithful to what the text is actually saying? But I was also, on the other hand, overwhelmingly relieved. In my experience thus far at that point in my life, I had thought the only option for reading the Bible faithfully was reading it very narrowly, taking from it only what was delineated by the black and white words on its pages. Kierkegaard demonstrated for me that this approach, too, can often be unfaithful. This is because it keeps us at a distance from the story itself, learning it, rehearsing it, and being vaguely bothered by it, but never really entering into it and submitting to its message. Reading the Bible as people of faith must surely entail our engaging it in such a way that we are transformed by it, and wondering and imagining are essential to the work of engagement that leads to such transformation.

Practically speaking, then, I am suggesting that we think expansively about the biblical witness by approaching texts with a willingness to wonder and imagine. What we are wondering and imagining, specifically, depends on what text we are reading. If we are reading Genesis 22, as discussed, we will wonder how each of the characters is feeling and how the story can possibly be synchronized both with the promise God earlier made to Abraham and Sarah, and with the character of God as good. From there we might imagine, as Kierkegaard did, various scenarios that will help us make sense of the story. If we are reading a different kind of text, say—Isaiah 40—on the other hand, we might stand in wonder in the face of a world where no one dies an untimely death and wolves are no threat to lambs. Now, *that* world takes a lot of imagination to draw to mind! It is an example, truly, of what Barth referred to as the "strange new world within the Bible,"[48] and how what we find there might be very different than what we expect.

Engaging Sources with the Bible as the Norming Norm

Another way we can prepare to receive what God will gift to us through Scripture is by attending more intentionally to how we engage the norms and sources that come into play as we seek to know, and speak about, God. The opening exercise to this chapter was geared to trigger reflection on how it is we actually work with and order our sources. What I am recommending here is taking the next step—attending to how we go about faithfully relating various sources to one another while valuing the Bible as the norming norm of them all.

The point of this is not to be rigid, or even always to order sources in exactly the same way. It is, rather, to have enough of a sense of what we are about, when we make statements about God or invoke biblical authority, that we can make persuasive arguments for our beliefs and be in productive dialogue with others about our, and their, convictions. If I can explain to a person with whom I am in conversation that the teachings of the church hold significant weight for me, when it comes to ascertaining what is meaningful or true, we will have a greater understanding of each other and why we disagree about something. This might be especially helpful, for example, if the person with whom I'm speaking values the discoveries made by scientific inquiry more than the theological arguments I tend to engage—at least they will know where I'm coming from! Where there is a problem being in dialogue with others about the most important things of all, it is often because we haven't been up front about what rules of the game we are operating with, or we have changed our rules mid-course without warning.

Allow me to give an example of where we have been having a problem in our conversations of late. In many churches, over at least the last fifteen years, there have been debates about the ordination and/or marriage of LGBTQ persons. Christians of all denominations and points of view have struggled to figure out what the Bible has to say about these issues. The challenge is: the Bible doesn't say a whole lot. What is said is, at face value, only condemnatory of LGBTQ sexual practices. The ordination or marriage of gay persons is not ever specifically mentioned in Scripture, one way or another.

Christians who are more literalistic have often argued that the Bible is clear in its condemnation and that, therefore, LGBTQ persons should not be ordained to church leadership or married in an ecclesial context. Many Christians, looking to think more expansively about these verses in the context of the biblical witness, point out that "homosexuality," in the biblical texts, was not associated with the monogamous, committed unions most Christian pro-LGBTQ supporters are rallying for today. Further, they argue, the Bible speaks clearly about God's love for all, and God's desire that we love one another. These central biblical themes, they hold, should be taken into consideration in developing biblical arguments for supporting LGBTQ persons.

Both the more literalistic person and the one who tries to argue for the Bible's central message of love may well be identified as people of faith who are trying to respect Scripture's authority. Regardless of the fact that they handle biblical texts differently and have different views about LGBTQ equality, neither refuses to push the Bible to the side in making assessments about issues of controversy in the church. But what if someone who claimed the Bible as the norming norm all of a sudden, in the course of an ecclesial debate or one-on-one conversation with a colleague, invoked an insight drawn from a source other than Scripture as a way of trumping a person making an argument with which she disagreed? If the self-proclaimed biblical literalist, debating with the person arguing for the centrality of love, suddenly brought into play that all the homosexuals she knew were promiscuous and unhappy, this would not really be fair, according to the very rules she had established. To reference her own experience as a higher authority than the biblical text, even as she was claiming to be doing otherwise, would be out of bounds. If the person arguing for love, on the other hand, suddenly left behind the work of wrestling with Scripture in order to leverage the fact that scientists suggest there is a genetic explanation for sexual preferences, this would also be less than fair. The point would be interesting, but it would change what the discussion was about. It would no longer be about what the Bible says about LGBTQ issues. It would be about drawing from whatever source works best to support LGBTQ people being ordained and married. Now, that might be a perfectly worthy discussion. But if one of the participants' views is ultimately grounded in her concern about promiscuity and the other is ultimately swayed by what science has to say about genetics, neither can accurately claim that the Bible is really their norming norm for all other norms in relation to this matter.

To engage the Bible as the norming norm even as other norms and sources are brought into play would mean having a manifest commitment to thinking through insights drawn from other sources in relation to biblical readings. These readings would not necessarily be limited to one's own interpretations, as though the only approach to taking Scripture seriously, as we debate important matters, would be to go off in a corner by ourselves, heavy-duty concordance in hand, and look up all key words related to whatever it is we are considering in an effort to figure out what the Bible says. While it is the privilege and responsibility of every person of faith to search the Scriptures for themselves, we don't go at biblical interpretation alone. On the contrary, we join in our exploration of the biblical witness with Christian believers from all over the world and from down through the ages. From the person sitting across from us at Bible study, to the pastor who preaches each week from the lectionary; from our grandmother who used to recite entire chapters by heart, to the new convert who identifies more with the person lying in the ditch than with the Good Samaritan who offers help;[49] from the community of biblical scholars who have labored over biblical commentaries, to the theologians who have, through the ages, worked to formulate Christian doctrines that take into account both the resonances and dissonances heard in the symphony of the sixty-six books that constitute the whole, to our forebears in the faith who developed criteria for what should—and should not!—be included in the biblical canon, we do not go at biblical interpretation in a vacuum. As we read, study, and explore we have all of these to turn to for conversation, insight, and guidance not only in relation to what the Bible has to say to various issues, but also to how multiple sources from real life come into play in relation to all our interpretations and discernings. To engage the reflections of others in the course of our own biblical study reminds us that we are part of a great, ongoing enterprise that people of faith have found to be life-giving, even if it is challenging at times.

An important and practical way into benefitting from the interpretive wisdom of our faith communities is to attend to the creeds and confessions made by Christians through the ages. While it is important to respect the fact that different Christian traditions weigh these more or less heavily, when it comes to granting them interpretive authority, they at the very least serve almost as "summaries" of the insights particular ecclesial communities have believed most faithfully draw from Scripture in relation to particular contexts and struggles. My own tradition, the Presbyterian Church (USA) has, as part of its constitution, an open collection of creeds and confessions called *The Book of Confessions.* Confessions can be added to *The Book of Confessions* whenever people of faith understand there to be something "new" God is offering to us, by way of Scripture, that speaks to a particular concern or context. The first confession included is one shared by Christians throughout the ages—the Apostles' Creed.[50] The Apostles' Creed came into being in the first century of the church, when Christian believers were developing a liturgy for baptism as well as moving toward developing the doctrine of the Trinity. "Do you believe in God the Father?" the baptizing pastor would ask. "In God the Son? In God the Holy Spirit?" The most recent confession to be adopted is the "Belhar Declaration."[51] Affirmed by the Dutch Reformed Church in South Africa in 1986, Belhar speaks firmly against apartheid, drawing from the biblical witness in making a case for inclusion and equality.

Church traditions—including its creeds and confessions—can serve as helpful checks and balances to particular readings of Scripture. If someone were to read the Bible and decide, for example, that the Bible is *not* trinitarian, the Apostles' Creed would offer a formidable challenge to that interpretation. This is because it represents the fact that Christians through the ages have recognized that the Bible teaches God is triune.

Interestingly, however, to hold that the Bible is the norming norm is to be open, at least in principle, to making adjustments even to our church traditions, if these traditions come to be understood as antithetical to Scripture. While challenges to God's triune nature, drawing from Scripture, have not held much sway, other challenges to church traditions, made by reference to Scripture, have led to significant changes in the traditions themselves.

Consider the church's tradition of ordaining only men, for example. This tradition, supported by reference to several biblical passages, is practiced by the majority of Christian churches around the world—Protestant as well as Roman Catholic. And there are also Christian denominations that have never imposed limits on who might be ordained. Wesleyan Christians, open to ordaining women as well as men, are fond of citing the verse from Scripture that reminds us "the Spirit blows where it wills."[52] Of particular interest are churches that were once convinced Scripture teaches ordination is for men only that now ordain women. My own church—the Presbyterian Church (USA)—is one of these churches. We reversed our thinking on women's ordination in the late 1950s precisely because we read the Bible, again, and decided our earlier interpretation was wrong. Certainly, emerging cultural values oriented toward the inclusion of women came into play in goading us to struggle, anew, with what Scripture had to say. But in the end it was not cultural pressure that was invoked as reason to change our church's tradition. In the final analysis, a biblical case was made that recognized the ecclesial leadership of women in Scripture, acknowledging (with the Wesleyans!) the inclusive movement of the Spirit and interpreting the New Testament household codes (i.e., that recommend women keep silent[53]) as applying only in particular and limited contexts. As important as tradition was as a source, in relation to this issue, it is the fact that the Bible was engaged as norming norm that led to the historic change.

Remembering this, as well as other instances when churches have changed positions on issues in light of their study of Scripture (in relation to, for example, infant baptism, divorce, and slavery), it becomes clear that the point of honoring the primacy of Scripture is not only to guard us against idolizing our own experiences and traditions, but also to give us a way of working for social change consistent with the convictions of our faith. When Luther and Calvin worked to get the Bible translated into the vernacular and into the hands of the people back in the sixteenth century, they were empowering members of the *priesthood of all believers* to read and interpret in ways that sought to understand not only how the will of God was understood in the course of history, but what God was saying in relation to their specific context. Similarly (and even more readily, in our day and age, with the books, educational opportunities, religious liberty, and leisure time to which we have access) we also have the opportunity to read and study Scripture, reflecting on what it has to tell us about the shape of God's Kingdom and how we can contribute to bringing what God desires to "earth as it is in heaven."[54]

Finally, the most important thing we can do to order our sources in relationship to Scripture is simply to read the Bible consistently and reflect on it often enough and with enough of our life energy to go deep. When we know the biblical canon—when we know it so well its stories become our stories and we hear its teachings in relation to ourselves and our own lives—it will then serve as a ready-at-hand arbiter, inspiring us as we ponder what can be learned from experience, tradition, reason, and the other sources that feed our lives.

To suggest that the Bible will begin to function as norming norm for us if we simply give it adequate time, attention, and energy might seem too simplistic, and perhaps even dangerous. Certainly, it is possible to know one's way around a Bible and still make all kinds of problematic claims. As we discussed earlier, to read the Bible is not to be guaranteed access to truth or a monopoly on right answers. To read and reflect on it is, however, consistent with living into our identity as those who have been gifted by the grace of God. What if we were to read Scripture habitually not because it is something we know we should do, or something we know we have to do in order to have any shot at living according to God's will, but because we are excited and curious about knowing what it says, and receiving its benefits? What if we approached our reading and study with gratitude and wonderment, amazed that we have had the good fortune to inherit it and the opportunity to join in conversation with those who wrote it and with all those who have read it along with us? What if we thought of reading the Bible as a way into understanding ourselves, our communities, and the predicament of and hope for the world in which we live? What if we engaged it with the interest of those eager to incorporate into our lives a life-changing gift? Then, it seems, honoring the Bible as the norming norm that norms all other norms would be for us a way of life, rather than a contrived method for ascertaining words about God.

Keeping Christ at the Center

A third way we can position ourselves to receive the gifts God desires to give us through Scripture is to keep Christ at the center of all our interpretations. A theological term for this is *christocentrism.* This is the idea not that every word in the Bible is, ultimately, about Jesus, but that what we know to be true of God in and through Jesus Christ cannot be rightly overturned by any particular biblical reading or interpretation. This idea has often been identified, in Christian traditions, as the *Rule of Love.* Specifically, it argues that any interpretation that contradicts what we know of God's love in the Gospel message of Jesus Christ must be rejected.

Allow me to give just one example of this. It is what to do with another 1 Timothy verse, an odd verse found at the end of a strange passage in which Paul calls on women to be silent because Eve, and not Adam, fell into deception in the Garden of Eden. Avoiding the temptation to exegete the entire passage and staying with our purpose here: 1 Timothy 2:15 concludes the passage by asserting that "women will be saved through childbearing" if they continue to live in a faithful manner.[55]

Now, if we read this verse only literally, we run into trouble. We run into trouble not because all literal readings are automatically bad (sometimes literal meanings work—when the passages are meant to be literal!) but because a literal reading of this verse violates what we know to be true in and through the person of Jesus Christ. In and through the Gospel, centered in Christ, we know that women are saved not through childbearing, but through God's redemptive work in the life, death, and resurrection of Jesus, as made known to us by the Spirit. Whatever this verse means, the interpretation that women who do not bear children are not saved is just plain wrong.

Thinking christocentrically, as we read and study Scripture, also helps us make sense of why we are disturbed by biblical texts in which God seems mean or unduly vindictive. Of course, we prefer the stories and passages in which God is more obviously loving and forgiving, because this is the kind of God we desire, the kind of God in whom we would put our trust. But choosing the loving God over the mean one because we like this

God better does not in itself help with the interpretation of the passages in which God seems to be less than loving. Invoking the Christ who stands at the center of our interpretations offers help because it gives us a basis, other than our own preference, for saying God acts in certain ways and not others. A Christ-centered approach might even serve as justification for reading some accounts of God's actions more as a community's limited interpretation of God's role in an event and less as an historical account of how God actually acted. An example of a case in which christocentric interpretation might helpfully come into play is in reading the prologue to the book of Job. In this prologue, God allows Satan to kill Job's family and torture him in order to prove Job's faithfulness. This is not something we like to imagine God doing. But it is also something that the God we know in Christ would not do. Applying the Rule of Love to our interpretation of Job's prologue, then, we have tended to understand it more as a creative setting of the scene for what will ensue than the recollection of an historical sparring between God and Satan.

Related to this, keeping Christ at the center of our interpretation helps us stay open to hearing all that God has to teach us through Scripture by making it possible for us to trust the text enough to be productively suspicious of it. Let me explain. What I have in mind, here, is what biblical scholars often refer to as a *hermeneutic of suspicion*. A hermeneutic of suspicion is a method of interpreting biblical texts that welcomes and encourages us to think more expansively (including reading between the lines) when something seems off in what we are reading. A classic example of this is given by Elizabeth Schüssler Fiorenza in *In Memory of Her*. Schüssler Fiorenza points out, in the framing story to this book, that when the New Testament woman anoints Jesus's feet with perfume and wipes them with her hair, Jesus promises that the story will be told in perpetuity, alongside the story of his death and resurrection, *in memory of her*.[56] Applying the hermeneutic of suspicion, however, Schüssler Fiorenza notices that we do not know the name of this woman who is to be remembered. We know the name of the crook in the story—Judas—but we do not know hers! Schüssler Fiorenza goes on to hypothesize that Jesus must have wanted us to know the woman's name, given what he said. But it has been lost somewhere, she surmises, in the historical, patriarchal shuffle. Applying a hermeneutic of suspicion allows us to think more expansively about the story in ways that are inclusive and hope-full, particularly for women who have been excluded.

While Schüssler Fiorenza does not identify her approach in her reading of the story as christocentric, it certainly is so. Christ is quite literally at the center of the story, and it is his presence and positive words about the woman that precipitates the productive suspiciousness about her missing name. It is because we trust Christ's affirmation of the woman that we have the wherewithal to be suspicious of the text, speculating that the name has been lost and thinking about what can be done with our interpretation of the text to honor Jesus's intention.

Keeping Christ at the center of our biblical study also ensures that our agendas do not become idolatrous ideologies, for they are continuously relativized by Christ. When we come to the Bible as though it has no central message, we tend to engage it as a kind of compendium of helpful resources that are compiled to address our questions and problems. There is a real danger we will treat it more as a blueprint or as a Fodor's guide that is there to be gleaned from for our purposes than as a coherent narrative. Barth wrote about this problem, playfully personifying the Bible in a voice of complaint:

> When we come to the Bible with our questions—How shall I think of God and the universe? How arrive at the divine? How present myself?—it answers us, as it were, "My dear sir, these are *your* problems: you must not ask *me!* Whether it is better to hear mass or hear a sermon, whether the proper form of Christianity is to be discovered in the Salvation Army or in 'Christian Science,' whether the better belief is that of old Reverend Doctor Smith or young Reverend Mr. Jones. . . you can and must decide for yourself. If you do not care to enter upon *my* questions, you may, to be sure, find in me all sorts of arguments and quasi-arguments for one or another standpoint, but you will not then find what is really here." We shall find ourselves only in the midst of a vast human controversy and far, far away from reality, or what might become reality in our lives. . . . It is not the right human thoughts about God which form the content of the Bible, but the right divine thoughts about [human beings]. The Bible tells us not how we should talk with God but what [God] says to us; not the right relation in

> which we must place ourselves to [God], but the covenant which [God] has made with all who are Abraham's spiritual children and which he has sealed once and for all in Jesus Christ.[57]

Part of what Barth so beautifully implies here is that a Christ-centered approach to biblical study understands that the Bible is always inviting us to participate in its story rather than promising to be useful to ours. An example comes to mind that illustrates the difference between coming to the biblical text for answers to our questions and submitting to being questioned ourselves. It draws us to reflect on a perennial controversy we have in our churches: Should we allow members of the congregation to clap after the children's choir sings?

I once got sneaky, breaking a class into groups and asking the class to explore what the Bible has to say to that question. We are, after all, "People of the Book," I told them. After breaking into groups and looking things up in concordances, we shared our results with the whole. All those who were *for* hand clapping said, with conviction: "Well... the Bible says 'the mountains and the hills shall clap their hands, so this obviously means *we* should too!'" And all those who were *against* hand clapping said, with the same amount of conviction: "Welll... the Bible says '*the mountains and the hills* shall clap their hands.' But it doesn't say anything about *us* clapping, so..." We had gotten nowhere by way of the exercise. Or so it seemed. But then I suggested, à la Barth, that perhaps the Bible was not all that interested in whether we clapped our hands or not. Thinking christocentrically, clapping our hands or not clapping our hands after the children sing has little to do with the message of the Gospel, one way or the other, it seems. Perhaps we should go to the Bible looking to see what important issues it would like us to address, rather than going to it with the idea that it will address the issues we find to be important?

A final benefit of reading the Bible christocentrically has to offer is that it reminds us we don't have to spend a lot of time trying to separate out the words of the book from the Word of God. As the Word became flesh in Jesus Christ in a way that the two are never separated, so the word and the Word, when we read and study the biblical witness, are inextricably joined, used together by the Spirit to communicate who God is, and who we are called to be. We can read the Bible with the confidence, then, that we do not have to figure out how to in some way get underneath the words in order to benefit from the deeper meaning. Whatever language study, historical study, and textual study we engage need not be devoted to dissecting words. Rather, we can enjoy the range of words and genres that come into play, as we read, wondering at how they are used to convey truths that cannot be confined to words, even as Jesus is truly known in the flesh that also cannot contain him.

Conclusion: The "Right Words" to Say

Earlier in this chapter I told the story of a woman who had become bored with her reading of Scripture. We also mentioned that there is a problem with biblical literacy in our American culture—we do not read the Bible, perhaps, because we find it boring, or confusing, or upsetting (e.g., because God does not always seem as loving as we want God to be). I have tried, here, to offer some ideas for faithfully engaging the Bible in ways that honor it as the norming norm. My hope is that these ideas will help readers engage the Bible in ways they find interesting, in ways that facilitate their participation in the wonder of the narrative. If the Bible testifies to the story we believe matters most to ourselves, there must be a way we can become more captivated by it! Again, Barth speaks to this matter of boredom and interest by recounting a story of his encounter with a colleague who was bored:

> A professor of theology once told me that he had learned much more from his devout mother than from the whole Bible. . . . It is all very well to realize, perhaps, that one may learn more from all kinds of greater or lesser prophets or apostles of a later period, or even of our own time, than from reading the Bible. Yet the issue is not where we learn most, but where we learn the one thing, the truth. . . . Let us presuppose that it really is Jesus Christ or revelation that is mediated to us; the question then arises how we know this, how we are to recognize it.[58]

Barth's quote helps summarizes the chapter and moves us forward to the next. It reflects, as we have, on the fact that there are all kinds of sources we are negotiating in this world, as we seek to discern what we can know and say of God. It suggests, further, as we have, that Christians have identified the Bible with the special revelation of God that gifts us with knowledge of the most meaningful thing of all: the truth of God's love, as revealed to us in Jesus Christ by the power of the Spirit. When the Spirit shows us God's revelation through the spectacles of Scripture, our audacious claim is that we really can say something about everything, something that gives hope and promise to each one and to all.

What, then, are the right words to say about God? They might be found anywhere, but they are always consistent with the story of the Christ who is at the center of the biblical witness. And so, we study the Bible, enter more deeply into its story, and set other sources that matter to us in conversation with what we are always discovering. It is from that vantage point that we live our lives not as know-it-alls, but as those determined to share something about everything in a world brimming with beauty, pain, and a perennial desire to know more.

Part Two

God Meets Us

Chapter Three

Where Does God Meet Us?

The Doctrine of the Incarnation

In the name of Jesus Christ...
wars have been fought,
witches burned, and
Jewish people exterminated.

In the name of Jesus Christ...
pacifists have turned the other cheek,
the hungry have been fed,
the value of all humanity has been upheld.

In the name of Jesus Christ...
people have been excommunicated,
and demons have been exorcised.

In the name of Jesus Christ...
women have been kept from ordination
and women have been ordained.

In the name of Jesus Christ...
missionaries have gone out to the ends of the earth
    and told people to be satisfied with their lot in life.
In the name of Jesus Christ...
missionaries have gone out to the ends of the earth
and have proclaimed God's redemption of the body
    as well as the soul.

In the name of Jesus Christ...
people have found encouragement
and people have been shamed;
people have been saved,
and people have been damned.

"All the armies that have ever marched
All the navies that have ever set sail
All the rulers that have ever ruled
All the kings that have ever reigned on this earth
All put together
Have not affected the life of people on this earth
As much as this
One solitary life."[1]

But it makes a difference
Who we say Jesus Christ is.[2]

Up until now we have been talking about what theologians like to call *prolegomena*, which literally means "words that come before." Technically speaking, we have been speaking the words and exploring the concepts that must be engaged before we move on to talking about the incarnation, the Trinity, and the Holy Spirit; before we discuss creation, sin, and salvation; before we consider the challenges of grace, Christian life, and church; before we ponder our vocation as well as what it means to be people of hope. We couldn't really consider all of these things, in good faith, without reflecting on how we are thinking and what approach we would take. Now that we have discussed the character of our theological language and the norms and sources we go to as we discern what words we will say about God, we are ready to move on to speaking about who God is. But how shall we begin?

Beginning with Jesus

Traditionally, theologians have been known to start speaking about God in at least a couple of different ways. Some start right in with discussing the attributes of God: God is *omnipotent* (or all-powerful), *omniscient* (or all-knowing), *omnipresent* (everywhere present), and *immutable* (unchanging), for example. After establishing what God is like, these theologians then go on to discuss how God reaches out to us by creating us, by becoming flesh and entering into existence with us, or by comforting and guiding us by way of the Holy Spirit. Thomas and Calvin are two theologians who take this approach. This is also the tack taken by many creeds and confessions that have been passed on, by, and to Christian believers through the ages. Consider, for example, the Westminster catechism, which by question #4 is asking students the weighty question, "What is God?" Interestingly, the prescribed answer speaks to the difficulty we have answering it, given our creaturely limitations. Rather, it insists that we—with Scripture in hand—may answer confidently that God is "a Spirit who is infinite, eternal, and unchangeable, in his being, wisdom, power, holiness, justice, goodness, and truth."[3]

The catch to this catechetical approach is that it can be easy to forget, in the course of learning and rehearsing very good theological answers to huge and complex questions, that it is impossible to know God in and of ourselves, on the basis of our own best logic. As we said in the last chapter, any knowledge we have of what God is like comes from God showing us what God is like. Even when we *can* list off the divine attributes, as we have learned them from Scripture (and perhaps the catechism), it is another thing to be able to say what these attributes mean about who God is and how God acts, as well as why they matter to our lives of faith. I remember, for example, how Peter is able to give the right answer to who Jesus is. But he actually has no idea what he is talking about. "You are the Christ, the Son of the living God!" he tells Jesus, who confirms that this answer is "from heaven."[4] But Peter makes a false assumption about what this means. He thinks that Jesus—and all who stand with Jesus, including himself—will manage to escape the persecution that is right around the corner. This, of course, is not the case. This story about Peter reminds us that giving the right answers can actually get in the way of understanding what they are all about, especially when we make the false assumption that, because we are "right," we are powerful and protected. As surprising as this is both to Peter and to us: to be the Son of the living God means suffering more, not less.

Even Calvin makes the mistake of over-knowing what God is like before he explores the content of God's revelatory acts.[5] This should give us pause, I think, given that Calvin is a theologian who so beautifully makes the point that we can know God only because God accommodates us when we are too bleary-eyed to perceive God on our own! God speaks baby-talk to us, Calvin says, as a caretaker speaks to a child, all for the purpose of helping us understand.[6] Yet Calvin at the same time does not hesitate to rehearse the attributes of God fairly early on in his *Institutes*, assuming his readers will grasp their meaning and significance apart from offering us any practical handles for understanding.[7]

The unintended consequences caused by beginning our talk about God with delineating and defining God's attributes are evident when Calvin reflects on certain biblical passages that seem to depict God in ways that contradict the description of God he has already presented. Calvin, at these points, seems forced to turn exegetical cartwheels in order to reconcile what he has already said about God's nature with the texts he is considering. Calvin assumes, for example, that God is *impassible*—unaffected by anyone or anything.[8] He says this because he surmises, alongside many theologians who have gone before him, that divine *impassibility*—the idea that God is unaffected by anything—is a logical extension of the divine *immutability*, the idea that God is unchanging. To be affected is to change, Calvin is thinking, therefore the unchanging God must not be affected, and is therefore impassible.

The problem is, there are many passages in Scripture where God *is* affected by us because God loves us and wants us to be faithful. God sends the flood in the Genesis story, for example, because God is affected by humanity's sinfulness and feels a need to act.[9] God listens and makes adjustments, when Abraham negotiates for the city of Sodom to be saved if there are a remnant of faithful left.[10] Jesus, whom Calvin believes is God incarnate, is affected by the death of Lazarus, weeping at Lazarus's tomb.[11] In an effort to reconcile cases like these with what he has already said about God's impassibility, Calvin proposes that the biblical writers are making use of *anthropomorphisms*. In other words, he suggests, the descriptions of God being responsive to what we hope for and feel are included in the biblical witness only for the benefit of our understanding, not because God *actually is* affected. This is a confusing and even dangerous proposal, from the vantage point of Calvin's own theological method. If we put on the "spectacles of Scripture" *before* attempting to describe God's character, it will be difficult to conclude God is unaffected by the creaturely world that God so loves.

In light of the problems created by defining the divine attributes prior to contemplating God's revelatory actions in human history, other theologians begin their discussions of who God is by reflecting on God's character always by way of God's acts. Elizabeth A. Johnson, for example, begins speaking about the God who is mystery by testifying to how God has met us, in our day-to-day lives, by way of the Spirit. Johnson begins with the Spirit, she explains, in part because she understands God's acts in the person of the Holy Spirit to be neglected, particularly in the theological reflections of the Western world.[12]

The most commonly engaged entry point for talking about the character of God, once we have eschewed beginning with a list of divine attributes, is God's dramatic entrance into existence with us in the person of Jesus Christ. Barth notes, along these lines, that the Word-become-flesh in the historical figure of Jesus of Nazareth is the central event of God's self-revelation. Barth's approach to ordering Christian doctrines, in contrast to Calvin's approach,[13] is to begin with God's self-revelation in Jesus Christ and to move on to discussion of the attributes of God only in the context of remembering Jesus Christ's life and work.

Here's one example of how beginning with Jesus, rather than with our very best definitions of the divine attributes, might make a difference: If we begin talking about God's power and then only after that consider Jesus Christ as the Word made flesh, we might find ourselves trying to figure out how Christ's suffering on the cross can possibly be reconciled with the portrait of a God who is the almighty and sovereign Creator. But if we reflect on what Jesus's suffering and death teaches us about the character of God before we try to articulate what it means to say God is all-powerful, then the cross and all it stands for will shape our understanding of what God's power is like. If we recognize that Emmanuel has entered into the depths of creaturely frailty and desolation, our understanding of what it means to say God is "all-powerful" will be informed and transformed. As Daniel Migliore notes, we will be far less likely to characterize God as a God of "sheer power" if we found our considerations in the story of Jesus Christ's life, death, and resurrection.[14]

The Witness of the Gospels

What words shall we say about the central mystery of the Christian faith, that the Word became flesh in the person of Jesus Christ? We might be tempted to begin straightaway with the New Testament Gospel stories about the historical figure, Jesus of Nazareth, whom Christians believe is God incarnate. But before we leap to those stories we will want to take note—following the lead of Matthew and Luke—that Jesus of Nazareth came from a particular nation, a particular people, a particular context—just as any other person who has ever walked on the face of this planet. Jesus was a Palestinian Jew, a member of the nation of Israel, God's chosen people from a time long before Jesus's birth. To remember this is to remember that the Judeo-Christian God is a God of real, on-the-ground history, that the God Christians know in Jesus Christ is the God of Abraham, Isaac, and Jacob—the God who has been involved in the workings of humanity since the very beginning. To be thinking of Jesus Christ in the context of the broad history of God's saving work is also to recognize that God acts even after the events of the resurrection. "The whole creation has been groaning" for redemption,[15] Romans insists, and the book of Acts, the Epistles, and the Apostles' Creed all bear witness to the movement of the Spirit in the life of the church, who waits and works for an historical manifestation of God's coming Kingdom.[16]

Where does the particular person of Jesus enter this expansive picture of God's salvation history? Looking at Matthew and Luke, we might well argue we should start at Bethlehem or a little earlier, perhaps at the point when Gabriel comes to Mary to tell her she will conceive by way of the Spirit. This is where the *incarnation* of God in the historical figure of Jesus of Nazareth begins, concretely—with God's determination to enter Mary's womb and be born. "The Holy Spirit will come over you," Gabriel says. "Therefore, the one who is to be born will be holy. He will be called God's Son."[17]

We don't know much about Mary before that announcement, but there is good reason to suppose she is utterly transformed by the news Gabriel brings her. She visits Elizabeth; she prophesies and sings. She realizes and testifies that everything has changed—the hungry have been filled; the rich have been sent away; kingdoms are reversed. Already, as the baby Jesus readies to be born, the incarnation of God in Mary's womb has begun the shaping of a new story that is not a different story than the story of God's redemption of Israel, but is more, I think, than simply the next chapter of the same story. Perhaps we might liken it to the beginning of a sequel that tells the same story from the vantage point of a different community in a different time and context. Mary is the Miriam[18] of the sequel. She, like Miriam of the first book, celebrates that the intervention of God in creaturely history means an overhauling of power structures that clears space for marginalized and underprivileged people to flourish.

"I will sing to the LORD, for an overflowing victory!" sings Miriam, celebrating the escape of the Israelites from the Egyptians. "Horse and rider [God] threw into the sea!"[19] Mary, basking in the good news that she is an essential participant in God's saving work, proclaims that God "has filled the hungry with good things and sent the rich away empty-handed."[20]

This beginning of the event we will eventually come to recognize as the incarnation next touches down in Bethlehem, where the baby Jesus is born. Converging on the scene there, as all the Western world knows, are the star, the shepherds, the magi, and the various and sundry animals who happen to carry family or friends of Jesus on their backs, tag along with the shepherds, or reside in the barn (perhaps, even, sleeping in the manger). Mary, Joseph, and Elizabeth may have experienced the beginning of something new when Mary conceived Jesus, but Bethlehem is the moment when a host of others begin to see everything differently. "A Savior, who is the Messiah, the Lord," has been born. [21] This is good news meant for the entire world.

When it comes to starting at the beginning, in relation to the incarnation, the Gospels of Luke and Matthew have far more caché with those who hold faith than does the Gospel of Mark. Mark's Gospel, almost certainly written first, does not have the angels, the shepherds, or the magi. It doesn't have the story of the Annunciation—the visit of Gabriel to Mary. Instead, it first notes Jesus's inextricable relationship with God about thirty years later, at the time of his baptism by John. The dove descends; the voice from heaven is heard; it seems that Mark's understanding of the character of incarnation comes close to *adoptionism*, the idea that Jesus was not yet the Son of God at the time of his birth, but that God the Father adopted Jesus of Nazareth as his child because Jesus was so faithful and true. While of course Mark's depiction of Jesus has as much value for our understanding of who Jesus is as the other Gospels, I have yet to see it used as the basis of an Advent play the kids present on the Sunday before Christmas!

It is interesting that Matthew and Luke, the two Gospels we believe were written next after Mark, make a special point of extending further back in time the coming of God to the world in the person of Jesus Christ.

Biblical scholars surmise that the inclusion of the stories centered in Bethlehem is accounted for, in part, by the fact that Matthew and Luke likely shared a text Mark didn't have and that we no longer have. (Scholars identify this hypothetical text as "Q").[22] But Matthew and Luke do more than simply include the birth narrative in their Gospels. They seem, actually, to *celebrate* the story, even as we celebrate it every Christmas. The story of Mary, Gabriel, Elizabeth, and Joseph; the story of the angels, the shepherds, the magi, and King Herod—these stories help make sense of who Jesus is and what he did next. Matthew tells the stories giving special attention to how they connect Jesus to what has come before, explaining how his birth fulfills the prophecies valued by the Israelites. Luke makes sure to highlight, for his part, that Jesus's solidarity with the poor and disenfranchised begins with his entering into this world as someone who is poor and disenfranchised—his birth occurs in a place clearly unsuitable, to a mother who would likely be viewed with disdain by those who pride themselves on being privileged.

If Luke and Matthew find it meaningful and even essential to begin consideration of Jesus's relationship with God by backing up to the beginning of his earthly life, John pushes back in time further, still. When you reflect on the prologue to his Gospel you can almost imagine John pacing around his desk and thinking to himself:[23]

> How can I get across, to my readers, just how far back this connection between Jesus, God, and the world they know and appreciate goes? Matthew and Luke did better than Mark, to be sure.... But I'd like to pull it back even further.... How can I convey that what is going on with Jesus has no beginning... that he reveals an eternal truth about who God is as well as what God has done...? Let's see... I've got it! I'll connect Jesus to what goes all the way back as far as our religious tradition has been able to fathom. I'll draw a parallel between talking about where Jesus came from and God's relationship to creation itself. Instead of starting with "in the beginning God" I'll start with "in the beginning was the Word." They'll never read Genesis 1 the same way, again!

I imagine John then sitting down at his desk to write, excited about drawing so many important parallels: between the creation of the world and the presence of the Word, both in the beginning; between the Word and the *logos*, both ways of naming the creative pulse of the cosmos; between the eternal Word and the historical figure of Jesus, the listeners' relationship to the latter making possible their relationship to the former, since Jesus *is* the Word incarnate. I imagine John writing in the hope that he will help us see the event of Jesus as essential to the beginning and ending of all things.

John and the Emerging Doctrine of Incarnation

Given that John associates the historical Jesus with the creation of all that is, it is not surprising that John is the Gospel most drawn upon to develop understandings of incarnation that emphasize the inextricable connection between the human and divine natures of Jesus. Jesus is the one in whom the "Word" (*logos*) became flesh, John says. This Word his readers would have recognized as the organizing principle of the universe. It is the power by which, it was thought, everything is made and operates. To connect this historical person, Jesus of Nazareth, to it must have seemed to some to be quite outlandish. For others who had experienced Jesus, it may have actually explained a lot. "Oh—that makes sense," I can imagine someone saying, as they begin reading John. "This helps me better understand the stories I've heard about Jesus."

Very important to John is that we continue thinking of Jesus as a historical, embodied figure even as we recognize his integral role in creation itself. John's goal, in introducing his Gospel, is in no way to reveal Jesus as some sort of God disguised by flesh, as though who he is as a human being is only a cover over his true self. Rather, what makes Jesus's connection to eternity so interesting to John, and what makes him think his readers' relationship to Jesus can transform them, is precisely the fact that the Jesus who indeed does "dwell among us" as a fellow human being is also essential to the existence of creation itself. Jesus has, after all, "dwelt among us" as one who is also "flesh."[24] As it says in 1 John (traditionally ascribed to the same author as the Gospel), Jesus is a historical figure whom we have "seen with our eyes" and "with our hands handled."[25] In John's distinctive telling of the good news, Jesus chats with Nicodemus and with the Samaritan woman at the well;[26] he cries, aggrieved, at Lazarus's tomb;[27] he shows Thomas, after his resurrection, his hands and his side.[28] Clearly, John has no interest in compromising one iota on Jesus's existence as a human being who lived on this earth as our neighbor, eating and visiting, feeling and relating. It is precisely this real-life one—this one whom we know because he shares in life with us—who joins us to God, John insists.

In sum, according to John's prologue, the one we know as the human being called "Jesus" was also around in the beginning, and the one who played a part in creating us from the beginning is the one who then became flesh in the historical figure, Jesus of Nazareth. This two-directional insight of John's probably did more than any other to provoke the formation of the doctrine of incarnation. By two-directional, I mean that the insight moves both from our knowing Jesus in the context of our world through to the truth of his connection with God; and from the reality of his eternal existence—before time was even created!—through to our knowing of him within the confines of creaturely history. We know Jesus, having encountered him as our neighbor; and it is just this one who was with God in the beginning—way before the fact of our knowing him. Conversely, it is the Word who was with God in the beginning who took on flesh so that we might come to be in relationship with him. Without his historic existence there would be no contact and therefore no clear perception. Without his eternal connection, our historical relationship with Jesus would offer us no immediate access to the life of God.

For John, as for the doctrine of incarnation, to know Jesus is to know God. "Whoever has seen me has seen the Father," Jesus tells Philip in chapter 14, going on to explain that he is in the Father and the Father is in him.[29] While people of faith have argued for centuries about what this statement means precisely, there can be no doubt that it connotes the closest possible relationship between God and Jesus. It is reflection on what constitutes the character of this relationship, what difference it makes to our understanding of God, and what difference it makes to our lives of faith that precipitated the earliest debates and decisions about doctrine. We will consider a couple of the most important of these now: the first is the framing decision that Jesus is of the same substance as the Father; the second is that Jesus is not half human and half divine, but fully human and fully divine. We turn now to considering each of these theological developments. As the Word became real flesh and walked around in history in the person of Jesus, so the teachings about him were developed on the ground—in real life, in the real early church, and with all the politics that come with real human beings when they come together to work out the details of something that matters to them all.

The Insight of Nicea

In the earliest centuries of the church, people of faith were of course invested in trying to figure out what it meant to confess Jesus as Lord. Who is this one the church identified as Savior, and how is it that we can claim him as the Messiah without compromising on our conviction that there is only one God? By the third and fourth centuries several Gospels were circulating, but Mark, Matthew, Luke/Acts, and John had already emerged as the four that were considered to be authoritative. These Gospels, particularly the Gospel of John, were cited frequently in the discussions and debates in which ecumenical statements about Jesus Christ's identity were formulated.

Athanasius, a fourth-century scholar, is one of the theologians who draws heavily on the Gospel of John, frequently citing Jesus's comment to Philip that "I am in the Father and the Father is in me" as he makes the case for the nature of Jesus's relationship to God.[30] Athanasius holds that Jesus shares in the very "stuff" or "substance" of God. The term he uses for this, a term that did not originate with him but with which he is associated because he argues for it so persuasively, is *homoousios*. This term means, etymologically speaking, "of the same stuff" (*homo* = "same" and *ousia* = "stuff or substance"). Athanasius noticed that Jesus spoke not only of being in close proximity to the Father, but of the two mutually indwelling one another, virtually sharing each other's lives and work. He offered his arguments for the *homoousion*[31] against a very persuasive opposing view: the teaching of Arius that Jesus was very near to God, indeed, but didn't, actually, share the same substance with God. Taking Arius's concerns and perspective into account and in contrast to the Athanasian *homoousion*, it was proposed that Jesus was *homoiousios* with God. Notice that this term is different by just one vowel—it has an *i* after the second *o*. To say Jesus is *homoiousios* with the Father is to claim he is of *like* substance, but not exactly the *same* substance. One of the strengths of maintaining that Jesus and the Father were different in substance, Arius and his followers thought, was that monotheism would not be jeopardized. They were concerned that saying Jesus was of the same stuff as the Father God would establish Jesus as a second divinity, and that Christianity would then shift away from monotheism, which everyone agreed would be deeply problematic. Eventually, the doctrine of the Trinity developed as a way of explaining how it is that people of faith confess Jesus is *homoousios* with the Father without compromising on the oneness of the Godhead. (Why this matters so much to our lives of faith is the subject of the following chapter.) Arius did not find tenable the idea that God could be at once both one and distinct.

Another concern raised, by those more inclined toward Arius's view[32] than the Athanasian *homoousion*, is that to think of Jesus as being just as fully God as God the Father would be to compromise on both his humanity and his divinity. If Jesus of Nazareth were of the same substance as the Father, Athanasius's opponents suggested, this would mean he couldn't really, actually, be human. Jesus would really be God-in-disguise, they posited, with all the human sorts of things Jesus did being more or less illusion. If Jesus were *homoousios* with the Father, for example, his suffering could not have been real suffering, since God is impassible and cannot suffer, Arius's supporters emphasized.

But Athanasius remained steadfastly against his opponents on this point, insisting that the *homoousion* compromised neither on the character of Jesus's humanity nor the integrity of his divinity. "He has not ceased to be God by reason of becoming human, and he does not flee from things human because he is God,"[33] he wrote. That humanity and divinity coexisted in the person of Jesus Christ with no compromise to either, Athanasius believed, was both the testimony of the Gospels and the Epistles and supported by logical argument about the necessity of the *homoousion* for salvation itself. Famously, Athanasius drew an analogy between the incarnation of God in Jesus Christ and a king moving into the neighborhood of his subjects. Just as the subjects of a king would feel protected by the presence of the king only if the king were actually the king and not only an especially benevolent neighbor, so Jesus Christ offers consolation to us only if and because he is God incarnate, not one who is only an awfully lot like God.[34]

At the Council of Nicea in 325, people of faith gathered, argued, and struggled with this question of the *homoousion* because they believed who Jesus Christ *is* matters to how they understood the character of their relationship to God. The idea that Jesus was of the *same* and not *similar* substance to the Father was received by the majority of those voting at Nicea as the measure of orthodoxy. The Nicene decision did not of course stop the debate about the nature of the Son's relationship to the Father, which raged on for centuries. But it did serve to anchor, and also to precipitate, many of the crucial doctrinal discussions and decisions made over the next 125 years. At the Synod of Alexandria (362 CE) and the Council of Constantinople (381 CE), for example, people of faith asked themselves the question: Is it only the Son who is of the same substance with the Father? Ultimately, they declared that the Holy Spirit, with the Father and the Son, was also and equally divine. At the Council of Chalcedon, in 451, people of faith returned to the specific matter of how to relate Jesus Christ's humanity and divinity. Having decided that the Son shared the same substance with the Father, this next question made sense. How is it, exactly, that Jesus Christ is human and divine at one and the same time, and what difference does this make to us, in our lives of faith?

The Wisdom of Chalcedon

At the Council of Chalcedon in 451, the order of the day was to figure out how it is that the two natures of Jesus Christ can coexist in his one person. What was at stake for those present was not to undo the mystery of who Jesus Christ is, as though Jesus were a kind of riddle that requires the best of our problem-solving energies. Rather, those who were present were people of faith seeking understanding; people who believed that grappling with this impossible-to-resolve theological question would facilitate their participation in the mystery of it. What was at stake at Chalcedon was, actually, the matter of perceiving and participating in salvation itself. The question "How can there be a perception of Jesus Christ and our being in Him?"[35] was layered just underneath the question of how we are to understand the human nature and the divine nature to coexist in Christ.

This very personal motivation for pursuing understanding of Jesus Christ's person is sometimes ignored as historical and theological details about Chalcedon are rehearsed. And yet the fact that a concern about salvation drove the deliberations is evident even in the final statement produced. This "Chalcedonian Statement," as it is known, recognizes Jesus as "one person in two natures" who is "begotten of the Father before the ages" in relation to his divinity and "born of the Virgin Mary, the Mother of God" in relation to his humanity. Crystal clear in the text of the Statement itself is that the fact the begotten one is born and the divine one is human is "for our sake and the sake of our salvation."[36] Salvation is accomplished, in fact, precisely by virtue of the fact that our one Savior is at once both begotten and born, fully divine and fully human.

The Statement then closes by giving what I understand to be a setting of parameters that are intended, at least in part, to help people of faith participate in the mystery of Jesus Christ's person. Noticing that there was a tendency of some, in the context of the Chalcedonian debate, to think of Jesus's humanity and divinity as "merging" or "mingling" together, the statement insists, correcting this, that Jesus is fully human and fully divine "without confusing" the two natures and "without change" to either of them.[37] Noticing that there was a tendency of some to try to find ways to protect the integrity of Jesus Christ's immutable divinity from his suffering humanity,[38] the Statement also proclaims that his two natures are related to each other "without separation and without division." Again, the authors' concern was not only to reconcile the opposing streams in the debate but also to reflect the consensus that Jesus Christ, in his very person, saves us.

In order to see the idea of *salvation* in the context of the statement as a whole, I offer here a significantly abbreviated version that draws together some key phrases relevant to the discussion we have had of it so far:

> Jesus Christ is . . . one person in two natures . . . fully human and fully divine. In relation to his divinity, he was begotten of the Father before the ages. In relation to his humanity, this very same one was born of the Virgin Mary, the Mother of God, **for our sake and the sake of our salvation**. The two natures are united without confusion and without change, without separation and without division.[39]

Notice that the explicit mention of salvation is made just after it has been emphasized that "the very same one" who was born of Mary is the one who is "begotten of the Father before the ages." Somehow, it is the person of Jesus Christ himself who saves. Below we will turn to the "so what?" of all this, seeking to lay claim to the value of Chalcedon for our lives of faith, today. But first it is important that we pause and notice that something we generally see as absolutely essential to any talk of salvation is notably absent. What happened, we might ask, to the cross?

The Emphasis of Chalcedon

We might well have expected that a statement concerned with salvation would somewhere mention Christ's work on the cross. Perhaps, if we had been asked to edit the statement, we would have suggested that one five-word phrase be added, so the statement would read: "this very same one was born of the Virgin Mary, the Mother of God; *he died on the cross* for our sake and the sake of our salvation." But those words are not there.

From where we stand in history, it might seem as though it must have been an accident to leave the cross out, if what is being talked about is *salvation.* However differently we interpret the crucifixion, we might remark, don't all Christians believe that it is by way of the cross that Jesus saves us? If so, why is it, then, that the Chalcedonian statement emphasizes salvation with no mention of the cross whatsoever?

In chapter 6 we will explore in greater detail the doctrine of the *atonement* and current controversies and creative suggestions for how to interpret the cross. For now, however, I'm hoping that if we simply notice that the way the Chalcedonians were thinking about salvation in relation to *who Jesus was* than in relation to *what he did*, we will become curious. Again, instead of talking about how Jesus saves us by dying on the cross and rising from the dead, Chalcedon speaks of Jesus's saving work being accomplished by way of his two natures being joined in one person.

Why is this the emphasis at Chalcedon? Isn't the important thing not so much who Jesus Christ is as what he did? In a world where we value doing and accomplishing almost to the point of understanding people to *be* what they *do*, it makes sense that we might want to move on quickly from Chalcedon to reviewing the events of Jesus's life, pondering his teachings, marveling at the miracles he performed, and standing, awestruck, before the cross and the empty tomb. We think that's where the real action is, don't we? We assume it is finally by way of what he *does* that Jesus accomplishes salvation on our behalf.

I have a pretty simple story that gets at this in a way that still shapes how I think about Jesus. I was a student pastor in a wonderful church in New Jersey, where I decided to do an adult education class on the topic "Great Doctrines of the Faith." I figured I would teach one doctrine each of six Sundays, really punching why each of the doctrines mattered to our lives of faith. Trinity, Creation, Jesus, Spirit, Church, Hope. I was proud because I was able to round up five to ten people who came each week. (Getting adults to come to Christian education classes on a Sunday morning in New Jersey was a lot more difficult, I have since learned, than getting them to come to church in Texas, where I now live!) Each week, with my little class, I held forth with a full measure of passion for these teachings of the church that have been so dear to the saints through the ages.

On the last day of the class, as she was heading out the door, my good friend and pillar of the church stopped to thank me. Nancy said she enjoyed the class but then, leaning forward, gave me her *real* assessment of the material I presented. "What I think, though," she whispered so that no one else could hear, "is that all these details about who people think Jesus is don't make much of a difference. Jesus showed us how to love each other, and that's all that really matters."

While I am certain Nancy meant this statement to be an offering of her view and not a criticism of the Sunday school class, it hit me hard. Were all these details I was learning and just beginning to teach about the development of christology actually irrelevant? I would have said then, and certainly believe now, that knowing every detail about who Jesus Christ is, as well as every verse in the Bible about what he said and did, is worthless if we miss the main thrust of his ministry. As 1 Corinthians 13 reminds us, "If I speak in tongues of human beings and of angels but I don't have love, I'm a clanging gong or a clashing cymbal."[40] My friend Nancy was correct insofar as she was remembering that Jesus *lived* what he taught, including that "all the Law and the Prophets... hang" on the two commandments "love the Lord your God with all your heart, with all your soul, and with all your mind,"[41] and "love your neighbor as yourself."[42] To love God and one another is, of course, the most important thing of all.

The question is, then: Why bother with all the other stuff? Why fill up a Sunday school class? Or six classes? Or, for that matter, *a lifetime* with reflection on detail? After all, even John in his Gospel says, about Jesus, that if everything he said and did were recorded "the world itself wouldn't have enough room for the scrolls that would be written."[43] Even the Gospel writers were selective in their depictions of Jesus. Granted, Nancy's Gospel would have been a bit short, but wasn't she challenging me not to overcomplicate the story, and its implications for us?

I went home from the class after church that Sunday and struggled with Nancy's comment, finally realizing I was bothered not only because I had failed, somehow, in the teaching of the class but—more importantly—because I sensed my very thoughtful and loving friend Nancy represented a mind-set that was hazardous. Late that evening I wrote the poem with which this chapter opens. What I hope it reflects is what I finally came to, as I struggled: that the details about who Jesus Christ is do matter because they shape our understanding of what love looks like, and how we commit to living it. Historically, people have acted in many different kinds of ways in the name of Jesus Christ and in the name of Christian love. It is a real question, in fact, whether more people have been helped or harmed; whether more life has been nourished or annihilated, in the name of the Christ who taught us to love God and neighbor. Who we say Jesus Christ is makes a difference to how we understand loving actions, as we will continue exploring as this book unfolds.

As we head deeper into exploring the shape of our faith, it will be encouraging and challenging to recall that our forebears at Chalcedon—for all their significant faults—thought it was obvious that how we live our everyday lives, as people of faith, will be shaped by what we think about the person of Jesus Christ. I believe they would have agreed, to put it in contemporary terms, that the salvation with which we are gifted in and through Jesus Christ includes not only "fire insurance" (i.e., escape from eternal punishment) but also a way of making sense of our day-to-day lives. They clearly held that Jesus *does things for us* that benefit us, acting in specific ways that are saving. But they also thought it was extraordinarily important to spend a great deal of time and energy reflecting on and debating who Jesus Christ is in his person. It seems clear they thought knowing *who Jesus is* benefits us by helping us accurately interpret the saving value of *what it is he did.*

With that in mind we turn, now, to considering what may have been at stake for those at Chalcedon, in this debate. But more important for our purposes than trying to get back to the intentions and motivations of our fifth-century forebears (if that were even possible) is to think about their legacy for us today. We join them in struggling with how to participate in mysteries that can never be exhausted with human words, but can nevertheless be glimpsed by way of words that can face us in the right direction and show us where to focus our attention. We join them in their journeys of faithful, passionate inquiry, asking some of the same questions they did but from a very different time and context, fifteen centuries later. These questions include: Who is this one, Jesus, whom we call "Lord" and "Savior"? In what sense do we understand him to be "God with us," and how would this save us, anyway? If God actually empties God's own self[44] in order to be human with us, how does this not represent a compromise in the very being of God? After all, if God is somehow less than who God really is in the incarnation, we can no longer say it is *God* who is with us in Jesus Christ. Conversely, if Jesus is, indeed, of the same stuff as the Father, does this make him in some way less human than the rest of us? Wouldn't this mean human beings are, in some sense, diminished by Christ rather than saved by him?

I will turn in a moment to pursuing some of these concerns, remembering that a worthy motive (shared with the best of our fifth-century forebears) is to understand why and how the person of Jesus Christ matters to us and our salvation, as people of faith. But before moving to this, it must be acknowledged that our forebears also had motives that were *not* worthy. The decisions at Chalcedon were often leveraged, and continued to be leveraged, in ways that set people in opposition to each other. As Constantine used the Nicene decision to promote homogeneity that he claimed was essential for unity, so leaders in the fifth century and beyond used the Chalcedonian Statement to force a like-mindedness that was convenient for the state, but left behind those who would not comply. As will be seen, I understand the theological logic of the Chalcedonian Statement to provide much more space for diversity than is reflected in the narrow political ways it has been used oppress and control. My insistence on retrieving and imagining the possibilities of Chalcedon even given the way it has been used to foster harm, historically, is a strategy I understand to parallel a Christian's insistence that Jesus Christ opens his arms wide to all despite the fact that his name has been used to divide, disparage, and even justify violence. Specifically, I am asking: how does who Jesus Christ *is* give way to the character of the love he extends to us, the love he invites us to enter into and share with one another?

The Fully Divine One Is Fully Human: God Is with Us[45]

The line from the Chalcedonian Statement that has more trickle-down influence than any other is the idea that Jesus is both fully human and fully divine. Even if church people don't say the phrase exactly like this, they commonly recognize Jesus as in some way both divine and human. This *both divine and human identity* of Jesus is so commonly presumed in Christian communities that sometimes people who have been going to church all their lives might not think to pause, ponder, and wonder at it. If someone does pause to consider, and then has questions about it, they might feel as though what they are thinking is not the right kind of issue to be raised in church. They don't discern any place for it, so they keep it to themselves. It might be that the Nones[46] and skeptics in our communities serve all of us well by asking us questions some of us are too afraid to ask, such as: Do you really believe Jesus was God? How does that work, exactly? Why is that important? And: How, exactly, can one person be divine and human at the same time? Or: If Jesus is a human being who is divine, doesn't that mean that all of us, in a sense, are divine?

To say that Jesus Christ is the fully divine one who becomes fully human is to say, in the words of that old song by Eric Bazilian,[47] "What If God Were One of Us?" It is to say that the Word, who exists in the beginning with God as the second person of the Trinity, actually put on real flesh and lived his life as a human being, right along with us. The original Greek found in John 1:14, in fact, is the phrase έσκήνωσεν έν ήμῖν, which translates literally as "pitched a tent among us." God has joined us in our regular daily lives, as fully human as we are.

What this means, for a start, is that God understands what it is to be finite. God understands what it is to be tired, because Jesus fell asleep on that boat and Jesus is God.[48] God understands what it is to be sad and grieving because Jesus's friend Lazarus died, [49] and Jesus cried in his grief, and Jesus is God.[50] God understands us when we don't want to do God's will because Jesus struggled with the will of the Father in the Garden of Gethsemane, and Jesus is God.[51] God understands what it feels like to experience God's absence because Jesus cried out on that cross: "My God! My God! Why have you forsaken me?"[52] And Jesus is God.

Because Jesus is the fully divine one become fully human, there is a point of contact created between humanity and God. This does not mean we are God, but that we are joined to the very life of God by way of Jesus's humanity because God has entered into our lives in the person of Jesus Christ. In and through Jesus Christ, we are not God, but God is human. Because Jesus Christ has entered into our existence, and lived for us, and died for us, and risen from the dead for us, our lives are "hidden with Christ in God."[53] In Jesus Christ, our sins have been forgiven and we are called to participation in what the Paul identifies as "the ministry of reconciliation."[54] We will discuss, in the section following, how full our inclusion in the work of God is, by virtue of the fact that the Jesus who is fully human is also fully divine, making a space for us—with him, by virtue of our shared humanity—as fellow heirs and co-partners. But all of this promise of us inheriting, and participating, and contributing to the kin-dom[55] rests first on the fact that Jesus Christ is God-with-us; that the real Word really became real flesh. Without the *kenosis* (the self-emptying of God, in Jesus Christ) there can be no *theosis* (lifting up of the human, in Jesus Christ). First the one who is equal to God takes the form of a servant and becomes obedient unto death (the fully divine is fully human); then the servant is exalted until every knee bends and every tongue confesses (the fully human is fully divine).[56] It is in relation to all of it, and the *kenosis* and *theosis* in *dialectical tension*[57] with one another, that salvation is worked out "with fear and trembling."[58]

Because this idea that Jesus Christ is both fully human and fully divine is a mystery, we sometimes try to simplify it by erring on one side or the other, thinking of Jesus as *only human* or *only divine.* We might be worried, when we hear people talk about Jesus as their friend, because we fear they might be forgetting that Jesus is divine as well as human. I once had this concern when someone introduced me to what they identified as a "Jesus doll." The idea of the doll was that kids could carry it around with them to remember that Jesus was with them. I worried that it might inadvertently communicate that Jesus is *only* human. That said, I admit I don't have any good suggestion for how to capture the divinity of Jesus in a doll!

An even greater danger for us, it seems to me, is that those who "hold faith" actually emphasize the divinity of Christ at the expense of his humanity. To do this is, technically speaking, to commit heresy of *docetism.* Docetism is in evidence whenever we think of Jesus as God in disguise—when we think to ourselves, *Those silly disciples! When are they going to realize who Jesus Christ is, underneath all that skin!* If we are thinking such things, we had better double-check ourselves, reflecting on what unintended consequences come with compromising on Jesus's full humanity.

If Jesus Christ is only God in disguise—a Clark Kent figure who at zip into a phone booth and change into who he really is—then God is not fully with us in him. If Jesus isn't human all the way through to his core, we cannot make the claim that God has entered the human condition in and redeemed it.

Reflect, a bit, on where docetism can be seen in our lives together, today. Think about Christmastime, when we sing "Away in a Manger."[59] "The little Lord Jesus, no crying he makes," we sing. Now, of course, this hymn is a lullaby, and lullabies are all about wishing a child peace, hoping for an end to tears and a good night's rest. We offer these well-wishes, also, in our singing of "Silent Night"[60] with the line "sleep in heavenly peace."

The problem comes when the "no crying" of the carol is taken literally, as though to serve as a clue to what certain insiders already know—that Jesus isn't just some ordinary baby. He is exceptional, of course (the problematic thinking goes), given that he is the only baby who has ever been fully divine. *Of course* he didn't cry, we might think piously. As the Son of God, he is better than all that ordinary baby stuff.

The thing is, if we assume Jesus the baby didn't cry because he was exceptional, or if we believe Jesus the friend didn't actually weep at Lazarus's tomb because he was aggrieved, or if we believe Jesus the Crucified One didn't cry out in anguish and genuine despair on the cross, just as any human being would; if we believe that there simply could not have been real tears at any point because this would have meant Jesus's divinity was compromised, then we are in real trouble. We are in real trouble because we are babies who really cry, friends who truly grieve, and people who know the anguish of believing the God who loves us has left us.

Another way in which we can more or less test to see if we err toward docetism is by asking ourselves (or those in our community) the question: Is Jesus human now? In my experience, if this question catches us off guard it is worth considering why. It is also worth trying to answer, reflecting on whatever it is we have to say. If we answer no, because it just seems too strange to us to think that Jesus could still be human, then when is it, exactly, that we believe Jesus ceased being in a human state? We confess that he rose, embodied, from the grave and that he then ascended, embodied, to sit on the right hand of God the Father. Did his body somehow dissolve away, as he ascended up to heaven to be reunited with his Father?

The problem with answering the question in the negative is that it treats the incarnation as a kind of "thirty-three-year experiment" rather than a revelation of who God is from and to eternity. Christian traditions insist on bodies, as cumbersome as they are, associating them always with human persons, and then by extension with the existence of God in the person of Jesus Christ. Thinking of Jesus as human now is, unquestionably, awkward. But then so is thinking of God entering the womb of a woman and being born, or thinking of the Son of God growing up and learning to build shelves in Joseph's carpenter shop, or thinking of the Word without which nothing was made that was made assuming the body of a man who is crucified, dies, and is buried. The awkwardness of the body, as it is associated with Jesus's full humanity, is not somehow overcome at the point of the resurrection (which the Christian confession inconveniently identifies as *bodily*). Why would we assume Jesus's physical body is only a past reality—and not a present one—just because we cannot fathom how it could possibly be true, literally?

I suggest we confess our docetism and consider what it means to say that Jesus is fully human, as well as fully divine, even today. It is only when we do so that we live into the fullness of our salvation.

Yet, such a suggestion immediately becomes tricky. This is because of something theologians like to call the *scandal of particularity*, or the idea that the humanity of God, known to us in Jesus Christ, is some things and not others. Like all humanity, it is one gender and not another, one ethnicity and not another, one height and not another, one race and not another. Jesus was male and not female, Palestinian and not Anglo, 5'10" and not 6'2".[61] These particularities have bothered people of faith some, even when they are applied to Jesus only in time. In other words, when we think about Jesus being male and not female for the thirty-three years he walked the face of this earth, it is easier to think of his sex merely in terms of "accidents," in the Aristotelian sense.[62] His maleness might be important, in these terms, to the way he interacted and accomplished his work. But it wouldn't make a difference to his essence as a human being. Johnson uses a funny example to illustrate that our accidents matter, though not to our essence. Jesus had to be male to accomplish his mission on earth, she says, because if he had died on the cross as a female no one would have noticed.[63] That's because women have, historically, always been known for and expected to give up their lives for others!

The benefit of interpreting particularities as accidents, and not essence, is fairly clear, from a perspective concerned with understanding the person of Jesus Christ in ways attuned "with us and our salvation." We can see it immediately and strikingly if we rehearse a point made by Gregory of Nazianzus, way back in the fourth century. To give you just a touch of context: following Nicea (325), a theologian named Apollinaris tried to interpret the *homoousion* in a way that came to be seen, by the church, as confusing the two natures of Christ.[64] He argued, in short, that the divine Logos *replaced* the mind of Christ in the historical person of Jesus Christ in such a way that the humanity of Christ was, functionally speaking, taken over by the divinity. Apollinaris's teaching was very popular, but was eventually condemned for being docetic (compromising on Jesus Christ's humanity).[65] Gregory of Nazianzus challenged head-on, in a single sentence, the problem with Apollinaris's view: "What has not been assumed cannot be restored; it is what is united with God that is saved," he said.[66] This statement, often expressed as "that which has not been assumed has not been redeemed," is one of the most well-known and frequently invoked insights in Christian theological history. Almost everyone—even those on opposing sides of ecclesial debates—invokes it as being true. And what statement could possibly link, more elegantly, Jesus's person to our redemption, the doctrine of incarnation to the doctrine of salvation?[67] The assumption of our flesh by the Word who is God accomplishes our salvation!

With this point of Gregory's in place, now, it becomes pretty clear that we must insist Christ took on the humanity of all in taking on the humanity of one particular person. We are in dangerous water, for example, if we say he assumed male humanity and not female humanity, because this would mean (according to Gregory's insight), that women are not by him redeemed. To put it another way, drawing from a popular book series: if men are from Mars and women are from Venus, women are in big trouble![68] Believing that women are redeemed in Christ, just as men are, it must be that there are not two kinds of humanity, but one: the humanity Jesus assumed is the humanity of women just as much as it is the humanity of men, even though the Word was made incarnate in a human being who was "accidentally"[69] male (and Palestinian, and Jewish, and a certain, singular height). There is only one essential humanity, and the Word has entered into it just as any of us do, with certain particularities.[70]

Once we start talking about the humanity of God being a revelation of who God is, was, and always will be, however, it becomes more difficult to keep in mind that the particular particularities of Jesus's embodied existence are not essential to his humanity. To be human is to have particularities, but to be human is not dependent on having certain particularities over others. Jesus enters into all humanity by entering into the limitations of what it means to be a particular embodied human being.

Shifts in our understanding about what constitutes gender will also change the way we think about Jesus's particularity as a male human being. Even though the so-called nature versus nurture debates continues, as we try to understand the relationship between the bodies people appear to be born with and how they understand their own gender and sexuality, few would deny that how we are socialized, as gendered human beings, plays a significant role in how we understand ourselves as male and as female. In twenty-first-century American culture, where Bruce Jenner is now Caitlyn

Jenner and most major airports have added gender neutral restrooms, our culture no longer thinks of gender as something absolute. Even if we are uncomfortable with the idea of gender fluidity, we recognize that someone who currently self-identifies as female will not necessarily always continue to do so. Even if someone is one gender and not another, then, the possibility of change might make us less likely to think about male humanity and female humanity as though these are fundamentally different things.

Still, if we are to say that the humanity of Jesus Christ is in some real sense an eternal reality, it does not work to say that *everything* about him, as a human being, should be thought about as accidents. We need to claim the truth that the Word enters into a *particular* human flesh, with all its particularities—and in so doing somehow enters into *all* flesh.[71] But what does it mean to be enfleshed, to be fully human? What would eternal humanity *look like*, exactly?

As we mentioned above, the biblical stories about Jesus are unrelenting in their assertion that who Jesus is now must in some way include a body. Speaking in terms of accidents may begin to address some of the problems precipitated by this (as we have discussed), but it still remains to say what does constitute our shared humanity. If the humanity shared by all human beings is not male, Jewish, and Palestinian, then what constitutes shared humanity, exactly? And why does getting at this matter to our lives of faith?

Calvin insists that one of the things shared by all human beings, including the resurrected Jesus who is eternally fully human as well as fully divine, is physical location. While Calvin holds that the divine Word is ubiquitous (everywhere present), he also believes that it is in one special location and not another at any given time, as it is incarnate in the historical figure of Jesus of Nazareth. Calvin thinks that the eternal humanity of Jesus Christ, which the Creed says is "sitting at the right hand of God the Father Almighty"[72] is critically important to understanding the shape of our salvation. It is not so much, he thinks, that the point of the Creed is that Jesus is seated in one place and can never move, but that the Jesus who is everywhere present is at the same time now in one place, and not another.[73] So central to the identity of Jesus Christ did Calvin think this seeming paradox is that he interpreted biblical texts and the meaning of the sacraments in relation to it. I will explain why this is the case, but first allow me to demonstrate Calvin's tenacity on this issue.

In interpreting the post-resurrection appearance of Jesus to the disciples, as the story is told in John 20, Calvin is clearly looking through a Chalcedonian lens. He is asking himself the question: How is this resurrected body of Jesus still a fully human body, if Jesus is now in a "glorified"[74] state? Probably he has running through his mind and heart the kinds of things we think about when we try to put all the post-resurrection stories about Jesus together into a coherent understanding: Jesus says "don't touch me!" as if he is a Spirit, but then he invites Thomas to touch his hands and his sides so that he might believe;[75] Jesus is unrecognizable to the disciples, but then is recognized;[76] Jesus is immortal but still able to eat. But when Calvin reads John 20:26,[77] where the text says that Jesus appeared "in the midst"[78] of the disciples gathered together in the Upper Room, Calvin draws a hard line. Because he believes that the ongoing humanity of Jesus Christ must mean something *concrete*, and because he believes what it means is that Jesus's resurrected body is not ubiquitous but physically located, he insists Jesus must have walked physically through a door. His explanation for John's phrasing is that the disciples were too full of grief to notice that he had come in, or been let in by someone who unlocked the door and opened it for him.

I can almost hear my friend Nancy sighing, reminding me that at this point maybe Calvin and I are getting too hung up on the details. But let me push on just a little bit more, because I think what Nancy missed, what I failed to convey to her, and what we all often overlook, in our day—is thinking through *why* Calvin would be so obsessed with this kind of detail. What was at stake for him?

Whatever it was, it was at stake for him as he wrote scores and scores of pages about why what happens in the sacrament of the Lord's Supper is *not* that the bread and the wine are *transubstantiated* into the body and blood of Jesus Christ. In some sense, his argument against the Roman Catholic Church of the sixteenth century is very simple: if Jesus is sitting at the right hand of God the Father, his flesh and blood cannot be physically located in the elements of the sacrament. True, he thought that

Christ's body and blood are "really present...by the 'bond of participation' that is the Holy Spirit."[79] But this, he thought, was a different thing than saying they are "locally" present. "In his flesh he be in heaven, which he has chosen as the abode of his human nature,"[80] Calvin insisted, speaking against the idea that Christ's body and blood could somehow be in every piece of bread and every drop of wine consumed in the Lord's Supper.

Again, though, why the big deal? We might appreciate the fact that Calvin took Chalcedon seriously enough to play out what the full humanity of Jesus Christ looks like, but was doing so really the best use of his time? What was at stake for him? How were these arguments, which we see in his interpretation of certain biblical passages and in his understanding of the sacraments, indicative of how he understood our salvation, extended by Christ?

Why the "Full Humanity" Continues to Matter

For Calvin what was at stake in all this was our knowing that God knows us. Following the line of reasoning that he began: If Jesus, post-resurrection, were not in some way identifiably human, we would not be able to say that, in and through him, we are in actual relationship to *God.* We would be able to say a lot, to be sure. We could say, for example, that God did something wonderful for us, in entering into existence in the person of Jesus Christ for that thirty-three-year time span. We could say we learned a great deal, through that event, about what God is like. We could say that Jesus Christ tells things that are true *about* God. But we couldn't say that we know God directly, in God's very own self, in the person of Jesus Christ who was, is, and always will be *fully human with us.* If Jesus's humanity were only a temporary condition, we would know God as the fully divine one who went out of God's way for us to do something extra special. To live with us so we would know God cares and understands. To die by our hand so that we would know we have been forgiven, even of the worst of sins. To rise for us so that we know the pains of this world are not, finally, the things that will endure.

We would know all these things, and we could be awe-stricken and grateful. We could bow, reverently, in the context of Christian worship, thanking God for all God has done for us. But we would miss out on the fullness of our salvation, because we would not know God directly in and through the fully human one. What we would know of God would only be whatever we could glean through the mediation of this one who took on our creaturely existence for a time in order to teach us, to show us, to demonstrate to us God's love. The humanity, in the case of a Jesus who is not human now, would be a pedagogical tool that would help us know about the God we are incapable of knowing directly.

Such an understanding of Jesus Christ's humanity would be quite logical, especially since it syncs with Christian convictions about the magnitude, mystery, and unknowability of God.[81] But it is not, finally, adequate to the task of articulating what, at the Council of Chalcedon, our forebears in the faith saw as the heart of the mystery: that is, that our salvation rests, somehow, in the existence of this one, Jesus Christ, whose very constitution, from the vantage point of human understanding, appears to be a contradiction. The very same one who is born from the Father before the ages in relation to his divinity is, in relation to his humanity, born of the Virgin Mary, the Mother of God. If we were to say that the Word "covered himself in flesh" or "disguised himself in flesh" or "became human temporarily in order to pay us a visit and teach us something about God," we would be compromising on the mystery in order to better understand it. The mystery is, precisely, that this one who is wholly divine is also wholly human, and that these two natures do not seem readily or logically to hold together. Instead of trying to understand how they do fit, we would do well, as people of faith, to explore the "so what?" of their coexistence. When it comes to the mystery of Jesus Christ being one person in two natures, we can't understand it, but we can know what it is about.[82] As Chalcedon bears witness, what it is about has something to do with us and our salvation. We are saved because in and through Jesus Christ—the one who is eternally fully human as well as fully divine—we know not only that God visited with us, at one point, but that God *is* with us—right now. We know not only that God has done and will do great things for us, because God has done them in Jesus Christ, but also that God *is* for us in God's very self. In Jesus who was and is fully human, we are privy to the humanity of God. In knowing Jesus who is fully human as well as fully divine, we know not only what God has done for us; we know and are in relationship to this God. In Jesus, the one who is fully human as well as fully divine, we know the God who is unknowable. And even as we know God truly by way of Jesus Christ's full humanity, we are drawn more deeply into the knowledge of God's unknowability. We stand in awe of the God who will not be limited to being unlimited, who will not be limited to being only divine, but has brought the limits of creaturely existence into God's very own life and says, with Mary: How can this be? We stand in awe of the God who does not do things for us in order to instruct us, but because God loves us. We stand in awe because it would be enough to believe our powerful God benevolently went out of God's way to instruct us and to offer us gifts. Instead, what the eternal humanity of God in the person of Jesus Christ conveys to us is that it is not so much that the Word became flesh in order to instruct us, but that the Word became flesh because God so loves us.

This changes everything, when it comes to us and our salvation. Instead of being servants who feel compelled to respond to the God who treats us so well, we are friends who are called by the One who loves us to "remain" in him and hold fast to his words.[83] Instead of being those who wait patiently at the edges of the Garden for our fully-divine-but-disguised-as-a-human Lord to confer with the Father God, we are shaken awake and asked to join hearts, lives, and destinies with this one who desires the companionship and partnership of fellow human beings.[84] Instead of being those who can be content, simply, to let go and let God, we are those who are charged to "carry out [our] own salvation with fear and trembling," knowing "God is the one who enables [us] both to want and to actually live out God's good purposes."[85] Because the fully divine one is fully human for all of eternity, it is both the case that God is with us no matter what and that we are included, as participants, in the life and work of God.

The Fully Human One Is Fully Divine:[86] Partnership with God?

One of the worthy concerns about the Chalcedonian Statement, raised in various ways by those committed to the work of social justice, is that thinking about Jesus as fully human as well as fully divine inevitably backfires, disempowering or excusing human agents by representing Jesus, ultimately, as the God who is able to do it all—including being the human being we are not able to be. The concern is that, in the final analysis, to speak of Jesus as fully human and fully divine will lead, ultimately, to a depiction of Jesus in which the divinity more or less trumps the humanity. The humanity is taken into the divine; there is, now, nothing that God does not have covered; human beings who are marginalized are encouraged not to act but to wait on God to do the work; human beings who are oppressors are excused from acting by way of appealing to the God who understands and who "works all things together for good"[87] in the end.[88]

In my view, these important critiques have validity and must be taken into account in the development of any christology. I understand them to apply to what I would say is an abuse of the Chalcedonian Statement rather than to its conceptual content. Chalcedon has been distorted whenever we speak elegantly about God's radical presence with us, in the person of Jesus Christ, without testifying with equal fervor to the truth that, because *God* is with us (the fully divine one is fully human), *we* are with God (the fully human one is fully divine). Consideration of this Chalcedonian idea—that we as human beings are in some sense through Christ integrated into the life and work of God—has consistently been neglected by those who have little interest in inviting people to think of themselves as the "hands and feet" of God.[89] The idea of the humanity of God, when understood to carry all of we humans into God's life-giving work of this world, is exhilarating for those who value egalitarianism and inclusion, but frightening for those who are more comfortable with hierarchical ways of thinking about who God's agents are in the world.

Consider Mary, again: Into her very womb God empties Godself in the baby Jesus Christ. She is lifted up, by way of this, to sing and prophesy about how God is acting to reverse the order of life as we know it: "[God] has filled the hungry with good things," she says, "and sent the rich away empty-handed."[90] This is clearly not what those who have worldly power want people like Mary to be saying. This may be one reason why, then, there has been a problematic tendency for ecclesial structures, when talking about Chalcedon, to emphasize that Jesus is the fully divine one who empties himself to be with us, but to neglect the idea that, in and through Jesus Christ, humanity is with God, participating in the divine life.

It might help to understand what is at stake here by coming at it another way. Chalcedon argues that, when Jesus couldn't heal when the people didn't have enough faith, when he was corrected by the Canaanite woman, when he cried at Lazarus's tomb, and when he called out with agony on the cross,[91] he did all of these things every bit as much as one who is divine as one who is human. While these examples might seem jarring to those who understand God to be unchanging and self-sufficient, I am naming them in an attempt to take the Chalcedonian insight seriously. To continue in this vein: according to Chalcedon, the one who fed the five thousand with lots of leftovers, the one who walked on the water and spoke so meaningfully and eloquently, the one who forgave sins and rose from the dead[92]—this one did all of these things as a fully human, human being as much as he did them as one who is divine. What does this say about our humanity, insofar as it is joined to the humanity of Jesus Christ? This Word that touched all flesh by becoming flesh shows us what flesh is capable of, in and through our participation in him. This idea, it seems, is even more unnerving to the status quo than the idea that (for example) Jesus, the divine one, weeps. But the potential, here, to "liberate the oppressed"[93] must be revisited and claimed.

God with Us and Us with God

Reflecting on the meaning and significance of the Chalcedonian Statement from various angles, Barth considers not only what we learn from recognizing the fully divine one as fully human, but also what we learn from acknowledging the fully human one as fully divine. If the full humanity of the divine Jesus leads us to think of *kenosis,* as it is described in Philippians 2:3-7a, the full divinity of the human one leads us to consider the implications for us and our salvation of *theosis,* as it is described in Philippians 2:7b-8. The fully divine one empties himself and is (also) fully human, becoming obedient even unto death on the cross. The fully human one is exalted by the Father and is (also) fully divine, lifted up from that pivotal moment on the cross to the glorious, inclusive reality in which no one is left behind—every knee bends, every tongue confesses, that Jesus Christ is Lord.

The "so what?" of Chalcedon, when considered from the vantage point of *theosis* (exaltation), is just as significant for understanding who Jesus is, and how he reconciles us to God, as is *kenosis.* If the confession that the fully divine one is fully human reminds us that *God* is ever *with and for us*, the confession that the fully human one is fully divine reminds us that *we*, therefore, *are*—in and through Jesus Christ—*with and for God.*

What this means is that we who are mere creatures, we who in and of ourselves often feel it is an amazing accomplishment just to have made it through another day—we are actually included, and even have the status of being "partners" with God. In and through Jesus Christ, the one who has entered fully into existence with us, we are lifted up and included in the life and work and God.[94] This is, as we will discuss later, the movement of baptism—Jesus Christ became sin, died, was buried, rose, and is exalted. We join him in dying to self and are lifted up to become new creatures—heirs together with him and partners with him in the ministry of reconciliation!

Now, this language of partnership needs to be handled carefully. After all, who are *we* to think of ourselves as *partners* with God? Barth noted that talking about the implications of the confession that the fully human one is fully divine could get us into trouble—that we might be accused of heresy, of compromising on the sovereignty of God, of thinking of ourselves as in some way divine. But the implication of remembering that the fully human one is fully divine is not at all that we, as human beings, are in some way divine. In fact, the implication is closer to the opposite of this. The fact that God has taken humanity into God's own life in the person of Jesus Christ, as borne witness to by Chalcedon, frees us to think of ourselves as partnering with God as the fully human, human beings we are. We do not have first to become better, stronger, and faster than before. We do not have to engage in spiritual practices that make us more worthy. We do not have to focus on being less human, less creaturely, less limited. We are worthy as we are, as the beautiful creatures God made us, as creatures joined in creatureliness by God in Jesus, as creatures included in the operations of God's household also by way of the Jesus who enters into our lives with us and then takes us along, with him, into the ongoing creation of life that is new.

To claim Jesus Christ is both fully human and fully divine means, then, that our relationship to God is not founded in a mere transaction—with God doing things for us and us, in gratitude, then trying our best to respond by doing things for God. Because God in the person of Jesus Christ doesn't simply do things for us but *is* for us, we can be for God and one another. Our relationship to God and to others, when we know what the person of Jesus Christ is all about, looks nothing like a transaction or a contract (in which we get the better end of the deal, but we do what we can and are grateful). On the contrary, our relationship to God and one another, when we are paying attention to the person of Jesus Christ as fully human and fully divine, looks a lot like the relationship of people who love each other dearly. The doing for is there, but it is an extension of the being for. The *being with* is the reality, but it is no burden whatsoever—it is a manifestation of the desire to *be with* that is had by a Lover for the Beloved. It is core, and unconditional, and tenacious, and never satiated. It is "love so amazing, so divine" that it "demands our life, our souls, our all."[95] It is the love in which we abide, the love we learn by way of the humanity of God, the love that, as John says, actually is God.[96] In the next chapter we will continue thinking about the love of God as it is expressed not only in God's acts on our behalf, but in God's own self-relation as Father, Son, and Holy Spirit.

Chapter Four
In What Ways Does God Claim Us?

The Doctrine of the Trinity

In the last chapter we considered the truth that lies at the center of our faith: God has met us in the person of Jesus Christ. By way of the Word made flesh God is with us, and in him we are included, we have said, in the very life of God. In the person of Jesus Christ, Christians believe, God not only meets us but also makes us God's own. We are claimed as beloved ones embraced by a lover, as children held by parents, as friends defended and believed in by one another. We are claimed as objects of a love greater than our understanding, a love that desires we participate, as conscious subjects, in the joy of its benefits. As Jesus asks Peter, so we, too, are asked, by God: "Do you love me?"[1] From a trinitarian vantage point, we might recognize this question as implicit in creation, if we understand God's creation of us, and the whole world, as an act of love. And we might understand it to extend from our response to Jesus's question out and into the shape of our lives, where we are driven by the Spirit to feed and to tend.

The God who meets us in Jesus Christ claims us, but the claim God makes on us is not something new or alien to God. As we will discuss in the chapter on salvation, God meets us in Jesus Christ, to be sure, in order to heal us. What is healed in Christ is not God's love for us, however, but rather our faulty perception of it. God's love, Christian traditions have consistently taught, is steadfast and unconditional. Even when we think we have been left behind, who God is argues to the contrary. When Jesus meets us, we are reminded of the claim God has always and consistently made on us. We are God's creatures; we are God's children; we are God's ambassadors. God desires fellowship with us; God wants to shower us with blessings; God calls us to participate in the ministry of reconciliation.

The claim made on us is multifaceted because the one God meets us in multiple ways. Traditionally, Christians have reflected on this by way of the doctrine of the Trinity, which holds that God acts, on our behalf, as Father, as Son, and as Holy Spirit. In this chapter we will continue exploring how it is that God meets us and claims us, not only in the person of Jesus Christ but also as Father and Holy Spirit.

A Note about Trinitarian God Language

A couple of comments about language, before moving on, to address one of the pressing questions of our day. Like it or not, we live in an era where there is much disagreement about God language. Debates about how to speak about God come into play especially strongly when we discuss God as Trinity, because the traditional language is, decidedly, male. But what, if anything, can and should we do about this? Even if we agree with the way Sandra Schneiders once humorously put it—that "God Is More Than Two Men and a Bird"[2]—it is nonetheless the case that male language for God is the most commonly used language of the traditions we have inherited. It has, in one way or another, shaped our experience of the faith that holds us.

I tend to use, in this chapter, the traditional apostolic language that God is "Father, Son, and Holy Spirit." I use this language because it is the language that connects Christian believers through the last two thousand years. It is the language of the Apostles' Creed—a Creed developed in the second century of the church's history, to be used in tandem with baptismal services: "Do you believe in God the Father? Do you believe in God the Son? Do you believe in God the Holy Spirit?" baptismal candidates were asked.[3] Since then and still today, children and adults are baptized in the name of the "Father, Son, and Holy Spirit." While there is nothing magical about any language we use for God, many Christians find it to be a very powerful experience to use the trinitarian formula that was used by the earliest Christians and down through the ages. Christians baptize in the name of the "Father, Son, and Holy Spirit," for example, in order to remember we are members of the one household of the same triune God, together with those who have been baptized for the last two thousand years. Church congregations generally recite the Apostles' Creed, which again is built on this apostolic formula, whenever the Lord's Supper is celebrated; this reminds Christians they are joined across both time and space—through history and all around the globe—to all other Christians who use the same Creed.

My intention in using the apostolic formula is, then, to be inclusive of all Christians everywhere. But I don't think good intention is enough to justify use of "Father, Son, and Holy Spirit" without acknowledging and attending to the fact that this language has been too often used either to exclude, or to establish hierarchies that privilege some over others. Most notably, the language of "Father, Son, and Holy Spirit" has been used to justify the superordination of men and the subordination of women,[4] the idea that men are the "leaders and initiators" and women are the "responders and followers."[5] It is likely no secret to anyone reading this book that Christian believers do not always agree about whether and how to address this problem. Some simply hold it should be enough to recognize that the use of "Father, Son, and Holy Spirit" is in no way meant to imply that God is male. Others think the roots of the issue run deeper, and that the problem of privileging men over women cannot be corrected simply by asserting that, in the case of God, the reference to "Father" is gender-neutral. As we have learned in numerous sociological, psychological, and linguistic studies, language is powerful, shaping the way we think as well as reflecting *what* we think.[6] Over the course of the centuries and even millennia, the almost sole use of male language for God has influenced how we understand God, and how we understand men and women to resemble and/or not resemble God.

My approach is to honor both the strengths of the tradition and the valid challenges made to the tradition. In the pages that follow, then, I will use the apostolic language of "Father, Son, and Holy Spirit," but I will also try to model an expansive way of engaging this apostolic language. I am influenced, in this approach, by at least two sources. First, by the argument espoused by Elizabeth Johnson, that the best way to make sure Father language is not misunderstood is to use other language for God as well. When we use "equivalent female images" for God,[7] for example, we are reminded that who God is cannot be exhausted even by the very best titles we might use. On this point even Calvin agrees, explaining that "no figures of speech can describe God's extraordinary affection towards us; for it is infinite and various."[8] Calvin insists, further, that God "has manifested himself to be both . . . Father and Mother," noting that God "did not satisfy himself with proposing the example of a father . . . but in order to express his very strong affection, he chose to liken himself to a mother, calling his people not merely 'children,' but the fruit of the womb, towards which there is usually a warmer affection." Interesting that a twenty-first-century feminist theologian and a sixteenth-century Reformation theologian would make such similar arguments. Clearly, they are both remembering that all of our theological language—even our most beloved titles for God—is analogical in character.

I am also influenced by a church document I had the privilege of working on several years ago. It is titled *The Trinity: God's Love Overflowing*.[9] After struggling not only for hours and days but even for a couple years about how to handle the matter of trinitarian God language, members of the committee who crafted this document agreed to recognize the language of "Father, Son, and Holy Spirit" as the anchor language of the church that cannot be replaced, but can be supplemented by language that helps clarify its meaning. Similar to Johnson and Calvin, *The Trinity: God's Love Overflowing* commits to using expansive language for God because to do so is consistent with God's very nature. But it recognizes at the same time that it is also true to who God is to be known in particular, concrete ways and relationships and not just in an endless number of ways that may seem good to us. Christian traditions have consistently identified knowing God with experiencing God's acts as "Father," "Son," and "Spirit."

"But wait!" we might say. "If God is infinite, why limit the ways we refer to God to only three?" In one sense, this is a good point. Who God is cannot be exhausted by even the best ways we have of speaking of God. God is more, even, than "the Word was made flesh"; more, even, than "Father, Son, and Holy Spirit." The *oneness* of God's triune character reminds us of the truth that no amount of knowing God can ever undo God's hiddenness; that none of God's acts—as true as they are to who God is—ever exhaust the divine being. But the *threeness*, with all of its specificity, reminds us of another truth equally descriptive of God, that is: God has entered into existence with us not only abstractly, as the one who in some sense gives us life, and loves us, and keeps us going through our lives. Rather, to say God is three is to remember that God has met us *concretely*, in the context of our own creaturely history. God the Father created us willfully and with desire. God the Son saved us by entering into a specific moment and person in time. God the Holy Spirit birthed the church, with all its various, specific peoples, languages, and gifts.

To think of the triune God in relation to the particular number three helps us remember that, if we thought of God as endlessly particular, we would lose track of the specificity and importance of the threeness itself. I remember when I first had the opportunity to think through this. I was part of a panel discussion on the Trinity in which someone presented a paper arguing that the problem with thinking about God in terms of Trinity is that three is not enough. The concern of the presenter, in many ways quite understandably, was that "three" is way too constraining of a way to think of the God who is all-in-all, the God who is infinite. But, I wondered, what *would* be enough of a number, when it comes to the infinite God? Would 5,834 be enough? How about 9,456,321,069? In the face of an infinite being, it seems to me there is no number that is enough, if enough means to in some way do justice to God and all God does. God is able "to accomplish more than we can ask or imagine"[10] . . . or count!

The irony is that, as soon as we think of the one God as present in an endless number of ways, we have forgotten the divine mystery. In other words, it makes sense that the God who is one, the God who is sovereign, the God who is all-in-all, the God who fills the very cosmos is present in more ways than can be counted, and certainly in more ways than are encapsulated in the "three" of the Trinity. What is truly mysterious (and this is what we are reminded of by the *three in one* and *one in three*) is that the God who is one, sovereign, all-in-all, and cosmos-filling is also three. Not 9,456,321,069. But three. Only three. There is an absurdity to this, to talking about the all-in-all God in such specific terms. A trinitarian thinker will say, in the face of such absurdity, "exactly." As we peer over the manger at the baby Jesus and marvel that nothing that is exists apart from this one born of Mary, so we look at the concrete number *three* and engage the specific acts of God the Father, God the Son, and God the Holy Spirit. And we stand in wonder at the mystery that the God who is unmanageably and incomprehensibly *one* meets us, and claims us, in these awesome, particular ways we can actually grasp, talk about, and share with others.

The Heart and the Skeleton

If we think of the incarnation as sitting at the heart of the faith we hold, the Trinity might be understood more as the frame or the skeleton of our faith. Even if we who hold faith don't give it a great deal of considered attention, we might notice it now and again, providing structure to our confessions and in a sense holding together the faith that holds us. In the Apostles' Creed, for example, there is no mention of the Trinity—but the idea that God is Father, Son, and Holy Spirit serves as the outline of what we commonly refer to as the *three articles of the faith*: First, that we believe in God the Father ("almighty…Creator of Heaven and earth"). Second, that we believe in Jesus Christ ("his only Son, our Lord"). Third, that we believe in the Holy Spirit (and all the benefits of our faith that follow).

In addition to noticing that the doctrine of the Trinity helps frame Christian belief, we might rightly have the sense that it reminds us of the mystery of God. After all, we realize just as soon as we start really thinking about it, it is not possible for something to be *one* and *three* at exactly the same time. No amount of mathematical somersaults can prove, without logical fallacy, the equation 1=3 or 3=1. To remember God is triune is, then, to remember God is mysterious, beyond our knowing.

At the same time, however, the point of confessing the Trinity is not to remind us that God is mysterious in such a way that we feel ourselves standing at a distance from God, intimidated by what is impossible to understand. Too often, people of faith have treated the doctrine of the Trinity almost as if its primary purpose is to keep us at bay, reverently tip-toeing around any claims we might make about who God is. But if we think the point of the doctrine is that we need continuously to qualify whatever claims we make about God, humbled by God's massive holiness, we may have missed what is the greatest mystery of all—that is, that to say God is triune is to celebrate the fact that the *God who is* has shown God's own self to us in multiple ways. In creating us, redeeming us, and sustaining us; by enlivening us, healing us, and empowering us to do God's work in the world, the triune God of life[11] does more than show us who God is. To confess God is triune is to recognize God actually shares life with us, inviting us to share life with God. Contrary to the stereotypes about the Trinity that associate it with some sort of esoteric piety, to confess God as Father, Son, and Holy Spirit is to insist God is *present* and *involved* in our day-to-day lives. As Catherine Mowry LaCugna suggests in her aptly titled book, *God for Us*, the Trinity is the most practical of all the Christian doctrines.[12] If the doctrine of the incarnation is all about God being *with* us, LaCugna and other contemporary theologians suggest, the doctrine of the Trinity is about God being *for* us.

Why does it matter so much, we might ask, that God is *for* us as well as *with* us? An analogy that might begin to get at an answer to this is that of a friend—let's call her Melissa—being *with*, versus *with and for*, another friend—let's call him Josh. Melissa can be *with* Josh, listening to his joys and his woes, helping him run errands when he is sick or cheering for him on Facebook when he accomplishes something wonderful. But it would be possible for Melissa to be with Josh without really being particularly *for* him. To be for him would be not only to participate in the assisting and the cheering, but also to act as his representative in the world: to insist that a space be made for who he is and what he can accomplish; to defend him in ways that enable him not only to survive in the world, but to thrive in it *as Josh*, as one who has a contribution to make to it.

The difference between being simply *with*, and being *with and for*, might also be compared to the difference between a parent who spends time connecting with a child who is struggling and accomplishing and a parent who is so committed to the child with whom he connects that he actively works at creating spaces in the world for her (e.g., by advocating for the child in relation to family members and teachers, by believing so strongly that she has something to contribute that he encourages her to speak, to act, to create, to practice). To be with, and only with, is to do pretty well by people—it is possible to enter into relationship to a child, or a friend, to rescue or to celebrate—and then return to our own familiar space, having paid a benevolent or supportive visit. But to be with as someone who is also *for* is not to visit with a friend or a child now and then, or even as frequently as possible, leaving them to live their lives independently of us between visits. It is not only to enter in and rescue a person in need, but to remain in solidarity, advocating for them in ways that make them present even when they are physically absent from the room or from the deliberations that are taking place. It is never to be separated from any of these, even when we are apart from them. It is to have them ever in mind and be ever making them present in conversations, in plans, in policies.

To say God is Trinity is to confess that the God who is with us in Jesus Christ is not only with us but also for us. It is to remember that what the incarnation is all about is far more than that a benevolent God paid us a visit and orchestrated a successful rescue operation on our behalf. It is to know the amazing truth that what we see in the person of Jesus Christ—and in the handiwork of God the Creator, and in the intercession of God the Spirit—is not only God *doing things* for us but God *being* for us. To be with, now and again or as much as is possible, is praiseworthy, helpful, and worthy of gratitude. It is to give benevolently, to share with those who reside outside of the sphere of oneself. To be with *always*, as one who is also *for*, is certainly worthy of gratitude. But there is an even more immediate response "being for" invokes, when one becomes cognizant of it—that is, a response of love. "If God is for us, who can be against us?" Paul asks, insisting that we love the God from whose love nothing can separate us.[13]

In the remainder of this chapter I will imagine what possibilities emerge when the trinitarian insight that "God is for us" is in play, exploring the ways in which this framing doctrine of the Christian faith really matters to our daily lives. First, as I did in the chapter on incarnation, I will consider briefly how the doctrine developed. It is my hope that this will help pique the curiosity of the reader who may have the impression that the doctrine of the Trinity is one of the more anachronistic doctrines. Believing we can learn from our forebears' passion, I want to ask: Why did people of faith, way back in the fourth century, care so much about understanding God as at the same time both one and three? What was at stake for them, and what is at stake for us in thinking through who God is—and we are—in these terms? Before we pursue these historical questions, however, allow me to set the context with a couple of anecdotes that will help us reflect on fourth-century debates about the Trinity in light of our own twenty-first-century context.

Story One: The Children's Sermon Scramble

When I teach theology classes, different groups of people feel more or less strongly about particular themes related to the doctrine of God. Presbyterians generally have strong views about God's sovereignty, for example. Pentecostals listen carefully and critically to what I have to say about the Spirit, and just about everyone comes into the lecture room believing they know at least most of what there is to know about Jesus.

When it comes to the Trinity, however, I encounter a great deal of ambivalence. It is almost as if people know better than to ask if we can skip over it, but can't for the life of them figure out how confessing God as one-in-three-and-three-in-one could possibly matter to their actual lives. Often the impression seems to be that talking about God in this way must have meant something in a bygone day, but really means very little now. Sure, some students concede, they like singing the hymn "Holy, Holy, Holy,"[14] but they don't really think much about what it's all about.

It is easy to get snagged by the temptation to treat God as a kind of puzzle. We ask: How can 3 = 1 and 1 = 3? There are all kinds of answers we can come up with, especially if we feel pressure to say something. One annual occasion that inevitably supplies such pressure is Trinity Sunday, the Sunday following Pentecost. Doing the children's sermon is often, for many, a dreaded assignment, but I would bet there is no Sunday that it is more actively avoided than on Trinity Sunday. How do you explain the Trinity to fifteen children gathered round? Hmmm. What *would* a children's sermon on the Trinity look like? Imagine this:

> Good morning, kids. Today we're going to talk about the Trinity. Can you say "Trinity"? Now I've brought along my Bunsen burner, and I'm just going to flip it on and—don't touch that, Hannah!—Let's all look in this saucepan. What do I have in here? That's right, ice cubes. And you know what? Ice cubes are also called H_2O. Can you say H_2O? Now I'm just going to put these ice cubes on the burner and . . . what's happening now? That's right . . . they're melting. What's in the saucepan now? Water? Guess what, boys and girls? Water is also H_2O. Can you say H_2O? Okay . . . now the water is getting hotter and hotter and (don't touch that, Hannah!) . . . what's that wispy stuff coming off the top of it? No, Johnny, not smoke . . . that's called steam. And guess what? Steam is also H_2O. Can you say H_2O?

And then you go for your big transition:

> God is kind of like H2O. Just like H2O can be ice, and water, and steam, so God is Father, Son, and Holy Spirit.

That afternoon, you receive a phone call. It is an irate parent:

> When my kid got home he opened the freezer and said, "M-o-m! What's God doing in here?"

And you realize you've failed to convey a meaningful point. Instead of expressing to those kids why it matters that we believe God is triune, you've treated the Trinity as though it is some kind of a puzzle, a mathematical marvel to be figured out. Even if we could come up with the perfect way of explaining the three-in-one—people have tried an apple (with core, flesh, and skin), a pie cut into three pieces, a family with three members—we still would not have answered the important question everyone is wondering about, which is: So what? Why does the Christian confession that God is triune matter to our lives of faith?

In trying to explain the mystery rather than participating in it, we have dropped the theological ball. Trinity becomes a colder, more calculated doctrine. Unable to figure out the mathematics of it, we might throw up our hands and cry: I don't know . . . it's a mystery! When we do this, we have actually betrayed mystery for "mystification."[15]

The problem with invoking the category of *mystery* in order to justify giving up on the pursuit of understanding is that it forgets the mystical character of mystery itself. Throwing up our hands and ceasing to try may be an appropriate response to failing in a task such as, for example, solving a Rubik's cube. We might decide it is just not worth the effort to figure out how to get each side of a cube a single color. When we give up on solving a Rubik's cube, it is not because the cube transcends the capacities of human understanding. We know there are people who can solve it even if we cannot or don't want to. When it comes to the doctrine of the Trinity, by contrast, there is no one who can solve the problem of how 3 = 1 and 1 = 3 because whatever these equations are doing, they are not trying to invite us into the challenge of problem-solving. Rather, what they are trying to invoke in us is an appreciation of the fact that who the triune God *is* is beyond any human formulations. The mystery is not the solution to the puzzle of how 1 and 3 can be made equal. The mystery we are invited into is, rather, that God is, at once, both equally one and three. What might look like a puzzle or a riddle is, actually, itself an answer: a statement of who God is. Our task is not to decipher it, but to recognize it participates in a deeper meaning than can be captured by any neat and tidy solution and to discern what it is about and how it affects us. As is the case with all mysteries, figuring out what the doctrine of the Trinity is about requires attention that, in turn, requires we create time and space for reflection and contemplation.

It is through thinking about the inexplicable mystery of the three-in-one that we can, in fact, come to participate more deeply in the "so what" of it. As Gregory of Nazianzus once put it: "I cannot think on the one without quickly being encircled by the splendor of the three; nor can I discern the three without being straightway carried back to the one."[16] The experience of Gregory doesn't yet get us to the "so what" of the Trinity in our day-to-day lives, but it is, I think, "thinking on the one," then "thinking on the three," then moving back to "thinking on the one" that is the necessary precursor to figuring out what the Trinity is all about.

Story Two: The Encouraging, Heartbreaking Letter

I remember the first time I tried to talk out loud about why the Trinity matters. It was hard. Harder, even, than talking about why the incarnation matters to our lives of faith. As challenging as it is to think through the "so what" of Jesus being fully human and fully divine, at least you are thinking about a *person* and not about syncing two different numbers.[17] So trained we are to try to solve puzzles or provide answers to equations that we are inclined to treat the nature of the triune God as if it is a conundrum to be solved, as in the case of the children's sermon imagined above. One of the strategies I used to try to think in a different way about the Trinity was to say out loud what my alternative children's sermon would be. In other words, if I wouldn't tell the kids that the Trinity is like H_2O, what would I say? Imagine this, as a Sunday morning children's sermon:

> Kids, today we are going to talk about the Trinity. When we say God is Trinity we remember God is "tri" or three: God is the Father who loves us, the Son we know as Jesus Christ, and the Holy Spirit who is with us right now,

> reminding us of God's love and grace in this time of worship. But the God who is three is also always one. That sounds kind of silly, doesn't it—that God is one and three at the same time? This doesn't make any sense to us because we cannot be one and three at the same time, can we? We can't understand it, but we can know what it is about. When we say God is Trinity, what it means is that God loves us because God is love. The Father loves the Son, Jesus—and Jesus loves the Father God the way we love our mothers, our fathers, and the people who take care of us and believe in us no matter what. And sometimes we think of the Holy Spirit as the way God reminds us that we are loved too! The God who is Trinity includes us in God's love. Isn't that great? We are not left behind, but included in the love of God's family. On Trinity Sunday, we remember that this is why it matters that we say God is three and one, all at the same time. To say God is "Trinity" is to remember how much God loves and includes us!

A children's sermon along these lines, which might be framed in several different ways, steers clear of trying to do bad or impossible math and attempting somehow to prove the faulty equation 1 = 3 or 3 = 1. Even if such a thing could be proven, by the way, what good would such a proof do us? We might gain the reputation for being mathematical wizards, but we would have lost the opportunity to think through how this fundamental confession shapes the way we understand God and our relationship to God.

Moving from thinking about how to convey the "so what" of the Trinity to children to thinking of what I would say to adults, I developed my first lectures on "Why the Trinity Matters" beginning about twenty years ago, giving them in my introductory theology class and at various continuing education events. I'll never forget a letter I received from a retired schoolteacher who had attended an event at which I had spoken about the Trinity. The letter is several pages long. After saying her eyes had been opened, by way of the lecture, to what the Trinity was all about, and after adding her own keen insights and implications to what she explained she had learned, this woman closed her letter by expressing great pain and frustration, almost grief. "I just don't understand why I never heard any of this before. I've been going to church my whole life, and I've always been one to ask a lot of questions. But no one ever said anything about this," she wrote. "I was told, only, that I had to accept the mystery of the

Trinity, but never how it made a difference to my life. If only I had known this years ago," she continued. "I think my life would have been different. I would have known how much I meant to God. I'm angry that no one ever told me, if you want to know the truth. I just don't understand why."

What this wise woman rightly recognized is that the main themes of my lecture were not composed of ideas to which only select people had the wherewithal to gain access. What she was hearing from me was not excessively brilliant, as though—again—I was sharing some hard-to-grasp method for solving a Rubik's cube. What I said was basic, but she recognized it as profound: to say God is triune, I taught, is to say God is love, God is relational, God acts, and God is knowable. All that woman needed from me, in the lecture that helped her, were a few gestures to the "so what" of who the triune God is in relation to her life of faith. She needed someone to point out the simple truth that to say God is love, related, acting, and knowable is to say God has met us and claimed us as God's own. The woman was frustrated, as she expressed it in her letter, because she recognized these connections as being fairly easy to make for anyone who has been invited to consider them. More importantly, she perceived them to be essential to her own—and to everyone's—spiritual well-being.

Every time I think about this woman's letter, I recommit myself to doing my best to invite people to see the connections between God's character as three-in-one and the claim God makes on each of us. I learned that this faithful woman died a couple of years after she sent me this letter. I may have helped her think about something she had always wondered about, but her legacy to me continues to be a reminder to me, over and over again, to help people quit trying to figure out how to explain the mathematics of the Trinity so they can focus on how the doctrine might transform the ways we think of God and ourselves. This is the joyous work of the remainder of this chapter. We will first retrieve a bit of the passion for the doctrine of the Trinity had by our fourth-century forebears, and then move on to considering how the doctrine of the Trinity undoes any conceptions of God that keep God and creation at a distance from one another. Instead, the Christian confession that God is triune invites us to participate in the beautiful dance of God's action in the world.

Getting to It: Fourth-Century Passion for Why the Trinity Matters

In the last chapter we gave brief consideration to two ecclesial councils: the Council of Nicea (325) and the Council of Chalcedon (451). While of course debates about the Trinity have gone on for centuries and still continue today, the time period between Nicea and Chalcedon was an especially rich period for development of the doctrine.[18]

As in the case of the christological controversies, the trinitarian debates were committed to honoring both God's unsearchable character and God's self-revelation in discrete moments and events of history. Nicea and Chalcedon were marked by the concern that Jesus's full divinity and full humanity were equally and wholly represented. Similarly, at the Council of Alexandria (362) and the Council of Constantinople (381) the operative concern was how simultaneously to honor both the unity of the Godhead and the particular contributions and actions of each of the trinitarian persons—Father, Son, and Holy Spirit. As was true at both Nicea and Chalcedon, there were two main schools of thought represented at Alexandria, the gathering committed to the work and debate that led to the development of the trinitarian formula that was adopted at Constantinople in 381.

On the Western side (which came, later, to be represented by Augustine—though he was only about eight years old in 362!) there was a great deal of emphasis on the *oneness* or unity of God. Westerners tended to focus their discussions about the Trinity, along these lines, on what became known as the *immanent Trinity*—God in God's own internal relationships to the triune self. The concern of the West was that, if we overemphasize God's distinct actions as Father, Son, and Holy Spirit, we will finally move too far astray of monotheism and be functioning as though we believe in three gods, rather than the one true God. By thinking of God first as one, and then as three, they thought, the Christian church could ensure we were not committing the heresy of *tritheism*, respecting the fundamental Christian insight that God is the one, undivided, sovereign being who is Lord of all.

The Eastern side, represented by the three Cappadocian Fathers (Gregory of Nyssa, Gregory of Nazianzus, and Basil the Great) agreed with the Westerners that God's oneness should be respected. They nonetheless took another approach to reflecting on this Trinity, beginning their discussion with the threeness of God rather than orienting discussion of "Father, Son, and Holy Spirit" around the divine simplicity. *Epistemological* concerns[19] drove the Cappadocians' agenda. For them, it didn't make sense that we could dive in and begin thinking about who God is as one without first recognizing God in God's acts on our behalf. God meets us by creating us, redeeming us, and sustaining us, the Cappadocians thought, and it is in these and other acts of God that we come to know the divine unity. Their emphasis—on the acts of God, rather than on the being of God, came to be identified as the *economic Trinity*. The Cappadocians defended themselves against the Western accusation of tritheism by developing a model, along the lines just described, that later came to be called the *social model* of the Trinity. It is a model that has been developed and is today espoused by theologians including Jürgen Moltmann.[20]

Even as they defended themselves, the Cappadocians made accusations of their own against the Westerners, complaining that the Western take veered dangerously close to the heresy of *modalism*. Modalism is the idea that the one God more or less "morphs" into each of the three persons as each is needed. God starts out as Creator, then takes the form of the Son when redemption is required, then finally is present as the Spirit when we need comforting. As the Cappadocians defended themselves against the charge of tritheism, so the Westerners insisted they had no intention of compromising on the fact of God's triunity. If the goal of the Cappadocians' framing of the doctrine was epistemological, the concern of the Westerners was *ontological*[21]—they wanted to be sure there was no compromise to the being of God in the way they formulated their understanding of the one-in-three.

Just as both sides, in the Chalcedonian debate of 451, agreed with Gregory of Nazianzus's position that that which is not assumed is not redeemed,[22] so there were major points of agreement between both sides of the trinitarian debates that took place at the council of Alexandria in 362.[23]

All reaffirmed, against the earlier Arian heresy, that the Son is the same stuff (*homoousios*) with the Father. Both sides affirmed the Holy Spirit is of the same stuff as well. All agreed, even though they had different starting points and emphases, that God is both one and three, both three and one, and that tritheism and modalism are heretical extremes that need be avoided. All agreed with what became a classic way of articulating how it is that the three persons are considered distinct from one another even as all three are considered equally to be God. "The Father is not the Son or the Spirit," the saying goes. "The Son is not the Father or the Spirit," it continues. "And the Spirit is not the Father or the Son. But all three are equally God," it concludes. This is a way of thinking that honors both the oneness and the threeness of God without compromising on either.

These significant similarities between the Eastern and Western churches might actually serve to accentuate the differences between them. I think of it this way: the people I fight hardest with are often those with whom I have the most in common. Because we share so much, I care even more that they share, or at least see the value of, my perspective. When I talk with people who are Muslim, I am happy to find points of similarity between what they think, spiritually speaking, and what I think. But when I talk to someone who is Christian, I take the similarities we share for granted, almost, honing in on our differences and trying to persuade them about matters I take to be of common concern. While part of the reason I try to persuade them is no doubt because I want the satisfaction of proving myself right, the better part of me goes after small points of difference between myself and other Christians because we are somehow drawn closer together when we debate doctrines for which we together share a passion. Arguing about points of difference is a tricky enterprise, as all of us know. It we push things too far, we can wind up divided further from those we want nearer to us. But if we ignore differences, never representing our views or trying to convince each other about the things that matter most, we can find ourselves living on opposite sides of a silent divide rather than manifesting the visible unity we claim is a characteristic of Christian community.[24]

The point of heated debate between the Eastern and Western churches is something that was seeded in Alexandria in 362 and developed until the point of the Great Schism between the Eastern and Western churches, which took place in 1054.[25] The focus of it might, at first, sound somewhat trivial. Sometimes it is lamented that, if a single vowel determines the difference between christological orthodoxy and christological heresy (*homoousios* versus *homoiousios*, as discussed in the last chapter) a single prepositional phrase has divided the body of Christ for over a thousand years. The phrase is "and the Son," commonly known, in the Latin, as the *filioque* clause.

The *filioque* clause was not introduced until 589, at the Council of Toledo in Spain.[26] Obviously, this is over two hundred years after the Council of Alexandria, but the concerns the Eastern church had about the Western church's understanding of the Trinity, and vice versa, continued to endure. At the Council of Toledo, the Westerners added the phrase to the Nicene Creed because they believed it helped preserve the unity of God. "We believe in the Holy Spirit, the Lord, the Giver of Life, who proceeds from the Father *and the Son,* and who with the Father and the Son is worshipped and glorified." The thinking of the Western church was that subscribing to the "double procession" of the Holy Spirit, from both the Father and the Son, helps us conceptualize the life of the triune God in a more coherent manner. It is more consistent, for example, with some of the Augustinian analogies for the trinitarian God that, by 589, were shaping Western Christendom. God the Father is the Lover, God the Son the Beloved, and God the Spirit is the bond of love between them, Augustine had taught.[27] The Spirit, Westerners believed, in a very real sense ensures the unity of the triune Godhead by bearing witness to the relationship between the Father and the Son. The idea that the Father *and the Son* together send the Holy Spirit further reinforces that they are united by way of the Spirit who continues their shared work in the world.

The Eastern church was and still is understandably chagrined that the *filioque* clause was added to the Creed, not only because they disagreed with what it represented theologically, but also because the Western church has acted poorly, from a political standpoint, when they voted on the addition without their agreement.[28] It is clear, however, that the Easterners would not have endorsed the addition even if they had been included in the deliberations. Suspecting the Western church of being modalistic, their conviction was that the *filioque* clause renders the Holy Spirit passive, and in this way compromises on the Spirit's status as equally God. The Father and the Son are actively engaged in sending, but the Spirit is, only, *sent*. The Spirit, moreover, seems finally to be an extension of the Father and Son's relationship rather than, truly, her own, distinct person. It is almost as if the Eastern church interpreted the addition of the *filioque* as a clear indication the Western church is "binitarian" rather than "trinitarian."

These debates that raged from Alexandria (362) to the schism (1054) continue to have an impact on the global unity of the church. Still today, those who subscribe to the *filioque* are not permitted to take Communion at the Table in Greek and Russian Orthodox churches, precisely due to the concern that only those who are trinitarian are members of the one body of Christ and are invited, by him, to partake. Efforts to develop ecumenical versions of the Nicene Creed that can be said with no finger crossing by both Westerners and Easterners have mainly failed. In one version, the *filioque* clause is included, but is set in parentheses, the idea being that those who want to say it can, and those who do not wish to say it may leave it out.[29] This is far from satisfying to either Eastern or Western Christian traditions, appearing to diminish the stakes of the debate itself.

More recently, there have been Westerners who have argued Christians should set aside the *filioque* clause for the sake of ecumenical unity. LaCugna argues, for example, that Westerners should return to the insights of the Cappadocians as a way of correcting theological errors emerging from overemphasis on God's *substance* at the expense of God's *person.* Clearly, LaCugna argues, the Cappadocians are right that we come to know God by way of God's acts. What is amazing, she thinks, is that God's acts give us clear and reliable insight into who God is in God's being.[30] Moltmann has advocated setting the *filioque* to the side, similarly, if only for the sake of ecumenical relations, because he believes the unity of the church matters. It is hypocritical for Christians to keep singing "they will know we are Christians by our love" without actively working to meet and claim others identified with the body of Christ.[31]

In addition to supporting ecumenical unity, Moltmann suggests setting aside the *filioque* creates space to explore differently the doctrines of the Christian faith. In *The Way of Jesus Christ: Christology in Its Messianic Dimensions*, for example, Moltmann considers how we might understand who Jesus Christ is and what he does differently if we interpreted everything about his life in terms of the movement of the Holy Spirit.[32] Teasing out the implications of this, it seems to me that, when we think of Jesus as being enlivened by the Spirit as he teaches, heals, and socializes, we find it easier to understand how it is that we may abide in him, and he in us—we are joined by way of the very same Spirit, the one who indwells us is the very one who indwells him, facilitating our participation. Moltmann ends his discussion in *The Trinity and the Kingdom* along similar lines, with the idea that the Spirit makes it possible for us not only to be "servants" of God, but also God's "friends"—partners with God in the ministry of reconciliation.[33] We will engage these creative possibilities in the chapters following, particularly in our discussion of vocation and hope. For now, the important point to notice is that the seemingly archaic debate about the relationship of the "one" and the "three," as it began at Alexandria and has been shaped in the course of the *filioque* debate, continues to matter to Christians who hold faith.

Acknowledging just how much our forebears cared about thinking in the very best way they could about who God is, and how Father/Son/Spirit—Creator/Redeemer/Sustainer—are at once both united and distinguished, we turn now to exploring the "so what" of this history to our lives of faith today. Even as aspects of these past debates seem silly to us, we might ask ourselves if we can concede that we have our own silliness: we do not talk *enough* about these things! Karl Rahner once joked that, if it were ever announced that "a fourth person of the Trinity has been discovered," it would cause "little stir"![34] As that retired woman who wrote to me after that lecture noted, it is time we started talking, more, about the difference the doctrine of the Trinity can make to our lives.

Scandalous Presence: The Trinity and Christian Life

In the preceding chapter I noted that Jesus Christ reveals God is not who we may have expected God to be. I mentioned the theological concept called "the scandal of particularity"—that the very idea the God who holds the waters of the universe "in the hollow of God's hand" enters into one, particular historical person is in some sense outlandish.[35] Kierkegaard used a word to describe this phenomenon that is usually translated "offense."[36] Saying we are "offended" by the way God meets us in Jesus Christ and by the way God claims us in the persons of Father, Son, and Spirit might rattle us even more than saying we are "scandalized." Who are we, after all, to be offended by God? But if we take a step back from our resistance to Kierkegaard's language, for a minute, we might be able to see that what offends us is not as much who God is as that God's self-revelation does not fit with how we expect God to act or who we expect God to be.

When I am trying to imagine or explain what being scandalized looks like, I sometimes think of that classic scene in *The Sound of Music* where Captain von Trapp returns home from a trip only to discover that his very own children have been running around in play clothes made out of old curtains. Such a thing just isn't done; not by *his* children, he thinks. He is at a loss even to grasp the reality of what is going on, so antithetical it is to how he understands things to be.[37] Another example that evokes the kind of core incredulity associated with scandal is the scene in *Monty Python and the Holy Grail*[38] when the cows are catapulted over a wall. Such a thing simply isn't done; to interpret it at all takes breaking out of all our usual categories of understanding and thinking in an altogether different sort of way. Finally, when I try to imagine being scandalized, I remember a little history: when Amelia Bloomer, one of the early American suffragettes, became tired of negotiating her hoop skirts, she traded them in for pants that were disparagingly referred to as "bloomers." Who could imagine any respectable woman ever dressing in such a way? Scandalous!

In the last chapter I considered how scandalous it is that God meets us by entering the womb of Mary, eating with tax collectors and sinners, dying on the cross, and refusing to leave behind his body—and all the bodies of this world, by association—at the point of the resurrection. Writing in particular about the scandalous character of the cross, Paul acknowledges the crucifixion as "a stumbling block to Jews and foolishness to Gentiles."[39] If there is anywhere we have difficulty believing God meets us, it is in the concrete experiences of our sufferings. On the one hand, as many of our early forebears would agree, it appears unseemly for the God who is self-derived and all-in-all actually to suffer. On the other hand, however, this experience of feeling scandalized or offended is, it seems, not something Christians would want to settle into, since their hope lies in the fact that, as Dietrich Bonhoeffer puts it, "only a suffering God can help."[40] Perhaps that is why, then, the incredulity Christians experience when they encounter an unexpected God, in Jesus Christ, ideally gives way to awe and gratitude.

The scandal of the incarnation is perhaps obvious, especially when we think about God in relationship to the womb and the cross. But what is so scandalous about the Trinity?

Here, the history of conflict between the Eastern and Western church gives us some hints. There is something about the coexistence of the *three* and the *one*, in the life of God, that seemed to everyone quite precarious. In a sense, the East may have overcorrected on one side of the dilemma, and the West on the other side. But it is harder than it looks, theologically speaking, *not* to overcorrect, when one is concerned about avoiding making theological errors that can lead to unintended consequences. How do we at all moments understand Jesus Christ to be fully human and fully divine? How do we actually think about God as simultaneously one and three? In the final analysis, many people of faith saw the solution developed at Alexandria (362) and adopted at Constantinople (381) as being of very little help. "God is one *ousia* in three *hypostases*," the statement said.[41] The language of "substance" and "persons" ("God is one *substance* in three *persons*") developed later,[42] and actually strayed pretty far from the original Greek terminology. What we know about the meaning of *ousia* and *hypostases* is that they were almost synonymous. It was as though the wisdom of the council was to say that both the Eastern side and the Western side of the debate had something of value to contribute that needed to be preserved and considered. While this confusing language frustrated many, Kelly describes the deliberation at Alexandria as "statesmanlike" because it invited conversation about what was meant, and kept people from both sides of the debate in conversation.[43]

What is so scandalous about the Trinity is reflected in the statement itself, I believe. It is that somehow, in the life of God, unity and distinction coexist, each wholly and without compromise. This is unfathomable to us, it seems, in part because, for us, "individualization" and "participation"[44] stand always in conflicting relationship to one another. Think about it: where the value of distinction is emphasized, achieving unity seems to be an almost constant struggle. Individuals, with their individual priorities, gifts, opinions, lives, and schedules have to be *convinced* to enter into communion with others, and even when they actively try to be part of a *one*, there are constant struggles and conflicts that get in the way of relationships being harmonious. Couples break up; families bicker; nations cannot see their way clear to set aside partisan politics and join together to create a common good. Ecclesial and educational institutions seem unable to emphasize frequently or strongly enough how important it is for everyone to make a contribution, for the sake of the well-being of the whole. If you, the reader, are a church leader or any kind of educator gifted at planning events for groups of people, you no doubt spend significant amounts of time and energy trying to figure out new ways to sell autonomously driven people on the idea that they should budget blocks of time to go to Bible studies and potlucks, fund-raising events and PTA meetings. "Please come if you can," we beg and plead, "it's really important; we really need you; you can make a difference." In our radically, autonomous twenty-first-century American culture, no case needs to be made for threeness, if threeness represents the distinction between members of the whole. The case we are constantly trying to make, on the contrary, is why commitment should be made to the one.

Rarely, in our culture, do we have to convince anyone to disengage from the community and to spend more time developing their autonomous selves. It is almost comical to imagine a pastor, for example, saying to members of a US congregation that they should be careful about going to *too many* church events since—as those made in the image of the triune God—they are responsible for nurturing their distinction from others as well as their unity with them. Nonetheless, there are the rare cases when someone is burned out by volunteering too much, giving too much of herself to the community. "You need to take more time for yourself," we tell that person. Which might perhaps be translated, in Trinity-speak, as "you have emphasized oneness at the expense of threeness and need, now, to reclaim and nurture your distinctiveness. You are being far more Cappadocian than Augustinian, and now it is time to take a step back toward the West!"

Well, you wouldn't say *that*, exactly. But perhaps you have some sense of what I mean.

The fact is, the way we think about God impacts profoundly the way we think about ourselves. This is how it should be, it seems to me, since we are made in the image of a God who did not morph from one to three somewhere between Malachi and Matthew.[45] We are made in the image of the triune God, and that means individualization and participation are not in conflict. Just as we see, when we look at the person of Jesus Christ, that sin is an aberration when it comes to our true humanity, so we witness something beautiful about ourselves when we stop to contemplate the harmonious relationship between the *one* and the *three* in the being of God. Made in God's image, the constant conflicts we have between living as individuals and living in community are the aberration. From the standpoint of faith, this is a pretty bold thing to say: that we are holding on to the hope that distinct individuals really do add to the strength of the one community, and that the one community allows for real distinction among and between individuals. Can you imagine if we believed this into being, in our everyday lives in this world? It would mean, among other things, that the fear of the distinct "other" could fall away, replaced by joyful anticipation of the way unity could be enhanced by communion together. It would mean that being united would not mean some getting lost for the sake of others to thrive—rather, each would be honored, in the context of the one. The unity of the Trinity reminds us, because it always stands in dialectical tension with the threeness, that neither our union with Christ in the life of God nor our union with one another, as members of Christ's body, is anything like being drawn into a continuum in which particular identities are lost for the sake of the whole. The oneness realized and opened up to us by the Trinity is different in kind than the kind of unity advocated by nation states, religious sects, and household structures that promise honor to those who sacrifice their particular identities; it is different in kind, to use another example, from the community of the Borg (on *Star Trek*) that forces loss of particular identities. "You will be assimilated," says the Borg. "Resistance is futile."[46] By contrast to this, life in the God who is triune promises we will *not* be assimilated, but will be valued as the unique individuals we are. Our lives, "hidden with Christ in God,"[47] are still distinguished from one another.

What is so scandalous about the doctrine of the Trinity, then, is that it completely undoes our conception of what kind of place the world really is. What the world *actually is,* to be sure, is broken by sin, characterized more often than not by conflicts between individual needs and desires and communal concerns. But the doctrine of the Trinity will not allow anyone who truly subscribes to it ever to be complacent or accepting of such tensions and conflicts on the grounds that "this is just the way the world is." On the contrary, to join the rhythm of the scandal is to keep moving back and forth between the *one* and the *three*, refusing to give up on the possibility that each can fund the other that is built into the fabric of creation itself. We are made, after all, in the image of the God in which individualization and participation are perfectly in sync.

Along these lines, I even think the doctrine of the Trinity has something to say about the way we think about heaven. Commonly, I hear people of faith speculating about whether or not they will be able to recognize others in the world to come. Some say yes to this with confidence, but others seem worried about overstating what heaven will be like. "I don't think we will be able to recognize each other in heaven," a woman at a church I was teaching in recently confided in me. "I think all of that will kind of dissolve, so that we will really and finally be 'one' in Christ." This woman did not seem entirely happy with that prospect, but her thesis came from really taking the promise of perfect unity seriously.

Interesting, but understandable, that the woman could imagine individuals and community only being in odds with one another, even in eternity. The doctrine of the Trinity, as we have been saying, gives another option. Somehow—we claim and we hope, when we confess the three in one—we individuals will no longer conflict with the unity that is the communion of saints. Yes, we will recognize one another. But our distinctions will only strengthen our connections, and our unity will only celebrate our distinctions. Now, that idea is truly scandalous!

Joining the Dance: The Trinity and Christian Community

Another way of getting at the "so what" of the doctrine of the Trinity is by way of a concept developed in the course of Christian believers trying to work out how, exactly, God can be three and one at the same time. The concept is *perichoresis*, a Greek term that is hard to decipher. While it is agreed upon that *peri* means "around," scholars disagree about which root grounds *choresis*. Is it *chorein*, which means something along the lines of "make room for"? Or is it *choros*, which means "dance"? Wrestling with these possibilities, *perichoresis* has been translated, variously, as "interpenetration," "mutual indwelling," and "dancing around." Given its unusual structure and infrequent appearance in the literature, at least one scholar has hypothesized that the word was developed as a technical term that we can better understand by attending to its usage than by analyzing its etymology.[48] What we do know is that *perichoresis* was used, during and after the debates at Chalcedon, to describe the relationship of Jesus Christ's two natures. As we discussed in the last chapter, since the concern was to speak of the natures as at once both inextricably intertwined and at the same time distinct from one another, it might be safe to say that the intention of those developing the word was to aim for both unity and distinction, oneness and distinction, participation *with* individualization.[49]

Mutual indwelling, understood with this dialectic between individualization and participation in mind, would be about sharing life, together, as distinct individuals. Sometimes, when I think of mutual indwelling, I picture translucent circles, each a primary color, overlapping one another. The red circle is always red, but when it is placed over the yellow color (which always stays yellow) it, in a sense, "indwells" the yellow insofar as the two, together, are orange. Another way of putting it, playing off another common way of understanding *perichoresis*, is to say the red makes room for yellow and the yellow makes room for the red. Similarly, of course, mutual indwelling is imagined as the red and blue share life together as purple, while still remaining red and blue (for example). And when and where all three together overlap[50] there is seen either white or black (depending on when the three colors are mixed by way of "additive" or "subtractive" color).

A very different example that comes to mind, when I think of mutual indwelling, is something my father used to say. He used to tell my two brothers and me, especially around the time when we were teenagers, that he always had the activities and schedules of the other members of our family playing in his head as he went through his own day. "I'm always thinking," he would say, "here's what your mother is dealing with right now; and this is the time of Cindy's math test, and I hope Scott is feeling better, and I hope Mark is having a good day." My dad often spoke, along these lines, of "little TV sets he had," each with one of us featured, in the background of everything else he was doing. "I never turn them off," he used to tell us. "You and what you are doing are always with me. I am always tuned into your channel. I am thinking about you very consciously and praying for your life."

There is a downside of any analogy to a mystery, and the downside of the TV set analogy I have drawn from what my dad used to say, as strong as it is in other ways, is that it does not capture the dynamic movement between the persons of the Trinity. This might be a weakness of the mutual indwelling model in general, by the way: it seems a bit static. The fact is, the Father, Son, and Spirit do not simply remember one another, or have one another in mind, or even overlap one another's lives (as the colors might). They actually work and act together.

Barth makes something of this when he argues that the triune persons who indwell one another perichoretically also actively *fellowship* with one another and participate in *partnership* with one another.[51] Because they are each distinct, they do more than make space for one another, the way members of a commune share common space. Rather, they share who they are and what they have to offer as distinct members of the community in ways that are reciprocally beneficial. I think, when I imagine the fellowship of the triune life, of a family in which members know one another's stories so well that the story of each one becomes the story of every one. The Son, I imagine, brings to the table (so to speak), his experiences of life on this earth, of the faithful disciples he meets along the way, of his suffering in the Garden and on the cross. The Father brings to the fellowship the experience of his grief, on the occasion of his beloved Son becoming sin so that we might become the righteousness of God. And the Spirit brings her story of enlivening Jesus throughout his life, first by "coming upon" Mary who then conceived, then also by driving Jesus into the wilderness and guiding his prophesying that he had "come to set the captives free,"[52] and then finally by coming to comfort those who are grieving, and to empower the church to continue in ministry. Like a family telling stories around a shared meal, I imagine each of the three persons of the Trinity telling distinctive stories about the crucifixion (for example) in ways that are really the telling of a shared story.

One more imagining of how God's intra-trinitarian fellowship might look could center on the story of the creation. The Father might speak, at the table, from the vantage point of Creator, remembering the joy of creating all things good, rehearsing the created harmonies between God and humanity, between nature and humanity, between Adam and Eve. The Son might remind the household of God of the central role of the spoken word to the creation itself. With words the Creator said, "Let there be light!" and there was light. And the Spirit might tag onto the story of the Son, reminding him that the Word was present, in the beginning, as Wisdom—present before anything that was made was made, working alongside the Creator, "rejoicing and delighting in the human race."[53]

This idea that Father, Son, and Spirit share in fellowship, and that this fellowship honors both the distinctiveness of the three and the unity of the persons, extends, then, into the activities of ongoing partnership. It is not only, in other words, that we should imagine the three sitting around a table reminiscing about the past. Rather, God is engaged, together in God's own trinitarian self, in God's work in the world—bringing God's Kingdom to earth, as it is in heaven. Perhaps, around whatever table there is, there is some current planning going on. How will we arrive at all tears being wiped away? And wolves and lambs lying down together? And no one being left behind?[54]

It is in relation to the life of the triune God being a partnership that the metaphor of the dance seems particularly apropos. I used to have a t-shirt, when I was a kid, that said: "God is not finished with me yet." That is certainly right—and also incredibly hopeful, when you think about it, in the face of naysayers who insist "people never change" or "that's just the way the world is," as if we shouldn't even bother imagining how things could be better. The Christian claim is that, even in the face of our less-than-perfect world and less-than-perfect history, the dance of the triune God continues. In partnership with one another, Father, Son, and Holy Spirit continue the creative work they celebrate in their fellowship—their work of ongoing creation, yet-to-be completed redemption, and faithful, 24/7 intercession. The God who made us did not leave us to then manage on our own, but gives us our breath and our life, new again every moment. The dance goes on; creation continues. The God who redeemed us continues working to "conform us to the image of the Son"[55]—a spiritual process often known as *sanctification.* The dance goes on; creation groans; we are one step closer to the mending of the world. The God who comforts us is not a kind of security blanket that operates, as expected, whenever we have need. Rather, God as Comforter, dancing around in shared life and partnership with God the Creator and God the Redeemer, goads us out of comfort zones that perpetuate the discomfort of our brokenness, and into new life. The dance goes on; creation is remade; there is new heaven, new earth, new us. We are still three and distinct, particular and precious; we are also one and united, mutually indwelling and whole. We are, in the dynamic, buzzing, moving actions of the dancing, triune God, completely and totally claimed and included. Like it or not, we are swept up. Like it or not, we are caught in an unconditional love that will eventually of course be about forgiving our sins and omissions but is now, and first, and even more primally, about laying claim to us as participants, as members of the household, as beloved ones, as children, as sons and daughters who are brothers and sisters of the child who is Christ. We are the adopted children who are chosen and brought home, who are made fellow heirs, who are given a key—and all before any frank conversation about sin or repentance, about gratitude or responsibility. We are brought into the dance not by a God who has acted benevolently and who is now giving us the opportunity to respond in kind, though in lesser degree. On the contrary, we are brought into the dance by the God who *is* love, the triune God who, in claiming, capturing, and dancing with us, is being exactly who God is.

As Father, Son, and Spirit indwell one another's lives and actions, sharing in fellowship and joining in ongoing partnership, so we who are claimed by the triune God of love are free to indwell the lives of others, entering into fellowship and partnership relationships with them.

We will return to considering the shape of our life together with others, as it reflects the image of the triune God, when we consider the doctrines of the church and Christian life (part four) and when we consider what we are called to hope for and to do, in this world (part five). But before we move on to thinking about how the lives and work of people of faith might look, as they dance together in the household of God, it is important to flesh out, a bit more, the narrative that is the story of our faith, and that helps us make sense of who we are not only in relation to God, but in relation to the historical conditions in which we find ourselves—the circumstances in which we live. The fact is that something has gone awry with the beautiful image of us dancing with the God who is love. How do we understand this, theologically, and what do we do about it as we consider how to form our daily lives, fellowships, and partnerships? We began this book, in the first part, by thinking through how we can possibly say words about the God who is infinite, and where we can go to find the right kinds of ideas and words to work with. In this part we have said a good many words about God, asserting that God meets us in and through the incarnation and claims us as the God who is three-in-one and one-in-three. In the next section, we will consider how the God who meets us continues to make us, even in the face of the very real problem of sin.

Part Three

God Makes Us

Chapter Five

Who Did God Create Us to Be, and What Went Wrong?

The Doctrine of Creation

Life in this world is often described as a hodgepodge of good and bad. At the end of any given day, we might tell our spouse, partner, friend, or parent what went well and what did not, what raised our hopes and what threw a wrench in our expectations because it went so poorly. We might attribute the good things that happen to effective planning, great luck, or God's blessing. We might account for the bad things by appealing to evil forces, or believing we are being punished for something, or reasoning that there is a certain amount of difficulty built into the world, and we sometimes happen to be in the wrong place at the wrong time. Whatever our way of making sense of the events of our lives, the idea that there are "good" and "bad" things that happen is commonplace. We might use other words; we might insist we understand good and bad more in terms of perception than reality; we might argue for the inclusion of gray areas that are, themselves, not all good and not all bad. The point is that we nonetheless immediately resonate when people describe their life circumstances in terms such as these because they reference the disparity we know is true to our common existence.

Many stories of creation also reflect our dualistic ways of describing our lives. They help us account for where we find ourselves. We can appeal to them to explain why it is that we sometimes witness and experience ugliness, violence, and suffering, and at other times enjoy beauty, compassion, and wholeness. They enable us to explore and formulate answers to questions we have, such as: Why is there suffering in the world? Are there good powers and bad powers it makes sense to hold responsible, or is creation subject to some kind of force that can be life-giving or can be destructive, depending on how we engage it? Or is there good and bad built in to all of us, leaving us do what we can to distinguish between them and evaluate their dynamics? How we think about these things influences how we expect ourselves to live and act as individual agents and how we structure societies in ways that both nurture the life-giving capacities and guard against the destructive propensities of their members.

In this chapter, we consider the Christian doctrine of creation and what it tells us about how Christian people of faith understand God's relation to the created order and the character of creation itself. Interestingly, consideration of the Judeo-Christian creation story,[1] as it is found in Genesis 1–2, usually precipitates more questions than answers, when it comes to the matter of negotiating the ambiguities of this world. This is because, as we will see, it leads us to understanding sin and suffering as adulterations of creation, rather than as following naturally from it. And so we begin to consider also in this chapter the Christian doctrine of sin, recognizing how heinously it disconnects us from the glorious goodness of creation as we realize our salvation in Christ (ch. 6).

The understanding of what it means to confess God as Creator, as it is presented here, builds on the themes related to the doctrines of Trinity and incarnation discussed in part one. The God who creates us is the very same God who both enters into existence with us and who invites us to dance, together, in God's own, triune life. How might we understand creation in the context of what incarnation and Trinity teach about how God meets us?

Creation as Interplay of Meeting and Making

The Christian faith holds that the God who meets us and claims us has always actually known us. When we say "God meets us" we are speaking not of a first meeting, but of a meeting in which one already knows the other very well, and the one who is well known might actually know the one they are meeting better than they imagine they do! God knows us and claims us, the Bible says, "before the creation of the world."[2] The psalmist recognizes that God meets him in all places and at all times, even before and outside of time. This God who everywhere and even outside of time meets him also, in fact, made him. "You knit me together in my mother's womb," the psalmist says, marveling at this.[3] "My frame was not hidden from you when I was being made in secret, intricately woven in the depths of the earth," he exclaims.[4] It is almost as if the psalmist recognizes his creation by God as taking place in the context of the divine embrace—as if he understands God to have met him even before he is made.

This idea that we met our Creator even before we were created is, admittedly, confused when we try to conceptualize such a meeting literally and in chronological time. Clearly, it seems, creation would need to take place first, before there could be the possibility of meeting. How could one meet another that does not yet exist? And yet even in human relationships, such out-of-order relationships seem to take place regularly. Consider these examples: A parent prays for the safety and well-being of her child's future spouse, a person who has not yet been met. A kindergartener tells everyone, with confidence, that she has a little sister—even before her future sibling is actually conceived. A couple loves the child they will eventually adopt so much that the child actually becomes their own, even before that child is born, in another place, to a woman they do not yet know.

I have a close friend who hoped for a child for several years before actually having one. When she was packing up Christmas ornaments one year, during this period of time, I noticed she had printed hopeful questions and happy welcomes on several of the cardboard storage boxes, directed to her child who was not yet conceived. "Are you here yet?" she inquired. "Welcome to your first Christmas! We are so happy to have you with us." It struck me, at this time before either of us had our children, that my friend had already met the one whom she would birth a couple of years later. She not only hoped that a child would come, but already loved the one who had not yet come. There is no question in my mind that these words, scribbled with magic marker on the outside of a couple of cardboard boxes, represented a meeting that participated in the making of the coming child's life.

There are at least a couple of classic children's stories that seem to follow this theme. In *Pinocchio*, the carpenter Geppetto, unable to have his own biological child, crafts a wooden marionette of a little boy. He makes the *marionette* by cutting and assembling pieces of wood, but the *boy* is made by quite another route—by the way of the father, Geppetto, meeting him and loving him as a son. He is made, through this tenacious meeting of Geppetto, a real flesh-and-blood boy.[5] Similarly, the stuffed rabbit in *The Velveteen Rabbit* becomes real—he is *made* real—by the habitual meeting of the boy who played with him, imagined with him, hoped with him, loved him.[6]

In *Star Trek: The Next Generation*, the android Data is made—in the sense of being "put together"—out of highly advanced raw materials. But then he is met, and met again, by colleagues on the USS *Enterprise* who make him, though their encounters with him, into an actual subject—a real person.[7]

This creative dynamic between meeting and making is probably best understood, analogically, in terms of relationships between beings. As many have noted, there is an "I" and a "Thou" that become who they are only in the context of the encounter between them.[8] But it is also evident in other forms of interplay. Artists describe themselves being met by ideas that demand they be realized by way of making. I once spoke with a sculptor who described himself as so overtaken by an idea for a project he had no peace until he actually made it. And so he searched for and found the perfect stone, working on his sculpture until he brought to life the idea that had met him. Interestingly, I noticed, the stone itself was at once both incidental to his encounter with the idea and critically important to it. The meeting between the sculptor and the idea was complete apart from the stone out of which the sculpture was eventually created, but without the stone being discovered and sculpted the meeting would also have been incomplete, since the meeting between artist and idea itself pressed for a concrete encounter.[9] To offer another example: In the movie *The Martian*, the botanist stranded on Mars figures out how to grow potatoes in order to survive.[10] He makes soil, he makes water, he creates heat, he constructs a safe place for the potato plants to grow. He has, in a very real sense, met and claimed those potatoes even before they come to exist. You can see this inextricable connection between creating and meeting especially well in the scene where the botanist discovers the first seedling pushing up from the soil. He gets down on his knees, gently cradling the stem between his index and middle fingers, palm up and just below the forming leaves. "Hello there," he says, with joy and tenderness.[11]

Hello, there, I imagine God saying to the creation God has made. *You don't know it, but I've already met you and claimed you. You are mine, and I am going to keep on making you. I'm so very glad you're here.*

A father takes his newborn child into his arms for the first time and says, "Hello. I'm your daddy, and I'm going to take care of you." A teacher walks into a classroom to meet her class of brand-new students. "Hello," she says. "Welcome to Introduction to Theology. I have the honor of helping you become theologians." A director welcomes the audience to a new production, hoping against hope that they will like it, happy for even the most remote connection insofar as it undoes, and remakes, both the participants in the art and the art itself. Such meetings are miracles—they are made possible never solely by the "facts of life" that lead to the baby, the excellent pedagogical methodology employed in the framing of the syllabus, or the fluidity of the actors moving in and out of worlds, enlivening minimalist sets. In each of these cases, there is an entity created in the context of the encounter that did not exist before the literal meeting—the child born becomes a son or daughter, the roomful of students becomes a class, those gathered to see the production become an audience entering into the play of new creation.

The claim of those who hold faith, then, is more than that the God who makes us in the beginning then goes out of God's way to meet us. It is more, also, than that the God who meets us then goes on to make us, offering us opportunities to be changed along the way, as we journey hand-in-hand, together. Certainly both the image of God traveling from a distance in order to be with us and the image of God meeting us daily as we journey through our lives hone in on the character of the encounter between God and creation: There is an "I" and a "Thou" that meet one another, and this "I" and "Thou" must first (and by definition) be distinguished from one another, if there even is to be an encounter, a relationship, a mutual claim, a subsequent transformation. But there is also an important synchronicity to celebrate, between the meeting and the making. The Word becomes flesh, entering into existence with us—and in this meeting itself there is making: all flesh is changed. The triune God acts, as Father, Son, and Spirit, and in these multiple actions creaturely existence is touched and transformed. The Holy Spirit "falls afresh" on us, "melting us" and "molding us" into new creations that can be "filled" and "used," as the popular chorus says.[12] God's creation of us is never accomplished at a distance from us, but always as the one who is meeting us, the one who is with us, the one who knows us and claims us.

This making of us by the God who meets us is something that is, of course, ongoing and that we always have in mind, in one way or another, when we reflect on doctrines including salvation, sanctification, and vocation—doctrines we will consider in later chapters. We will be able more fully to celebrate and participate in God's everyday and ongoing making of us, however, when we understand it as a kind of continuation of what God has been up to from "the beginning." When we are able to relate how it is that God is making us into "new creations"[13] to how God created us, salvation may be understood not as God replacing who we always before have been, but making a place for who God created us to be from the beginning. As we will discuss further when we explore the doctrine of salvation, the old that passes away[14] when we are newly created is not the oldest selves we are, but the sinful selves that have impinged on our being who God created us to be.

As soon as we begin reflecting in this manner, however, the tough questions of why we find ourselves so mired in that which is "not good" come rushing in. Reflecting on our own less-than-good behaviors or reading the daily headlines in the newspaper, we might doubt that creation is as inherently good as the Christian faith claims it is, asking: If we were, indeed, created good in God's image, what happened that has left us, now, in need of re-creation? How could we who were created good and in the image of God possibly be so adept at *de-creation*?[15] That is to say: How are we so good at undoing what God did so well? What, exactly, went wrong?

These are, of course, crucial questions that must be taken into consideration. The trick is to remember, while doing so, not to set our created goodness to the side for the sake of making sense of our situation now. This might be tempting. If we claim we are not all good, but in some sense good *and* bad, it is far easier to explain why we do things that are *not* good. "There's good and bad in all of us," we say, sounding commonsensical enough. Disturbingly, however, what happens when we explain things in this way is that we inadvertently make a bit of acceptable room for the suffering of the world as part and parcel of what life is all about; we create an opening for letting ourselves and others off the hook for the ways we are complicit in causing harm and perpetuating injustice. "That's just the way people are," we might declare.

There is a lot of truth in this statement, descriptively speaking. A problem emerges, however, when we misunderstand these words as being *prescriptive* in addition to being *descriptive*. In other words, it is one thing to say that the creatures of the world, and the creation itself, has its problems. Similarly, it is one thing to say that human beings do, actually, sin. But it is quite another thing to suggest there is no way around the problems and the sin—that this is just the way we were created and almost, in a sense, who and what we were created to be. To say not only that there is sin (descriptively speaking) but that sin is necessary (that God prescribed things to be the way they are) is to compromise on our created goodness as well as the goodness of God. We are not all good, but good enough to be better than we've been, we might say to ourselves, by way of consolation and challenge.

By contrast to this, when we lay claim to the goodness of creation, as God made it whole and complete, we no longer have a ready answer to why there is sin and suffering. Unable to explain these things away, we begin to realize sin and suffering are even bigger problems than we had thought. They are, indeed, actualities that characterize our existence in this world. Their existence is, of course, problematic in the face of our desire to live full and abundant lives. But the very fact that they are not prescribed, willed, or desired by God makes them far worse, even, than they would have been if they could be interpreted as the necessary downside of a generally acceptable world. Calvin goes so far, in fact, as to describe sin as an "aberration."[16] It is an aberration *because* it is the antithesis of what and who God created us to be; it is contrary to the reality of our created goodness. To describe ourselves as sinful and the world as broken is to grieve all the more because it is, in fact, unnecessary to be so. Not God's intention. Not God's will. Not God's plan. Not who we are. Not good.

Reclaiming the goodness of our creation will mitigate neither our sin nor the brokenness of the world. It will, in fact, serve to underscore how awful these things are, compelling us to take a prophetic stand against them. In the context of recognizing and naming the troubled character of our historical existence, we may join hands with others who hold faith, resisting all that runs counter to God's creative and redemptive intentions. We may work as Christ's partners, by the power of the Holy Spirit, to reconcile and restore.

Look at the Heavens!

There is no better way to reclaim the goodness that is God's gift than to open our eyes wide and stand in "wonderment" in the face of God's wondrous works.[17] Each of us should ask ourselves: When is the last time I contemplated the beauty and intricacy of the created world? I imagine that there will be a great range of ways readers answer this question. Some might say, "Why, it was just this morning, on my morning run!" For others, the answer might be harder coming. I myself am one of those people who might manage to take a walk and still miss out on genuinely contemplating creation, so caught up I can get in synching family schedules, grappling with the implications of something I just read about in the newspaper, or finishing a book chapter on creation and sin. Some of us need to be quite intentional not only about getting out into nature, but about making space and time to reflect on what it teaches us about who we are and who God is.

Whether it comes readily to the psalmist or not, she takes time to contemplate the glory of the world around her. "What are human beings that you think about them?"[18] she asks. This question spills over from her awe as she revels, before God, in her surroundings: "the heavens . . . the moon and the stars that you have established . . . the birds of the air . . . the fish of the sea,"[19] she rehearses. I like to imagine myself standing next to the psalmist and peering up into the night sky with her. My bet is that standing outside and gazing at the stars was her habit, and that at an earlier point she asked a question that was even more basic than this one. I imagine the question being something like: Where did all this come from; or Why is there anything at all? Or, as philosophers have commonly put it: Why is there something rather than nothing?[20]

This is the question I write on the whiteboard at the start of class, just as my introductory theology students are gathering to hear about creation. Some students wait with anticipation when I read it out, hands poised over their laptop keyboards or pen touching point to paper with readiness, prepared to write down whatever I will say next that they expect will approach an answer. Others look at me with eyes full of fatigue, wondering what possible use it is to bother with such a question, given that we're here and have to find ways of moving through our days whether we contemplate our existence or not. Usually, I ask the students to put down their pens or override their weariness to consider the matter, just for a bit, even if it seems superfluous. To create space for such contemplation is to open ourselves to the possibility of transformation, to being the kind of people

God can find,[21] meet, and make, I tell them. It is to be in good company with forebears in the faith such as Augustine, whose exploration of the question and its answers (as he describes his journey in his *Confessions*) leads him to convert to Christianity.

Why is there something rather than nothing? The answer, from the vantage point of faith, is short and sweet: because God made it. But its implications are profound, framing the way we think about just about everything, including how we interpret scientific discoveries about the natural world, how we understand God's motives and purpose for creating us, how we negotiate an existence that seems to be characterized by struggles between dueling powers, and how we think about our own nature as *good*.

Divine Sovereignty and Evolution

Some people of faith find the assertion that there is something rather than nothing "because God made it" to be quite satisfying, insofar it seems to give us a way out of trying to navigate between theories of evolution and biblical stories of creation by affirming the sovereignty of God in the face of all else. For others, this answer might seem to be evading some of the pressing, modern questions that are before us today. After all, they may note (remembering Paul's charge to "make your defense to anyone who demands from you an accounting for the hope that is in you"[22]), that there are debates going on all over the United States[23] about whether and how the stories in Genesis 1 and 2 should be included in public school curricula, and what their relationship is to evolutionary theory. Surely, they might insist, we can do better—as people of faith—than simply saying that creation exists "because God made it."

I agree that the conviction that God made all things should never be used as an excuse for blocking ourselves off from knowledge or reflection. The truth is that this confession about how things began is not in all ways incompatible with scientific claims about origins, and can often work in tandem with them. For example, the fact that creation is here "because

God made it" does not preclude the possibility that God made it by way of a Big Bang, as described by evolutionary theory. The study of evolution might actually deepen our appreciation of how intricate and beautiful God's handiwork is. The doctrine of creation, in turn, might well supplement logical gaps in evolutionary theory. For example, the Big Bang theory might explain *how* there is something rather than nothing. But it doesn't explain the why. My impression is that scientists are quite aware of this and that most do not see any need to go further back, in their explanations, then to the Big Bang itself. They have plenty to study and engage, certainly, from that point forward! Still, there are some who do want to pursue the question of *why* there is something rather than nothing, and these might find the Judeo-Christian answer to the question interesting.

Some scientists, along these lines, have hypothesized that there is something "unstable" about nothingness, itself.[24] People of faith might find this thesis interesting to engage, insofar as it seems, in ways, commensurate with the idea that God is intrinsically driven to commune with others because God is, in God's own triune life, already a community. Clearly, describing God as unstable would be problematic because it would seem to compromise God's sovereign character and steadfast love. But to think of God acting freely, in creating—and to understand this free exercise of creating as an act that manifests God's being, as Father, Son, and Holy Spirit in relation, is to present God not as unstable, but as utterly consistent. It is not God, but nothingness, that is unstable. It is destabilized by the God who is eternally about relationships and ever about "something" that requires meeting, dancing, indwelling, affecting. So, again, there might be some interesting ways willing theologians and scientists could talk with each other about these issues that matter so keenly to them both.[25]

Those people of faith who would rather not engage in conversation with the hard sciences about matters related to creation still have plenty to think about, after asserting that there is "something, rather than nothing... because God made it." Why did God bother creating, Christians often ask, if God is self-sufficient and has no needs? Why did God create a world so prone to sin and brokenness?

The Divine Sovereignty and the Divine Motive

In relation to the very common question about why a sovereign God would bother creating, trinitarian insight is again quite helpful. Instead of moving from whatever ideas we have about what the divine self-sufficiency means to trying to understand how creation fits this understanding, we would do better to begin by thoughtfully attending to God's acts (Consider "the work of God's fingers!"[26] Meditate on God's wondrous works![27]) and then thinking about what God's acts have to tell us about God's character. After all, people of faith believe, what God does is always consistent with who God is, because God is perfectly free. The very practical gift to us, in this, is that we can look at what God has done, concretely, and learn things that are true about who God is (even though they never exhaust who God is). When we consider the character of God by way of meditating on God's wondrous, creative works, we would do well to note that, whatever it means to say that God is self-sufficient, the definition must take into account God's meeting us in the making of "each little flower that blossoms; each little bird that sings."[28] The doctrine of the Trinity is, again, helpful here because it shows that being in relation is not something extrinsic to the divine life, but who God actually is. Explaining why God would bother creating is only an issue when the creating is seen as something inconsistent with God, something God goes out of God's way to do. When God is known as three-in-one and one-in-three, God's creating is not assumed to be a bother, but understood to be a free expression of God's own (relational, dynamic, eternally-meeting-us) self.

God's motive for making us, then, was not to have something to do with all God's free time, or to show off God's power, or to have sentient beings with whom to be in fellowship. God made us, in a sense, because God had already met us in God's own, eternal life. God made us to make us, the way an artist creates art for its own sake—not in order to impress, or even to express who the artist is. The art that is created *does* impress, and it does express, but the artist's motive for making the art is inseparable from the making itself. When the creative work of the artist is so much in continuity with who the artist is that the "why are you making that?" question seems redundant or even absurd, there we witness freedom. And the artist that is free in this sense mimics the artistry of the Creator God who always creates in continuity with God's very self.[29]

Sovereign Creator, Broken World

The question of why the sovereign God created the world with the capacity for brokenness and sin haunts any discussion of the doctrine of creation. This is, most people of faith will agree, a question that has never been satisfactorily answered and likely never will be. Calvin, frustrated with people who ask this question not only because he can't answer it but also because he thinks it distracts from reflection on more important spiritual matters, is known for reminding questioners that "God created hell for those who engage in idle speculation."[30] Contemporary theologian Moltmann, counseling people who demand answers to the unanswerable, frequently explains that we cannot know the answer to the "why" question. But we can know the answer to "where."[31] As reasonable as Moltmann's redirection of the question is, it does not remove our compulsion to ask why. This is for good theological reasons: if we have accepted that God is both good and sovereign, it seems logical to us that such a God had to have been capable of creating a better world than the one we know.

This problem of sin and brokenness comes up any time we stand in wonder before God's beautiful creation. How can we help but be completely brokenhearted when we witness creation as it really is? This whole world, teeming with life, brimming with food, humming with harmonies, bent eagerly toward possibilities—this is the character of the real world, as God made it in creation and as it exists, whole and complete, in the eternal reality of the kin-dom. Glimpsing again this reality, in the course of our contemplation, we become even more chagrined at the actuality, insofar as it is characterized by dehumanizing forces, a paucity of resources, constant conflict, and stymying hopelessness. God's ongoing creative work, people of faith believe, is to get the actuality of our historical existence more in tune with the reality of God's creative and redemptive will.

Reclaiming Our Created "Good"-ness

In the beginning, the Christian faith teaches, God created us good. The word *good* is used liberally in the creation story in Genesis 1–2, along with "not good," but then "very good," used in relation to human beings.

The idea that creation is good is, actually, a fairly radical one, from the vantage point of twenty-first-century American culture. Not that we think of human beings as bad, exactly. But, as we discussed in the preceding chapter, we tend to think of ourselves and one another as "not all good, not all bad." The sense seems to be that this *dual nature* we recognize in ourselves is, somehow, our default setting—the way we were put together. Often it seems to be accounted for, vaguely or explicitly, by reference to the evolutionary process. We all have the instinct to survive, as members of the animal kingdom. That instinct is understandable, to a point, serving to justify certain more selfish behaviors, even when they are engaged at a cost to others. But it becomes a problem when significant harm is done.[32] The goal of noting that people are both bad and good seems to be to foster awareness of the dynamic, so we can work to fan the good into flame.

The idea that there is some good and some bad in all of us makes a great deal of sense, when seen as a way to understand how the world works. After all, we read the newspaper and see violence and lies, deceptions and abuse. But we also see people demonstrating kindness. The same thing is true when we go through our days—there are those who do damage for seemingly no reason, and those who go out of their way to be helpful even when it is not clear they receive any immediate benefit for doing so. The not-good things that surround us, it would seem, would be well explained by positing that there are ambiguities in the fabric of creation itself.

This is the tack taken by some creation narratives. Often, these stories feature multiple gods, goddesses, and other powerful beings who might have varied motives for acting the ways they do. These motives are often associated, as they generally are for we human beings in this world, with having a certain sense of entitlement and/or desire for power over another. In the story of the *Enuma Elish,* a Babylonian creation myth written during the same time period as the book of Genesis, the world is formed in a context characterized by violence associated with struggles for dominance. Eventually the world and the sky are formed out of the body of Tiamat, a goddess associated with salt water who has birthed many gods, but who—in the course of trying to avenge the death of her first husband, Apsu—has come to represent chaos and danger, even taking on the form of a sea monster. The ruling god, Marduk, goes on to murder Tiamat's second husband, Kingu, forming human beings out of Kingu's blood.[33] Human beings, like the world they inhabit, are, in this story, made from materials that might not be all "bad," in and of themselves, but that certainly are not "all good" either. Given the range of human behaviors evident in the course of history as well as in any day's newspaper, the narrative of the *Enuma Elish* has significant explanatory power.[34]

This is not true of the creation stories in Genesis, where all the emphasis on goodness might lead us to look elsewhere for stories more connected to the brokenness of our actual lives. The heavens and the earth are not made out of broken bodies, but by way of the command of the Creator God, who speaks a word and makes it so. Traditionally, the Christian tradition has emphasized that there was no chance of anything being compromised in the raw materials used by God in the making, since God created anything and everything *ex nihilo* (out of nothing) to begin with. Augustine, again in his *Confessions,* puts great emphasis on the idea that, since God is good, and God created everything–and God created everything *ex nihilo*–everything God created has to be good, in its substance.[35] The question again comes rushing in: Where did all the brokenness come from, if God made everything good? But another question, and one that will be helpful to address before considering the matter of our brokenness head on, is: Why did Augustine, and so many people of faith who followed him in the course of Christian history, see confession of the creation *ex nihilo* not only as an important idea, philosophically speaking, but also as beneficial to our lives of faith?

The short answer to this question is that people of faith have consistently seen the church's teachings about creation *ex nihilo* as inextricably intertwined with the affirmation of creation as good, and therefore with the recognition that we, as creatures, are ourselves "good," despite our obvious shortcomings and sin. Here, roughly, is the logic many of our forebears employed that connected the idea of creation *ex nihilo* with the affirmation of the created goodness:[36]

(1) First, they began with the Judeo-Christian confession that there is only one God.

(2) Second, they affirmed that there is no ambiguity or capriciousness in this one God—God is, they held, entirely good.

(3) Third, they posited that, because there is only one God, everything that exists must have come from this one God who made it.[37]

(4) Fourth, they concluded that, because all things originated with the one good God who made all things, therefore all things are completely and wholly *good.*

(5) Fifth, then, the confession of the creation *ex nihilo* simply and in one clean theological sweep affirms the goodness of creation by reminding people of faith that the one, good God made all that is, with no additives or ambiguities included.

Some people of faith reject the association between the creation *ex nihilo* and the goodness of creation, arguing that emphasis on God creating "out of nothing" in fact disparages creation by imagining that God creates it from afar, in a solitary, nonrelational mode that avoids having to deal with any of the messy stuff of creation itself. There are worthy arguments being made for how it might benefit us to imagine that chaos pre-existed creation. Catherine Keller suggests, for example, that to think of God fashioning creation out of pre-existent chaos is consistent with understanding God is with us in relation to the messy, chaotic things of this world. Even more importantly, to think of creation as something that is in process is to be positioned to consider what we can and must do to contribute to its improvement.[38] Keller, Thomas Oord, and others point out, further, that to associate chaos and ambiguity with things that are negative or not good is problematic.[39] Such connections are founded in a less relational understanding of God that understands perfection in terms of God being unaffected by the created world.[40] Why would we want to imagine God creating by verbal command, from somewhere at a distance from the substance of the creation itself? Better to have God getting God's hands dirty, so to speak—working with the chaos that is the stuff of our world. Such an image of God, Keller, Oord, and others have suggested, takes better into account traits that have traditionally been identified as maternal than does a God who creates *ex nihilo*. Like a mother who births and nurses; like a father who changes a diaper while heating chicken nuggets in the microwave while simultaneously telling a made-up story to an older child who is hungry for lunch and attention, so God forms and creates in and out of the beautiful chaos that is the stuff of creaturely existence.[41]

Addressing the concern that the rejection of the creation *ex nihilo* leaves open the threat of dualism, those following in the trajectory of Keller and Oord are clearly not proposing creation by multiple gods. Rather, they are challenging us to think in a different way about creation, a way that does not try to account for the origin of the chaos that existed "in the beginning," but rather accepts it as an indication that creation is a process that encompasses ambiguities indicative of life in this world. This more process-oriented approach[42] to the doctrine of creation does not concern itself with the beginnings and ends of creation as much as with the ongoing, collaborative work of creation itself. The question "who made the chaos?" that existed in the beginning is, in this flow of understanding, not an important one, except insofar as it draws us to participation in mystery.

Certainly, these critics are right that we mustn't imagine God the Creator phoning it in—creating the world from materials so sterile they are unrecognizable in the context of our actual lives. The God who meets us in the making of us must be the incarnational, trinitarian God who enters into the messy beauty of creaturely existence ("the Word became flesh"[43]) and is invested in the dynamic vulnerability of life that is shared (trinitarian *perichoresis*). What we should not overlook is that those people of faith who have upheld and even shaped our understandings of incarnation and Trinity simultaneously insisted that God created *ex nihilo*. This doesn't mean, of course, that they were automatically right in their assessment of how God must have created. But it does mean that we might learn something important by trying to understand how they reconciled their conviction that God is near with their understanding of the character of God's creative work. Despite the fact that the idea God created *ex nihilo* is not self-evident in Genesis, these forebears in the Christian faith insisted the creation *ex nihilo* works in lockstep with the confession that God meets us and claims us. What led them to hold these convictions so closely, and what practical implications did they understand the idea of the creation *ex nihilo* to have for helping us live lives of faith that are, obviously, influenced by chaos?

A brief, beginning answer to this question might be: That our forebears thought the idea of the creation *ex nihilo* upheld the integrity of both God and creation. It reminded them, as has been mentioned, that God is not simply the most powerful of gods, but that the God Christians trust is without rivals; there are no demigods or devils that pose any threat to God's reign or God's promises. There is only one God, not many or many parts. It reminded them, also, that the creation made by this God is similarly whole and intact: free itself to act creatively without being bogged down by any elements derived from traumatic, violent, or otherwise damaging influences.

As a corollary to rejecting the creation *ex nihilo*, Kelly, Oord and others insist that we emphasize God's relational character when we articulate a doctrine of creation. But are there any ways in which adhering to the creation *ex nihilo* can actually support and advance important values emphasized by process-oriented thinkers? Let me mention three possibilities. The first corrects the impression that there is a necessary connection between subscribing to the creation *ex nihilo* and portraying God as standing at a distance from creation. The second argues that, insofar as the creation *ex nihilo* upholds monotheism, it makes possible a critique of any and all would-be gods that would pull us away from doing the work of justice in the world. The third argues that creation *ex nihilo* actually promotes a relational understanding of God by positing a more immediate relationship between God and creation, and then between fellow human beings, than it is possible to have when there is *stuff* that stands between God and our very existence.

First, the idea that God created *ex nihilo* has certainly been used to portray God as being at a distance from the created order, painting a picture of God that overemphasizes the *divine transcendence* (God's distinction from creation) at the expense of the *divine immanence* (God's presence in creation). That is, it has been associated with a portrait of a God who is separated off from creation instead of standing with it and even in it, or at very least with a portrait of God who is first and foremost at a distance and only secondarily enters into communion with it. But creation *ex nihilo* need not be interpreted as *separating* God from creation. When understood more as *distinguishing* God from creation than as *distancing* God from creation, the creation *ex nihilo* actually makes it possible to envision God's radical fellowship with creation. This is because distinction is necessary for relationships every bit as much as nearness is. Think about it: When two are utterly separate and at a distance from one another, there is no relationship, or at least no intimate one. But where two have lost a sense of where one begins and the other ends, relationship has also been forfeited. To be radically present to another is a wonderful thing, unless and until one's distinction from the other is lost. Then the relationship becomes more of an unhealthy problem that needs resolving than something to be celebrated.

From the vantage point of our daily lives, then, this idea that the God who creates *ex nihilo* and who admittedly stands in clear distinction from the created order can and does enter wholly into creation itself helps us think more deeply about the character of all intimate relationships. Any good relationship will of course reflect a blurring of certain lines, emotions, and experiences as those who are partners empathize with each other and share the stuff of life together. But for a relationship to be healthy, it also needs distinction and boundaries. The fact is that we, as human beings, cannot truly be met except by a "Thou," by one who is distinct from us however, much is shared. This is, in fact, the backdrop of Adam and Eve's meeting: Adam looks upon the one so different from himself and is amazed at how much they share; it is their distinction, it seems, that allows him to celebrate what they have in common. "You are bone of my bone and flesh of my flesh," he tells her.[44] Like the Son in relationship to the Father, they share the very same stuff even as neither one is the other. To uphold the creation *ex nihilo*, then, is to confess that we really have been met by the Other, in our creation. "You knit me together while I was still in my mother's womb," says the psalmist,[45] recognizing the Creator as simultaneously right there with him and clearly transcendent to him, knowing his days. There is something about the utter distinction of God that, in fact, makes God's nearness to the psalmist all the more possible. The God who creates *ex nihilo* is the ultimate "Thou" who—unencumbered by any external metaphysical necessity or need—is ready to meet us in perfect freedom, carrying nothing along with Godself that can get in the way of being with us and for us. Clearly, the psalmist experiences the Creator's distinction from him as part and parcel of their extraordinarily intimate relationship. The divine transcendence is anything but the opposite of the divine immanence. It does, in fact, give way to it.

Second, to affirm the creation *ex nihilo* is to have a reference point for condemning injustice. The idea that there is only one Lord of All, and that this Lord is absolutely not threatened by any would-be lords or rivals, has been drawn upon through the ages not only by those who are trying to justify imperialism, but also by people of faith seeking theological justification for taking a stand against it. Scripture tells the story of how Shadrach, Meshach, and Abednego refused to bow down to powermonger King Nebuchadnezzar, for example, because they believed there was only one God—and the king was not that God![46] Martin Luther, claiming victory in Christ, is rumored to have thrown inkwells across the room at Satan in order to remember that God has no real rivals. Barth invokes the sovereignty of God to argue that we are "always wrong" if we think our only choice is to be stressed out all the time.[47] And Jacquelyn Grant notes that "to claim Jesus as Lord is to say the white slaveholder isn't."[48] In none of these four examples is creation *ex nihilo* mentioned explicitly. But in each of these four a major corollary supported by the creation *ex nihilo*—that God has no rivals—is clearly in evidence. Only God is God—Nebuchadnezzar isn't, the devil isn't, our stress levels are not, white slaveholders are not. All of these, as well as all other would-be "gods," are prophetically denounced by appeal to the God who is Creator of all.

Third, and something that is not often noted: to affirm the creation *ex nihilo* is to highlight the direct and immediate character of creation's relationship to the divine. Creation out of something envisions God putting us together in a way that might be somewhat akin to Geppetto choosing the very best materials to craft Pinocchio. In such an endeavor, there might be no lack of love, attention, or self-sacrifice, but there would be something standing between the Creator and the created: that is, the constructive work of the creation itself.

We are most godlike, I think, when we glimpse what it is to create *ex nihilo.* We are not God, so of course we cannot create out of nothing. But there are times when, in our creating, we become so caught up in what it is we are doing we are lost to the details, including the materials we are using. This happens to me, most often, in the moments when I am lecturing and I get so caught up in the beauty and mystery of what I am talking about that I lose all sense of time, but more importantly, that I lose all sense of self-consciousness. This is very hard to explain, but let me give it a try: in these moments, what falls away is whatever ordinarily stands between the words coming out of my mouth and the reality in which these words participate. I (and the Holy Spirit, if I may be so bold) am generating or creating the words. I have studied the content of what I am saying, thought about how best to present the ideas, and have generally created an outline of the lecture that listeners hold in their hands. I have researched who my audience is, given attention to what I am wearing, and arranged for amplification so I can be heard. In other words, the creation of the lecture and the presentation of it is certainly out of *something.* But there are those moments when the something is forgotten, where there is a transparent, immediate relationship between me and the creation that is the lecture. In those moments, creation feels like perfect participation in something that is real. It feels like relationship itself.

This, I think (though I imagine it on a far greater scale!), is what is experienced by great artists. They paint, they sculpt, they compose with all kinds of methods and papers and paints and tools, but finally what they produce is not the sum of their raw materials, or even their materials *plus* something more, but actually something that is, almost, indifferent to the materials that give it expression. I imagine Leonardo da Vinci stepping back from the *Mona Lisa*, much as I have done, wondering at its goodness. I or others might comment on her enigmatic expression as a way of recognizing the mystery that is before us: *Is she smiling, or isn't she?* Da Vinci's question, I am guessing, would be even more basic. *Where did she come from?* he might ask, paintbrush still in hand, standing in wonder before that which he meticulously created, but which he recognizes—much to his surprise—has its own, discrete existence that transcends even his best efforts and highest hopes.

To claim that God created *ex nihilo* is to recognize God as an artist who is in immediate relationship to his or her art, relationship that is not mediated even by materials used. God is the artist who makes neither from materials that are outside God's own self or are part and parcel of God's own self, but from out of nothing. God is therefore able, as Creator, to be immediately present to what is made both because there are no raw materials standing between Creator and creature *and* because what is made is, as we mentioned earlier, truly distinguished from the God who made it.

What this means, simply put, is what we said at the beginning of this chapter: that God meets us as God makes us, and God makes us as God meets us, directly and wholly. What I have tried to add, in deepening this point, is the idea that God the Creator meets us and makes us as artists meet and make their creations, only (if you will) more so. To be a craftsperson or an engineer is a wonderful thing—it is to be someone who takes raw materials and puts them together into something beautiful that gives joy and/or that changes the way people live. To be an artist, on the other hand, is to be someone who makes use of raw materials in order to participate in something that is not bound to those materials. As artists frequently testify, they are first captured by an idea that they then work to convey or conceptualize by way of working with raw materials. Salvador Dali, for example, was taken by the idea that time marches on relentlessly, deciding to explore and represent this idea by way of melting clocks.[49] The assembly of materials serve, then, for Dali and for other artists, as invaluable portals into a greater reality they have already met. But artists know that any given work of art fails to capture the reality of what they have met, in all its fullness. That is why they keep on making works of art—Dali, for example, made sculptures and paintings of melting clocks throughout his life. Just as theologians shape and reshape the words of the theological tradition in order to better speak of God whom they have met but have never exhausted, so artists work within the limits of what they have ready at hand in an effort to get ever nearer to that which they have met.

To illustrate this: In *My Name Is Asher Lev*, by Chaim Potok, a young Hasidic boy who is an artistic prodigy wants to shade a picture of his mother, but is given no supplies to do so by the community that discourages his art. Driven to find something at hand that will move his picture closer to the truth, he uses cigarette ash he finds in a nearby ashtray. His mother is astounded when she sees he uses the ash to depict the sweat stains that were under her arms when she was rowing a boat. "Why did you do this, Asher?" she asks. "Because that is the way you look," he replies, innocently. Asher uses what he can find to create art that facilitates participation in what is real.[50]

Unlike any other artist, God's creations are not approximations of some greater reality, nor are they attempts to imagine or participate in something beyond their inevitably inadequate material components. God's creation is, in fact, *the* reality in which other artistic creations strive to participate. Creation *ex nihilo* reminds us of this. It insists that there is a direct, and not an indirect, relationship between all creatures and their Creator, God. It holds that the making of us does more than make possible our meeting of God; it reminds us that our making *is* the meeting. Nothing needs to be negotiated; creation is itself already in intimate communion. This is, I think, why creation is deemed "good" and "very good." These declarations are not meant to imply that creation is perfectly quaffed, neat, and well-ordered. Where "all things bright and beautiful"[51] are existing—the flowers, the animals, the humans; the "birds of the air and the fish of the sea"—there is bound to be a kind of chaos. And if there is—and where there is—it is not lordless. It is, with the rest of all creation, made and met by God and therefore part and parcel of the "good."

Evil as Not Good and Sin as Aberration

All of this might sound, at this point, like a bit of a fairy tale. After all, the fact of God's intimate relationship with nature is often far from apparent. Just a few moments ago my middle-school–age son looked over my shoulder, read a few of the preceding paragraphs, and said, "Mommy, you know what saying I don't like, that we say in church? 'God is good, all the time. All the time, God is good.' What in the world does that *mean,* Mommy, when so many bad things happen in the world?"

Exactly the question we all have. Once we say that everything that exists is good because it was created by a good God out of nothing, it might seem difficult (perhaps impossible) to explain why and how there is so much that is *not* good. It is so difficult, in fact, and the pressure to account for suffering so great, that we wind up adjusting to account for the seeming discrepancy between what we claim about God and God's creation and the problematic things that are in evidence all around us. We might assert, given God's sovereignty and goodness, that things can't be as bad as they seem.[52] Or we might conclude, given the depths of the world's suffering, that God is not as powerful as we may have thought; perhaps God "cannot do everything."[53] Or perhaps God is not altogether good,[54] creating us with flaws that have to be navigated. The problem with any and all of these "solutions" to the problem of suffering is that they set aside the promise of creation—that God makes us and meets us, wholly good and perfectly present. In Genesis, as we have said, this utter goodness is emphasized, and God is present in our midst, walking in the Garden. When sin enters the story, it is viewed as an aberration and adulteration, utterly inconsistent with what God has made, what God desires, and what God intends.

There is a way, however, of accounting for the suffering of the world without compromising on the goodness of either God or creation. Augustine got at it by asking (after affirming the goodness of creation as made by the good and singular God): Then where did *evil* come from? Augustine recognized that he could posit neither that evil was made by God nor that it was made by one other than God without running into theological difficulties. He struggled to find another response to the problem and finally arrived at what has ever since been a defining way theologians have framed evil and sin. What approach did Augustine take?

Augustine's brilliant solution to the dilemma of how to account for suffering in the face of the created goodness is to define evil as "the absence of good."[55] Evil has no substance, he argues. It was not created. It could not have been created, he thinks, since everything that was created is good. Evil, he thinks, is the antithesis of the good creation. When we turn away from the reality that is good and turn toward the "not good," we have turned toward the evil that Augustine identifies with the absence of good; the absence of God; the antithesis of the overflowingly beautiful, gracious world of resources and possibilities that God proffers to us as a gift.

To turn away from the goodness of creation—to ignore our own created goodness—is to lose sight of who God is and who we are. It is to lose track of the fact that we live in immediate relationship to God. It is to feel and to live as those defined by a falsity, forgetting the reality that God makes us and meets us.

Liberation theologians have raised concerns about the Augustinian definition, pointing to incidences in history when understanding evil as "absence" has led to minimizing heinous, inhuman behaviors. Some of the questions they ask are: Is it adequate to describe Hitler's murder of ten million people as a turning away from his created goodness? If we understand evil as the absence of good, what is it, exactly, that we can say to those whose lives were devastated, for example, by the slave trade in the United States? If I understand the harm I have done someone to be inconsistent with who I am, won't I run the risk of minimizing my own sin, even as I confess and apologize?

James Cone is among those who suggest that, while Augustine offers a rational understanding of evil that helps us make sense of evil's origin in light of what we believe about the nature of God and creation, it fails in at least two ways. First, it does not adequately address the anguish of the sufferer. A mother whose son has been lynched experiences evil not merely as the absence of good, but also as something substantive and real. Second, it does not attend to the political structures that make for human suffering and that must be addressed and transformed, prophetically and with legislative changes that promote justice.[56] Cone suggests, and I agree, that we be careful not only to have Augustine's definition in hand when thinking about evil, but that we attend also to the many biblical stories that tell of ways oppressed people of faith were empowered by God to confront destructive principalities and powers.

In my view, laying claim to the truth of creation's goodness and understanding evil as the antithesis of all that God intends and desires readily funds our resistance to oppression with one proviso: that we do not convolute *evil* with *sin*. This is critically important. If we understand evil to be "the absence of good" as that it is *without substance*, we must emphasize that sin is something very different. Sin is not identical to evil. Rather, it is the *distortion* of the good that is quite definitely substantive. When I sin, I in my substantive goodness have turned away from what I am, and the good world God has made, and turned toward what I, and my world, am not. When I sin, I am not evil, but I have turned toward evil—toward the nothingness that is not God.

With this understanding of sin in play, it is clear that when we confess our sins and ask for forgiveness, we are confessing behaviors that are substantive and that need to be renounced and corrected. It is also clear, when we witness institutions and systems that are corrupt and oppressive, that these have turned away from God and God's good creation and have acted in concrete, twisted ways that not only reflect a distorted understanding of the reality God has given us, but also contribute to the distortions. In other words, it is not only the case that sinful institutions are lured, by the demonic, into turning away from God's creative intentions. It is also that they, themselves, become distorted and demonic, drawing sinful human beings into their wake and forgetting, altogether, what it should mean for our actual existence that we have been met and made by God.[57]

In the next chapter we will pick up on this understanding of sin and then move to considering how God redeems us from it, both personally and corporately. I will show how our salvation restores us to living in tune with who we really are, as the God who meets us has made us and is making us to be.

Chapter Six

Who Is God Making Us Into?

The Doctrines of Sin and Salvation

I like to think there is at least a moment in each of our lives when we see ourselves as God sees us. What I mean is that we glimpse that we are beloved, beautiful, and whole as those who are created and claimed by God, despite the fact that our "on the ground" perception of ourselves is quite antithetical to this. I imagine this realization as a kind of revelation, simultaneously both of our created goodness and value and of the ways in which we fall short of this—the ways in which we, in fact, sin. "All have sinned and fall short of God's glory," says Romans.[1] And we were made in the image of this glorious God, a "little lower than God," the psalmist says.[2] To see ourselves as God sees us would fill us, no doubt, with joy, gratitude, and peace. But it would also quickly accentuate the fact that we have fallen short not only of God's glory, but even of our own. Our joyful recognition of our belovedness, taking in our inconsistent behaviors, would quickly dissipate into Paul's lament that "the good that I want to do I do not do, and the evil I don't want to do I do! O wretched [one] that I am! Who can save me from this body of death?"[3]

Notice that Paul does not think he is an evildoer, plain and simple. Rather, he testifies that he is someone who, in reality, wills to do the good.

The fact that he wishes he could act in ways other than how he is acting does not make the fact that he finds himself unable to do the good he wants to do any less of a problem, however. There is a way it even makes it worse—once we see ourselves as God sees us, we can never claim "it wasn't meant to be" as an excuse for not doing the good we want to do. This is because to see ourselves as God sees us is to see precisely that the evil we do was *not* meant to be—we were created good and should, really, be able to act in accordance with who we are in Christ. I'm sure Paul did not follow up his lament by reminding himself that, *Oh, well. It really wasn't realistic to expect myself to do the good, anyway. After all, it's not like I'm superhuman.* As it turns out, the fact that we are made and equipped to do the good makes it a bigger problem when we cannot do it. For me not to return a tennis ball for an entire game would be no big deal to anyone who knows me; for Serena Williams it would be inconceivable precisely because it would contradict who she is at her very core. We are made for doing good even more than Serena Williams was made to play tennis—so it is a real problem when we can't do it!

This realization that there is a disparity between how God sees us and how we actually live certainly gives way to lament and remorse about sinfulness. It also yields to a deep yearning for healing—the desire to bring our daily lives and behaviors back in sync with the reality of who we are, as those met and made by God. It is here that the doctrine of salvation comes into play. Salvation, in this understanding, is not about rescuing us from being bad, but restoring us to being the good people we were created to be. Included in the work of salvation, then, is *forgiveness* of certain out-of-sync actualities—the sinful behaviors in which we have engaged that are contrary to the reality of our created existence.[4] Included, also, are the redemptive actions of God accomplished by Jesus Christ, often referred to, in the history of the Christian faith, as *atonement theories.* Finally, what cannot be forgotten is the ongoing work of the Holy Spirit, who continues saving us by *sanctifying* us. The Holy Spirit, as it turns out, never gives up on reconciling who we really are (as those who have been created in the image of God and made righteous in Christ) with who we actually are (as those who act in ways that are neither good nor righteous).

To be aware of our salvation and to want to live more fully as those who are being met and made by God, is, I would say, close to whatever it means to be "saved." *Salvation,* I am thinking, is the ongoing process of perceiving, and living in continuity with, our redemption in Christ. Paul suggests salvation is something we "work out . . . with fear and trembling."[5] Kierkegaard, wanting to emphasize that holding faith is not always the easiest thing to do, would never simply call himself a Christian. Instead, emphasizing the character of salvation as ongoing, he liked to say that he was in process of becoming one.[6]

To realize the discontinuity between who we are in Christ and how we live and act in our day-to-day lives is risky, because it can lead us to discouragement and even to despair. This is because part and parcel to the realization itself is the recognition we cannot correct the problem on our own. Given this, it makes sense that we who are determined to be good and productive people tend to hold the realization at arms' length, redoubling our efforts to bridge the gap. Instead of resolving the discontinuity, however, we tend to instantiate it by trying to override our wretchedness (or at least by trying to cover it up). The net result of this dynamic, too often, is that we find ourselves living as hypocrites—desperately trying to convince ourselves, and others, that we are the people we know we should be, but actually are not.[7] Ironically, it seems to me, the hypocrisy of us Christians is usually founded in a sincere desire for a kind of consistency we (with Paul) just don't seem able to pull off. In other words, most Christians don't become hypocrites by trying to fake people out about who they are. Rather, they start out trying to be who they think they should be, but inevitably fail to be good enough. This failing to be who we want to be, when it is not admitted, confessed, and corrected, is what hardens into hypocrisy.

We have mentioned that hypocrisy is cited as a major reason the Nones are uninterested in being involved in institutional churches. They generally recognize churchgoers as hypocritical, not living out what they claim to believe. To the degree to which this analysis is accurate, churchgoers need be corrected. Hypocrisy is something Jesus also has no patience for, comparing those he identifies as hypocrites with "whitewashed tombs,"[8] or coffins that look good on the outside, but actually have corpses rotting on the inside. The path out of hypocrisy—the path toward salvation—Jesus teaches, begins with the confession that how we live and act doesn't begin to measure up to who we are in the eyes of God, in and through Jesus Christ. Jesus is always trying to precipitate such admittance from hypocrites not in order to shame them, but to free them to move toward recognition of who they are, as children of God. When they want to stone the woman caught in adultery, for example, Jesus suggests that "the one who is without sin" throw the first stone.[9] "First take the log out of your eye," he instructs, "and then you'll see clearly to take the splinter out of your brother's or sister's eye."[10]

Encouragingly, religious people are often quite eager to rid themselves of hypocrisy, both in themselves and in their communities. It is common to hear, for example, in evangelical Christian circles, the exhortation to "walk the walk" and not just "talk the talk." Similarly, the WWJD movement I mentioned previously insists Christians act in ways consistent with who they claim to be, as disciples of Jesus Christ.

In ecumenical circles, similarly, the challenge is often made to demonstrate "visible unity" to the world.[11] Again, there is the acknowledgment that it is not enough to claim "they will know we are Christians by our love"[12]—we need, actually, to show the world we *do* love by way of loving acts. Taking seriously the charge of hypocrisy, members of the World Council of Churches and the World Alliance of Reformed Churches (for example) work to discover and promote common worship practices among Christians as well as to host bi-lateral dialogues where representatives of different worshipping bodies can come together to discuss how common commitments to justice can push us forward in acting lovingly in the world.

Following these lines of thinking, salvation at its fullest might be understood as the healing of the discontinuity with which we struggle to the point where the details of our historical existence are completely in sync with the reality of our created goodness. This would mean that the redemption for which "all creation groans"[13] is the state in which all creation can be itself, as God made it and intended it to be.[14] It would be—finally—the granting of what we cry out for when we say the Lord's Prayer. "Thy Kingdom come!" we demand. "Thy will be done, on earth as it is in heaven." The coming of heaven to earth is what salvation looks like when each of us is so attuned to who we are in Christ that we actually do what God wills we should do.

Salvation as Freedom

Understood in this way, salvation is also freedom. The Apostle Paul, I believe, would cry "Amen" to that. I say this because what he describes, when he calls himself "wretched," is the common experience we people of faith have of being *not* free—unable to be who we want ourselves to be. Martin Luther describes our predicament, in this regard, as "bondage of the will."[15] We are not able, Luther thought, in and of ourselves, to garner together enough wherewithal to overcome our propensity to sin and be who we are as created by God and redeemed by Christ. Our wills are freed to act in accordance with who God created us to be only by way of God's graceful action, the work of salvation.

One of the challenges we have in grasping how freedom frees us is that our cultural understanding of freedom is different than how we are defining it here, in relation to the spiritual disparity in which we find ourselves. The Western world tends to link freedom, for good reason, to the availability of choices. The more options we have, the more freedom we have—or assume we have—particularly in American culture. Think of car commercials, where purchasing certain vehicles is associated with being able to drive anywhere one wants to go. To buy a certain car is to buy freedom, we are told, because this car expands our range of options. To have fewer or no choices is, by contrast, to be in a kind of bondage—confined, limited, and certainly less free than one *could* be if one had the right car!

Spiritually speaking, the bondage that is antithetical to freedom cannot be accounted for simply by lamenting a paucity of choices. As aggravating as it can be not to have options, what is most maddening of all is not to be able to make choices we do have, but somehow aren't able to take. Paul cries out in anguish, apparently faced with options that are right before him but that he is somehow not able to embrace. Strangely but commonly enough, he behaves instead in accordance with what he does not want. Nothing is stopping him from choosing the good, in other words, except his own propensity to choose the evil he does not want to choose. It is this choosing—against who we are and what we want—that is the bondage of personal sin as Paul is describing it. Salvation from such sin, by contrast, looks like us being able to choose in ways that are consistent with who God made us to be and who we want to be, in our actual lives. People of faith have long hoped for the day when our salvation is complete because it is then that we will suffer no longer even one iota of wretchedness—we will be so utterly free to choose to be who we are that making choices against who God created us to be will not even be a possibility. As Augustine describes it, at this point of completion we will be "free to choose for the good always."[16]

There is another kind of bondage that can result from personal bondage to sin. This bondage affects not only those who cannot (and often do not even want to) make the right choices, but also those who are affected by the bad choices being made. It is the bondage of some by others who, acting in accordance with their own bondage to sin, actually work to limit the options and choices of those around them. Classically, for example, slaveholders work to limit the choices offered to slaves in order to keep them captive.

Whatever redemption is, I believe it includes the healing both of the bondage of our wills and the oppression of some by others. Sometimes, theologians associate these two kinds of bondage with *personal sin* and *corporate sin* (or *systemic sin*), respectively. This can be useful as long as it is remembered that the two cannot be separated—it is the personal sins of individuals that shape corrupt institutions in which the lives of some are used up to enhance the lives of others. But then, to be sure, institutions and systems take on a life of their own, or at least it feels that way. They are dependent on the flourishing of hypocrites, those who are best able to ignore or justify the harm they are doing, and so they promote bondage of the will as a way to fund oppressive dynamics that ensure the most powerful continue to have power over others.[17]

The idea that God desires *both* personal sin and corporate sin to be redeemed is consistent with the biblical witness all the way through. In the Old Testament, for example, there are requests for personal healing, such as David's appeal that the Lord "create... a clean heart, filled with right desires." And there are commands, throughout, to take care of those who have been impoverished by broken systems. "Establish justice," Amos tells us, for example, warning us that neglecting the "poor" and the "needy" will have dire consequences.[18] In the New Testament, similarly, Jesus's work of redemption touches and heals both sinners and those who are sinned against. "I've come to set the captives free," he says, listing the poor, the blind, and the oppressed as those who will be "released."[19] Interestingly, Christians in good faith have interpreted Jesus's words, historically, both as applying to personal sin and as applying to corporate sin. Sometimes they have even argued about which is Jesus's greater concern. My view is that this in particular is something of a wasted argument, since what is clear is that both personal and corporate sin are symptoms of brokenness, and both are and will be healed.

Is Salvation Really Necessary, if All Are Met and Made by God?

At this point it might be important to step back for a moment from different types of sin and acknowledge straightforwardly that the understanding of salvation that is operative in this chapter and this book is not one founded in the idea that some are simply *in* and others are simply *out*, when it comes to the Kingdom of God. As has been suggested in prior chapters, the hope is that all have been met in the coming of the Word made flesh, and that all have been made good in the image of the triune God. In relation to the incarnation and creation, then, all are accounted for.[20] On the basis of this confession of God's grace Barth is reported to have suggested to Christians that they "hope everyone makes it in the end and preach as though hell is real." Supporting this recommendation is an interpretation of Philippians 2:10-11 framed not in terms of Christian triumphalism, but rather by God's relentless determination to include everyone. "Every knee will bend; every tongue confess,"[21] the Scripture says, which we might do well to interpret as meaning no one will be left behind. Now, it is important to be clear: a human being is no more authorized to declare that everyone makes it in the end than he or she is licensed to determine who is *in* and who is *out* of whatever constitutes God's eternal Kingdom. It is only the sovereign God who decides such matters. If we are to hope that everyone is included, it is solely because we understand full inclusion to be consistent with the character of the sovereign God who is unconditionally loving and unfathomably gracious.

The redemption of sin, however, is in the business of something more than issuing "fire insurance," as I sometimes like to joke. In other words, it is not only—and perhaps not even primarily—concerned with the matter of creating a way for people who deserve to go to hell to go to heaven instead. Rather, it is God's work of making it possible for people to be the beautiful creatures God made them to be, in fellowship with the triune God, by way of their brother, Jesus Christ, in the power of the Holy Spirit. "Fire insurance" will—I hope!—be included in all this, but the focus of redemption should not be merely escaping punishment, but also enjoying God's gift of abundant life. God's work of redemption saves us not only *from* something but also *for* something—life in God, through Jesus Christ, by the power of the Holy Spirit.

Salvation and Universalism

If the understanding of redemption being presented isn't in the business of dividing up those who are somehow *in* and those who are *out*, some may ask, isn't it simply a form of universalism? If all are, objectively speaking, met and made by God, doesn't this mean all are, whether they know it or not, already "saved"? And if our conviction is that the salvation of all is, in reality, already accomplished, what is left to do? Why even think about salvation at all?

Already we have begun to answer this question, at least indirectly, in the first few pages of this chapter. Salvation is not only about God making provision for us, but also about us living into an awareness of what it is God has done. We are in bondage when we do not remember that we have been made and met, when we forget that we are created good and claimed by God in Jesus Christ. Insofar as we know ourselves before the God who has met and made us, on the other hand, we are able to live the abundant life God desires for us.[22] There is a sense in which we who are saved by God no matter what are also *not* saved whenever we lose sight of who we are. This does not mean that if we were to die in the moments of our forgetting we would go to hell. What it does mean is that we are less free in our daily life whenever we lose sight of God's meeting and making of us.

Karl Barth explains it this way:

> Reality which does not become truth for us obviously cannot affect us, however supreme may be its ontological dignity. . . . It will necessarily remain unattested on our side—a word which has no answer, a light which has no reflection. Unrecognized, the love of God in Jesus Christ cannot awaken and summon us to its attestation and therefore to a response of love.[23]

A word with no answer; a light with no reflection. It is hard to imagine how this could be the case, but there is a definite sense in which we human agents have the power to contribute to the dynamics of the divine revelation by way of whether or not we recognize the reality of God's love.

The character of any decision we make regarding our own salvation is explained quite straightforwardly by Barth. What we decide, he explains, is not whether or not we have been met and made by God, but whether or not we will live our lives in light of the decision that has been made on our behalf. While this life decision is really ours, Barth explains, "it . . . cannot precede but can only follow the decision already taken in Jesus Christ."[24]

I have been helped, in trying to envision how God's redemptive work is and isn't related to our conscious participation in it, by the following analogy: Imagine, if you would, that you love someone (a lover, a child, a friend) with a love so great that nothing can take it away—even your beloved one's rejection of it. But now imagine that the person whom you love is not living their life with an awareness that they are loved by you. You have told that person that you love them in all the ways you know how, but somehow they don't seem to have absorbed it. You genuinely believe—you *know*, in fact—that if they only recognized how much they are loved by you, their whole life could be different, better, richer. Imagine that your primary concern, in proclaiming your unconditional love for this one, is not to receive the "I love you return"[25] (although of course you want this). It is, rather, that that person know the gift of your unconditional love, and all the blessings that correspond with it.

Your love for this person, it is clear, will endure whether this person recognizes it and lives in relation to it or not. But imagine what would happen if and when this person acknowledged it. In one sense, nothing would be different (because the love you have would be the same love that was present even before the recognition). At the same time, everything would be different (because the person would be transformed by the love extended to them, which would give you great joy).

God's love for us, demonstrated in the ways God meets us and makes us, is the reality that frames our existence whether we recognize it or not. But when "the reality becomes truth for us,"[26] everything changes. We experience life abundant. It is when we recognize the reality of God's love that the blessings of redemption are ours, and that we have the hope of living free lives that are consistent, in actuality, with who we really are as God's children.

Interestingly, this way of understanding salvation avoids buying into an easy universalism while at the same time eschewing any problematic tendency we might have to divide the world up into insiders and outsiders. Avoiding an easy universalism is important to those of us who have experienced and witnessed the ways faith claims make a difference to our lives and the life of the world. To say, simply, that "everyone makes it in the end, so why worry, really, about the space between here and there" does a disservice not only to the legacy of Christendom but also to the transformative experiences of those who have "held faith" down through the ages and found that their conscious Christian convictions have shaped their very lives. People of faith from contexts as wide-ranging as the fourth-century African-born theologian Augustine to the fifth-century Greek mathematician philosopher Pythagoras of Samos; from the eighteenth-century philosopher René Descartes to nineteenth-century American slaves who sang, "we've come this far by faith";[27] from philosopher Simone Weil to Pulitzer prize-winning author Marilynne Robinson—all testify to the ways in which experiences of Christianity made specific, life-changing demands on their lives and their plans.

What Keeps Us from Being Saved? Sin and Finitude

If salvation is about syncing who we actually are (in our day-to-day, on the ground lives) with who we really are (as those created by God and beloved), what's the big hold up? Shouldn't the fact that we are met and made by God facilitate the syncing? Why can't we just realize what it means to be met by the one who has entered into existence with us and made good in God's own image, living our lives according to these framing ways of self-understanding? If being met and made by God is, finally, both a done deal and consistent with who we really are, why is the reality, reassurance, and challenge of it so difficult to lean into? Why is it so hard to recognize the reality as truth for us? What keeps us from being saved, if salvation includes recognizing the redemption that is already ours?

Traditionally, the answer to this question has been: sin gets in the way. We don't want to give up control, we hypothesize. We would rather be the gods of our own life than to recognize ourselves as those who are met and made by God, and therefore as mere creatures. To know ourselves before God is to know we are *not* God, we explain. This is a problem if we imagine we want to *be* God, or at least a god to ourselves. In wanting to be our own gods we are guilty of pride, we say, treating pride as the fundamental sin. So closely aligned is pride with sin, in fact, that sometimes we understand the two to be synonymous.

There is probably a lot of truth to the idea that what keeps us from knowing our redemption is primarily the sin we know as pride. But saying "pride gets in the way" of our acknowledgment of who we are in relation to the God who has made and met us oversimplifies the condition from which we need to be redeemed. For one thing, not all sin can be described as pride, as we will discuss further in a moment. Additionally, identifying and describing our sin—whether as "pride" or as anything else—still doesn't get to its root. What is it, exactly, that plagues us? If we indeed want to be in control, *why* is this the case? Why do we play God rather than receive the true freedom that is extended to us, freedom that allows us to be the wonderfully made, beloved and claimed creatures we are?

It may help, in answering this question, to think of sin as emerging from the condition of bondage in which we find ourselves, as the Apostle Paul testifies and as we have been describing it in the last few pages. The theologian Paul Tillich, along these lines, identifies sin with *estrangement*—the experience of feeling alienated from the source of all things, the "Ground of All Being" with which we desperately desire to feel connected.[28] Tillich notes that, while we of course *are*, in reality, inextricably connected to the "Ground of All Being," we inevitably feel as though we are not. Why is this? Because, he says, when we encounter this one who is infinite, our limitations as creatures are accentuated. Because of this, we inevitably feel distanced from that to which we are inextricably connected. The Ground of All Being is immortal, but we, being mortal and finite, will die. This troubles us since—face-to-face with the unlimited One—we realize death is not the only possibility. Somehow, it just doesn't seem right to us that we should die. And so, we fight our creatureliness.

I like to use, as a humorous example of this, a clip from the popular 1980s sitcom *Cheers*. In the scene, psychiatrist couple Frasier and Lilith are sitting at a bar, discussing their will. "So, who gets the wok?" Lilith asks, all business. "Look, darling," Frasier says, "I find this entire will discussion troubling. It's not easy to talk about one's mortality. . . . We're talking about death here! My death, your death, the end of everything! . . . I know it's irrational," he admits, "but I can't help feeling that if you talk about it, it'll happen." "Well, Frasier," Lilith says, "it *will* happen." "Stop it!" Frasier cries. "What?" Lilith insists. "Do you think if I hadn't mentioned it, you'd live forever?" "Well," Frasier responds, "now we'll never know, will we?"[29]

What makes this exchange funny is that many of us can resonate with it. We often avoid facing our mortality—the mortality of ourselves, of others, and of all things—because, oddly enough, given that everything comes to an end—death seems "out of sync" with how things should be. And so sometimes we deal with it by not talking about it, as if that would make our mortality go away. I have a friend, Tina, fifty-three years old with stage-four colon cancer and a great sense of humor. She tells me that many people either avoid mentioning her cancer or talk as though she will soon be cured when they talk to her, as if they can keep her alive a little longer if they pretend what is happening isn't really happening. Contemplation of our mortality, as Frasier points out, is upsetting. But, as Tina insists, to let go of our denial allows us to live freely and joyfully as the limited but beautiful creatures we are.

Tillich argues, along these same lines, that when we resist the freedom that comes with recognizing we are creatures who are met and made by God, we are actually resisting our *finitude*.[30] Made in the image of God, we recognize and value the infinite and so try to overpower that which is antithetical to it. While the finitude itself is no sin, fighting it leads us to sinful behaviors. Denying our finitude because we want to be more like the Ground in which we participate, we pump ourselves up and act as if we are immortal (Tillich calls this the sin of *hubris*, or pride). Or we might conceptualize everyone in orbit around us, or imagine ourselves as movie stars around which all other actors in a movie need be orchestrated, attempting to draw others into our narratives more as supporting players than as agents in their own right. Tillich calls this form of sin *concupiscence*, a term that is rarely used in common parlance, today, although the sin itself appears to run rampant. Or we might try, Tillich notes, simply turning our backs on God altogether. On some level, he suggests, we hope that *turning away* will get the infinite out of our line of vision so we don't have to process our finitude, by contrast. The sin of "turning away" looks the most innocuous but is actually the most serious of the three instances of sin, in Tillich's conceptualization, given that it ignores our grounding in God.

What keeps us from living in light of being met and made by God, then, according to Tillich, are indeed the sins of *hubris*, concupiscence, and turning away that are manifestations of our resistance to being who we really are as God's beloved creatures. But the setup to all of these is, again, the fact of our creatureliness itself. While there is nothing wrong with finitude, since it is part and parcel of God's good creation, we really don't like it. Some have suggested that the struggle we have with mortality, as those who are cognizant of the divine, is what is distinctive about being made in the image of God. Cats don't seem to pause and reflect on the fact that they will one day die, wishing that they wouldn't. Though they may misbehave, it is hard to argue that they actually sin, at least in the ways Tillich delineates. They seem to have less trouble being who they are as cats, than we human beings do being human. Perhaps there is an alpha cat who appears to be guilty of the sin of concupiscence, placing other cats around him. But it would probably be pushing our luck to argue that the reason this cat is so self-glorifying is because he is looking for ways to deny his finitude.

Because Tillich's approach to the problem from which we need redemption focuses more on the condition of our sinfulness than on the particular sins rooted in it, his reflections on the human condition often resonate with groups of people who feel estranged, including those whose sins look quite different than pride, concupiscence, or unbelief. James Cone writes, for example, that American blacks understand what Tillich means when he talks about the "existential risk" associated with being people of faith, insisting that "the meaning and fulfillment of our lives is at stake." This is because, Cone suggests, "in the black world, no one takes life for granted: every moment of being is surrounded with the threat of nonbeing."[31]

All of us are finite beings, but we manage our finitude in varying ways. Those in positions of privilege tend to deny their finitude on the basis of whiteness, maleness, or material wealth. Those who are consistently discriminated against on the basis of race, gender, or class are more likely to be overcome by the forces of finitude or to be unable to hide it by way of hypocrisy. For people who are black, Cone, Martin Luther King Jr., JoAnne Terrell, and other African American and African theologians suggest, the recognition of finitude and its corresponding mortality can be so overwhelming that there can be a kind of "giving up" that looks quite the opposite of pride, concupiscence, or turning away. Nelson Mandela commonly named this form of response to feelings of estrangement, when exhorting audiences comprised primarily of black persons in South Africa. Making famous a poem written by Marianne Williamson, he on a number of occasions asserted: "Our greatest fear is not that we are inadequate. Our greatest fear is that we are powerful beyond measure." "We ask ourselves," he would continue, still using Williamson's words, "Who am I to be brilliant, talented, fabulous? Actually, who are you not to be? You are a child of God. Your playing small doesn't serve the world."[32] Clearly, the sins Mandela named with these words looked very different than the sins named by Tillich, even if they all grew out of experiences of estrangement.

This idea that the sins that seem to stand in the way of our recognizing we are met and made by God can vary, depending on who we are and what demographic we come from, has also been noticed and developed by many feminist theologians. As far back as 1960, in fact, Valerie Saiving published an article that suggested women do not resonate as readily as men do with the idea that the fundamental sin is "pride."[33] Judith Plaskow, twenty years later, applied Saiving's thesis to Tillich and Niebuhr, arguing that the theologies of these formative male theologians could be expanded to take the experiences of women into account, in teachings about sin and salvation.[34] In showing what this would look like, Saiving and Plaskow identified the sins they thought were more common to women as *feminine sin*. They argued that women are much more likely to think of themselves as *less* than they really are, rather than as *more* than they are. If men tend to attempt to override their estrangement by acting as though they are god-like, Saiving and Plaskow suggest, women tend simply to fold in the face of it, so convinced of the truth of their unworthiness (relative to the infinite God) that they act as though it is pious and humble simply to give up.

In my experience in teaching theology, I have found this category of "feminine sin" to be very useful because it resonates both with women and with men. Women are relieved to have a way of articulating, in a way that seems more consistent with their experiences and feelings, that which stands in the way of recognizing their redemption. Men who care about women—particularly men who are pastors and want to minister to women whose experiences are in some ways different than their own, feel they now have a broader way not only of naming sin, but of understanding a range of human experiences and spiritual struggles. And—very importantly—just as women can be and often are guilty of pride, so men are sometimes guilty of self-deprecation. In other words, "feminine sin" isn't only a sin with which women struggle, even if it is more commonly identified with women than with men.[35]

What stands in the way of our living into our redemption, then, is whatever keeps us from recognizing the reality of who we are as those who have been met and made by God. Whether we try to be our own gods or we melt down in the face of God's gracious claim on us, we have not yet experienced the fullness of salvation that is only ours once we appropriate it. The bottom line is that the reason we have so much trouble recognizing that we are met and made, beloved and good, is because we—unlike God—are finite. Our limitations, as creatures before God, are not readily accepted as *good*, which is why we respond either by trying to override them or by giving up. Following Tillich's reasoning, to work out our salvation entails embracing our finitude, reveling in the gifts of our creaturely existence.

This is what Jesus did, as the one who entered fully into our creaturely reality with us. When, early in his ministry, the devil tried to tempt him to override his limitations by turning stones into bread, Jesus resisted the sins of pride and concupiscence. When, at the end of his life, he was struggling in the Garden of Gethsemane, he did not simply dissolve in the face of the

Father's will. Rather, he held on to a strong sense of self even as he submitted to the will of God, saying not "my will is irrelevant and pointless," but rather "not my will, but yours be done."[36]

With Jesus, then, we who groan for redemption might work, in our spirituality, at neither blocking out the conditions of our estrangement nor collapsing into them, but rather recognizing who we are as those who have been met in these conditions by the Christ who reminds us of our goodness and value. This said, there is still a piece we have to consider, and that is: What is the place of Christ's actual work—his life, death, and resurrection? Is there a need for *atonement*, related to salvation? Or is salvation mainly about following in Christ's footsteps, working to live as who we are rather than committing sins on one side or the other of our creaturely existence?

Salvation and Atonement[37]

People who hold faith have always recognized salvation is not accomplished by sheer consciousness-raising. If it were possible for us simply to ward off all manner of sins and realize who we are as beloved and good creatures, we would have done it by now. People of faith have noted that this problem of wretchedness Paul describes, even as it is parsed out later by theologians such as Tillich, is impossible to conquer on our own. Calvin believes we have nothing whatsoever to contribute to our redemption, naming our incapacity to recognize God in our own total depravity. Aquinas and Wesley, however, both think we have something to contribute to the redemptive process: Aquinas thinks we have the capacity to discern an intelligence behind the natural world; Wesley thinks we *decide* to reach out and take God's gift of forgiveness. But all these theologians agree that, regardless of humanity's capacity or incapacity to contribute to their salvation, we cannot accomplish it on our own. All agree, in fact, that we need the help of God, as it is extended to us in God's many gracious acts. Most explicitly, however, they argue that we need the help of God as it is extended to us in the acts of God in Jesus Christ. It is through his life, death, and resurrection, they believe, that atonement is made for our sins. It is this atonement that makes it possible for the barriers of all sins to be broken and for us to know where we stand in relationship to God.

Today, there is a great deal of controversy surrounding the doctrine of atonement and its relationship to salvation. If salvation is in the business of healing whatever is broken about our relationship to God, atonement would be about paying any of the costs that emerge in the process of that healing. At the extreme, there are those who argue that atonement theories are not really needed, that no costs need to be paid, that it is in fact damaging to talk about atonement for sins because it works against the idea that nothing could ever separate us from God's love for us and presence with us—certainly not any penalties, which God would have the capacity to forgive, anyway. What we need, they say, is less emphasis on our sinfulness and more on our created goodness. If we can focus more on what is good about us, without spending such a great deal of time wallowing in our sinfulness and debating about how it is that Jesus saves us from it and how he doesn't,[38] some argue, we will be able to more productively focus our energies on promoting life, rather than protecting ourselves against punishment and death by covering ourselves with guilt and shame.[39]

A major concern of those questioning atonement theory is the history of ways in which the cross has been used to justify or perpetuate abuse. Historically, the cross has been carried by the Crusaders of the Middle Ages, by members of the Ku Klux Klan, and by Nazi soldiers. Survivors of domestic violence frequently testify that pastors have sent them back home to their abusers with the instruction that they should "bear the cross" they have been given, even as Jesus has. And the idea that the Father would send the Son to die, and that this was somehow necessary for the Father to be able to forgive us, has been identified by some thinkers as "divine child abuse."[40] While this might seem like an extreme statement, its antecedents were recognizable all the way back in the twelfth century, when Peter Abélard complained about Anselm's theory.[41]

Faced with these ambiguities related to the cross, what tack should we take in exploring what it means to be redeemed, and what role Jesus's life, death, and resurrection plays (or does not play) in this process? I propose that a good place to begin is with the three most well-known atonement theories themselves. What do each of these tell us about how Jesus saves us? What can be learned, and what should be discarded as unhelpful or, even, destructive? In my view, each of the major approaches to atonement has something valuable to contribute to our understanding of salvation, and they are not mutually exclusive. When all three are considered in tandem, in fact, we have a much fuller and richer understanding of the ways in which we are healed, in the course of our redemption in and through the saving work of Jesus Christ.

By way of background: unlike in the case of the doctrine of incarnation and the doctrine of the Trinity, there has never been a church council that has determined a standard of orthodoxy for understanding atonement theory. In other words, when we think of the relevance of the "Word made flesh," we consider it in relation to the Nicene idea that Jesus Christ is *homoousios* with the Father and the Chalcedonian ("fully human; fully divine"). When we think of God's triunity we bear in mind the statement that God is, simultaneously, the one who is three and the three who is one ("one *ousia*; three *hypostases*"). But when we consider atonement, as it relates to redemption, there is no council that made any determination, no statement that serves as a reference point. The reference point is the cross itself, and the life, death, and resurrection of Jesus Christ in which it is situated.

Thinking about this figure of Jesus Christ, who he is, and what it is he saves us *from* and *for*, Christian believers have, through the ages, tried to articulate the faith they hold in many different ways. There have been three approaches that have emerged as "most common" among atonement theories as people of faith have developed them in conversation with Scripture. Christ is viewed as: (1) the One who died so we can be free to live and serve (e.g., Rom 8:3-4; Rev 1:5-6), (2) the One who goes ahead of us to teach us and represent us (e.g., Matt 28:7; Heb 12:1-2), and (3) the One who empowers us on the journey itself (e.g., Phil 4:13; 2 Cor 12:9). Theologians such as Calvin, Wesley, and Barth have tried to take all three of these into account in considering Jesus Christ's atoning work, often identifying him, in relation to each of these three, respectively, as "priest, prophet, and king."[42]

Christ as Priest: Anselmian Atonement

In his book *Cur Deus Homo* (1098), Anselm of Canterbury explains why it is that God became a human being in Jesus Christ.[43] According to Anselm, our sinfulness dishonored God. The God who is perfectly righteous and holy cannot look upon sin because to do so would be inconsistent with God's righteous character. But the holy God is also a God of order who desires to restore the damage done by sin. Because of who God is, then, God can only turn away from sinners, and God will find a way to be reconciled to them. In order for God to enter back into relationship with us, Anselm explains, the debt to God's honor has to be "satisfied." Since we, as sinners, are not capable of satisfying God's honor, and since a human being has to pay the debt accrued as a consequence of human sin, God becomes incarnate in Jesus Christ. Because Jesus takes the penalty of dishonor upon himself, as the fully human, sinless one, God's honor is restored. Jesus is offered a reward for his sacrifice, a sacrifice he was not compelled to make, being sinless. But because Jesus is also fully divine, he does not need the reward. He offers the reward to us. The reward is our salvation.

It is interesting to note that Anselm's understanding, now most commonly known as *substitutionary atonement*, did not emerge until the end of the eleventh century. It is informative to ponder how those who hold faith were thinking about the role of the cross in redemption before that time. What seems to be the case is that, earlier in the church's history, it was clearer to believers that God's entrance into human existence was itself redemptive. Recall, along these lines, Gregory of Nazianzus's assertion that what has not been assumed has not been saved, which takes as its corollary that what *has* been assumed *is* saved. Notice that Gregory–and all those from the fourth through the eleventh centuries who appreciated his insight–understood salvation to have been accomplished by way of the Word become flesh (which includes, but is not limited to, the cross).

Our thinking has changed since the time of Anselm. Today, we tend to look at the incarnation of God in Jesus Christ at Christmastime as a kind of means to an end. After all, Jesus had to get down here somehow, so he could grow up, die on the cross, and save us—right? I remember, as a child, sitting in the back of the church and hearing the preacher say that "Jesus died for me." I remember wondering: How did Jesus's death on the cross, so long ago, get from him to me? How did his dying help matters any? These are the kinds of on-the-ground questions Anselm was, to his credit, attempting to answer.

Anselm's theory does a fine job of upholding the divine sovereignty. According to Anselm, God does not demand that the Son die because there is any external metaphysical necessity imposed on the being of God. The need for satisfaction stems from the *divine aseity* or the divine freedom, Anselm held. In other words: God becomes flesh because God's very being demands it in order to be in relationship with us, not because God is following rules that compel God to do this. As David Bentley Hart explains it, Anselmian atonement does not represent Christ's sacrifice as required by the "laws of the universe." Rather, the sacrifice of Christ "belongs . . . to the infinite motion of God's love, in which justice and mercy are one and can never be divided one from the other."[44] The payment for our sins, then, is not made to the devil, which would imply that the devil had some power in the workings of the universe. Satisfaction is made to the one true God, for whom there is no rival.

Another strength of Anselmian atonement, not often noted, is that it takes very seriously God's relationship to the created order, particularly to human beings. The closeness of God to us is seen not only in God's decision to enter into our reality in Jesus Christ, making amends for our sinfulness. It is also seen in the fact that God is affected by us—so profoundly affected that God has to turn away; so affected that something has to be done to preserve God's character.

As has already been suggested, there are many weaknesses to the Anselmian view. Both in the theological guild and also in many church pews it is coming under severe attack. People of faith are asking serious questions about whether it does more harm than good, when it comes to understanding who we are in relation to the God who meets and makes us. Does it actually heal our feelings of estrangement, we might ask, or does it serve only to deepen them? Many are concerned that this model glorifies human suffering and so promotes both shame and the sin of self-deprecation. If the Father-God sends the Son to die a violent death in order to satisfy the Father-God's honor, they ask, how can we not see this as abusive?[45] Connected with this is frustration regarding Anselm's insistence that God's honor has been violated, as if God would be more willing to sacrifice God's only child than to sacrifice God's honor. And why, many people of faith want to know, couldn't God just forgive human beings, without demanding a sacrifice at all?

This is a question that, as we have mentioned, was raised as far back as the twelfth century by Peter Abélard (ca. 1130). Abélard wrote that he did not even recognize Anselm's God as the God he loved and worshipped. He, like feminist thinkers who would follow, thought Anselm also engaged in faulty logic, asking: "If the sin of Adam was so great that it could be expiated only by the death of Christ, what expiation will avail for the act of murder committed against Christ, and for the many great crimes committed against him or his followers? How did the death of his innocent Son so please God the Father that through it he should be reconciled to us?"[46]

For Abélard as well as for many who hold faith today, the idea that God would require death in order to forgive is antithetical to what we confess about God's unconditional love and graceful, ongoing creation. In fact, I also reject this proposition. I do not believe the Father required the death of the Son.[47] I am in good company. While Calvin emphasized Anselmian atonement (the priestly office of Christ) more than the other two approaches, he, too, seemed to struggle with how to reconcile God's "wrath" with God's loving character:

> Since our hearts cannot, in God's mercy, either seize upon life ardently enough or accept it with the gratefulness we owe, unless our minds are first struck and overwhelmed by fear of God's wrath and by dread of eternal death, we are taught by Scripture to perceive that apart from Christ, God is, so to speak, hostile to us, and his hand is armed for our destruction; to embrace his benevolence and fatherly love in Christ alone.[48]

Clearly, there are troubling themes in this particular citation from Calvin. Significant, however, is his desire to convince us that the wrath of God is not really part of the divine character, but a pedagogical tactic for the sake of our salvation.

One further, and important, critique of Anselm is that he tends to reduce Jesus Christ's atoning work to the substitutionary work on the cross. According to feminist theologian Dorothee Sölle,[49] this raises certain questions: If Christ is only our *substitute*, what happens to us? Was Christ's only purpose in becoming human to die as the penalty for our sin? Did the incarnation, the teachings, the life of Jesus Christ contribute nothing to our salvation? If Christ is only the One who substitutes for us, and not One who lives for us and enters into partnership with us, Sölle holds, the atoning work of Christ is not accomplished for our benefit, but only in order to replace us. And replacement, she thinks, is not salvation, but annihilation.

Christ as Prophet: Abélardian Atonement

Having critiqued Anselm's understanding of atonement, Abélard was fair enough to present his own view, commonly known as the *moral exemplar theory* or, sometimes, *representational theory*. According to Abélard, we are not saved primarily through Christ's death on the cross, but through the example of Christ's life, which includes his suffering and death on the cross. Abélard thought the Gospel testimony presented such a compelling portrait of Jesus Christ—his love for God, his submission to the Father's will, his concern for those to whom he ministered, his desire to live a righteous life—that we who ponder these stories will be compelled to respond in kind. In contrast to what he believed was a skewed representation of God by Anselm, Abélard founded his understanding of atonement on his belief that God is a God of love, and that the example of this love is Jesus Christ. The cross, too, is primarily a manifestation of the divine love, the perfect realization of the divine friendship with us: "By the faith which we hold concerning Christ, love is increased in us, by virtue of the conviction that God in Christ has united our human nature to himself and, by suffering the same nature, has demonstrated to us that perfection of love of which he himself says: 'Greater love than this no man hath. . . .' "[50]

For Abélard, Jesus Christ is not just a nice example, a leader in a game of Simon Says whom we are called to emulate. For Abélard, Christ is the one who constrains us to love: the best friend, the parent, the mentor—the person who will not let us go, the advocate who is always working to make a place for us to be who we are. The desire to emulate Christ above all else, he thought, is a mark of spiritual maturity.

Abélard's understanding is helpful insofar as it does not reduce the person and work of Jesus Christ to the event of the cross, but understands the atoning work of the cross to be efficacious only in the context of Jesus Christ's entire life and ministry. In this regard, Abélard's understanding of the atonement returns to the early church's emphasis on the saving value of the incarnation. God in Jesus Christ has entered into existence with us, and in so doing has redeemed us. We are not replaced, as in the case of a solely substitutionary view. Instead, our place is held by Christ.

Abélard opens the door, then, for us to consider what Jesus's teachings and interactions with others in his ministry communicate to us about our salvation. Given Christ's prophetic example, how shall we then live in relationship to God and one another? Following Abélard, looking to Christ as our representative might lead us away from seeking to locate the cross in the story of the Samaritan woman at the well or that of the prodigal son.[51] Instead, we note that Jesus's concern for the woman compels her to respond to him and to reach out to others; the father's overwhelming love urges the elder son to give up thinking only about what is fair and instead participate in the realm of grace. When seen through an Abélardian lens, salvation in both of these stories is holistic—revealing to us what it is to live in the Kingdom of God in the here and now.

Similarly, an Abélardian reading would not attempt to make sense of Jesus's cry of dereliction[52] by understanding it as a necessary means to the end of paying the penalty for our sin. Instead, a representational reading helps us to hear the cry as an affirmation that God really suffers with us, and so understands our suffering. God loves us enough to meet us in the most heinous dimensions of estranged human existence with us, and this identification with us is itself redemptive, apart from anything Christ then does or doesn't do for us.

The idea that we need to consider Christ's atoning work on the cross in relation to the incarnation, the rest of his life, and the resurrection/ascension was emphasized in the Reformation period and is still a strong theme in Reformed theology today. Calvin asks: How has Christ abolished sin, banished the separation between us and God, and acquired righteousness to render God favorable and kindly toward us? He doesn't answer this question with "by dying on the cross" but "by the whole course of his obedience."[53]

In a context in which we are suspicious of those who claim to be our representatives (consider, for example, our attitude toward our political and legal representatives), it might be difficult to resonate with Abélard's depiction of Christ as our Representative. Abélard's greatest contribution to us might then be that he communicates so clearly what it is to be represented and to represent. Surely, because Christ our Representative is for us, living with awareness of our salvation must entail that we be for one another as well as do for one another.

The critique frequently made of Abélard is twofold: First, those who have learned from Anselm's view are concerned that Abélard does not take into adequate account the character of God. To argue that God may simply forgive if God wants to is to ignore God's self-revelation as the perfectly holy One. God does not do whatever God wants to, but only that which is consistent with God's own character as holy and righteous.

Second, some critics wonder if Abélard has given much thought to the depraved character of human beings. How can he be so sure that we are equipped to respond to the love demonstrated for us by Jesus Christ? Someone who is simply "a good example" cannot redeem us, they argue, for our salvation then ultimately rests on our capacity to mold ourselves in to Jesus's likeness, and we are not capable of doing this in and of ourselves. Human beings need more help than this, critics argue.

One further critique made of Abélardian atonement is that it, like Anselmian atonement, can perpetuate violence and abuse. This is because the cross is still interpreted as a demonstration of love, by way of self-sacrifice.

Resisting this, many feminist and liberation theologians argue that the model of conformity to Christ for marginalized persons can no longer be one of self-sacrifice. The marginalized need, rather, to learn that they are God's precious children and to stand up for themselves. They need to look, perhaps, not to emulate Christ's work on the cross, but to respond to the command of the risen Christ to follow him to Galilee.[54]

Christ as Victor: Christus Victor

The *christus victor* theory cannot be ascribed to any single thinker as readily as the Anselmian and Abélardian views. Often Irenaeus (2nd c.) is credited with its earliest articulation, and the theory is later reflected in theologians including Luther (16th c.) and Wesley (19th c.). It has been promoted most recently by twentieth-century theologians Gustaf Aulén[55] and C. S. Lewis.[56]

According to the *christus victor* theory, God and the forces of Satan are in battle with one another. There is no question of who will ultimately win, *christus victor* proponents argue, and in this sense the battle is therefore not a real battle. There is no God above God, Irenaeus insists, which is why Christ was able to "overthrow Satan by means of [God's] words and commandments."[57] Nonetheless, *christus victor* clearly acknowledges that, while never tenable rivals to God, Satan and Satan's demons have real power along the way to the coming of the Kingdom. "Jesus opposes [the forces of evil] during his life, is apparently conquered by them in his death, but triumphs over them through his resurrection."[58]

God and Satan are at war because human beings sinned. In sinning, we succumbed to the power of Satan (the "fallen one"). Christ came to release us from the bonds of Satan, and to bind Satan to sin. As Irenaeus explains:

> For as in the beginning Satan enticed human beings to transgress their Maker's law, and thereby got them into his power; yet Satan's power consists in transgression and apostasy, and with these Satan bound humanity... so it was necessary that through a human being Satan himself should, when conquered, be bound with the same chains with which he had bound humanity.[59]

According to Irenaeus, Christ "carried off a glorious and perfect victory" by paying the ransom that was owed to Satan for our salvation.[60]

The *christus victor* theory presumes that we continue to struggle against demonic forces even though victory has been achieved in Christ. Luther believed that Satan has no real power over us, in the sense that we could ever be "kidnapped" from the grace of God. But he thought it was spiritually beneficial that we be continuously reminded of this. Luther thought, for example, that remembering our baptisms would help guard us against the wiles of Satan, enabling us to live in conscious awareness of God's grace. Consider, for example, the third verse of "A Mighty Fortress Is Our God":[61]

> And though this world with devils filled,
> Should threaten to undo us,
> We will not fear, for God hath willed
> His truth to triumph through us.
> The prince of darkness grim, We tremble not for him;
> His rage we can endure, For lo! his doom is sure,
> One little word shall fell him.

Clearly, Irenaeus and Luther found it to be spiritually valuable to name their experience of the principalities and powers in their midst, testifying always to the superior power of God.

A frequently noted strength of the *christus victor* theory of atonement is that it is honest about naming the presence of evil in the world for what it is, being clear that it is not something that will simply *go away* without intervention. For this reason, liberation theologians often resonate with it, emphasizing that the work of atonement is "ongoing."[62] The *christus victor* theory is reflected, for example, in Peruvian theologian Gustavo Gutiérrez's comment:

> Redemption implies a direct relation to sin, and sin—the breach of friendship with God and others—is a human, social, and historical reality which originates in a socially and historically situated freedom. . . . Sin demands a radical liberation, which in turn necessarily implies a political liberation.[63]

A strength of *christus victor* is that, in unabashedly naming sin, it can support dynamics of change. Transformation can only occur if sin and/or oppression is identified; once we identify it, we can repent of it, disarm it, and work to put in place personal and institutional structures that are consistent with the salvation we claim.

In many mainline Christian denominations in North America, there is not much emphasis on *christus victor*. There are at least three reasons for this. First, *christus victor* is often thought to compromise, however unintentionally, on God's sovereignty: If Satan has power that needs to be undermined, and God must act in order to thwart the will of Satan, then God is not all-powerful, but only mostly powerful. To hold that Satan must be attended to is, finally, to reveal that one believes in more than one god, even if Satan is only a lesser power.

Second, as Aulén explains, the benefits of *christus victor* have not been seriously considered in the modern period because we understand this theory of atonement to be too "dramatic" for conservative theological thinkers who thought it did not reflect a "clearly worked-out theological scheme" and was therefore unhelpful. For liberal theologians, Aulén argues, *christus victor* was too "mythological," "grotesque," and "lurid," unable to address, concretely, the realities of life.[64]

Third, there is the concern that *christus victor* is too triumphalistic. To insist that Christ conquers sin and evil can be to deny the reality of sin and pain. The victory of Christ and his followers has too often in history come at the expense of others, as in the case of the Crusades. The victory of Christ and his followers is meaningless and oppressive in the face of heinous crimes such as have occurred, for instance, at Auschwitz, during the Inquisition, in Bosnia, and in Rwanda. To sing "Onward Christian Soldiers"[65] is not, according to this concern, to live our salvation in Christ. It is to use our identification with Christ as a weapon against others.

While liberation theologians often understand *christus victor* to open up the possibility for speaking and acting prophetically against injustice in the hands of the oppressed, they are concerned that it supports imperialism in the hands of the oppressor. For those who are looking for a way out of working to bring God's Kingdom on earth as it is in heaven, *christus victor* can serve as a justification for passivity. This is because, though the threat of Satan is real, the victory of God is still a foregone conclusion. If it is inevitable that God wins in the end, one might reason, why even fight?

Expansive Salvation

How does consideration of these various approaches help us better articulate what it means to be saved, if salvation means living into the abundant life offered to us by Christ? It might be tempting, at this point, to choose our favorite of the three, arguing for why, all things considered, it is the best approach. But I have suggested that we resist the urge to reduce our understanding of atonement to any one theory, believing, as Leanne Van Dyk puts it, that a "range of theories attempts to focus our attention, illuminate the truth, and point beyond themselves to God."[66] As the portrayals of Jesus vary in the four Gospels, each shedding fresh insight on the figure of Jesus Christ, so the various approaches to understanding the atonement challenge us not to become overly confident in our ability to summarize what God has done for us in Jesus Christ. Instead, keeping the three in play can open us to marveling ever-anew at the working of grace, drawing us into deeper participation in the mystery of our salvation.

Thinking of these approaches to atonement in an integrated fashion, then, should not be done in the spirit of trying to harmonize them into a master narrative. Rather, setting them side by side enables us to see what each contributes, and what they all together contribute, to our understanding of our relationship to God.

What all these theories have in common is, of course, that they attempt to elucidate how our salvation is accomplished by way of the life and work of the fully human, fully divine One, Jesus Christ. The starting point of each theory is "The Word became flesh." While Anselm, Abélard, and Irenaeus disagree with how, exactly, the coming of the God-Human saves us, they are in perfect agreement that what God did for us in the work of atonement must also involve a remembering and recognizing of who God is for us in Jesus Christ. As George Hunsinger notes, citing Thomas Torrance, "It is all one indivisible act . . . in one indivisible Person. . . . The atonement is identical with Christ himself. . . . It lives forever in the person of the Mediator. He is the Atonement."[67] When we understand this, we can begin to look at these approaches to the atonement not only as explanations of what God did, but who God is; not only as clues to what we receive, but who we are in relationship to God. The full benefits of grace that are ours in and through the atoning work of Christ are not handed out to us from the windows of the divine being. Rather, through the work of the One who is with us and for us as the Word made flesh, our salvation is our being drawn into the depths of the one who is triune. Atonement theory, understood as grounded in the person of Jesus Christ and communicated by the Holy Spirit, enables us to glimpse the *how* of the reality that we abide in Christ, and he in us.[68] Our lives are, indeed, "hidden with Christ in God"[69] precisely because in Christ, God has acted. These atoning acts of Christ, utterly consistent with the being of the One who loves in freedom,[70] reveal to us that we, through Christ, by the power of the Spirit, participate in the very life of God.

"I don't call you servants any longer, because servants don't know what their master is doing," Jesus says. "Instead, I call you friends, because everything I heard from my Father I have made known to you."[71] The mystery of God's will is revealed to us in the atonement, in the person of Jesus Christ who encounters us by revealing who God is in his actions on our behalf. In him, the Word made flesh, we as flesh live and move and have our being. Because he is one with the Father, we are one with God. Salvation is living in this synchronicity, in this mutual abiding. It is not in claiming the gift that God is handing us—via Christ's death on our behalf—apart from living with Christ, who has entered into death and life with us. It is not in claiming that Jesus is the Messiah, the Son of the living God, and thinking that we know what this means apart from knowing him. And knowing him, again, is knowing his atoning work: the work that reveals who he is because he—as the God who is one of us—always acts in a way consistent with the divine being, bringing us along.

This abiding in Christ and he in us is known in our baptisms—in him we die to sin, are buried, and rise to new life. Apart from our union with Jesus Christ, apart from his entry into human reality with us, atonement theory is meaningless. To understand Jesus Christ as "doing something for us" in the work of atonement is to overlook our salvation; to thank God for coming and dying for us without recognizing that God drew all creaturely existence—in its dismal as well as lively colors—into God's life is to miss that the abundant life *is* our salvation.

The three approaches to atonement theory, in short, reveal to us who God is in relation to us, and who we are in relation to God. In Jesus Christ, we learn that God is for us through what God does for us in the free exercise of God's love. When understood in the context of the incarnational event, both the concern that human beings are replaced by Jesus Christ (critique of Anselm) and the concern that we replace Christ (critique of Abélard) is appeased. Our salvation, realized in and through the incarnate One, is accomplished not only by way of our replacement by Christ, not only by way of representation by Christ, and not only by way of our empowerment by Christ. As a parent's embracing love for a child is manifest in the various roles a parent takes on in relationship to that child (disciplinarian, model, coach, for example), so God in Jesus Christ enters into our reality and exalts us to the very life of the triune God, saving us in a multiplicity of ways.

In his substitutionary role, Christ reveals that God is for us by taking on the burdens that we cannot handle. He does this precisely in order to save us, to free us to engage in "other more important and more happy and more fruitful activities" than being caught up in our own guiltiness.[72] Christ's representative work communicates that we do not live out our salvation as lone rangers, but as members of Christ's body[73] who look to the Author and Perfector of our faith, the One who has gone ahead of us and prepared a way. Practically speaking, to work out our salvation[74] is to pray constantly in the name of the One who has gone before, the One who understands, the One who is never without us, for he has gone into all places, even into Hell. And *christus victor* reminds us that to be redeemed means that God has promised to give us strength for the journey. While *christus victor* has been used to support imperialism, in the life of the saved it must function as a constant critique. As we work our way along the path cleared for us by the Pioneer, *christus victor* reminds us that we are not the victors, for Christ is.

Understanding Christ to be *for* us in the event of the cross cannot remove from it the pain and the violence. The concern of Abélard, feminist theologians, and others that atonement theories promote violence can, however, be more adequately addressed when the three approaches to atonement are held in play. Substitutionary atonement, when seen in relationship to the representational view, argues that we are replaced on the cross precisely so that we can have a place in running the race that is before us.[75] When seen in relation to *christus victor*, substitutionary atonement becomes a prophetic claim that God died on that cross in our place so that we do *not* have to die for our sins or the sins of others. Christ is the victor who dies; we are the disciples who can therefore offer ourselves as *living* sacrifices.[76] To direct a victim to suffer as Christ suffered is to deny our salvation and separate the cross from the incarnation and the resurrection, to see the crucifixion as "something God did" that must be done over and over again because it takes place only in time. On the contrary, the cross is once and for all because it is eternally realized (in the priestly role of Christ) and conquered (in the kingly role of Christ) in the life of the triune God.

Salvation, as the recognition of our redemption, then means this: in relation to our sinfulness, we are replaced; in relation to the course we are called to follow, we are represented; and in relation to the nitty gritty details of the journey itself, we are sustained. Salvation is neither something that is completed (only justification), something to be waited for (only glorification), or something that is in progress (only sanctification). Salvation is not even all of these three, though all three are included. Rather, salvation is living in and with the One who accomplishes it for us and with us, the One who continuously meets us and makes us by way of his life, death, and resurrection.

In the next chapters we turn to what it looks like to live as those who know their salvation in Christ and are consciously claiming the presence and guidance of the Holy Spirit, in the context of the community of faith, to guide them in their spiritual growth, their work, their relationships, and their life-shaping decisions. The God who has met us in creation and incarnation not only continues to make us anew, but promises to bless us all along the way, even as we struggle to interpret and negotiate the many ambiguities that characterize our world. How do we "hold faith," in the real world of our daily lives, as those who remember, together, the reality of our salvation?

Part Four

God Blesses Us

Chapter Seven
Where Is Our Home?

The Doctrine of the Church

The Blessing of the Spirit; the Blessings of the Church

Christianity teaches that the God who meets us and makes us also blesses us. The blessings of God are often associated with the nurturing, sustaining, and sanctifying work of the Holy Spirit, who fosters our joyful awareness of our salvation so that our lives might be transformed accordingly. The Holy Spirit might move in anyone, anywhere, at any time, but is never anyone's personal possession. The Bible and the creeds of the church testify that the Spirit who—like the wind—"blows wherever it wishes"[1] is also reliable and consistent, showing up when the people of God gather and watching over them even when they are too disillusioned, or frightened, or skeptical to hold faith. Where the Spirit is present in the context of a community of believers, there we find the church.

Of all the analogies I think of when I think of the church, the one that stands out is a bit dangerous: I think of church as "home." The reason the analogy is dangerous is, as so many in our culture are pointing out today, because the church more often than not falls short of being the safe and nurturing place it promises to be and that people hope it will be. Given this, a good argument might be made for setting the metaphor of "home" to the side and lowering expectations for what church has to offer. Then, perhaps, people of faith would be less likely to be labeled hypocrites when church communities don't deliver.

I vote for a different approach: calling the church "home"—even when the term doesn't quite fit, descriptively—as a way of naming, and holding to account, what the church is called to be. Just as we do not always live and act as who we are in Christ, so the church too falls short of who it is and will be, as the bride lifted up, holy and without blemish,[2] by the bridegroom, Christ.[3]

My pastor friend, Laura, models holding the church to the highest ideal and working to make it so. At the beginning of every church service at which she preaches and presides she leads a procession of youth down the center aisle. Each carries something essential not only to what will happen in the service to follow, but to the identity and for the comfort of every person in the room. There is a huge pitcher of water almost too heavy to carry, a freshly baked loaf of bread, a beautiful flask full of wine, a been-there-since-the-church-was-founded Bible with a musty, leathery smell and fancy type, and candles that are hard to light and drip all over the place, but that everyone always likes. She places the Bible in the pulpit and lights the candles, heaving the pitcher up and pouring the water splashily into the font; she arranges the elements on the beautifully laid-out Communion Table. Then she takes a big loaf of bread, breaks it in half, extends her arms to the people of God with half a loaf in each hand, and says—with a huge smile on her face—"Welcome home!"

The Church as Home

"Home is where your heart is," the saying goes. Most of us agree with this statement, I bet. Even when we work hard to make our houses or apartments comfortable, safe, accessible, warm and hospitable, we know our home isn't, finally, the actual building we live in. What makes for a home is the community we call our own. A place, as the old *Cheers* sitcom celebrates, "where everybody knows your name."[4] A place where people who know you "warts and all" not only love you, but believe you have a God-given purpose in this world and insist on helping you discover and embrace it. A home is a place where you are met by those who love you and made more into who you are, in and through relationship with them.

Sometimes children seem to understand what a home is better than adults. I had a friend who discovered this in the context of doing a children's sermon, as part of the regular Sunday morning worship service, on the subject of "church." He told me his plan the night before: he would start off with an old favorite: "Fold your hands like this," he would say, interlocking his fingers and turning his palms downward, with knuckles facing up. "Now, put the tips of your index fingers together to make a point. There you go. 'Here is the church; here is the steeple.' Good. Now, keep your fingers locked together but turn them palm-side up. Pull your thumbs apart. Now wiggle your fingers back and forth. That's it! 'Here's the church, here's the steeple. Open the door and see all the people!'"[5] His plan was to then ask the children what he thought was a fail-proof transition question to his fresh, new take: "Kids," he would say, "what is the church?" And then he would sit back, waiting for them to give the answer he was sure they would give. "The church is this building we are sitting in," they would say, he thought. "The church is the place we come to for Sunday school and worship." My friend's plan was, then, to lean in, in good pastorly fashion, and gently explain to the kids that, though this answer was good, the church is even more than the place we go for Sunday school and worship. It is, he would tell them—and at this point he would add extra emphasis—*the people of God.*

"What is the church?" my friend asked, on the prescribed Sunday morning. And immediately a very little girl chimed out her answer. "The church is the community of believers!" she proclaimed. "That's right," my friend responded, clearly surprised and at a loss for what to say next. "But did you know some people think it is the *building*?" he finally said.

Often it is adults, even more than children, who strongly associate church with bricks and mortar, walls and ceilings—even to the point of identifying the buildings, instead of the people, as "home." When neighborhoods change or congregations shift, suggesting that a move to a new location or smaller building would be in order, some of us would risk our church slowly dying off rather than relocating. Maybe this is because we feel sure, rightly or wrongly, that a move to a new building would mean the certain and sudden death of what we hold dear. We want to perpetuate for as long as possible all the life that has happened in that building, all the resources we have invested. We also associate buildings with our desire to increase church membership, organizing capital campaigns that emphasize additions or improvements to the brick-and-mortar that bank on a kind of "if we build it, they will come"[6] philosophy. Budgets and stewardship campaigns are pitched in relation to what we dream of building or what we have already built that must be paid off. It can be helpful to the growth of a church and the sustaining of the people of God, of course, to add an education wing or to make the sanctuary more hospitable. It is perhaps too often the case, however, that improvements in programming and staffing or efforts to reach out to those in need are sacrificed for the sake of buying bricks and mortar.

New church initiatives often name the problem with over-associating church with buildings. Internet churches[7] and other new church communities,[8] for example, actively remember that the first communities of believers generally gathered in homes, pooling their talents, food, and other resources as they celebrated and shared the good news of Jesus Christ. They don't want to be bogged down by raising money for building projects or by paying off building debt, which they view as taking away from more important aspects of their ministry, such as caring for their membership and ministering to people outside the walls of their meeting space.

To share one anecdote, along these lines: Several years ago, I learned a great deal from a brief visit with the pastoral staff of an internet-based church. While I suppose we could have had our meeting online, in a chat room or as avatars interacting with one another, we actually met face-to-face in a plain, square, inexpensive-to-maintain building they affectionately referred to as the "God-box." The staff explained to me that their church had members from all over the world, and that they were joined together as one local community by way of their shared participation in a common worship service, posted weekly online (along with Bible studies, inspirational videos, and other resources).

"Why this building, then?" I asked them.

"We've found," they said, "that some people want to worship with others instead of home, by themselves, on their computers. So, the church helps interested groups of people buy cheap buildings that people can go to worship together. They sit together in the 'Assembly Room' and we project the service on a big screen."

We visited the Assembly Room. It seated about six hundred. "How many people do you get every week?" I asked.

"About 2,100," they said.

"Wow, that's a lot!" I replied. And then I added, reflexively, "You must be looking for a bigger building."

They got me on that one.

"Oh—no ma'am," they said. "We aren't interested in bigger buildings. We're interested in people. What we do is offer multiple worship experiences so we can accommodate everyone. Everyone is participating in the exact same service, regardless of whether they come here or if they are worshipping at home. This is because they are all hearing the same sermon, music, and prayers—except at different times."

I confess that I did challenge their idea that worship is the same regardless of whether you worship with others or not, for reasons I will expand on as this chapter unfolds. But mainly I left the meeting feeling less like I had offered them something from my store of theological wisdom and more like they had extended to me a productive challenge. Quit putting so much emphasis on buildings and put it on people instead, they were telling me. And in telling me this, they were building on a truth that we shared, a truth that all Christians claim to believe—the truth that was stated by the little girl at the children's sermon. The truth is this: that the church is the "community of believers," disciples gathered in one way or another; in one place or another; rather than in a certain kind of building with a steeple.

The Church Expanded

Many Christians today might be quick to suggest we need to be careful not to reduce church to "buildings"; we also should avoid defining "believers" too narrowly. Traditionally, a "believer" is someone who confesses faith in Jesus Christ as "Lord." Such a person would be identified by Calvin as part of the *visible church*, and by Gutiérrez as a member of the *ekklesia*. But both Calvin and Gutiérrez insist there are those who are not currently confessing "Jesus as Lord" who should still be considered part of the Christian community. Calvin talks about the *invisible church*, along these lines, arguing that the invisible church includes those who are chosen by God but have not yet come to recognize this. He thinks Christians should treat everyone as though they are elect, since you never know in whom God has planted a "seed" of faith.[9] Gutiérrez argues, similarly, that the church is present wherever the Holy Spirit is at work. When a person gives a cold cup of water to someone who is thirsty, the Spirit is present even if that person has not made a confession of faith. Gutiérrez calls the church in this broader sense the *koinonia* (meaning "fellowship"), in contrast to the *ekklesia*.[10]

While Calvin understands the invisible church to be the context in which confessing Christians do the work of evangelism, Gutiérrez holds that the *koinonia* often offers a corrective to the *ekklesia*, acting as the "true church" in relation to the church that is a corrupted institution. In short, while Calvin thinks the church evangelizes the world that is the home of the invisible church, Gutiérrez thinks the world (as *koinonia*) often evangelizes the church.[11]

Church, Technology, and Changing Understandings of Community

How we conceptualize what constitutes a church community has always been shaped by the way we understand the relationship of the worshipping community to the movement of the Holy Spirit in the world at large. These days, notions of what constitutes church continue to be broadened by changing understandings of "community" in our globalized, connected, twenty-first-century world. In recent times, social media has made possible the formation, maintenance, and nurture of communities never before possible, comprising people located in multiple places and time zones. Fifty years ago in the United States, when friends and relatives moved across the country from one another, the avenues for keeping up their relationships were limited to investing in expensive long-distance calls, writing letters that took several days to deliver, and making sporadic visits. This was, of course, in many ways an improvement on the possibilities of 150 years ago, when there were no cars, planes, or telephones and it took eighty-three hours to travel by train from New York City to San Francisco.[12] Today, in a world in which more people have cell phones than toilets,[13] it is possible for the first time in history to talk and text for hours on end every day, send pictures, or even put out-of-state (or country) grandparents on Facetime so they can be present at their granddaughter's fifth-grade awards ceremony.

As we are all aware, however, a live and hotly debated question in contemporary American culture is whether we actually *do* use our technology to maintain and deepen relationships. Anecdotally, we often hear people grumble that they don't have any desire to go on Facebook to find out what everyone ate for lunch. The suggestion, of course, is that social media interactions promote superficiality rather than relational depth. While those who value the ways social media have helped them keep up with friends far and wide will understandably push back against this stereotype, surely they will agree that texting does becomes a problem when it interferes with having meaningful, face-to-face conversations with those in physical proximity. It is safe to say that few people actually think it is a great idea to text one's date from across the table in a restaurant, instead of actually talking.

If we stereotype social media users as not caring about community and never having relationships with any depth without opening ourselves to genuine consideration of their views, we may well miss out on learning how understandings of "community" are shifting and expanding. I can't help but wonder if our disparaging stereotyping stems from fears about these shifts and feeling threatened by how committed to keeping up with others many Facebook users actually are. The fact is, social media users care *so much* about their communities that they carry them around with them—in their pockets and purses; on their iPhones, tablets, and laptops. And they nurture them constantly, feeding them "likes" and life updates and photos.[14]

Again, there are both up and down sides to this. Twenty years ago, as a professor, I could assume that students coming into my classroom were committed to investing in the community of the class, at least for the hour and twenty minutes, twice a week, that they were there. Now I can make no such assumption. Students come into class with Facebook running, and it becomes my job (whether I want it or feel it should be or not) to make a case for why they should privilege the possibility of a classroom community (which will exist, as such, for twelve weeks at three hours per week) over the established community of Facebook friends (which they have been building for years). It is by no means obvious to everyone who is walking through the classroom door, smiling down at whatever screen they are monitoring, that Facebook is a more superficial context for developing relationships. Questions I ask myself, especially right at the start of a new theology class, are: How do I make a theological case for why students should invest in this particular community? Why should they attend to the people in the room—listening to what others have to say and vulnerably sharing their own stories? Why should they risk setting their expectations high, hoping that something can happen in those thirty-six hours that is not only about meeting course requirements and getting a good grade, but also developing the kind of deep relational connections that lead to formation and transformation?

Perhaps you would point out that there is more reason to invest in the church than the classroom, given that there are not the same kinds of time constraints at church. Also, while a classroom can function quite efficiently even with students who have not signed up for transformation, this might not be quite as true of church, where the expectation of transformation, while not a requirement, is hopefully not considered alien or intrusive. And yet church leaders, too, work hard to make a case for investment in community, particularly in the United States, these days, when membership is on the decline. What kinds of promises can we honestly make about church that might lead folks to invest? Here are some pitches I've seen on church billboards along the way (I bet you can add to the list): "We Are a Friendly Church!"; "Imperfect People Welcome!"; "Doubters Welcome!"; "Church isn't church without 'u'!"; "Free Coffee* and Fellowship (*we serve Starbucks)!"; "There Are Some Questions That Can't Be Answered by Google"; "Don't Ignore God's Friend Request"; and "Blah blah blah. Just come to church." In these days of declining memberships, religious leaders are scrambling to convince folks that church communities are worth investing in. There are conflicting sentiments about what is needed, in marketing the church, and where we have crossed the line from extending invitations and treating the church more as a commodity to be sold than a community in which to participate.[15]

One arena in which different understandings of how to go about inviting others into the community of the church are showcased is in debates about whether entering into membership is still a valuable rite of passage into the community. There are always those who cannot understand why so many are resistant to joining, telling stories about how many years they have been members and how meaningful membership has been to them. But there are others who think it is not at all obvious they should become members of a church, even if they are involved in one. Some seem open to being convinced, but when they ask *why* they should become members, they are not given convincing answers. Often, they are told membership is a mark of commitment. But when they look at who seems most involved, there is not always a correlation between membership and involvement, or even membership and giving. Sometimes the most active members of church communities are, in fact, non-members. My pastor friends often share with me the ways in which this can interfere with the functioning of churches. For example, how do you know who to send the pledge cards to, they ask, if you don't have an accurate roster of those who have publicly committed to extending their support (i.e., when they officially and before the congregation became members)? One pastor friend told me he couldn't have the committee of elders he wants to have because his denomination allows only members to serve in this capacity. His most invested and gifted participants in the community, in other words, are not allowed to take on the very leadership roles for which they are most suited. He got around the problem by forming a "Vision Team" of non-members that meets regularly to brainstorm ideas with him. The pastor meets once a month with the elders, and once a month with the vision team.

There is certainly a place for grieving the losses to community associated with our social-media focused culture. It is also important to name its limits—a Skyped meeting is not as effective as a face-to-face meeting, and when everyone is only half invested in the important deliberations going on in a conference call because they are surreptitiously typing emails or cleaning Cheerios out from under the couch cushions, it might possibly have been better to have no meeting at all.[16] That said, we can't ignore how helpful technology is for those who are not trying to shortcut their participation, but are rather working to keep their place in the community. Reflecting on church, in this regard, isn't it wonderful that people who are unable to get their bodies to Sunday morning worship due to illness or work commitments may tune into a service online rather than missing out altogether?

The Church and Bodies

"Can my avatar take communion?"[17] is a newer question related to who is invited to the Table. Can you have Christian community without bread? Without wine or juice? Without bodies?

Historically speaking, the church has not imagined such a thing until recently. It has always been in the business of gathering together actual bodies. We bring our bodies to church to sing, pray, listen, see, eat. The sacraments of baptism and the Lord's Supper use the basic stuff needed for bodily existence: water, bread, wine. In churches people join their bodies together in marriage; into churches we carry the bodies of our beloved ones, hoping for resurrection. Social media has not yet usurped the church's work of building communities made up of bodies.

That said, we do need to acknowledge that some people now go to church online. It is possible, for example, to create an avatar of oneself and to enter into the life of a virtual church community. One fifty(ish)-year-old pastor friend of mine recently shared that he himself is a member of a virtual church. He shares that the conversations he has, as an avatar with other avatars, are more authentic than most conversations he has—in physical church—with people whose real live bodies can be seen, touched, smelled, and embraced. My friend testifies that the church community he has joined online is in many ways more of a community than the physical church he still feels obligated to attend.

I'm not sure what to say about this. On the one hand, I'm glad my friend is finding community online, since I can tell this is meaningful to him. On the other hand, though, there is something about bodies that cannot be indefinitely left out. Something about living and breathing bodies, breaking bread together and stepping on each other's toes. What is it about actual bodies that is—or at least should be—so important to community? Maybe it's that we *are* bodies, and can therefore be fully known to one another only *as* bodies.

The Lord's Table is a locus, in church, where bodies are front and center. The body and blood of the ascended[18] Jesus Christ are at the center of everything that happens, reminding us that Jesus Christ is "bone of our bones and flesh of our flesh."[19] And as if this isn't strange enough, we *eat* Christ's body, and *drink* his blood. It's no wonder that Christians in the early church were sometimes accused of being cannibals! Even we who know better than to make such an accusation are little put off by the intimate, boundary-less treatment of bodies around the Table. Perhaps it seems somehow sacrilegious to do too much chewing and gulping, which is why, I am sure, it is so often the case that only very small cubes of bread and only a few drops of grape juice are served. Some might even imagine it is more pious not to chew the bread at all, but simply to swallow it.

There is a christological heresy that is relevant here. It is the aforementioned heresy of docetism—the idea that Jesus was divine, but not really and truly human. In contradiction to the Chalcedonian Statement (see ch. 3), docetism thinks of Jesus's humanity not as something true to who he is, but as a disguise he put on to cover up his divinity as he made his way through life and ministry. To try not to chew the communion bread, as though it is not actually bread, is actually a way of denying the humanity of God in Jesus Christ. It is, however inadvertently, a way of resisting the Christian confession that the Word was made flesh, that God is with us in the ordinary aspects of our days, and that our daily meals can actually facilitate our participation in Christ. When we believe God is with us, we can see the beautiful things in ordinary creation as holy. We tear off a big chunk of that bread—taking several bites, chewing and swallowing, remembering that Jesus Christ walked as a human being through history, died in body on the cross, and rose embodied from the grave. To have something to chew and swallow is always a great blessing to us creatures who need food in order to stay alive, but it is a particular means of grace on those occasions when we have trouble believing. All we have to do is chew, and swallow. These things we can usually do, even on days when we feel empty of faith. And doing these things, the communion liturgy reminds us, leads to our hearts being lifted up by the power of the Holy Spirit at work through the shared meal. Indeed, I have known more than one person who thought they had lost their hold on faith who found healing via the simple but profound gestures of eating and drinking at the Table of Christ.

The sacrament of baptism also deals intimately with bodies. It is a bath that washes away the dirt and stains (and in front of members of the community, who serve as witnesses) even as our new life in Christ is announced. I had a teacher in seminary who told us again and again that when we became ministers and baptized we should "always use a lot of water" and "make sure it is cold." "When you baptize a baby," he used to say, "crying is a good sign, not something to be avoided." My teacher's point was that making use of the blessing of ordinary cold water would have an extraordinary impact, heightening our awareness that something life- and world-changing happens every time a person is baptized.

The Church as One Community among Many

For better and for worse, technologies make it possible for us to avoid leaving one community for another, and to continue developing communities even of people who have never seen each other face-to-face, and perhaps don't even aspire ever to have such a meeting. If we cannot participate physically, we can at least be present virtually, and that's better than nothing. The problem is, of course, there is a limit to how many communities we can invest in—isn't there?

Thinking about this, I counted up the number of communities I consider myself to be part of and that regularly ask me to contribute service hours or (more commonly) financially. I did *not count* the couple dozen organizations that, in my view, are simply trying to lure me to donate because they know I care about their cause. My initial count is: five institutions of higher learning, eight schools and clubs my kids have participated in, and at least fifteen churches and church-related missions/outreaches in which I have had some kind of direct involvement. (My guess is that there are many of you, reading this, who would run similar numbers.) All claim to identify me as a member of their community, and seem to share resources with me as well as to request donations. But it is, frankly, impossible for me to give, financially, to every one of these communities—and even more impossible for me to invest in each of them the kind of time and life energy it would take to benefit from the resources they are extending to me.

Given the reality that finite beings do not have unlimited time and resources, I wonder: If a person has ten hours of time a week to invest in communities other than family or workplace,[20] how many of these hours should be committed to the church? If someone commits to donating 10 percent[21] of their income to charity, what percentage of that money should be given to the church? What theological argument would we make to support whatever answers we give to these questions? How is social media reshaping the ways we think about stewardship?

People who were invested in church communities in the United States back in the 1950s, 1960s, and 1970s yearn for the glory days when people were not continuously moving in and out of multiple communities, but settled into the communal life of a particular church. Gone is the time, it seems, when a family might go over to "the church on the corner" on several occasions a week—for worship, youth group, choir rehearsal, a meeting, a potluck supper. Who has time for that, today—we often reflect—with myriad communities making demands on our time and other resources?

People of faith recognize there is work to be done to figure out what it means, these days, to think of the church as a community of believers. What exactly is the nature of church community in this day when people are likely to invest a great deal of time, share the tough and joyous events of their lives, or agree to be mutually accountable for living holy lives before God? And is it hazardous to call the church a "community of believers" if we want to be sure to include people who do not believe—skeptics, seekers, partners, visitors, spouses?[22] The desire to honor both inclusivity and particular identity in our thinking about church is an admirable one, but at some point these values might come into irreconcilable conflict.

Church as Community of Believers *and* Seekers

Perhaps we should understand the church not only as a community of believers, but also as a community of faithful seekers. Understood as "the community of believers and seekers," the church would be composed, then, of those who affirm God's claim on them and those who, as yet, do not; of those who have already been baptized and those who have yet to be baptized; of those who express strong convictions about what they believe and those who are more skeptical; of those who have the "great faith" of the Canaanite woman[23] and those who, like Nicodemus, have difficulty signing on but who keep showing up.

To think of those who are not yet baptized joining with those who are to together form the community called "church" will understandably raise the eyebrows of some. Baptism has traditionally been seen as the rite of entry *into* the church. This is true in the case of both infant baptism and believers' baptism,[24] despite how much disagreement there is about which practice is more faithful. When infant baptism is practiced, there is often a declaration made, at the time of baptism, that the child has officially become a member of the church community. When believers' baptism is practiced, there is often mention made that the angels are now rejoicing, for the person has joined the church universal. While it is certainly the case that baptism marks the entry of individuals into the church, the point of it shouldn't be to set up an exclusive club or leave others behind. Those who are not yet baptized are invited to join the celebration the way guests join in celebrating the love of those who are being wed. The guests in the wedding are not left out, but what they experience is different than what is experienced by the couple getting married.

What Makes Church

This is not the first time in history we have struggled to figure out what constitutes "the church," even if our current challenges are shaped, in unprecedented ways, by access to transportation, ubiquitous cell phones, and social media. In the sixteenth-century church reformers re-thought the traditional *four marks of the church*, as they were confessed in the Nicene Creed,[25] because they were concerned that the Roman church of the day was invoking them in ways that detracted from recognizing the church as a concrete entity that exists in this world. The church is, as the Creed says: (1) one, (2) holy, (3) catholic ("universal"), and (4) apostolic, but it is seen and experienced "visibly" in this world, Calvin says, wherever and whenever "the Word is proclaimed and the sacraments rightly administered."[26] People of faith therefore can have confidence, when they go to worship and interact with members of a worshipping community, that—even when it is difficult to see the four marks in evidence—they are participating in the real thing, "true religion,"[27] the body of Christ.

As was mentioned in the introduction, in the context of discussing the increase in the number of people in the United States today who do not affiliate with any religious tradition, one of the most common criticisms of church communities is that they feel fake or hypocritical. Christians present themselves as having superlative values such as unconditional love, a forgiving spirit, and acceptance of all, yet the actual people *in* a church, on any given day, might act quite unloving, unforgiving, and unaccepting. The Reformers abhorred ecclesiastical docetism, insisting the community is real even when it harbors bad behaviors and even when its claimed identity seems distant from its on-the-ground life. By this they in no way meant to excuse incongruities, but rather wanted people to be able to lean into and see the beauty and possibilities for this world, a world that is more than a placeholder for what will someday come. The church is, they thought, a flesh-and-blood real-world community of struggling, hopeful people who confess belief in Jesus Christ, who repent of their sins, who together seek understanding of what it means to be "one, holy, catholic, and apostolic," and who do these things concretely, by gathering to hear the Word and by partaking in the sacraments of baptism and the Lord's Supper.

Made up of "come as you are" people of hope, the church is an unusual place insofar as it claims us at one and the same time as sinners who are still in the process of working out our salvation and righteous ones who are already made whole in Christ. Church is not like the workplace, where we likely feel pressure to cover up or justify our sins and even our mistakes for the sake of avoiding litigation or ensuring our success. Nor is it like the proverbial after-hours hangout spot, where we join up with friends to vent our frustrations and, possibly, overindulge in ways that do not represent the better part of ourselves. The church, ideally, is a place where we are at one and the same time embraced as exactly as who we are and challenged to be the new creations God has made us.[28] Again, this dialectic between acceptance and challenge is reminiscent of what we hope for from any home; to be a member of such a household is, in itself, one of the greatest of all blessings.

And then come the blessings upon blessing. When we participate in a church where we are accepted and challenged, benefits[29] are extended that minister to us in the current moment of our living and actively draw us to participate more deeply in relationship to God, through Christ, by the power of the Spirit. Through worshipping God, confessing our sin, listening to the sermon, praying for ourselves and others, affirming our faith, partaking of the sacraments, and being sent forth into the world, we have the invitation, opportunity, and support to practice being who we believe we truly are in Christ. God blesses us through the church with the resources we need to "work out" our salvation so we can know—and live out—the "good, acceptable, and perfect will of God."[30]

Where God Is Worshipped

The church is where God is regularly worshipped in the context of Christian community. The people of God gather on Sunday morning or at some other point during the week and focus their attention away from themselves and on the majesty of the God who made them. Sometimes, the Decalogue (Ten Commandments) is read as a celebration of the goodness of God's Law. As disciples forgiven for breaking the law, those gathered for worship are now free to obey it,[31] believing it is so beautiful and true that it can help us imagine, and step into, the Kingdom God so desires.[32]

Often, a hymn of praise is sung to begin the worship service. The presence of the Holy Spirit is invoked, even though Christians understand the Holy Spirit already to be in some sense the one who has gathered[33] the people together and is hosting the entire event. The invocation serves to orient worshippers toward the reality of God's power and blessings they believe already surrounds them but they desire better to perceive. "Spirit of the Living God, fall afresh on me," worshippers sing,[34] wanting to be open to whatever transformation God has in store for them as they listen for God's Word and participate in the sacramental rites.

Worship takes place in the church, and the church is also present wherever worship takes place. If someone is out on a hike, "meditating" on the "wondrous works" of God,[35] they might well be the only human being on the trail. Still, they are not worshipping alone. Standing in wonderment in the "theatre of God's glory,"[36] they are in company with the great *communion of saints* who are worshipping 24/7 before the throne of God. Any one of us and any particular congregation or worshipping community in any given instant might join explicitly in this ongoing worship, but we are part of it even when we are not worshipping—even when we cannot pray, sing, listen, wonder, or chew. And when we do engage in worship, we represent brothers and sisters who might not on that occasion be locally present, but to whom we are nonetheless joined, as members of our shared community, by the power of the Holy Spirit who makes us one. The whole church is, therefore, included in the worship of any one person or any particular congregation, and the worship of one never takes place apart from the whole.

Where Sins Are Confessed and Forgiven

The church is where sins are confessed and the forgiveness of God is declared. It is also the place where we recommit to living in forgiving relationship to one another. While Christians from different traditions order worship differently, it is common practice to include a prayer of confession and *assurance of pardon* (or *declaration of forgiveness*) in the earlier parts of the worship service. This is no accident. A benefit of confessing sins at the beginning of the worship service is that confessors who have been reminded they have been justified in Christ will continue in worship as those who have been reoriented: they can see themselves, again, as God sees them. They are prepared, now, to receive the blessings that will subsequently flow. When the minister assures the people of God that their "sins are forgiven," the way is clear for worshippers to be the new creations they are;[37] to hear God's new Word, to be strengthened anew at the Table; to participate in God's vision for a new heaven and a new earth.

Confession and forgiveness of sins are meant to be regular practices in the life of the church, according to the third article (third part) of the Apostles' Creed. Here, the Creed testifies to the reality of "the Holy Spirit, the holy catholic church, the communion of saints, the forgiveness of sins, the resurrection of the body, and the life everlasting." If we had the idea that God is the one who brokers all forgiveness on our behalf and think to ourselves that this is a good thing, too, since we would never ourselves be capable of it, we had better take another look. Certainly, forgiveness is the work of God. But it is also our work, to be accomplished in the context of our home, the church.[38]

One of the reasons we get nervous about promoting forgiveness in the life of the church is because the doctrine of forgiveness has too often been leveraged in ways that have done harm rather than promoting healing. When a survivor of abuse is pressured to "forgive and forget," for example, this causes further brokenness to the person who has already been sinned against. It also harms the entire community, and is probably indicative of the fact that the church is trying to avoid getting involved in the work of restoration. But getting involved is the responsibility of all members of the household. Jesus is clear that the burden of forgiveness, in the context of the church, should not lie on the person who has been harmed, but rather on the community as a whole. Forgiveness, as he talks about it in the Gospels, is more of a dynamic process than a punctiliar action directed by one to another.

In the Gospel of Matthew, for example, Jesus tells the story of a king who forgives a servant a debt too great to fathom.[39] But then the servant demands a fellow servant pay back to him a much smaller debt. When still other servants in the community witness the first servant's treatment of the second, they report what has happened to the king. The king reacts by throwing the first servant in jail until he can pay back what he owes.

This parable is rich and worthy of close examination, as we work to formulate a theological understanding of forgiveness that serves to heal in the context of the church community. Notice that the participation of every character in the community of the story is necessary to the dynamic of forgiveness. Forgiveness is not up to the king alone. It is not enough that he forgives the debt of the first servant—forgiveness also requires that the first servant "step in" to what the king has done. Without the participation of the servant, the dynamic is incomplete; forgiveness has not yet occurred.

The community of servants that witnesses the bad behavior of the first servant is also essential to the dynamic of forgiveness. It is only because they are paying attention to what is going on around them and have a heart for the marginalized that they spot the unmerciful act of the first servant toward the second. They take the risk of being told to mind their own business; they go and tell the king. This shows us once again that forgiveness is not something that is the responsibility only of the two people we surmise are the most obviously involved. Clearly, it is important, in the life of the community, that we watch out for one another and hold each other to account.

It is also the case that forgiveness, realized in the context of a community, does not at all require us to set justice to the side. On the contrary, the dynamics of forgiveness, properly understood, up the ante on the doing of justice and the loving of mercy. Consider this: in the story, we see that the forgiveness of the king actually changes the responsibility of the first servant to the second. If the king had not forgiven the first servant, what the first servant did to the second would have been okay. But the fact that forgiveness is opened wide to the first servant changes the rules, broadening the scope of mercy and justice. If only he had entered the dynamics of forgiveness, he and his behavior would of have been transformed.

What would churches be like, I wonder, if we all stepped together into the dynamics of forgiveness, forgiving one another as God forgives us? What difference would it make if churches could bring such practices into the life of the world? I suppose the short answer to this is: we would live in reconciled and reconciling relationship to one another, insisting on justice and extending mercy to all.

Where the Word Is Proclaimed

The church is where the Word of God is proclaimed. For Christians who come from "active way" or *kataphatic*[40] traditions, the sermon is often considered the centerpiece of the service. Having opened worship with praise and been forgiven for our sins, we are now ready to listen for what God would like to say to us through the biblical witness. The preacher puts on her spectacles of Scripture and represents the people to whom she is preaching by helping her listeners look through the text at the world God desires to meet, make, and bless. Together the preacher and the people of God witness to where God is present and how God is at work. Where the Word is heard, the people of God are strengthened in their faith and challenged to act for God and on behalf of others.[41]

Where There Is Confirmation and Intercession

The church is where our faith is strengthened and we are upheld in prayer. In the context of the community, the Holy Spirit "confirms" in our hearts and minds that we are the children of God, so that we can live our lives secure in that knowledge.[42] This happens every time we witness a baptism, every time we partake of the bread and cup, and every time we hear or bear witness to the presence of God in our midst.

The church is where prayers of intercession are continuously offered. They are offered for all members, and they are offered for the whole world. As the children of God, we can pray about anything we want, at any time, and God promises to hear. Calvin called prayer, along these lines, the "chief exercise of faith."[43] And even if we cannot pray—if we are too weak, or too doubtful, or too unbelieving, we are still recipients of blessing. The Spirit promises to "intercede with groans and murmurings too deep for words" whenever we are stuck.[44]

Where We Are Bathed

The church is where we are bathed. We are bathed by the water of baptism, in which our old selves are drowned and out of which we emerge to new life in Christ. To remember our baptisms is to live into our identity as children of God. In rituals of *baptismal renewal*, Christian believers remember their baptisms by renouncing evil and recommitting to living lives of discipleship.

Some Christian denominations engage habitually in another kind of bathing: footwashing. Mennonite Christians are among those who hold that footwashing is an ordinance disciples of Jesus are to practice regularly, following Jesus's instruction to wash one another's feet even as he washed the feet of the disciples.[45] There are also Christians who engage the practice of footwashing once a year—on Maundy Thursday. While the waters of baptism identify us as the children of God, the waters of footwashing identify us as servants of one another, joined by our Lord who is Servant of All.

Where We Are Fed

The church is where we are fed with Christ's body and blood. While Christians understand in a variety of ways the relationship between the physical elements we chew and swallow and the actual body and blood of Christ, they agree that the Communion Table at which disciples partake is a place where we remember Christ's life, death, and resurrection and we anticipate the promised Kingdom to come. Just as importantly, the Table is a place where we eat bread and drink wine or juice. Even when we have trouble believing Christ is present, we chew, we swallow, and our "hearts are lifted up . . . to God"[46] by way of these concrete, physical actions. Further, justice is always in evidence at the Table. In a world in which one in nine people are starving,[47] all are fed around the Table. To celebrate the Lord's Supper is in this sense nothing short of a revolutionary act.

Those who care both about inclusivity and Christian identity recognize that these two values often stand in tension in the dynamics of the Table. The pressing question is: Who is the meal prepared for? Historically, many churches have held that the meal is intended for those who are baptized, only. The idea of this is not as much that baptism is a requirement for entry to the meal as that there is a logical order to our life together in Christian community: First, one is baptized into the communion of saints and then, one sups with them and with Jesus around the Table. Because, in our era, we value inclusivity, we are often critical of churches that are thought to "fence" the Table. Some churches, including the United Methodist Church, invite anyone who will to come, believing God might well choose to use the communion meal itself to draw a person to belief.[48] Many churches have pastors who invite to the Table not only those who have been baptized, but also anyone who confesses faith in Christ. In the Presbyterian churches in which I am very involved, there is not any screening to determine who is baptized and who is not, to discern who believes, and who does not. The bread is served to all who come, but this after an invitation is issued to all believers.

I do think the Table is meant for believers, specifically. When Jesus told the disciples to "do this in remembrance of me," he seemed to be assuming that those gathered around the Table would have a vested interest in who he is and his saving work.[49] I also do believe it is possible to set the Table for Christian believers while still being inclusive. Last November I helped make a Thanksgiving dinner for my extended family members, not for everyone in general. I made three kinds of pie so everyone would have their favorite, and I was sure to serve my father's mushrooms and my mother's gravy. The meal was for my family, so I called my family (not anyone else) to the dinner. I like to think that, if someone showed up at the door who wasn't invited, I would pull up a chair and give them a plate. They would partake of the meal, but they would be eating food that was prepared with my family in mind and extended to them. Similarly, when I as a minister preside at the Communion Table, I prepare for and invite those who self-identify as disciples of Christ. But when others come, I encourage the sharing of food, even as I believe Jesus himself would have.

Where We Are Comforted and Exhorted

The church is where we are both comforted and exhorted. We are assured that our sins are forgiven in Jesus Christ. When we are sick or aggrieved we are supported in prayer. In some traditions we might be anointed with oil and experience the laying on of hands. Through these and other practices, members of a church community actively seek the healing action of the Holy Spirit for the bodies and spirits of those who are sick and broken.

As those who are "forgiven, healed, and made whole,"[50] we are charged to live as the children of God we are, obeying God's laws freely and serving one another in love. We are affirmed in our gifts and then challenged to develop and to share them. The church is where all gifts are considered equally essential to the life of the community, but where those called to the ministries of preaching, teaching, or pastoral care might be ordained and charged to the particular work of pastors, elders, and deacons.

Where We Work and Hope

The church is where we work and hope in freedom, remembering that all of our efforts are provisional. In other words, the church has neither the capacity to nor the burden of speaking univocally about God or what God is up to in the world. The church does speak and act, but sometimes makes mistakes, and will never bring the Kingdom of God to earth as it is in heaven on its own. This is a relief and a blessing for the church, which should therefore feel no pressure to be some smaller version of the Messiah—that job's been taken! To remember that we await the coming of the Christ who is absent, to watch and pray and do the work we believe is of God, without the burden of trying to prove we're always right, is a true blessing. And it will be followed up with another. Our efforts might be provisional, but the promise is that they are also essential to the divine work. Thus, when Christ returns again (whatever form that takes) he will turn to the church and say, "Well done, my good and faithful servant."[51] And the church's joy will be complete.[52]

Where We Are Charged and Blessed

The church is the place where we are charged and blessed, sent forth to share the benefits we have received with the world that God so loves. When we are charged, at the end of the worship service to (for example) "do justice, love mercy, and walk humbly with God"[53] we are reminded that the blessings we enjoy as members of the household are not our own personal possessions, but God's gifts to all. What we experience in church is "a parable and a promise to the whole world... a provisional representation of all humanity justified and reconciled to God."[54]

At the end of the Christian worship service, the charge is always followed by a benediction, or blessing. Often it is trinitarian in structure: "May the grace of our Lord Jesus Christ, the love of God, and the communion of the Holy Spirit be with us both now and forever more." The benediction signals that the instruction the church gives us to go out into the world does not serve to "pause" God's presence with us, as if we came to church to be refueled and are now headed out to use up our resources, at which point we will return. On the contrary, this blessing of the church reminds us that God is with us wherever we go, empowering us by way of the Spirit to do the work of Christ's disciples.

The joining of charge to the blessing of Christ's presence is evident throughout the New Testament witness, particularly in Matthew 28, frequently called the "Great Commission." Here, just before Christ's ascension, he commissions the disciples to "go and make disciples of all nations,"[55] immediately assuring them that this work is not to be done in response for God's good gifts, but as an extension of their relationship to him. It is because we have and will always have the blessing of God's presence that we are able to go forth. "And behold I am with you always," Jesus promises, "even unto the end of the age."

In the next chapter we continue discussing the ways God blesses us by considering the doctrine of the Christian life. While this chapter on the church has reflected on the matter of how God blesses us by way of our embodied engagement in the practices of Christian community, the next chapter takes a slightly different and more meditative approach. It reflects on the journey and struggle we have as human beings seeking to live as those we claim to be. It acknowledges how difficult it is to walk through a day, week, or lifetime remembering one's baptism; knowing one is loved; believing one is forgiven. What does it look like, really, to be filled with the Spirit, to abide in Christ, to walk humbly with God? How we live in light of the faith we hold is, for many of us, the most pressing question of all.

Chapter Eight

What Does It Mean to Be God's Children?

The Doctrine of the Christian Life

An Essential Meditation

The tone of this section is a bit different than the other chapters. It is more deliberately contemplative or meditative. If the prior chapter considers how it is that God blesses us by way of the church that is our home, this chapter attends more to the struggle we have to accept and live in cognizance of these blessings, as those who desire to hold faith. It is out of living mindfully, in relation to our faith, that we are then called by God to live and act in the world as people of hope, as we will discuss in the final section of this book.

Barth thought a question that should be "addressed to . . . every theologian" is: "How are things with your heart?"[1] While understanding ourselves as members of the community of believers is crucial to appropriating our identity as God's beloved children, cognizance that we stand "personally" before God should also be nurtured. Each one of us, Barth thought, is the one whom God makes an "'I' by addressing... as a 'Thou.'"[2]

This chapter deals with matters of the heart. But that does not mean it should be treated as an antidote or even a supplement to what comes before or after it. Rather, it explores an essential dimension of what it looks like to live a theological existence.

We begin with a statement and challenge Kathryn Tanner poses at the start of her book, *Jesus, Humanity, and the Trinity*: "In order to witness to and be a disciple of Jesus Christ," she says, "every Christian has to figure out for him or herself what Christianity is all about, what Christianity stands for in the world."[3] Over fifty years earlier the teacher of Tanner's teachers—Karl Barth—had made a similar radical point. Sick and tired of the fact that Christians in Germany baptized their children unthinkingly, as a kind of rite of social passage, Barth had begun advocating for adult baptism. Barth said that infant baptism, as it was practiced in that context, "was one of many symptoms that the church is not alive and bold, that it is afraid to walk on the water like Peter to meet the Lord, and [that it] does not seek a sure foundation but only deceptive props."[4] Barth insisted that, if the emphasis were taken off the baptism of children, "every individual would then have to decide whether he or she wanted to be a Christian."[5]

The language of "decision," "want," and the church "walking on the water... to meet the Lord" might seem quite jarring, coming from a theologian who thinks God, and not humans, initiates and funds every revelatory moment. But Barth was not turning away from a lifetime of commitment to the sovereignty of God, in saying what he did. On the contrary, he recognized that the God known to us in the One who is fully human as well as fully divine includes we who are human in the very act of God's own self-disclosure. The Word is made flesh, and we enfleshed ones—in and through Jesus Christ—are exalted as "genuine subjects" in the revelatory event.[6] Our decisions and our wants in the face of God's living, challenging Word shape the kinds of people we are, and the kinds of communities we form. It is because Barth and his colleagues *decided* to be Christians; because they acted *mindfully*, *intentionally*, and *habitually* in relation to this decision, that there was a Barmen Declaration, a confessing church movement, and a neo-orthodox renewal of the church.

The Christian life, simply put, is life lived before God. It is life lived with the awareness that we are known, claimed, called, and sent by the sovereign God who meets us in Jesus Christ by the power of the Holy Spirit. In this book thus far we have talked about living with the awareness that the God of all things meets us in our creaturely reality, that this God made us and continuously heals and enlivens us, and that this God blesses us in the context of the community of faith, the church. In this chapter, we will consider how God blesses us by shaping in us an awareness of God's presence, salvation, and gifts. We will gain inspiration, along the way, from biblical forebears who also strove and struggled to hold faith, including Nicodemus, Ruth, Orphah, the saints in Rome, the elder brother from the "parable of the prodigal son" in Luke 15, the sheep from Matthew 25, and Mary the mother of Jesus.[7]

How are things with your heart? To be Christians, ideally, is to live as those who truly know God and know ourselves in relation to God. To live the Christian life is to be so transformed by awareness of the reality in which we participate that our gratitude spills over into faithful actions, contributing to the transformation of the world. To live the Christian life is to see ourselves as God sees us: as beloved children God has made and continues to make by the power of the Spirit; as friends declared righteous in Christ who are called to join as partners in the joyful work of reconciliation.[8]

Troubled Awareness

We have spoken candidly throughout this book about the fact that many find holding faith to be challenging. Sometimes it seems, even, an impossibility. And it is difficult not only for skeptics, but for those who have made professions of faith. With Nicodemus, even we who testify to having been "born again" lose sight of our experience of new birth and have difficulty fathoming how we could possibly get from where we are to spiritual renewal. For reasons that may elude us, we are even reticent to engage in practices of faith that we know would be helpful to us, such as Bible study, prayer, and worship participation. How do we get so stuck? What is it that keeps us from being "born again"? What keeps us from living in light of the reality of God's claim on us?

Sometimes I imagine the challenge of Christian life in relation to the metaphor of a swimming pool (which for me is reminiscent of a baptismal font).[9] If the water in the pool represents the reality of God's grace-full presence and salvation, in relation to us, the question is: Why do we spend so much time off to the side of the pool instead of swimming in the water? How do we jump back in, surface, and begin to swim?

Jump? The Risk of Holding Faith

Some of us might be more apt to hold faith if we could simply reach out and take grace without risking a leap into it. As we discussed in chapter 6, discipleship requires we risk putting ourselves to the side in order to see ourselves anew, as God sees us. This poses difficulty for all skeptics who, with Nicodemus, are concerned about taking a leap of faith because they can't know, before they jump, exactly where they will land. I picture Nicodemus, wanting to engage with Jesus, respecting Jesus but feeling a bit irritated with the line of argument being presented. And so he blurts out a sarcastic question: "Can one enter a second time into the mother's womb and be born?"[10] Now, this is obviously *not* a real question. Nicodemus *knows* there will be no climbing back into his mother's womb. He's asking this question in an attempt to gain some strength in the conversation. And Jesus is clearly up for this kind of edgy exchange, having a knack for meeting people where they are. "You're a leader of Israel," Jesus chides Nicodemus, "and still you don't understand these things?"

Sometimes I wish Jesus had been a little easier on Nicodemus. Instead of telling Nicodemus he should "*understand these things*" Jesus could have told Nicodemus he was trying *too hard* to understand. *To be born from above" is a heart thing—not a head thing,* Jesus could have said. *To try to understand the mechanics of it is to undermine the process of being reborn by the Spirit.* Jesus does say that "the spirit blows where it wills."[11] So why doesn't he simply tell Nicodemus to "let go and let God" rather than challenging him to figure it all out?

But Jesus refuses to punt on understanding. He scolds Nicodemus for not understanding practically in the same breath in which he concedes the Spirit's work is not understandable. Jesus is not going to let Nicodemus—or us—get away with hiding behind astonished questions. He wants Nicodemus to get closer to the mystery of God's grace; to dive into it; to revel in that which he cannot manage, that which he cannot track.

Nicodemus will never understand grace, but Jesus wants him to understand something of what God's grace is *about.* And Nicodemus seems interested in this, too, going out of his way to pay Jesus a visit in the middle of the night. A pastor once told me, in a surprised voice, that the members of his congregation "keep coming back... week after week!" Nicodemus and my friend's parishioners both want to know what grace is about, and so do we. But we all find ourselves nitpicking and dissecting rather than actually taking the plunge.

What is it that keeps us from jumping into the pool of God's grace? What is it that makes us climb out even after we've been fully embraced? Little kids just learning to swim have real and understandable fear. Maybe fear is in play for Nicodemus as well—and maybe even for us. After all, the same water that supports us when we float can also, potentially, drown us. And—even if we *do* survive the jump—it is different living wet than living dry. On the outside of the pool, we can be warm, presentable, and self-possessed. We can even doll ourselves up a little and pay a visit to Jesus, sitting across from him and engaging in polite, logical, respectable conversation. There would be no need for sarcasm here, since a Jesus-kept-at-arms-length would never make us feel uncomfortable.

But being born from above—jumping from the known, dry edge into the mysterious deep—requires a conscious letting go of control. To get wet is to be affected. To be "born of the Spirit" is to be melted and molded, not simply tweaked or improved. Nicodemus is not looking to be melted and molded.[12] His spiritual goal seems to be, admirably enough, to "be his best self now."[13] Clearly, Jesus's insistence on the necessity of transformation disturbs Nicodemus. It rocks his boat, so to speak—and he doesn't want to fall into the water.

Surprisingly, Jesus doesn't do anything but exacerbate Nicodemus's discomfort. I mean—as if Jesus's testimony to the mysterious work of the Spirit isn't disconcerting enough—Jesus then starts in on his own relationship to Nicodemus's spiritual quest. It is hard to know what is more decentering: the unchartable blowing of the Spirit or the trackable manifestation of God's love for the world in the historical figure Jesus of Nazareth. "We speak of what we know and we testify to what we have seen," Jesus tells Nicodemus, "and you have not received our testimony." The Son of Man has descended from heaven and will be lifted up—as Moses lifted up the serpent in the wilderness—that all who look upon him will have eternal life.[14] The Kingdom of God is seen in the particular face of Jesus, the Son sent by the God who so loves the world. Nicodemus had to be taken aback even further by these words of Jesus. Can you imagine? You come to Jesus, acknowledging him as a teacher sent by God, and he not only tells you that you must be born again by some unpredictable Spirit, but that he himself is the one through whom the world will be saved.

It is no wonder Nicodemus has trouble getting into the pool. He is sitting there, listening to Jesus, looking over the edge, thinking about what it might be like to jump into the water. The chaotic character of the Spirit is off-putting, but one might be able to gather enough courage to leap anyway and hope for the best. But then there is all this talk about Jesus himself. The unpredictable, unknowable Spirit is joined by the particular, known event of Jesus Christ. And Nicodemus—as I imagine it—moves from not jumping in because he is afraid of the chaos, to not jumping in because he is suddenly offended. *You're telling me,* he might well have said to Jesus, *you're telling me that my way to seeing the Kingdom of God is you? You—specifically?*

I mentioned, in chapter 4, that Kierkegaard uses the startling language of "offense" to describe our reaction to God. He might say it is our *offense* that most often keeps us from jumping into the water of grace.[15] Contemplating the water, we *think* we are offended by what the incarnation says about God. To insinuate that the omnipotent, omnipresent, immutable God who created the universe can be known in a singular event, in a particular person, is scandalous. We think we know what God is like, and God is not a baby squirming in a manger, a man who eats with tax collectors and sinners, a criminal who dies a disgraceful death.

We think we're offended by what the incarnation says about God, Kierkegaard suggests. But what offends us, in fact, is what it says about us. Because if it really is the case that God became flesh because God so loved the world, this means that we matter to God. We are loved by God. We are precious in God's sight. And to be viewed as beloved by God is almost unbearable, given that we so often perceive ourselves as *un*lovable. My offense, like my sarcasm, creates distance between me and my rebirth, between me as I know myself to be and me as I really am in Christ.

It might seem a funny thing to be talking about jumping into a pool of grace, for those who believe they have been claimed by God regardless of their cognizance of this reality. But even Calvin, who emphasized predestination, was a strong advocate of people living with an awareness of their salvation. He thought that *perceiving* we belong to God "in life and in death" was God's earnest desire for us. Contrary to popular stereotypes, Calvin thought the doctrine of election was deeply *reassuring*. Because being born again is the Spirit's doing, and not our own, he thought, we can be confident that we are God's own. Listen again to Calvin's definition of faith, with this in mind: "Faith is the firm and certain knowledge of God's benevolence toward us, founded upon the truth of the freely given promise in Christ, both revealed to our minds and sealed upon our hearts through the Holy Spirit."[16]

So, how is it, exactly, that we make the move from being afraid and offended to taking the plunge? As Christian believers, we should know better than to exhort one another simply to "have faith" and "jump." We cannot be born again on the basis of our own efforts or we would have done so by now. Faith is not something we need a little bit of *in addition to* grace. Rather, faith itself is a *form* of grace. As Karl Barth put it, our belief in Jesus Christ is, actually, a kind of surplus grace—constitutive of the gift itself.[17]

But we would be mistaken if we understood the journey from the edge of the pool into the water to be all about God and not at all about us. We would be forgetting to take into account the particular manifestation of God's love as it has been made known to us, by way of the testimony of the Spirit, in Jesus Christ. Jesus saves us not by becoming a hero who rescues us, but by entering into existence with us and thereby including us in the life and work of God. Our jumping is all God's work and just as completely our own because—in and through Jesus Christ—our work is included *in* God's work.[18] Our lives are "hidden with Christ in God";[19] "everything God has is ours."[20]

And so, Jesus exhorts us, too, to set aside our sarcasm, our distancing questions, our fear, and our offense. He urges us to jump into the water of grace. To remember—anew—that "God so loved the world."[21] To be born "from above." To risk being born—again.

Splash! The Cost of Holding Faith

So we take the leap. But we are not yet wet. Imagine that we have gone over the edge and are about to break the water's surface. By the grace of God we have jumped, and—whether we like it or not—there's really no turning back.

Have you ever experienced a moment of regret just before you hit the surface of the water in a swimming pool? "Oh... no... here we go! It's about to get *really cold*.... And wet. And—well... I didn't even *have* to do this. I know grace is irresistible, but this doesn't mean we have to go overboard—does it? It seems to me I could be standing back on that nice dry edge right now, safe and composed."

To jump into the pool is to risk transformation; to break the surface of the water is to pay an actual price. It costs us something to be born of the Spirit. We were suspicious that we might be getting into something serious, by jumping into the pool. And our suspicions, as it turns out, were right on target. Grace is not cheap for God, and it is not cheap for us. "Love so amazing, so divine, demands our life, our soul, our all."[22] As we hit the water, for just that split second, we know this for sure. The splash represents a moment of urgency; we are about to break through into a new reality. We are about to go under. And so we prepare, as best we can in that fraction of a second, for the dangers we are about to experience. We squeeze our eyes shut; we seal our lips tight. We brace for impact; to be buried underwater; to be cut off from the air that sustains us.

It's hard to imagine a more solid jump than Ruth's pledge in relation to Naomi in the book of Ruth. "Where you go, I will go," Ruth says. "Where you lodge, I will lodge; your people shall be my people, and your God my God. Where you die, I will die—there will I be buried."[23] Now, I recognize that the text does not record Ruth's thoughts and feelings. But I still have to wonder, as a real human being learning from the faith journey of another human being, if Ruth had any second thoughts, however fleeting. I wonder if she woke up the next morning, replaying her speech to Naomi with just a touch of regret. Could she possibly have thought to herself, *Rats! Well—now I've really gone and done it. There's nowhere to go but into that water. Why did I have to be so . . . well . . . definitive?*

Of course, that's the way real commitments are, aren't they? They don't leave a lot of wiggle room. There's no such thing as a three-quarters-of-the-way jump. And so, if we are as righteous as Ruth, we follow through *despite* our emergent doubts.

D. L. Moody once wrote that "the problem with a living sacrifice is that it keeps crawling off the altar."[24] I just love this quote because it is so descriptive of the reality of our spiritual journeys. Of course we have second thoughts even as we make contact with the water of grace, the site of our transformation, the substance of our commitment. We'd be crazy *not* to have second thoughts, given that all things are about to become new—including us. This is why Paul finds it necessary to *appeal* to the justified-by-faith-alone Christians at Rome. "I *appeal* to you...to present your bodies as a living sacrifice,"[25] he says. Splashing into the water will always remain a counterintuitive moment, even for the most graceful among us. It is not easy for us to continue climbing back up onto that altar, because to climb back onto the altar entails a cost.

Ruth seemed well aware that grace, though free, was never cheap. The costs of her commitment were many: she risked never getting married again, which made her both economically and physically vulnerable. She risked living out her life as a stranger in a strange land, as a Moabite living in Judah. And, she risked the unpleasantness of living her life with a "Naomi turned Mara." Who wants to share their days with a bitter mother-in-law who has every reason to be depressed? But Ruth—fully aware of the risks she is taking—goes ahead and makes her countercultural, counter-logical, and counter-ambitious move. She takes the plunge because she is willing to make sacrifices for the sake of her family.

It is usually harder than we think it's going to be to defy the expectations of the world and to be melted and molded by the transforming work of the Spirit.[26] Too often we imagine we are following God's creative leading when, really, all we are doing is perpetuating the status quo, strengthening the empire. Our ambition leads us away from the edge of the pool, away from the risk, toward drier and more manageable terrain. We are actually standing over in the picnic area, over there—next to Orpah (Naomi's other daughter-in-law, who chooses to turn back and go home to her people).[27] We may *think* we respect Ruth's commitments, but really, we are doing so only in a hypothetical sense. In actuality, Orpah is our model; Orpah is clearly better at minimizing loss and managing long-term investments.

It is those of us who are just now splashing down into the water to whom I believe Paul is speaking in Romans chapter 12. He is speaking to those who have been born of the Spirit,[28] those who believe that God is for us in the person of Jesus Christ.[29] And Paul is exhorting us not to pull back from the splash, even if our intuition tells us to. We are to hit that water head-on, offering ourselves as living sacrifices, holy and acceptable to God.[30]

But what does this really mean for us? I think Paul is here speaking with us very candidly about the cost of our new life in Christ. He seems to be giving us the "bottom line"—a "peek" at what things will look like after we've paid off our educational expenses. Holy. Blameless. Hmmmm...what happened to "sinful"? "Well...let me explain that," Paul might say, pulling a mechanical pencil out of his front shirt pocket and circling something on a scrap of paper. "'Sinful identity' is the major thing that has to go. You just can't afford it anymore, now that you've been made righteous in Christ."

Now, of course Paul knows we continue to be sinners even after we've splashed into the pool. What he wants us to give up is claiming our sinfulness as our primary *identity*. He wants us to think about sin more as an aberration than as a given. He wants us to take seriously the fact that transformation entails the *cost* of dying to sin and the *promise* of being made alive again in Jesus Christ. He wants us to present ourselves to God not as sinners, but as "holy and acceptable" living sacrifices.

It's amazing how difficult it is to give up our identity as sinners. It is a huge cost for us to put aside our sins of pride and self-abasement and stand clothed with nothing but the righteousness of Christ, with nothing but *relationship to* Christ. A sinful identity provides more coverage, you see, than a "holy and acceptable" identity. There are, simply, a lot more accessories in the wardrobe of the sinner than the wardrobe of the saint. A lot more protection against getting too carried away with this transformation stuff. A lot more buffer between ourselves and the overpowering claim of God's "good, pleasing, and perfect will."[31]

Who are we, anyway, to even presume we can be holy and blameless? We might ask ourselves this, feeling very pious, even as we hit the water. Surely, one can be wet and still hold on to at least some sins. As we mentioned in the prior section, both the Spirit and Jesus seem interesting in drowning us, if necessary, for the sake of new life. Our sins, you see, could act as life preservers to keep us afloat. Can't you just *see* Paul, with this image in mind: the Christians at Rome *finally* knowing what it's about, grabbing frantically for a way to hold on to parts of their old selves, parts of this world. "Be not conformed to this world,"[32] Paul tries to remind them.

One of the stories I tell that illustrates how we have trouble letting go of our sinful identity is about a former professor at Austin Seminary named James I. McCord. One of the things Dr. McCord was known for was the way he greeted students as he entered the classroom. "Good morning, saints," he would say. "Good afternoon, saints."

Now, I love this greeting, theologically speaking, especially when I reflect on it in tandem with Romans 12. But try it out the next time you lead off a meeting at your church. If your experience is anything like mine, you will find that people will resist answering, laughing and shaking their heads as though the very idea they could be saints is absurd. And it is not only the case that people *don't* think of themselves as saints; they also don't want to. Like I said, the suspicion is that sainthood does not come with enough accessories—what if all you get are one of those thin monk's robes with a cincture?!

How is it that we who are just breaking into the water can put off the urge to grab a life preserver? How can we sacrifice our identity as sinners? The answer is simple, but hard: by trusting Jesus as Lord, and giving up our own lordship. As those who are guilty of the sin of pride, on the one hand, we are still thinking we can somehow manage our entry into the water even after we have taken the leap. We're great with Paul's exhortation to live; we're resistant to being living *sacrifices.* As those guilty of the sin of self-deprecation, on the other hand, we have the opposite problem. We're perfectly willing to be overtaken by the water, to sacrifice ourselves in our unworthiness. What we have trouble with is the idea we are called to be *living* sacrifices. To trust Jesus as Lord, when our sin is self-deprecation, is to recognize that Christ removed from us our very unworthiness. As Barth, again, so well put it, the judge was judged in our place so that we might engage in "other more important and more happy and more fruitful activities" than the judgment of ourselves or others.[33] To know Jesus as Lord is to know the cost of laying down our sinful, prideful, self-abasing identities.

There is another cost as well. An even higher one, especially for those of us who are wealthy, educated, and/or socially well-adjusted. It is the cost that comes with renouncing conformity to this world and being transformed by the renewing of our minds. And just as it is a little nerve-wracking to think about putting aside our sinful identities, so it offends our pious sensibilities to assume *we* can know the "good, and acceptable, and perfect will of God." Talk about presumption, we think, exclaiming (with an air of humility) that *we don't really know* what *God desires* even when we actually have a pretty good idea. Such false humility is, again, a barrier to our transformation. And so Jesus keeps shaking us awake, begging us to pray with him for an hour, beseeching us to join with him in accomplishing the will of God in this world.

The WWJD?[34] movement, for all its faults, seemed genuinely interested in the renewal of Christian life. "Walking the walk, and not just talking the talk" takes the splash, as well as the jump, pretty seriously. It takes into account the costliness of grace.

You might be aware that the WWJD slogan was taken from a book, first published in 1918, titled *In His Steps*.[35] The author of the book was Charles Sheldon, a leader in the social gospel movement of the early twentieth century. In this novel, a town is transformed as a result of all the Christian members of the town asking themselves the question: "What would Jesus do?" and then following through. My only criticism of Sheldon's book is that he makes doing what Jesus would do seem too easy. Sheldon suggests that once we figure out what Jesus would do, it is simply a matter of deciding to obey. But I have a story that illustrates just how difficult the follow through can be.

It was early in the spring semester of a class I used to teach titled "Theological Reflection in Contemporary Society." On the way to class I stopped by my mailbox and found an oval, one-inch WWJD lapel pin that had been sent to me by a religious marketer. The special thing about this pin was that, when you pressed the button under the lettering, a little red light on it would blink on and off.

On a whim, I pinned this thing on my jacket, turned on the blinking light, walked into class, and began to lecture. A few minutes into my lecture, one of my students interrupted to ask why I was wearing that "very annoying" light pin. "What—this?" I asked, with exaggerated surprise. "Why—this is a WWJD pin. Do you have a problem with that?" I then launched into guiding a class discussion that I thought beautifully displayed my brilliant pedagogy. We talked about whether or not we would do what Jesus would do, if and when we knew what it was. Of the twenty-nine students who were there, every single one agreed that, when we *do* know what Jesus would do, we should certainly do it.

I then turned—spontaneously—to what was in that week the hottest Austin news story. You may remember it: Karla Faye Tucker, a convicted murderer and rehabilitated born-again Christian, was due to be executed shortly. There was unbelievable pressure on the governor to commute her sentence, since her rehabilitation seemed real and since she would become the first woman to be executed in the state of Texas.

We took a vote, and twenty-nine of the twenty-nine students agreed that Jesus would *not* execute Karla Faye Tucker.

But then something strange happened. Twenty-seven of the twenty-nine students in the class suddenly reneged on their commitment to do what Jesus would do. They declared that we *should* execute Karla Faye Tucker, arguing that it would be presumptuous to think that we could ever do what Jesus would do. One of these students actually proposed that, in all humility, we wear buttons with a different set of letters: "WWJWUTD"? ("What Would Jesus Want Us To Do?"). Clearly, the student argued, Jesus would want *us* to execute Tucker, even if he wouldn't do it himself. Jesus is at liberty to forgive and extend mercy; we, with our sinful identities in place, can only do the next best thing.

I am telling you this story not to make a case against capital punishment,[36] but because I believe it offers a blatant example of how difficult it is to stay with the transformation process, even for those of us who—by the grace of God—have managed to take the leap. When what we believe contradicts what we think, it is time to leave behind what we "think" as part of the cost. As part of the cost of discipleship. As consistent with the work of grace, which is not cheap, but costly.[37]

"The problem with living sacrifices is that they keep crawling off the altar." Our toes have barely broken the service of the water and already our necks are craned back around, looking toward Orpah. Looking—most commonly—not for debauchery, or gluttony, or titillation. But looking for the most reasonable, practical, marketable, acceptable, and respectable things this world has to offer. When we conform, we generally conform to the very best things of this world—don't we? And it is our Achilles heel to think what we are conforming to is therefore OK, and to defy any of our brothers and sisters to tell us otherwise.

To be perfectly honest: at this point I can hardly wait to get to the next section so I can talk about the happier stuff. Because the jumping in, and especially the splash that follows, is pretty rough. It's the splash that signals burial; it's the splash that is the grueling pain of labor, the cry of dereliction, the death of self. The death of *our* selves. As it turns out, when Paul was making his appeal to the believers at Rome, he was also pleading with us. I'm considering putting a little reminder of this in my own Bible—circling the first two verses of Romans 12 and drawing an arrow to the sentence: "This means you!"

How dare we assume we are Ruth when we are not. How dare we assume we are being somehow transformed when the water has hardly been disturbed, when no sacrifices have been made, when no cost is in evidence. To splash into the water of grace is to let go of such hypocrisy and be renewed with a right spirit. It is to move closer to having a faith-full answer to the essential question, *How are things with your heart?*

Surface: The Promise of Faith

Let's take a look at what some see as a paradigmatic story of the love of God: the so-called parable of the prodigal son, as it is told by Luke.[38] I'm guessing many of us can sympathize with the characters in this story, especially with the elder brother. (This might be because most people who would read a book like this *are* the other brother. Even if you were *once* a prodigal, you are likely an elder child now.)

Elder siblings that we are, we naturally feel guilty. We know, you don't have to tell us—we *should* just go to the party, even if we don't feel like it. We know we need to be more forgiving—like God—and we're working on it. Let's put aside our guilt, for a minute, and take a second look at this character with whom we likely identify. (If you are unfamiliar with this story, you might want to pause and read Luke 15:11-32.)

The elder son makes a pretty good argument, in this passage. He really speaks his mind. While the father clearly has some of the worst boundaries of anyone in the New Testament (in our day we would surely recommend therapy!), the elder son is clear about his expectations and what he wants. The younger brother had received his half of the property no questions asked, with poor consequences to follow. The elder brother feels entitled to at least a party, especially since he has run circles around his younger brother in terms of showing up and taking responsibility.

Many of us probably identify with this elder brother, thinking he makes a pretty good case. Some do argue his question betrays a misunderstanding of inheritance law.[39] But this line of argument seems to miss the point. It's not as though the father could have reminded his older son that the fatted calf was his to give away, and the elder son would have apologized for having been confused about the law, and the problem between them would have been cleared up. The elder son isn't interested in making a technical point about inheritance. He's telling his father how hurt he feels, and how unfairly he believes he's been treated. "Look!" he says. "I've served you all these years, and I never disobeyed your instruction. Yet you've never given me as much as a young goat so I could celebrate with my friends." What the elder son can't swallow is that his irresponsible, wasteful, inconsiderate brother is being thrown a party by his friends while *he* never has. And we, the readers, can't make much sense of this either. I mean—it's one thing to pay a person the same wages for working an hour that you pay someone who has worked for a day. But this situation, from the elder son's perspective, is more like paying the person who worked for an hour a year's salary, and giving the person who has worked for a year nothing at all. In other words, the elder son isn't begrudging his little brother a party as much as he is saying that he wants one too. If the undeserving one gets a party, surely the deserving one should get one.

The father's response is also difficult to understand. "Son, you are always with me, and all that is mine is yours," he says. I continue to struggle with what this means. I used to think that the father was more or less explaining where he was coming from, but without really addressing, directly, his son's complaint. I even wondered if the son's concerns were being minimized, as though knowing that the father's possessions are his is an equivalent alternative to enjoying these possessions in a rip-roaring celebration with friends. Now I wonder if the father might actually be saying that of course his son can have a party. *Did you think you had to wait around for me to give you a goat? I thought you knew that everything that is mine is yours! We can start making plans at any time—just give me the word.*

Regardless of what the father is saying or not saying about a party for the elder son, one thing is clear: these two are on different wavelengths. The son is thinking of his relationship to his father in terms of fair transactions, the father in terms of the sharing of life. The son is operating in accordance with the "order of justice," the father in accordance with the "order of grace."[40] The son is sitting, with a calculator, at the table by the side of the pool. The father is in the pool, yearning for his sons to perceive they are in there with him.

The promise of grace, as we break through the surface of the water, is exactly the father's promise to the elder son: everything God has is ours! In and through Jesus Christ, the one in whom we believed when we jumped, we participate in the very life and work of God. Having splashed into the water and died to our own sinful identities, we rise again to the surface, claiming the new life—and the new selves—God has promised.

The promise is not that we emerge sinless, but that sin no longer has the power to incapacitate us, to keep us from knowing the good, and perfect, and acceptable will of God. Martin Luther explains it this way: he says that *surfacing* Christian believers should "sin boldly, and love God more boldly still."[41] The promise of God is that sin has been dealt with, that to be sinners is to turn away from who we really are in Christ, and that one day sin will be no more. To sin boldly, for Luther, means not that we don't sin, but that sin cannot and will not incapacitate us, if only we enter immediately into the God-given cycle of confession, repentance, and restoration.[42]

In our surfacing, we follow in the pattern of Christ in the great kenotic hymn of Philippians 2. With Christ we have died, and with him we have been raised. This, I believe, is a version of double predestination that makes a little more sense than Calvin's version.[43] He—Christ—is both the reprobate and the elect one. God made Jesus "to be sin who knew no sin so that in him we might become the righteousness of God."[44] In and through him we acknowledge that we are at once both incapable of making any contribution and fully included as essential participants in the divine work.[45]

This is not the way the elder son is thinking about it. He's more practical about his capabilities and contributions than all this. He'd be the ideal employee for writing up an annual self-assessment, wouldn't he? He'd list out everything he had done for that year, and his expectations for how the administration should respond. You can almost imagine him going into his annual review meeting, a coffee cup in hand that reads: *Do your best, and God will take care of the rest.* Or, maybe, he'd modify it a little to: *I'm doing my best, and* my *best is pretty darn good.*

And that's the problem, we might suspect, with the elder son. He's a little too full of himself. He's like that rich man—you know...the one who *says* he has kept all the commandments since the day he was born?[46] (*Oh—come on!* I imagine you are thinking. *You can see that he hasn't. After all—he just lied!*) We might suggest to the rich man that what he needs to do is tone it down a bit. To realize that living a life of obedience is about acknowledging we can do *some* things, but not *all* things. What we need to do, we might advise him, is recognize our unworthiness and humbly trust God might be able to use our meager contribution somewhere along the line.

But that's not really quite right, is it? To emerge from the depths of the water, to live as children of the promise, is not only to believe God will accomplish significantly more than we might expect, and that somehow we will have some small role to play in whatever God is up to. It is, rather, to believe God will accomplish what is utterly impossible, and that we will have essential roles to play in the divine accomplishing. *Just remember,* we might imagine God saying to us elder children. *Remember that you are my child; we live and work together; everything I have is yours.* As it turns out, to be theocentric in our reading of salvation history is not to sideline ourselves in pious recognition that it is *God*, and not *us*, who accomplishes God's purposes. To buy into an either/or, in this matter, is to be thinking in a transactional, rather than a participatory, manner. Thinking in this way is a humbler version of the elder son's mistake. Refusing actually to be in the pool, it negotiates between what it is that *God* does, and what it is that *we* do. The strictest Calvinists among us might say that God does it *all*, and we do *nothing*. Most of us, worried that this might foster passivity in relationship to Christian life and work, want to be able to say we do "just a little something." God is 99 and 44/100th percent sovereign, we seem sometimes to be thinking, but there needs to be just a little power for us—56/100 of a percent, or so. "I can't do much," we say to ourselves, "but I hope to do a *little something*."

In contrast to this, the promise and miracle of grace is that we who can do *nothing* in and of ourselves can do *all things* in Jesus Christ who strengthens us.[47] This is the promise we are charged to lay claim to, even in the midst of all of our wretchedness.

We've suggested that Abraham and Ruth understand this—the two of them seem to be in the pool, reveling in their inheritance even before their wealth is in evidence. But another person who is really keyed in is Mary, the mother of Jesus. Mary shows us what it looks like to live in the pool. "How can this be?" she asks, contemplating the water. "Let it be unto me as you have said!"[48] she says, jumping in. And—splash!—she lets go of defining herself in relation to her limitations as a virgin and is newly created as the servant of God through whom—and with whom—and, certainly, *in* whom—the impossible is made possible. Mary can do nothing in and of herself. She is a virgin. Totally depraved. Aware that, by virtue of her own good efforts, she can contribute not one iota to the coming of God's

Kingdom to earth as it is in heaven. And simultaneously she also recognizes she is an essential, creative contributor to the divine work. She is, in fact, the Mother of God—the one who bears God to the world. She jumps into that water as one who submits to her role in the divine plan, and she is exalted. When Mary surfaces, she does not do so as a passive vessel who may have a little something to contribute, but as a true heir of everything God has and partner in the divine work.

Mary sees herself as God sees her. She rises up out of that water not only as a virgin who has contemplated the risk, not only as a servant who, diving in, has paid a price, but now as the Blessed One who participates in God's saving work in the world. "With all my heart I glorify the Lord!" Mary sings. God has "filled the hungry with good things" and "sent the rich away empty-handed."[49] We see, in the example of Mary, that the promise of God is not that we will be used, as passive vessels, if we only submit. The promise is that we, in our submission to the God who is able to do "far more than all we can ask or imagine"[50] will ourselves become creators of life. We will be poets, we will be prophets, we will bear God to the world.

It would have already been a benevolent thing if God had offered us just a small portion of the Kingdom. Just a small mansion on the corner. Just enough daily bread. It would be more than we deserve, and it would be manageable and understandable. If God had done that much, Christian life could then have been about "offering back to God a small portion of what God has given us," and we could have spent our time deliberating about what that might look like, about how we might achieve the proper balance.

But then God had to go and give us the whole farm. And now God wants our help in running it. And not so much because God sees value in doling out chores. God believes we, like Mary, have something essential to offer to the work of salvation. Even more significantly, God desires that we participate in the divine life and work for the same reason God entered the world in Jesus Christ and fills the world with the Spirit: God wants to be actively with us, and wants us to be actively with God.

Swim! The Practice of Holding Faith

Could those sheep in Matthew 25 have been any dumber?[51] I mean—if *I* had been invited to enter into the Kingdom of God, I certainly wouldn't have stood there going: "Huh? Who—me? When did *I* feed you? When did *I* clothe you? When did *I* visit you when you were sick and in prison?" If I were one of those sheep, I wouldn't have just idled before the king, trying to "recollect." I would have *run* through those pearly gates before I was found out!

Instead of worrying that I am a goat, as I used to do, I instead devote my energies to imagining I'm a sheep. *Of course you want to be a sheep*, you're probably thinking. *Who doesn't? They get to go to heaven.* Well . . . I'm as interested in going to heaven as the next person, I suppose. But the reason I want to stand with the sheep is not as much because they beat out the goats as because they just seem so God-honest *free.* They don't seem to be burdened by carrying around a list of what they believe, and what they have done (and for whom), and what their position is on x, y, and z issues (however important x, y, and z issues are). They seem to be living out their faith in a considerably less tense and clenchy sort of way.

Have you ever suddenly realized you were living as though life were a never-ending series of obligations? *I've got to get up and take a shower, I've got to get the kids to school. I've got to get the dishwasher loaded, and those papers graded, and that trip planned. I've got to take a break, to take care of myself, or I'm not going to be able to keep going like this.* Have you ever found yourself processing your relationships like a caller on the circa-1990s Dr. Laura radio show? *Dr. Laura, I'm calling to find out what my obligation is in relation to "person x." Am I obligated to such-and-such?* Or, *My daughter will be eighteen next week. How will that change my obligation to her in relation to "y"?* The thing is, if everyone met their obligations, if everyone were half as responsible as the elder son, if everyone were attentive, for example, to the demands of distributive justice, the world would be a much better place. Transactions, when they are fair ones, can be almost transformative.

I hate it, especially, when I find myself carrying out my vocational duties because it is my *obligation* to do so. *I've* got to *teach; I've* got to *preach; I've* got to *meet with that student about her paper; I've* got to *visit that guy in the hospital; I've* got to *run that meeting.* Let's face it: the better part of all of us does not want to help others merely because we feel a deep sense of *obligation* to do so. We got into this life—this calling—not because we felt obligated but because we experienced grace. Remember? We are here because we loved Jesus, and wanted, therefore, to feed his lambs and tend his sheep.[52]

On the other side of the spectrum: Have you ever had someone thank you for something that you didn't even realize you had done? So often we who are apt to reach out to others have to go begging for a word of appreciation. We hardly know what to do when it comes unaware, and certainly when we don't think we've done anything we need to be thanked for. In French, by the way, the equivalent of the English "you're welcome" is *de rien*. Literally, *de rien* means "it was nothing." But—let's face it—usually, even if we tell someone it was nothing, we really think it was a little something. I'm talking about those times when *de rien* means *de rien.* When—in the language of sheep—we really are bewilderedly bleating: "Huh?"

I think I know what is going on when thank-yous confuse us. We are swimming. We have surfaced in the pool and claimed God's promise that everything God has is ours. We are holding firmly to faith. And we are reveling in the treasures that are our inheritance. To shift to a metaphor I have used elsewhere in this book: We are sitting in the center of the treasure trove, running gold coins through our fingers and hanging pearl necklaces around our necks. Everything God has is ours. The beauty of the earth. The power to admonish, and to forgive, and to heal. As Calvin put it, we are free to use God's gifts for God's purposes.[53]

So why don't we exercise this freedom more regularly? Maybe one reason we fall into the trap of begrudgingly meeting obligations is because we are spending out of our own personal bank account, rather than from the superabundant resources God shares with us. I probably don't have to tell you that burnout, when it comes to matters of faith, is a big problem. I'm thinking one reason it is such a big problem has to do exactly with what we've been talking about—that is, we have been operating transactionally, rather than gracefully. If we imagine ourselves doling out portions of what God has so generously given us, if we imagine that what we need, to prevent burnout, is to make enough time to spend with God ourselves so we can then receive from God enough to continue doling out to others, well . . . if this is the way we are operating, it is a losing battle. Not to mention a human-centered one, instead of God-centered. Christian life becomes all about what *I* am able to gather and deliver. As if I'm a kind of "carrier pigeon," rather than a partner with Christ in the ministry of reconciliation.

It's no wonder that, in this position, I am counting up thank-yous, protecting my energy, adding and subtracting what I have left. I'm sitting there, at poolside, next to the elder son, doing calculations. Those stupid sheep, meanwhile, are splashing around in the pool, having a great time. (And I'm saying this with an awareness that sheep can't even swim, having learned it from one of my country-born friends.)

Barth says we are "always mistaken" when we think there is "no other way" for us to be than stressed out, no other approach we can take than to "work tensely." We could apply every one of the fabulous suggestions we come up with for living the Christian life and still miss out on grace. The trick to staying in the pool isn't coming up with the right method, or even with the right metaphor. It is not to put aside the word *response* and come up with some other word, although doing so might well be more theologically accurate. What staying in the pool is about, rather, is living into our only true identity; seeing ourselves as God sees us; knowing ourselves as beloved children before our sovereign God. We live and work, as Christian disciples who know they are beloved, before the God who holds the waters of the cosmos in the hollow of God's hand *and* calls each and every one of us by name. And when we engage our work *in the pool*, with an awareness of this God, according to Barth, we can "work 'with the relief and relaxation which spring from' our recognition of God."[54] This is "serious play, but play nonetheless." Our resources will not dry up, for we are tapped into the life of the one who is infinite, the one who is Life Itself. We meet those we serve, then, with joy—not with strain—inviting them to revel with us in the inheritance that belongs to us all. We act not out of *obligation* to the other, but because we *are* for and with them, even as God, in Christ, is for and with us.

Along the same lines, one of the things Paul says he desires—and prays—for the church at Philippi is that their "love may abound more and more, in knowledge and depth of insight."[55] Not that they would just manage to survive, not that they would just "hang in there," somehow, until Jesus comes back. Not that they would just faithfully continue to meet their obligations to each other. Not that they would simply "do their best." What Paul desires is that the love of Christ's disciples *abound* and *overflow*, that the grace of God in which we swim pour through and from we who know and want to share—ever more deeply—what matters most.

Gutiérrez has developed the idea that the poverty of the Western world is a spiritual poverty, not the economic poverty Paul is usually talking about.[56] We work very hard, we are overextended and stressed, and we have an inflated sense of self-importance, all because we've lost sight of who we are and what life's about. We struggle with our self-created paucity of time, our self-created need to gain ever more wealth, and our interest in moving to ever more powerful jobs from which we feel pressure to rush into early retirement, where we do not know what to do with ourselves. We don't know how to swim in the pool, Gutiérrez would say. And then he would add: but those who are truly poor—the economically poor—often do.

Someone asked me a question, recently, about Christians who preach about how God takes the side of the poor and marginalized then drive off in their fancy cars to their clearly privileged lives. This person made the good point that we who have wealth need to recognize our complicity in the power structures that be, if there is to be any hope for change. And part of our confession, as those with more, is that we don't want change if it means giving up our nice cars, or houses, or securities.

Maybe part of the problem is that we're thinking in zero-sum quantities again—in transactional ways that get us stuck, rather than in grace-full ways that open us to the resources of God. The thing is: those with material wealth are called to give to the poor not because they *should*, not in order to meet an *obligation*, but because they are *with* and *for* the poor who also have something to share with them. God's ways drive me crazy, sometimes, and one of those times is in relation to how I approach serving the sheep. It's hard enough for me to make some kind of effort to feed the hungry, clothe the naked, visit the sick and those in prison—or even load the dishwasher or grade a paper, for goodness' sake—as a responsible person meeting my obligations. But God wants me to do these things so freely that I don't even know I'm doing them. God desires that my service to others springs from who I am. Overflows from who I am, in fact, as a child of God swimming in the water of grace.

I've heard Gutiérrez jokingly say that, if we can get ourselves to write a check only by way of guilt and obligation, he'll still take the check. He'll take it because the economically poor can use it to eat. He'll take it because it will help alleviate poverty and hunger. But it will not relieve spiritual poverty, no matter how many checks are written, no matter how obediently obligations are met, if those writing the checks are still sitting at that table, six feet from the edge of the pool.

Maybe what the sheep teach us is that, from the vantage point of grace, our focus should be much less on *doing things for each other* and much more on *being with and for each other.* After all, what is most extraordinary about God is not that God has done great things. God is omnipotent, to do "great things," for one who is omnipotent, is par for the course. What is extraordinary—what is, in fact, the greatest miracle of all—is that this one who does great things empties Godself to be with us, and keeps insisting on being for us, drawing us into the divine work.

Do we want to be with one another? Are we, really, *for* one another? For our families? For those to whom we minister? For the poor? Is our frenetic focusing on meeting our obligations getting in the way of our knowing what all this is about?

To swim is to recognize there are others in the water. To share with them, to splash with them, to play with them, to *love* them. To live the Christian life means continuing to increase in a love for others that overflows so freely that our service becomes an extension of who we are, an expression of our freedom in Christ.

When this happens, we are ready to answer the question, "How are things with your heart?" with conviction and joy. "I am blessed," we will say, in whatever words we use. "I am blessed, indeed."

Part Five

God Sends Us

Chapter Nine

WHERE ARE WE HEADED?

The Doctrine of Christian Hope

As members of the church visible and invisible (ch. 7) who at times struggle to accept the blessing of God's grace (ch. 8), Christians have a definite focus. It is not on our own agenda, but on God's promises. Specifically, it is on God's promise to complete "the good work" God has begun in all of God's children,[1] to accomplish the redemption for which all creation waits with eagerness.[2] In this final part of the book we consider what Christian hope looks like and how Christians participate in it as those whom God sends out into the world to share the good news. Following the patterning of the Lord's Prayer we consider, in this chapter, the character of God's promised Kingdom. "Thy Kingdom Come!" Christians pray, imagining a new earth in which all are given daily bread, extended forgiveness, empowered to forgive, and delivered from evil. In chapter 10, the final chapter, we focus on another imperative issued in the prayer. "Thy will be done," Christians pray. But what is it that we are called and sent by God to *do*, exactly? And how do we get busy living into the promised Kingdom, even today, in a way that helps bring its eternal reality into our day-to-day living in this world?

Who Is Hope For?

We ended the last chapter (ch. 8) imagining that we are swimming in grace, cognizant of our identity as God's beloved children and loving and serving one another not as a matter of obligation, but freely. This essential meditation on Christian life, in exploring the dynamics of how we come to live in conscious recognition of our belovedness to God, is itself more individualistically than communally focused. It is meant to be read in tandem with the chapter on church that preceded it (ch. 7), where the church is the place and people with, among, and from whom we experience the blessings of God. God blesses us as individuals, but always as individuals in relation to others: individuals who find their home in particular communities with particular convictions and practices.

Christian hope is, similarly, not only for individuals, though it is experienced, in one way or another,[3] in the lives of every disciple. Christian hope is the hope of the whole church, and even beyond: it is the hope of the entire world. As the church is a "parable and promise of the kingdom of God"[4] so the hope Christians hold is not their own personal possession, but the property of all. To the degree Christians can glimpse the Kingdom breaking through and into this world they are called to point it out to others. Insofar as they are ever open to perceiving God wherever God might be self-revealed they are also called to respond when others do the pointing, when those from other communities or other faith traditions claim to have caught a glimpse. Preachers watch for and bear witness to where they see the Spirit present and at work in the *ekklesia* and the *koinonia,* that the people of God might be encouraged. Mentors listen and testify to the ways in which God has worked even in and through the difficulties of their lives, making a way where there was no way.[5] Parents learn and then tell their children stories about how God has acted in history to save and to claim unlikely individuals, families, communities, and nations.

Many Christians have hope that God is with us that is based not only in their conviction that God broke into history in the burning bush and at Bethlehem, but that God breaks into our time, our lives, our world, again and again. *Chronos* (created, chronological time) gives way to *kairos* (eternity breaking into chronological time). People of faith have tasted this in their lives, and it only makes them yearn for more. And so they pray, again, that God's will be done on earth as in heaven. And they go to church, again, hoping that something will happen to remind them that *kairos* will one day undo the mortality and sin connected to *chronos,* and every tear will be wiped away.

As many instances of hope that can be found, another common experience in this world, and among people of faith, is hopelessness. Hopelessness is, unfortunately, often quite understandable, given the tragedies in our lives and the life of the world. I write these words on the day after yet another school shooting in the US. It is a difficult day to write about hope. The last thing we need to be doing on days like today (which are certainly too numerous) is trying to overwhelm grief and frustration with upbeat, religiousy-sounding aphorisms that, however well-intentioned, seem geared, primarily, to managing everyone's despair so the economies of our lives together don't suddenly come to a screeching halt. This, in contrast to what might really help: meeting people with the strength of God's promises in ways that empower them to stomp their feet and pray once again—*Thy Kingdom come, already!*—recommiting to doing the will of God that will help bring the Kingdom to fruition.

It is this more authentic, tenacious, stay-in-the-game version of hope we could use more of, in this world. This is the kind of hope Christians claim to have in Christ, by the power of the Spirit. But sometimes it is harder to hold, show, and share than we want it to be, so distressed are we by the suffering of the world. If there is truth to the stereotype that people of faith are more liable to "shout" rather than to "laugh,"[6] it might be because shouting is the more appropriate response people of faith and hope should have to events like school shootings. To hope, when our hope is founded in the promises of God, looks sometimes like shouts of "No!" against injustices we can see are *not* what God desires. To hope, when our hope follows our commitment to "whatever is honorable . . . just . . . pure . . . pleasing . . . commendable . . . excellent . . . and worthy of praise,"[7] is to be disappointed a lot of the time. What we are sent by God to do in the world, in the face of all that is painful and disconcerting, is not to cheer everyone up, as though we are in some way the world's court jesters. It is, rather, to share God's promises, which hold nevertheless, even when it appears they are nowhere in evidence.

People of faith, then, are not sent by God to be the world's cheerleaders. And yet to walk around morosely, as though the fate of the world is solely up to us, and we are failing in our task, is also problematic. Barth once asked, in a sermon he preached one Ascension Day (1956),

> Why don't our faces shine? . . . Why are the faces we show each other at best superior looking, serious, questioning, sorrowful and reproachful faces, at worst even grimaces or lifeless masks, real Carnival masks? We are in the world not to comfort ourselves, but to comfort others . . . yet the one and only genuine comfort we may offer to our fellow human beings is this reflection of heaven, of Jesus Christ, of God himself, as it appears on a radiant face. Why don't we do it?[8]

Barth is hard on people of faith, here, reminding us that the work of comforting others is not really about ourselves. What we are sent out to share are not our honest opinions, our authentic feelings, our life experiences, or our best practices—as important as all of these things are. We are sent to share Christ, who is God with us no matter what.

Isaiah suggests that, when we comfort others by testifying to God's presence, we help them navigate their despair over difficult circumstances. "How lovely on the mountains are the feet of those who brings good news, who announce peace and bring good news of happiness, who announce salvation, and say to Zion, 'Your God reigns!'"[9] Peace, happiness, and salvation: these promises of God are so much more concrete and actionable than wishful thinking or vaguely asserting that, somehow, things are all going to work out if only we trust in God, work harder, or both. Jeremiah insists, along the same lines, that the hope we share has distinctive shape and perimeters: "I know the plans I have in mind for you, declares the Lord;" Jeremiah writes, "they are plans for peace, not disaster, to give you a future filled with hope."[10]

Christian Hope in the Present

Traditionally, the final doctrine considered in any Christian theological system is *eschatology.* "Eschatology" means, literally, "words about the end." And some approaches to eschatology have, consistent with this, focused more on what people of faith have thought of as end-of-time issues than on what eschatology means for the flourishing of human life in the here and now. A very popular manifestation of a kind of end-of-time oriented eschatology is the international, bestselling Left Behind book series, authored by Tim LaHaye and Jerry Jenkins.[11] The focus of these books is not as much on God's promises in the present as on what God will do in the future and how we can get ready. If we do not do what it takes to get ready for the rapture, the Second Coming, the tribulation, and the millennium, the books convey, we will be "left behind"—excluded from God's Kingdom. In direct contrast to this, the idea of eschatology presented here, focusing on Christian hope for this world, is premised in God's outlandish promise to be with us no matter what. Even when appearances seem to argue to the contrary, we have *not* been left behind. This world is not a testing ground for the real world to come, but the place in which God promises ever to be with us.[12] Following this, to be people of hope is to cling to the promise we have *not* been abandoned, regardless of our circumstances.

Theologians are generally determined that eschatologies be shaped in ways that address important matters related to our existence in the here and now. And most theologians, believing there is or at least should be a connection between this world and the next, make some attempt to work at the interface of the "now" and the "not yet." The conversation in this chapter assumes, therefore, that an eschatology that cannot speak hope to the present is no real hope at all. It is, rather, an *escape*—an escape from the struggles of the present world that God so loves, that God is with, and that God refuses to abandon. Any notions of "hope" that are grounded solely or primarily in the future actually rob us of the hope against hope that lies at the heart of our faith—the hope that leads us to live abundantly in the here and now, the hope that makes it possible for us to participate in and contribute to this world in freedom, the hope that empowers us to hold faith *despite* the ambiguities that surround us, the hope that promises inclusion for all God's beloved creatures.

So important is the idea that eschatology must have something to do with our real struggles that, when I lecture on this doctrine in the classroom or in the church, I hand out index cards before starting and ask participants to write "What do I fear?" on one side of the card, and "What do I hope for?" on the other side. Then I ask them to write their responses. Often, I collect the cards and read everyone's fears, and then everyone's hopes (anonymously, of course). I always say, before I start the lecture that follows, that however we think of the doctrine of eschatology, it better have something to do with our real-life fears and hopes.

I can't resist giving you an example of one of the "ah-has" that often occurs when I do this exercise: two of the most common "fears" that different people commonly write on the card are "afraid to die" and "afraid to be kept indefinitely alive." Resurrection speaks to both of these fears. To those who are afraid to die the doctrine of eschatology brings the promise of resurrection. This world is not the end. The end of earthly life does not mean the end of all life. Christ rose, and we will rise again with him.

But the doctrine of eschatology also has something to offer to those who are afraid they will be kept alive indefinitely. These people fear being kept on life support until the inheritance they have worked hard to save for their children is completely used up. They fear endless suffering. They fear being remembered for who they are in their final weeks, lying in a vegetative state. Resurrection speaks to this fear by saying that indeed it is OK to prepare DNR (do not resuscitate) orders for your loved ones to use when the time comes for you to die. To believe in the resurrection means that there is no reason to cling to life in this world as if that is all there is, as precious as life in this world can be. We can let go of life when it is time because resurrection promises that life continues.

To hold faith is to be people of hope. And to have hope is not to engage in wishful thinking, but to desire and enact what it is that God desires and does in the context of our very real fears and hopes. How do we begin to imagine what Christian hope is supposed to look like, so that we can live into it and, even, contribute to its coming?

CHRISTIAN DOCTRINES: INFUSED WITH HOPE	
Revelation:	We know the unknowable God.
Incarnation:	God is with us and for us in Jesus Christ.
Trinity:	God's love for us is true to God who is love.
Creation:	The gifts of life are good and to be enjoyed.
Providence:	Creation is ongoing; God enlivens every creature in every place at every moment.
Humanity:	We are created in the image of God.
Sin:	Sin is an aberration; finitude is not a sin.
Salvation:	We are forgiven; we can live in cognizance of grace.
Holy Spirit:	God intercedes for us, empowers us, and gifts us with faith.
Church:	We imagine God's Kingdom and claim it for the world.
Sacraments:	God blesses us through ordinary means.
Resurrection:	Death does not have the final word.
Ascension:	We participate in God's life and work.

Hope and the Cross

Traditionally, Christian hope is identified with the resurrection, ascension, and Second Coming of Jesus Christ. As we discussed in the chapters on incarnation and salvation, the one who entered into life with us when he was born to Mary in Bethlehem and held nothing back from us when he died on the cross at Golgotha drew us into the very life of the triune God by rising from the dead and ascending into heaven. The resurrection and the ascension signify a triumph over death, oppression, sin, and suffering in this world. Paul writes, reflecting on this victory, that all death will lose its "sting" when our "perishable bodies put on imperishability" even as Jesus Christ's body put on immortality in the resurrection.[13] Jesus himself tried to comfort his disciples with reassurances that he would "come again" and "take them to himself" so that they would never again be apart. And he wanted the disciples to know, even before this "coming again," that he had them in mind. He was "preparing a place for them," he told them, planning for reunion.[14]

Especially since the rise of science in modernity, we have wondered how to think about bodily resurrection. There are still today many Christians who point to Paul's words in 1 Corinthians 15:17 and say it is necessary to hold to a literal reading of the resurrection of the body, else "our faith is in vain" and we are without hope that sin and suffering will be overcome.

But the idea of the resurrection of the body can also be crucial to people of faith who are reticent about relying on a purely literal understanding.[15] To say that Jesus rose bodily from the dead is to insist, as I have mentioned, that the incarnation is not a thirty-three-year experiment. Whatever it means to say that Jesus Christ is "God with us" in the flesh, it does not end on Easter morning. To confess the bodily resurrection, ascension, and Second Coming (as Christians do every time we say the Apostles' Creed) is to remember that Jesus didn't leave bodies behind when he rose. On the contrary, he took these bodies, this world, our lives along with him into the life of God: into the promised kin-dom for which all creation groans and hopes.[16] The hope we have that is oriented around bodily resurrection is the hope that astonished us when the "Word became flesh,"[17] the hope that grew when Jesus announced his ministry would concern itself with freeing *bodies* from captivity,[18] the hope that, whatever Christian hope is about, it does not ask us to set aside concerns about hunger, abuse, violence, lack of medical care, or enslavement as incidental in the face of what is to come. On the contrary, to confess bodily resurrection is to insist, as Jesus did throughout his ministry, that bodies and souls are inextricable, and that bodies always matter.

The problem comes when we associate Christian hope with the resurrection but not with the cross, even though it seems fairly natural to do so. After all, human beings regardless of their circumstances or degree of suffering are eager to be free of all pain and the struggles of this mortal life. "It may be Friday, but Sunday's coming!"[19] writes Tony Campolo, trying to offer a word of encouragement to those who feel stuck in the suffering of Friday night.

The reality is, though, that the exhortation to "just hang on" for a couple of days is not all that useful on Friday night, when Sunday-morning resurrection cannot yet be seen. Even if it was seen in some way by Jesus himself, for that matter, the promise of resurrection did not seem to alleviate pain, but exacerbated it. Knowing what the Kingdom of God looks like can deepen our experience of the sufferings of this world, so dissonant are they with what has been promised. Images of those suffering in Dante's *Purgatorio* come to mind; I have always imaged that the sight of Paradise in the distance deepens their agony.[20] Araceley de Roccietti describes Christians fighting for justice in Latin America as living "between profound wretchedness and astounding hope," suggesting that the vision for a world marked by equality, safety, and shared resources for all people makes it impossible to ignore any "violation of rights."[21]

Concerned that we extend hope to those who are in the midst of suffering, theologians insist that we understand the cross, as well as the resurrection, ascension, and Second Coming, as a symbol of hope. Contemporary theologian Jürgen Moltmann has made this a major emphasis of his life's work. In *The Crucified God*, for example, he explores how the cross offers hope because it shows us not only that God suffers with us, but that suffering is included in the very life of the triune God in and through the ascended, crucified one, Jesus Christ.[22] Suffering is not only something God did for us two thousand years ago; the suffering of the world *today* is somehow, by way of that cross, taken up into God's life and plan. This idea is incredibly reassuring, Moltmann holds, on the Friday night before resurrection. It reminds us that God is present to us, and we are present to God, even before suffering is no more.

Having included the cross as a symbol of hope, we now turn to exploring the resurrection, ascension, and Second Coming of Christ. How do these hard-to-understand and sometimes hard-to-believe eschatological doctrines shape and empower Christian service in the lives of people who hold faith?

The Resurrection and the Ascension

Theologically, resurrection and ascension are inextricably intertwined. If the bodily resurrection of Christ reinforces the fact that the Word made flesh at Christmastime remains incarnate in Jesus Christ even when he rises, the ascension of Christ emphasizes, again, that the incarnation is not just something Jesus Christ does, but who he actually is—for all of eternity. The creed, in fact, insists that Jesus is "sitting at the right hand of God the Father Almighty" even now! It's almost as though Christian doctrines somehow know they cannot remind us often enough that the God who is with us in our very flesh is determined to take creaturely existence along wherever this God is going.

Resurrection and ascension might be inseparable, but it can seem even harder to talk about the "so what?" of the ascension than it is to talk about the relevance of the resurrection. With resurrection we kind of get it, even with the difficult problem of a person coming back to life. It is about death being overcome. It is about the forces of good winning out over the powers of darkness. It is the stuff great movies are made of.

The story of Jesus floating up into the clouds,[23] however, is a tough sell. It's one of those stories Christians have tended, even, to be a little embarrassed about. "You Christians believe all sorts of crazy things, don't you?" someone sitting next to me on a plane once said, when I made the mistake of pulling my Bible out of my bag. "Is it true you think Jesus started out in heaven, then came down to earth, and then sort of just 'floated up' again?"

How do we find our way "in" to the strange story of the ascension? What are we supposed to do with it? This one who was born, and ministered, and died and rose is "lifted up in a cloud" and "taken out of the sight" of the disciples. And this time there is no appearance of heavenly hosts, singing "Gloria" to help us out with what's going on. There is no weeping or crying out to guide us in how to respond. There is no wine made out of water or baskets of overflowing food, to drink and eat as we marvel at Jesus's miraculous powers. There is no stone rolled away to speculate about: Did someone steal the body, or did he *really* walk out? In the event of the ascension there are absolutely no distractions; there are no helpful hints, there is not much we can do but *look up* and wonder. And so we stand there, staring up with the disciples, as Jesus simply floats away. And we wonder (how could we help but wonder?): What does this mean? And: What do we do now? Or even: What will I ever tell the guy next to me on the plane about *this*? And to add insult to injury, by the way, two men in white robes walk up and start chiding us. *Whattya doing, staring up at the sky?* they say (more or less). *Don't you know Jesus will come back the same way you saw him leave?*

Oh, yeah—well, now that information really helps. Thanks so much.

OK... so: it seems things are a little trickier, all of a sudden, than they were around Christmastime, and especially since Easter morning, when we thought we had everything sorted out. The One Who Is With Us and The One Who Is Risen is suddenly and in mid-sentence leaving the world, and the Holy Spirit isn't due to arrive for over a week. We're about to find ourselves in a kind of a dead space, again. We felt it before, in the days between the cross and the resurrection. If Jesus is gone, and the Holy Spirit has not yet arrived, how are we supposed to connect with God?

As panicked as we might feel, when we put ourselves in the place of the disciples on Ascension Day, at least Jesus doesn't leave, this time around, with a cry of despair. Instead, he exits in glory, making two promises as he goes: first, that the disciples will be baptized by the Holy Spirit soon, and second, that he will return—well, *sometime.*

Jesus's departure reminds me, in some ways, of what it looked like when I left my children, when they were too little to read a calendar, to go on a trip. I may have ascended by taking a plane, but was certainly flying all over the place—you know: packing my suitcase, and organizing the stuff my kids would need for school while I was gone, and printing my boarding pass, and stocking up the refrigerator. And all the while I was reassuring my children who seemed—just when I needed to be flying around!—to be always at my heels: "Don't worry," I'd say, "Daddy is going to be with you. You're going to be OK." And "Mommy's coming back in just a few days." I made the same two promises, really, that Jesus makes to us: (1) that there will be another nurturing presence when I am away, and (2) that my absence will only be temporary.

I have a gripe with Jesus, as a child waiting for him to come home: Jesus has been gone for too long. How in the world could he leave us with *no idea* of when he was coming back? When *I* went on trips when my kids were small, I told them over and over again how many nights I'd be away so they'd know exactly what to expect. You know what I did, to help them understand the timetable? I went to the Container Store and bought a bunch of little boxes, the size that are meant to hold toothpicks. They're made of lucite, and they come in all different colors. What I did was put Hershey's Kisses in the boxes—one per person, for every person who was at home—for the number of nights I was away. Three kisses for each night: one for my spouse Bill, one for our son Xander, and one for our daughter, Jessica. And then I'd put one extra box, with four kisses, that we would share together the night of my return. We put all the boxes up on the mantel, so the kids could see how many nights more before I would be back.

Now, don't you think I did a better job than Jesus, in this? Of course, he did leave us something to chew, and something to swallow—something to remind us of our connection to his very body.

And this is what we want, isn't it? We want to be connected, in some way, to his very body. We want to stay joined to the body of the one who joined himself to us by being born of Mary's body, and dying as a body broken, and rising—embodied—to break bread with us again. "I am bone of your bone and flesh of your flesh," Jesus tells us, by his actions, time and time again. And so we believe we are somehow connected to this body being lifted up, this body floating off—and into—the clouds. But how? How are we still connected?

How are we connected to bodies that are absent from us? What does it mean to be members of the "communion of saints"—those who in this world had bodies, and who Christians believe are, somehow, bodily resurrected from the dead?

These questions are impossible to answer, but fruitful to ask. They draw us to a truth greater than any explanation. The truth is this: we are joined to certain bodies even when we are separated from them, even when we haven't seen them or touched them in a very long time. Our deepest intuitions testify to this. A grown man, dying on the battlefield, cries out for the tender touch of his mother. Two lovers, briefly separated, anticipate their next opportunity to embrace. A three-year-old girl, in her day care center, lies down for nap time with a photo in her grip: she looks at a picture of her father and her mother, her big brother and her cats, her grammy and her granddad. A nursing mother, her body begging for reconnection, wills her infant child to awake. A father watches out the window for his teenage son still not home, overwrought by his distinct, but irrational, sense that his very heart is out there—somewhere—walking around in the body of another. A widow helps her grandchildren create an avatar of their dead grandfather, so they can play games with him on their Wii. Yes, indeed—we're still connected, all right. Connected to the bone.

The Ascension and Christian Hope

As difficult as it is to watch Jesus ascend, the most painful experiences of life, it seems to me, are not about negotiating the distance between our bodies and the bodies of those we love. This can be done, and we constantly find new ways. We phone and we e-mail; we Skype and Facetime and iChat; we visit and we remember. Our grief at being separated is somehow bittersweet. Our most painful experiences come when the bodies we love resist us—when they leave us looking up with no promise of return. And this brokenness, this pain, is all around us. It is not the only story that defines us, but it is a major one. It's a common story in this country, it's a story of this world; it's the story of the sin that moved Adam from his glorious exclamation to Eve that she is, indeed, "bone of my bone and flesh of my flesh" to his disparaging remark that *she made me do it! It's her fault!*[24] The brokenness of the world is seen in Adam withdrawing his body from Eve's by ceasing to uphold her, holy and without blemish.[25] Adam abandons, and the two are separated. From each other, and from the earth. From the earth, and from God. And we've been trying to get back, ever since, to the physical unity we once knew, as creatures in God's good creation.

Jesus doesn't want us to think he is abandoning us. The last thing he is about, of course, is contributing to our brokenness. Jesus is, after all, in the business of healing. And so he is a little worried, near the end of his life, about how we might interpret all his comings and goings. He wants us to know that he yearns to be connected to us the way a parent wants to be connected to a child. "Do not let your hearts be troubled," he assures the disciples, in John 14. "If I go and prepare a place for you, I will come again and will take you to myself, that where I am you may be also."[26] And in John 17, right at the end of his life on earth, he seems to be down on his knees *begging* the Father to help us understand just how near he is to us, and how near we are—therefore—both to God and to one another. "As you . . . are in me and I am in you," he prays, "may they also be in us." "The glory that you have given me I have given them, so that they may be one, as we are one," he insists. And finally: "Father, I desire that those also, whom you have given me, may be with me where I am."[27]

While what Jesus is saying in John 17 might be difficult to diagram, at least one thing is clear: Jesus wants us to be with him where he is, and not just in the future, but *right now*. And so this is what he requests from the Father. Now, in one sense, this might seem a funny thing for Jesus to ask for, just as he is heading out for the clouds. He is *leaving* the earth we live on, so how can we be with him? But in another way what Jesus says isn't all that surprising, given who he is. For Jesus is the one who entered deeply into existence with us; the one who held nothing back in offering his very body. And now the one who entered in with us wants to lift us up out of the brokenness and into life with him. The one who sacrificed himself wants to make us living sacrifices, reflecting his own *kenosis* (self-emptying). He reaches in, in the incarnation and the cross. He lifts us up, in the resurrection and the ascension. At all points, he manifests a love that will not let us go: a love that glorifies us by exalting us, righteous and holy and beloved.

These are the kinds of things we think about in relation to the ascension. That God has raised us up, with Christ, to be united with God and with one another. That God exalts us to a life that insists separation, and brokenness, and abandonment are not the end of the story. That though we are tired of waiting for Jesus to come back, we will still keep watching and waiting (this week I myself want him to clean up the school shootings, violence in the Middle East, climate change, racial violence, and sexual harassment). The doctrine of the ascension reminds us to think about living lives that refuse to give up on the hope that bodies are related to one another and that the world, therefore, can be transformed.

We might not understand the story of Jesus's ascension, but we know what it is about. It is about being connected to the bone. It is about being connected not only because Jesus enters into all aspects of our lives and circumstances with us, but because he also lifts us up, with him, into full participation in the very life of God. And from up there, with Jesus, in the ascension, we have a really nice view: we can see the glory of God in all the dappled, shiny, colorful, or plain things in creation and in the faces of all who had once seemed pained. From up there, with Jesus, we can also know our own glory: the glory that comes with seeing ourselves as God sees us; the glory we experience when we know we are loved, the glory of those whose bodies are precious, the glory of those who—in life and in death—belong to God.

The Raising of Christ and the Coming of the Kingdom

The resurrection is a symbol of Christian hope not only because of what it promises to resolve, but also because of what it is determined to invite. It promises to resolve the problem of sin, suffering, and death, as Paul celebrates in 1 Corinthians 15. But it also invites us into a new way of being: to live more fully into the Kingdom of God that Jesus is always talking about; to wait in Jerusalem,[28] where the Holy Spirit will empower us to participate more fully in what God is up to in the world; to ourselves imagine, enact, and contribute to the coming of God's Kingdom to earth as it is in heaven.

The resurrection, connected with the ascension and Second Coming, bespeaks a new reality—a reality into which we have entered, but which is not yet here. What does it look like for us to "watch and pray" for its coming? How do we begin, even, to imagine a "new heaven and a new earth" in such a way that we can live into it and, perhaps, even make a contribution to its realization?

Hope and Imagination

Some things are just hard to imagine.

I have trouble imagining, for example, the existence of a Krispy Kreme donut that does not contain hydrogenated oil, even though our local Krispy Kreme advertises that such oil has been removed. I have trouble imagining that every room in our home could be tidy at the same time, even though my friends say there will come a phase in my life when our kids are in college, when we will have fewer responsibilities, and when comprehensive room tidiness will be easier to achieve.

Some things are just hard to imagine because we know something about what the world is like, and we know . . . well, we know how we are. I once had a student drop an 8:30 a.m. class she had with me—an elective class she really wanted to take—because she could not imagine waking up early enough in the morning to make it. She tried a couple of times, finally bringing me her add/drop slip. She told me, in a breaking voice: "Dr. Rigby, I just know myself too well. I'm not going to be able to do this." As I signed the slip, I remember commenting to her that it really was a shame. She had signed up for the class, so there must have been a time when she would have imagined she could do it. Where had her imagination failed?

Many of us would say we know how she feels. Maybe not about how hard it is to get up early in the morning, but about any number of other perfectly ordinary yet seemingly insurmountable elements of daily life. We know enough about our own weaknesses and about the idiosyncrasies of those whom we love to assess what can reasonably be imagined, and what, really, we should not even bother imagining. Things simply are what they are, we might say, matter-of-factly. People don't change, we might add. And these might be acceptable conclusions if we didn't want things to be different. But when we do need and even want to make a change, and finally give up even imagining being able to make it because to do so is "just not possible for me" or "not the way things work," is, to be honest, something of a shame.

Sometimes we resist imagining something different because we, on some level, don't really want things to change. We might not like things the way things are, but at least we understand them. *I don't even want to imagine my husband changing in relation to X, because that would mean I'd have to change in relation to Y,* we might say to ourselves. *And then I wouldn't even have X to complain about!* Or maybe we think to ourselves, *I don't want to even imagine my church becoming ______________, because that would mean I would have to ______________. And I know how I am, and I know I'm not going to ______________, even if I should.* A faithful church person once told me, for example, that her church had wanted to hire a particular young woman to be the congregation's pastor, but the committee couldn't get past their suspicion that she might soon want to take parental leave, noting that she was newly married. "We just didn't want to get into all that," the committee member confessed, demonstrating a terrible lack of imagination.

While we often resist imagining something different because we don't really want things to change, I think it is even more often the case that we resist imagining because we are afraid. We are afraid to set our expectations high because we don't want to be disappointed. We know ourselves well enough to be aware that, as Paul wrote, "we do not do the good we want, but the evil we do not want is what we do."[29] Perhaps it is better to set our expectations low, and not to imagine too much, we tell ourselves. Then we won't be disappointed.

Which leaves us in a bit of a pickle, when it comes to Christian life as we described it in the preceding chapter. This is because to be a Christian is to be constantly imagining something altogether different than how we are, and how this world is. Every time we pray the Lord's Prayer, we ask for God's Kingdom to come "on earth as it is in heaven." This prayer that Jesus taught us invites us to imagine a world characterized *not* by hunger, conflict, and sin, but by daily bread, forgiveness, and deliverance from evil.

Scripture invites us to imagine a world—the New Jerusalem!—in which every tear is wiped away from every eye.[30] Where there is no more weeping. Where people do not die before their time, and everyone's time is one hundred years or more. Where those who build houses get to live in them themselves, rather than handing them over to those who are richer, and going home from working on a mansion to themselves sleeping in a trailer park. Where those who plant and cultivate the pineapples can actually eat them, rather than handing them over to Dole or Del Monte. Where the children we birth are at no risk for calamity, but instead live into the fullness of life that we desire for them. Where stomachs will be full without violence; the wolf will eat with the lamb; the lion will eat straw rather than killing the ox. Where the One who is Alpha and Omega will dwell in our midst, quenching our thirst with the water of life.

If I cannot make it to an 8:30 class, how am I supposed to imagine such things? I know how I am, and I know how you are, and I know something about what this world is like, and—I'll tell you—from what I know, and where I stand right now, and what the newspaper says this morning, this just isn't going to happen. Why set our expectations high? Why set ourselves up for disappointment? I'll tell you something: as far as I can tell, we've been praying that Lord's Prayer for over two thousand years, and so far I haven't seen a single wolf hanging out with a single lamb. Perhaps we need to modify our demand that God's Kingdom come a little, just to be on the safe side. Perhaps we could ask, instead, that our kingdoms be *improved* so that everyone could get a little bread, say, once a week. Instead of forgiveness, we could request tolerance. Instead of deliverance from evil, we could ask for a skill set that would help us manage it better. After all, God knows how we are.

I remember, once, when I thought God was using me to lift a church out of its cowardly self-improvement mentality and into living in recognition of the new heaven and new earth to which Scripture bears witness. I was twenty-two years old and working as the youth director in a relatively small church in northern New Jersey. When I got there the church had four kids in the senior high youth group. Directly across the street from the church was a high school. While the church was made up predominantly of persons who were white, the school was about equally balanced between students who were white and students who were people of color. One day, a black fifteen-year-old boy killed a white fifteen-year-old boy on the playground. I went to the principal and asked if I could invite any interested students to our next youth group meeting so that they would have opportunity to discuss their grief.

The next youth group meeting was attended by one hundred high schoolers—more than the average attendance at the Sunday morning worship service. I recruited help from church leaders. Everyone in the church was energized. We all began to imagine the ministry we could have to the community in which the church was located.

For seven weeks in a row, we had about a hundred kids a week. On the first and second weeks, in the eyes of the church, I was a hero. We imagined the possibilities. We had all kinds of meetings to discuss what kind of programs were needed. We agreed that we had the opportunity to experience the Kingdom of God together with these grieving kids.

By the third week, our imaginations began to sag. The four kids in the original youth group were naturally becoming disgruntled by our lack of attention to them, given the need to attend to the one hundred. We were having trouble with the high schoolers spitting tobacco into various cups and containers they saw sitting around the church. The extra adult volunteers we had recruited, after two weeks of service, were already running out of steam.

I was no longer a hero. As I tried to keep the program going almost singlehandedly, resentment grew. Finally, the students from the high school were told directly, by someone in the congregation, that they were not wanted. On week eight we went from a hundred attendees back to the four members of the original youth group. And the pressure was on to forget what had happened and try to get back to the way things were "before."

That student wanted to take my 8:30 class, but couldn't imagine actually getting up. We wanted to help those kids, but couldn't imagine actually finding a way to do it. As they say back where I'm from (on Long Island): "So whaddya gonna do? You know how people are."

People of faith, stepping into hope, have had higher expectations than this. Consider our forebear John Calvin, for example. Or Julian of Norwich, Martin Luther, John Wesley, Martin Luther King Jr., or Rosemary Radford Ruether. It's hard to imagine that any of these people of faith would have signed that drop slip the student handed me. And I'm betting they would have kept at those church folks, and kept at those high schoolers, far more than I did.

Calvin, for example, wasn't big on excusing folks in Geneva for missing class, or missing worship, with the excuse that "you know how we are." You see, Calvin *did* know how we are. He knew, as a person of hope, that who we are is actually different from how we act, at least most of the time. He believed sin was an aberration inconsistent with God's creative and redemptive plan. He believed our lack of imagination is a symptom of a problem, not a reasonable excuse. Do you know that Calvin was far more open to being changed than many of us are? John Calvin, that one who has a reputation for being so dour, set his expectations high. He believed human beings can change, and he believed we are called to implement change in this world. Contrary to popular belief, he had a high view of human nature. He loved to look out at this majestic world that God has created and meditate with wonderment on the fact that the God who made *all* dearly loves *each and every* creature.

It is in and through contemplating and rejoicing in God's works, in and through imagining all that God is about and all that God has promised, Calvin thought, that we come to be included; that we come to be changed. With the psalmist, Calvin marvels that the God from whom there is no escape, the God who occupies the heavens, and dwells on the other side of the sea, the God who is present even in the depths of Sheol, also attends to us. God knits each one of us together in our mothers' wombs; God knows every day of our lives before one of them comes to be.[31] "When I look up at your skies, at what your fingers made—the moon and the stars that you set firmly in place—what are human beings that you think about them; what are human beings that you pay attention to them? You've made them only slightly less than divine, crowning them with glory and grandeur."[32]

So, you *can* find a way to get out of bed and make it to class, I'm sure he would say. And you can tell those kids not to chew tobacco in the youth room, or put up with the fact that they do. And you can pray that Lord's Prayer for what it actually says. And you *can* bear to imagine a new world so beautiful it is almost unbearable. And in imagining it, you may very well find that you become a vehicle of transformation in it. Don't aim to change the world, I think Calvin would instruct, but *do* aim to live in ever-deeper recognition of the world that God desires—of the Kingdom God has promised.

Live with the reality of God's world in mind, and this world will become something new. When we are imagining a world in which weeping is no more, we work—even harder—to alleviate suffering. When we are imagining a world in which all injustices are resolved, we ask ourselves questions about everything from the buying of pineapple to the building of our homes. When we are picturing a wolf and a lamb eating side by side, we cannot help but think differently about violence, war, and even how much meat we eat.

And all this *can* be pretty exhausting. Reflecting on who we are in relation to God's wondrous glory, participating in the New Jerusalem who is the well-prepared bride watching for the arrival of the bridegroom takes genuine effort. Anyone who has ever prepared to get married knows that it takes energy, particularly on the days leading up to the wedding. It takes energy to prepare, and it takes even more energy to expect. To courageously hope that dreams will be realized does not come naturally. Hope must be fed, or it will surely die. And it is fed, precisely, by courageously watching for the One who will return and preparing to live in the new heaven and the new earth that God is in the process of creating.

The book of Revelation urges us not to be "cowardly," but instead to live our lives as those who, together with the whole church, await reunion with Christ.[33] To imagine this Kingdom that is our inheritance, and to live in expectation of it. To believe that the God who has entered into existence with us in Jesus Christ will somehow meet us again and bring all that has been promised to full fruition.

And this one who is the Alpha and Omega will not come as one who asks us to step aside (so he "can show us how it's done"). He will come, rather, as *our God*, as *our bridegroom*, as one who claims us as his own. The one who is seated on the throne will leave the throne, and enter into our lives, and make them into something new. The one who emptied himself and entered the womb of Mary will wipe away our tears. The one who entered into death for us will, finally, put an end to death. The one who rose in body will join his body with ours in final consummation.

Now, I'm not sure I can spell out the details of what all this means. (As I said way back in the introduction, I have to love that guy who told Jesus, "Yes, Lord, I believe," but then added, "Help me, Lord, with my unbelief"!). We are not asked to draw lines from the concrete sorrows and joys of our life on this day to the images in these beautiful passages and then figure out how to move from "point A" to "point B." You see, there is no strategy that can move us from the many tears of this world to the no tears of the kingdom. The movement cannot be *from* here *to* there. As my grandfather liked to joke, whenever anyone asked him for directions, "you can't get there from here." Rather than starting from *here*, these images invite us to start from *there* and see what happens. To imagine the Kingdom of God that (quite frankly) Scripture gives us a lot of help imagining. To give the Holy Spirit a fighting chance to work in us so that we can become the new creations we are in Christ. To stand in wonderment, before the majestic God who has entered into existence with us, that we are fully included. To believe that God, in Christ, is making all things new. A new world without sorrow; a new world without violence. A new world in which everyone gets to live in the houses they have built, and everyone gets to eat the food they have grown. A world in which there is enough work, and enough life, to go around.

Can you imagine?

DISCUSS (IN THREE PARTS):

(1) Brainstorm some things that are hard to imagine, but we want to hope for. For example, we might say:

- It's hard to imagine putting a complete stop to global warming.
- It's hard to imagine an end to all war.
- It's hard to imagine the absence of all racism, sexism, classism, and heterosexism.
- It's hard to imagine food being distributed so equitably that no one dies, any longer, of malnourishment.

(2) Consider the ways we put aside our hopes for things that seem impossible in favor of being practical and realistic. For example, we might say:

- We can't put a stop to global warming, but we can significantly decrease our contribution to it.
- We will never end *all* war, but perhaps we can work toward disarmament.

- Human beings will never stop discriminating against each other, but we can create better laws and processes to protect people.
- We won't be able to feed everyone, but we can walk in the Crop Walk and raise funds that will be used to get more food to more people.

(3) *Reflect:* Are we hoping for *less than* the Kingdom of God, in the name of being realistic? If we do focus on being realistic and practical, what loss is there to the faith we hold and to what we have to offer the world as people of hope?

Hope as "Playing Toward" the Kingdom

I experienced a kind of conversion recently.[34] I was changed, for a time, into someone who remembers how to find my way into hope for this world. It happened at a band concert given by Murchison Middle School students in Austin. The performance of the seventh and eighth graders was way above average. The final band in the program—the wind ensemble in which our son plays the clarinet—deserved a standing ovation. So I stood, but no one else did. Perhaps I am biased, or maybe just overly affirming. Enthusiasm is both my strength and my weakness, I know. Laughing at myself, I sat back down, still lightly clapping, looking to grab my bag so I would be ready to head out with my family.

But there was another part to the program, Ms. C., the band director, was explaining. The band, next month, will perform in a competition where they will be required to sight-read a piece. They will be given the music on the spot, then given eight minutes to prepare, then asked to play it through. Ms. C. asked us to watch as the band practiced for this sight-reading event. We all nodded courteously at this request, glancing at our watches to calculate what impact an extra quarter hour would have on our schedules.

The music was handed out and each kid placed it meticulously on his or her stand without opening it up. Poised on their seats with instruments in the "resting" position, they focused entirely on Ms. C., who was now facing them and trying to settle a music stand that kept slowly sinking down. The assistant band directors scrambled to change it out a couple of times, with Ms. C. making a joke of it all. But the stand kept creeping toward the floor.

Ms. C. decided to start anyway. She opened the piece on her stand and said something like, "OK, open your music and let's play." The students opened their music, but made no move to put instruments to lips or produce any sounds, which made me, I admit, a bit anxious. Ms. C. nonetheless began to conduct, arms raised and moving, humming and gesturing, drawing the students into the piece, measure by measure. The students went right along with her. With instruments still in resting position, their eyes darted back and forth from score to teacher. "Here is the melody; there, a hard rhythm; careful—that's a B natural; now play up the crescendo. Watch me for the cutoff; engage here with more passion. And now, measure 90—don't play B-flat! That's a natural, again." Every student still riveted, though now not as much to Ms. C. Somehow, you could tell, they had entered the music itself. The audience forgotten, Ms. C. had ushered her students and fellow musicians into a piece they had never seen, had never played. And when the eight-minute timer sounded, Ms. C. stopped, pulled her music stand up again, and invited her company to make the beautiful music that first had claimed them and now had become their own. And they—these thirteen-year-old kids—played out loud, for the very first time, the piece they already knew. They played the music Ms. C. invited them to hear, the music they had entered, the music into which they were now inviting us.

My tears surprised me, pushing me to interpret the event as an act of grace. I remembered that it is indeed possible for us to be joined in celebration and creation of what is beautiful. I remembered that the way to create beauty is first to participate in it. I remembered that formative teaching doesn't focus first and foremost on "best practices" or utilizing tools that heighten the possibility of success. It is attuned, rather, to the truth, beauty, and goodness of the subject matter. It insists that we must play B-natural or watch the crescendo in measure 30, for example, not as much to create beautiful music as to synchronize with it. Most importantly, it reminded me that to be people of hope is to "watch and pray" for the Kingdom of God to come, actively looking for it along the way. I almost missed going to that concert, and am so glad I was able to be there, and to be inspired, as a witness to grace breaking through in space and time. What remains is to reflect on how we do even more than witness and imagine the Kingdom, which already takes energy and attention. How do we "lean into it," even making a contribution to it? How does the hope that is in us affect our engagement with, and contribution to, the keeping of God's promise to the world?

We turn to the final chapter with these questions in mind, continuing to examine what it looks like to participate in the Kingdom of God by way of the doctrine of Christian vocation. What might it look like to imagine the Kingdom that manifests our hope, allowing our imagining to give way to action? How do we imagine it so strongly that we believe it into being in what we do? How do we hope so fully that we are transformed into those who contribute to its coming?

Chapter Ten
What Are We Called to Do?

The Doctrine of Christian Vocation

In a 1954 Christmas sermon[1] preached to the prisoners at Basel, Karl Barth warns us not to miss "the hour of this fire right here and now." It sounds as though he is describing a crisis situation and calling people to action, which is something he often did. In the very same sermon, in fact, he says that the expression "wait and see" is dangerous, since we can't be sure we will be around tomorrow to hear the message of the Gospel we are hearing today!

But the fire to which Barth refers in this case is not a fire that needs to be put out, a fire that is hazardous to our existence. Rather, it has a positive connotation—it is the fire of life. Barth quotes the Swiss writer Jeremias Gotthelf, who points out that "life is not a light," because "a light can be kindled again." Rather, "life is a fire given by God to burn on earth, just once and never more."[2]

There is something about that sight-reading exercise described at the end of the prior chapter that shows what it looks like to take seriously this hour of fire that is our lives. Many days we are handed music we haven't before seen. We can set it to the side, humbly referencing our ineptitude, feeling bad that we aren't ready and recommitting ourselves to developing more skills, eating a better breakfast, or doing whatever it takes to be prepared, next time around. Or we can open it up and plow right in, "doing our best and letting God take care of the rest," hoping to cobble together, with zeal and perspiration, something that might make the world slightly better tomorrow than it is today.

But to take either of these approaches is to forget we are already members of God's household; inhabitants of the Kingdom of God; musicians who have ways of hearing the music, even when it is not playing. It is to forget that our job is not to play *toward* something beautiful, but to play *out of* what we know to be real. Our job is to live and act in this world ever-attuned to the music of God's reign, ever-ready to sight-read any music set before us because we have access to its reality and are eager to actualize it in the world.

What would it take, I wonder, to live like this? How do we go about participating without ceasing in the music of God that seems, right now, to be so hard to hear? Jesus taught us to ask that the Kingdom come and God's will be done "on earth as it is in heaven." But how do we go about imagining the reign of God so keenly that we hum it into actuality, feeling the very rhythms of it, respecting those edgy "naturals" so we've got 'em when they come—joining in the Spirit's nimble ways and surprising work?

My beginning answer is that we need to do a better job of creating the space and time to imagine God's Kingdom, so that we are ready to play its music whenever we are called upon. And here's where I default to the standard Christian advice we pastoral types dole out to anyone interested in being a faithful disciple: We need to pray. Read our Bibles. Go to church.

I know we know these already. But we need to reclaim them in a new way. What if we thought of prayer, Bible reading, and going to church as ways of creating spaces, in our frenetic lives, to imagine the music of God's Kingdom? In praying we remember we are already part of the reality that we desperately want to help actualize on earth. In seeking God's Word through reading the Bible and listening for proclamation we learn the details of how the music is working, becoming players, as well as listeners, in the process. In the context of Christian worship we enact the transformation we seek, setting a table around which there are not bipartisan loaves, but one loaf from which everyone, united in Christ, is fed. Playing the music, we leave the sanctuary humming, eager to share it with others.

To stand up for what we believe, we need be ready to play what is set before us.[3] And to be ready starts neither with boosting our qualifications nor rushing headlong in, despite ourselves, determined to do our best. It starts with creating sacred spaces in our lives to imagine the reality of the Kingdom of God with clarity and consistency. Insofar as we can envision the peaceable Kingdom in which wolves and lambs lie down together and every tear is wiped away from every eye, I believe we will be driven by impatient hope to do the will of God that makes it actual on this earth.

Making God's Desire Ours

When we focus on imagining what it is that God desires, as people of hope, we emphasize that the work does not and cannot begin with *us*, but rather is grounded in God. We work hard to do our part, as participants in the labor of God, impatient to witness the coming of God's Kingdom to earth as it is in heaven. We are impatient for the Kingdom to come not because we have any right to be but because God has promised. And the basis of any action we take to manifest God's Kingdom in and to this world is the reality of God's unsurpassable grace and unconditional love. On the basis of our own efforts, we might be able to make the world a better place. But we won't be able to make wolves lie down with lambs, or wipe every tear away from every eye, or ensure that every child in the world goes to bed every night with a full stomach. At best, we—in and of ourselves—can make a small difference. We can "practice random acts of kindness and senseless beauty"[4] that might in some small way touch the lives of others, but we will know better than to try to attempt to transform things at their very core. When we focus on our own capacities, our best hope is that somehow God will take the limited things we are able to do and maximize their impact.

When our work is founded in the promises of a graceful and loving God, our focus is not on what we can and can't do, but on what God intends to do, and on how God desires to work with us. While we (on our own) can only upgrade the actual, God (with us) makes the impossible possible. A stuttering man leads the chosen ones into the promised land; a virgin bears the Savior of the world; fishermen and peasant women receive the Spirit and become the church.[5] It is the graceful, loving God who makes possible the impossible dreams God has promised. And this God includes us in bringing these possible impossibilities to fruition. As God used Moses, Abram, and Sarai; as God used Mary, and Peter, and Paul—so God uses us. Essentially. Irreplaceably. We who can do nothing, in and of ourselves, are fully included in the divine life and work. We can do more than tweak, more than improve, more than contribute a little something we hope, somehow, will make a small difference. Rather, we can engage the bold work of participating in the coming Kingdom of God because we have faith that we who can do nothing in and of ourselves can do all things in him who strengthens us.[6]

With echos of chapter 9 in play, we move now, as people of hope, to consideration of how we might contribute to the Kingdom's actual *shape*. To make this move takes some imaginative effort. This is because the Kingdom is not something realistic or self-evident. It is fundamentally impractical, defying the realities of our daily existence. It represents, as I have said, not simply a "tweaking" of this world, but a world that is altogether different from everything we know.

Every time we pray the Lord's Prayer, we remember and profess our hope that God's Kingdom will come. So confident are we that this will happen that we even demand it. "God's Kingdom come!" we cry, following up with: "Thy will be done." To be people of a hope that is not escapist is to insist on jumping in and contributing to its realization. All of us probably agree that it is harder to know and to live according to God's will than we might have hoped. Most Christian believers have asked, on more than one occasion, "How do I know what God's will is?" Consistent with the emphases in the prior chapter, the basic answer to this question assumed here is: "We know what God's will is when and insofar as we participate in the desire of our gracious, loving God to bring God's Kingdom to earth as it is in heaven." Well. That makes it sound relatively simple. Except, of course, that we know it is not. "But how, exactly, do we participate in the desire of God?" we ask. "How do we participate so deeply and freely in the life and work of God that our doing of God's will is simply an extension of our participation?"

Building on our discussion of "hope and imagination" in chapter 9, I suggest that one path to the kind of deep participation in the life of God that gives way to the doing of God's will is *imagining* God's Kingdom. In the context of our imagining the Kingdom God desires, I believe, the Holy Spirit forms us into doers of God's will. In short, our imagination serves as a vehicle through which the Spirit works to facilitate our participation in the promises, grace, and love of God in such a way that God's desires become our desires, and our desires break forth into concrete actions that advance the coming of the Kingdom. I have in mind, in relation to this, the first two verses of Romans 12. Here, Paul exhorts us to "present our bodies as living sacrifices," to resist "being conformed to the world," and to be "transformed by the renewing of our minds." It is right here that I see imagination in play. Through imagining the Kingdom of God ("setting our minds on things above"), our minds are "renewed." And it is at this point, precisely, that "we discern what is the will of God—what is good and acceptable and perfect."[7]

I realize that talk of "imagination" will raise some suspicions. First, we might understandably say, doesn't imagination concern itself with the "not real"? The last thing we, as people who hold faith, want to do is portray the Kingdom of God as that which is a nice idea, an inspiring metaphor, but not something that will actually come to be. Too often, in the history of Christendom, eschatological concepts have been misused to establish not-real imaginary worlds in which people can "escape" from the painful realities of the "real" world. Allow me, therefore, to be very clear about this: when I talk about imagining the Kingdom of God, I am not advocating we imagine a world that is fun and inspiring but will never come to be. I am recommending, in fact, that we imagine a Kingdom that is both future and present, a world that is at the same time both the Kingdom of God that is coming to be and the "real reality" that contrasts, even now, to this painful world that is not our home.[8] The kind of imagining I have in mind, unlike the kind Christopher Robin engages until he is six (when he becomes too old for such frivolity) is not devoted to creating worlds that will not, and do not, actually exist. The Kingdom of God is not an imaginary place in which not-real talking animals get stuck in honey pots, rescue each other from the "rain rain rain" that comes "down down down,"[9] or make last-minute plans for birthday parties. The kind of imagining I have in mind is not the kind we should grow out of, as we become more conscious of, and responsible for, the realities of this world. Of course we do grow out of it, too often, as our exposure to the world's atrocities render us increasingly hopeless and cynical. But this is a bad thing, we hold, as people of faith. And so we work at the Table to revive our imagining; to recapture the Kingdom we claim is real; to remember our real home is characterized by all receiving bread, and all living in reconciled relationship, and none succumbing to temptation. While such imagining is, in one sense, at least as far-fetched as imagining Winnie-the-Pooh and the Hundred Acre Wood, it is grounded in the promises, grace, and love of God and not in our own wishes and desires. It is imagination that participates in the reality of God rather than advancing our own projected realities.

There is a second, related objection we might have to thinking about accessing the hope of our faith by way of "imagination." In short, we are worried that "imagining" the Kingdom of God will lead to the creation of idols. What is to prevent our imaginations from running amok, from leading us to create and desire worlds that are of our own making, rather than God's making? What is to ensure our imaginations don't pull us away from the reality of the Kingdom of God, as God has established it, toward trumped-up versions of kingdoms of this world? Certainly, a quick survey of history uncovers example after example of earthly Kingdoms formed through the exercise of imagination. Some of these kingdoms have preserved and advanced life as much as possible, but not completely; most have expended the life of some to benefit the lives of others who are more powerful; none are the Kingdom of God in which *all* have life and *none* are expended for the sake of others.

What ensures our imaginations will not lead us to create kingdoms of this world, but rather contribute to the real reality of the Kingdom of God, is attentiveness to starting point. Our starting point for imagining (and our ending point, for that matter!) is God. What we are imagining is not first and foremost what *we* desire, but what *God* desires. What we are envisioning is not the most fabulous kingdom that would be possible *if* this world granted us more resources and certain superpowers, but the Kingdom that is not of this world, that is qualitatively different from this world, that is of the God who is *totaliter aliter* ("totally other") than this world. We are, in fact, imagining that which is beyond anything we can imagine, because it belongs to the one "who is able to do far beyond all that we could ask or imagine by his power at work within us."[10] The imagining I am talking about here is imagining founded in that one who has claimed us as God's children: the one who makes outlandish promises, the one who continuously remakes and restores us, the one whose love is poured out and into us so fully that it spills over into works of love.

Calvin, I believe, had precisely this kind of imagining in mind when he instructed people of faith to "proclaim the majesty of God." He honestly thought this should be the agenda of every sermon, of every Christian education class, and of every confession of faith we make in the context of private conversations. When speaking with members of the "visible church" (those who know their election in Jesus Christ)—*proclaim the majesty of God.* When speaking with those who might very well be participants in the "invisible church" (those who are not yet cognizant of their election)—*proclaim the majesty of God.* We are called to proclaim the majesty of God, according to Calvin, both to edify the established Christian community and to evangelize those who might one day become members of it. It is his firm conviction, in fact, that as we bear witness to God's majesty, the Holy Spirit draws hearers more deeply into participation in the life and work of God.

We gave some consideration, in the preceding chapter, to how Calvin employs imagination in his proclamation of the divine majesty. Again, he does not imagine his way from himself to God. Rather, he begins with God's self-revelation, contemplating God's acts playfully and joyously. Calvin writes about God's actions on our behalf as though he is a kid in a candy store. He insists, for example, that "there is not one blade of grass, there is no color in this world that is not intended to make us rejoice"[11] and that therefore we are "not only to be spectators in this beautiful theater but to enjoy the vast bounty and variety of good things which are displayed to us in it."[12] Reveling in the bounty that is God's gift to us, Calvin watches a nanny speaking tenderly to a baby and imaginatively proclaims the majesty of God: God, our loving caretaker, "lisps" to us. Borrowing a creative quote from Gregory of Nazianzus, Calvin testifies to the majesty of the Trinity. "I cannot think on the one without quickly being encircled by the splendor of the three"; he cites, "nor can I discern the three without being straightway carried back to the one."[13] In these three quotes alone we witness Calvin bursting with imagination: celebrating grass and colors, identifying the world as the theater of God's glory, envisioning God as the nanny who speaks baby talk to us, and utilizing Gregory's majestic imagery to make the important theological point that there is "distinction, but not...division" in the life of the triune God.[14]

Calvin's creative proclamation of the majesty of God, I believe, is grounded in his conscious participation in the life of the God who meets us, makes us, blesses us, and sends us to share with the world. In other words, his imaginative language is not one strategic element in a system he employs to be a more winsome theologian or a more effective preacher. I'm certain he does not have, stacked on the corner of his desk, a pile of books instructing him on how to use catchy, marketable language to captivate one's congregation or audience.[15] Rather, Calvin's imaginative language itself both extends from and bears witness to his participation in the life and work of God. Calvin proclaims the majesty of God as one who reflects habitually on his relationship to God; in the context of his life of prayer he imagines what it is that God desires, both for himself and for this world. And he comes to participate ever more deeply in it, in such a way that God's desires, by the power of the Spirit at work within him, continuously form—and correct—his own.

And Calvin's participation in the work and will of God, facilitated by such imagining, then gives way to world-changing action. Submitting to the exhortations of a Christian brother,[16] he tears himself away from his safe circumstances and goes to Geneva; he writes the *Institutes* and the treatises of the Reformation; his prose contributes to the shaping of modern French. He supports separation of church and state[17] and advocates for more humane methods of criminal punishment.[18] He makes such strong provision for education that his vision extends to the Western world. Concerned to minimize the possibility of disease in the city of Geneva, he is also largely responsible for the installation of a closed sewer system.[19] All these things Calvin accomplishes, it seems, with an eye toward the coming Kingdom of God, never forgetting that "grace alone brings about every good work in us."[20]

If Calvin's example of how to do justice in the world without wavering one iota from a God-centered theology isn't enough to license the use of our imagination, consider the example of Jesus. Jesus has the habit of using whatever is ready at hand to proclaim the majesty of God, inviting others to participate so fully in it that their very participation contributes to its coming. Jesus encourages a Samaritan woman to deepen in her faith by referencing something she needs, and she carries, every day—a bucket of water.[21] The woman begins to *imagine* never again having to draw or to drink. Jesus invites a religious leader named Nicodemus to think of spiritual renewal in terms of the everyday occurrence of childbirth. Nicodemus begins imagining what it would be like to be born again.[22] Jesus challenges the disciples to feed those who are hungry with what is ready at hand.[23] He calls them to *imagine* that the contents of the lunchbox of one little boy can feed all those people.

Now, we know that the Samaritan woman was a good imaginer, and that her capacity to trust Jesus (to imagine and to believe that what he was saying was true) led her, in turn, to proclaim the good news to her townspeople. Unrelenting in her insistence that they "come and see" this one who tells her "everything I've done,"[24] the townspeople finally give in, eventually testifying that they have come to believe, "for we have heard for ourselves."[25]

Nicodemus and the disciples do not appear as able as the Samaritan woman to imagine the Kingdom in which Jesus is inviting them to participate. Nicodemus and Jesus apparently part ways, on the night after they have the conversation about being "born again," with Nicodemus appearing still to be deeply skeptical.[26] But he goes on to make two additional appearances in the Gospel of John, both which indicate he is stepping out of the kingdoms of this world and into the Kingdom of God. First, in chapter 7, he reminds his fellow Saducees, and the temple police, that Jewish law "doesn't judge someone without first hearing him and learning what he is doing."[27] Second, in chapter 19, he assists Joseph of Arimathea in removing Jesus's body from the cross, embalming it, and burying it in Joseph's own, newly hewn tomb. Joseph, it seems, provided the tomb and the linen. Nicodemus, for his part, provided the spices—seventy pounds of myrrh and aloe. Like Mary before him, his gift is excessive.[28] Because Nicodemus (alongside Joseph) is able to imagine a different reality than the one in which Jesus is nailed to the cross, Jesus's body is not left on the cross to decay, but is taken down and treated respectfully.

Like Nicodemus, the disciples find it difficult to imagine that God's desire for the people surrounding them might actually be realized. Concerned that the time for the evening meal is drawing nigh, they urge Jesus to recommend they break for the evening so individual families can go into town and buy food for themselves. They recognize they do not have the resources to feed such a large crowd of people—in one Gospel, they note it would take six months' salary to buy enough bread for every person to have just a taste.[29] But Jesus insists the disciples find a way to host the people. While each of the Gospel accounts suggests the disciples receive Jesus's plan with skepticism, they in no evident way resist his concrete instructions. They collect the bread and the fish, they organize the people into picnic groups, and they have enough faith not to turn on their heels and walk away from the scene, scandalized by the absurdity of it all. They have enough faith, it seems, to begin imagining what they clearly know is unimaginable.

Each of these figures in different ways shows us what it looks like actively to live into the Kingdom of God. The Samaritan woman imagines the living water Jesus tells her about, and is drawn through the work of the Spirit into deeper participation in the life of God. Her imagining gives way to action: she goes back to her town and does the work of an evangelist, insisting that her townspeople come and see this one she has met,[30] to participate in relationship to him, and to enter into the fellowship of the Kingdom. Interestingly, the passage makes a big point of telling us that the townspeople are moved to trek out to the well and meet Jesus specifically by the woman's compelling testimony that "he told me everything I've ever done."[31] Clearly, this woman is not only good at accepting Jesus's invitation to imagine; she is also herself gifted at inviting others to imagine with her. "Could this man be the Christ?" she asks.[32] She draws them in; they can't resist; they go to the well; they meet Jesus; and *then* they come to believe because they have "heard for ourselves."[33]

Nicodemus continues to reflect on what Jesus has told him; the imaginative "born again" imagery is used by the Holy Spirit to draw him even more deeply into relationship to God through his relationship to Jesus himself. I like to think that Nicodemus's ongoing engagement with the beautiful and truthful metaphor of Jesus gave way, finally, to his participation in the work of the Kingdom. His giving of the spices and participation in the embalming and burial, I think, certainly serve to promote justice on at least three levels. First, he who is presumably well off (financially speaking) shares his wealth with Jesus, a man who is (economically) poor. He cares for the Good Teacher whom many dearly loved, the Teacher through whom he comes to participate in life eternal. In providing for the care of Jesus's body, he participates in Jesus's ministry to bodies that thirst, and hunger, and groan for the completion of their redemption. In caring for Jesus, Nicodemus makes an actual contribution to the coming of the Kingdom. He quite literally tends the body that will rise again on Sunday, walk and talk and eat with the disciples, ascend to heaven to sit on the right hand of the Father, and come again to take us to himself.[34] In caring for Jesus's body, Nicodemus is participating in the resurrection that has not even happened yet. He is living into, and thereby advancing, the new life Jesus has told him about.

And then there are those concerned, practical, initially unimaginative disciples. I try to fathom what must have run through their heads as they handed Jesus the five loaves and two fishes. They must have been expecting him to shake his head, woefully, as he agreed with them that it was time to bring the evening to a close. Instead, Jesus instructs them to have the people sit down for a meal. I tell you what—something had to have shifted, in the disciples, when Jesus gave them this instruction. Something led the disciples from thinking *obviously we can't feed them* to *let's all sit down, now, and get ready to eat.* The way I see it, you have to have some imagination operative if you are going to have the guts to run around organizing five thousand plus people for a meal that is, for all intents and purposes, nonexistent. You have to have some hope that this man who has been healing bodies and teaching bodies can also feed bodies out of nothing. To have such hope is at least to have a glimpse of the Kingdom in sight: the wedding table of the Lamb around which all are gathered, at which all are fed, at which none go hungry. And the disciples clearly helped them bring this Kingdom to earth, as it is in heaven, with their organizing and collecting. In their imagining, which enables them to participate, they contribute to bringing it into being.

Vocation, Mission, and Risk

We've mentioned Barth's thinking that "if we think there is no other way" than to be stressed out, "we are always wrong." To think it is OK to put off imagining what God is calling us to, for a time, so we can get all our other stuff done, is to deny the sovereignty of God. It is to neglect the freedom we have to act courageously and take creative risks precisely because God is in charge of it all. To do, do, do all the time is—in a sense—to imagine we make it all happen. To do the Word of God—by contrast—is to remember it is God who is in charge.

When we prioritize getting a lot of stuff done over hearing God's Word and doing it, we miss out on participating in God's mission in the world.

I once heard Allan Boesak speak along these lines.[35] Allan Boesak is a black African theologian who helped fight apartheid in South Africa. What Boesak said in his lecture took me off guard, a bit. He said that, if you miss the chance to do God's Word, you've missed it. The chance will never come back.

"Huh?" I asked him, in a luncheon discussion following the discussion, a dreadful ache growing in my stomach.

And here is my paraphrase of his life-changing reply: "We have to be ready to hear God's Word and do it, or we will miss doing it. You Americans think God's Word will wait for you until you're ready to obey. You treat it the same way you treat ideals like 'liberty and justice.' Like they will always be there. You take them for granted. But it is important that American Christians learn that the transformative work God is calling us to do will not always be available. We must be ready to hear, and ready to act, or it will be gone."

My mind raced to how the Scripture describes the character of God's Word. God's Word isn't static, we believe. It is "living, active, and sharper than any two-edged sword." It is steadfast and unchanging, but it is—at the same time—living and dynamic. It keeps on meeting us, ever-anew, in each particular moment, in each particular situation, in very particular ways. When we preach (or listen to preaching), we're trying to discern and bear witness to the word's particular shape, to us as particular people, in this particular moment. The word doesn't just hang out in here. It's not hunkered down in a corner pew, inviting us to come by and chat "whenever": whenever we are not busy. Actually, the Word is the one who is busiest of all; the Word is doing; the Word is working to make all things new. We listen for it, we hear it, and then—then!—is the moment to join in the doing. Creating all things, showing Abram the stars, leading the Shunammite woman to build Elisha a shelter; entering the womb of the virgin, eating with tax collectors and sinners, suffering on that cross. Sending the

Spirit, coming again—the Word has entered our history not in general, not in the abstract, but in flesh and in blood and in time and in space and with us and in the now. Right now. Will we hear it? Will we do it? Can we clear away our doing, so we can be doers of the Word, even now? Or will we turn again from the mirror, forgetting? Missing the opportunity for our doing, burned out by our own inside-out hypocrisy? [36]

As Boesak spoke, that ache in my belly became identifiable grief as I faced the reality that I have been so busy doing, at times, that I have forgotten to be an imaginer of the Kingdom and a doer of the very Word I have heard and even, myself, proclaimed.

Without taking away his hard point, Boesak helped by gently explaining that, in his observation, we American Christians are so caught up in doing that we are not positioned to hear the specific things God is saying to us and calling us to do. Christians are as consumeristic, he said, as the rest of our culture—so obsessed with trying to make something of ourselves and our churches that we miss what God is trying to make us into.

He told a story[37] of when he once let an opportunity go by, when he and his colleagues heard the Word, but did not do it. He explained that there was a moment when he and his colleagues could have voted to reunite the Dutch Reformed Church in South Africa, but that they didn't call for the vote because they thought there might be a better time, a time that was more politically expedient. But things got worse, and there was not the chance to call for such a vote again. Not acting in that moment, when they had the opportunity, meant that there would not be another chance for at least a generation, Boesak insisted. He exhorted us to be ready, today, for whatever God calls us to do.

Vocation and This Moment

Boesak's words still scare me. I am afraid we are missing opportunities to gain life because we are afraid of losing it. I am afraid not only that we will hesitate in some future "big" moment when we are asked to sacrifice, but that we are already hesitating, for the sake of being politically expedient, for the sake of keeping everything in equilibrium. Again, being politically savvy and keeping things in equilibrium are important values, until they keep us from doing what God would have us do. Are our "right answers" keeping us from doing the will of God?

What sense can we make of *this moment*, as a moment of discipleship? What are we being called upon to do and to be right now, today? For it is right now—today—that the Messiah asks us to join him in doing power differently, in hoping against hope, and in holding nothing back for the sake of those whom God so loves. It is not that the moment might come, or even is definitely coming, at some point. That moment is here, in some particular way we need to ascertain. Will we let it pass by, or will we respond? Will we go with Jesus, or will he rebuke us—we who are the rocks, we who are among his beloved? Will we join in what God is doing in the world, or will we cling so fiercely to the understandings we have cobbled for ourselves that we don't even see the cross we are supposed to carry? Will we join in with what God is up to, or will we just get in the way? What we have to gain are lives that participate in a world that is new; in the world God promises; in a world that is wide and free; in a world where everyone is included and all tears have been wiped away.

The Hard Actuality

In every era, people have experienced crises in faith. Our time is no different, though our crises have, as all crises do, particular shapes.

Globally, we have lost confidence that we know what to do to keep people safe and healthy. All around the world, there are people who start every day by picking up a newspaper and scanning it for the latest terrorist attack. We breathe air that is impacted by pollution, we absorb sun's rays made dangerous by the erosion of our atmosphere, and we are surrounded by chemicals our bodies work to manage until they succumb to cancers or other diseases. Too many people are hungry; too many are homeless; too many are incarcerated; too many lack basic medical care. Even our identities are at risk, susceptible to cyberattacks that, we are told, are becoming a kind of "new normal." We grope for ways to survive, but whatever efforts we can take seem to pale in comparison to the threats that surround us.

Nationally, many Americans have lost all faith in political leadership. The common perception is that this crisis is bipartisan—there is a failure on all sides to represent, to care for, to work together, to tell the truth, to look out for those most in need. There is an unwillingness even to listen to the voices of others and a kind of insistence on operating according to fears based in destructive stereotypes. There has been, of late, a resurgence of concern about ongoing racism and sexism. This is in one way a hopeful thing, but it is also painful to realize that those we have until recently held in high respect have been living lies, engaging in acts of violence and profound disrespect that have done great damage both to other human beings and to our world at large.

Ecclesially, as we have discussed, there is a crisis in faith in organized religions and religious institutions. This is related to our global and national faith crises, since churches often reflect and have a hand in shaping the dynamics of culture. As we have discussed, a particular form the current faith crisis is taking, as described by the growing numbers of the Dones as well as the Nones, is that Christians claim to be different from the world and then actually are not. As Letty Russell once put it, instead of being "in the world and not of it," as the New Testament instructs, Christians are "of the world but not in it."[38] This crisis of faith is articulated in the form of testimony to an experience of betrayal: the Nones were once hoping people of faith would model a different way of being, believing this is what they had promised. But people of faith failed to come through, they say, as witnesses to a way of being that honors all life.[39]

In each of these spheres, there is a great deal of fear. Fear that we are not safe; fear there is very little we can do to ensure the safety of others. Fear that, no matter how hard we work, it will be impossible to advance—economically or socially. Fear that we are losing ground, in relation to power, influence, wealth and numbers. Fear that, if we risk opening ourselves up to new people and possibilities, the dissipating cache we have left will be lost.

Given all this, I recognize that to imagine a single book can make a difference is a pretty big stretch. But I do believe there are certain ideas—I would even say truths—that can change everything when we hold onto them, in faith, in the midst of crisis. My greatest hope is that you have found even just one such idea in this book. For me, the most transformative ideas of all are that we have been met by a God who has entered into existence with us, and we are lifted up by this God into the ongoing work of being made and making, of being blessed and blessing, and of being sent to be with and for one another even as God is with and for us. I try to hold on to these ideas as the framing reality of my life and all lives, but (as discussed in chapter 8), it can be difficult not to let them slip out of head and heart.

When our faith is shaped and reshaped by the truths that have sustained our forebears through the ages, we gain a "new capacity" for living in relation to the circumstances around us, according to Barth. This new capacity is, in fact, faith itself—gifted to us by God as an overflow of grace. While faith does not exempt us from circumstances, it does release us from incapacitating fear. It can free us, Barth says, "from any fear of the world or life or sin or hell."[40] How? By keeping our "gaze firmly fixed on Jesus" who has "overcome the world."[41] The surprise twist on all this is that Barth is not referring, this time, to Jesus Christ overcoming the world by way of the cross, resurrection, and ascension. He is reminding us that Jesus also overcame the world, on a day-to-day basis and before all the eyes that were present to see, through the performance of miracles.

I find it helpful to think of faith as a "new capacity," a manifestation of God's grace, in this difficult world, that is nothing short of miraculous. And what is so appealing about the miracle of faith is that it is not something "out of this world," standing at a distance from everyday life. As Jesus's miracles occurred in the middle of crowds, or conflicts, or terrible pain or walks on a beach, so our capacious faith is exercised, and can and will be exercised, in the context of this teeming, dangerous, fearful world that surrounds us.

Allow me to close with a brief exhortation, as we together seek to hold on to this new capacity, this miracle that is faith.

Daring Faith

The day before I graduated with my PhD, the then-president of Princeton Seminary looked me straight in the eye and made a startling remark. "You'll never again know as much as you know right now," he said. "I trust that you'll get a lot wiser," he said. "But you'll never know more." As my understanding of what it means and why it matters to know things has changed over the years, I believe I've experienced what he meant.

You are finishing this book knowing a lot, with a lot to hold on to.

The most important thing I'm hoping you know is that Christianity teaches that God is not simply God in general, but the God who chose us, who loves us, who will never let us go. Now, this is the kind of knowing you may have had since you were a child and feel you have basically held on to, in the course of all your theological escapades. Or it may be something you just can't buy into, given the state of the world or your skepticism about an omnipotent God paying attention to particular persons. Most of us likely fall somewhere between these two ways of describing ourselves—sometimes confident in God's presence; sometimes skeptical that it is as real as we want it to be.

The psalmists, by and large, seem to share the "up and down" experience of holding faith. One of the things they tell us is that knowing the God of all is also our God takes a lifetime of attention. We need to take the effort to *be still* in order to know again. And again. "Be still, and know that I am God."[42] We talked, in this book, about how difficult this can be in twenty-first-century American culture. It is no easy thing, in this crazy-busy world, to create time and space for stillness. It's hard enough not to check our texts in the course of a worship service, never mind being still enough to experience knowledge of God in an altogether new way.

Acknowledging that holding faith can be kind of a "roller coaster" experience, I'm hoping you are ending this book with a commitment to staying on the train, seeking ever to know and re-know who God is and what God is up to in the world. Again, the specifics of what God desires are not always easy to ascertain, and there is always the chance we who think we know them have misunderstood and will have to be corrected in our understanding, seeking again. But there are things we do know: God is with us. We are loved and forgiven. God is opposed to all injustices. God's Kingdom will come, and people of faith are included in the work that will bring it. Paul, in his letter to the Romans, talks about people who hold faith "being transformed by the renewal of their minds."[43] If being still creates a context for re-knowing God, renewing our minds carves a space for knowing God's will so we can go out into the world and help to make it so.

In the final analysis, people who hold tight to the faith that embraces them are never done gathering knowledge. This is because they are in the business of bearing witness to a God who is known, in each moment, ever-anew. The learning continues; and I mean not only experiential learning. I mean book learning. I mean focused theological, liturgical, exegetical study. I mean the kind of study that leads us to be still. I mean the kind of study that creates sacred spaces for us to think, to contemplate, and to re-know the somethings that matter to everything: that God meets us and continues to make us, that God desires to bless every life and the life of the world, and that God sends us to share all that is meaningful with one another.

NOTES

Preface

1. Phil 4:8.

2. See, for example, Lydai Saad, "U. S. Confidence in Organized Religion at Low Point," *Gallup News*, July 12, 2012, http://news.gallup.com/poll/155690/Confidence-Organized-Religion-Low-Point.aspx?utm_source=google&utm_medium=rss&utm_campaign=syndication, which reviews a 2002–2012 Gallup poll on this subject.

3. See, for example, Gary Laderman, "America's Religious Future: Dechristianization (Not Secularization)," *Huffington Post*, September 21, 2013, http://www.huffingtonpost.com/gary-laderman/religion-in-america_b_3632516.html.

Introduction: Transforming Theology

1. More about this in ch. 3.

2. The Contemporary English Version of Ephesians 2:4-5, for example, reads "God was merciful! We were dead because of our sins, but God loved us so much that he made us alive with Christ, and God's *wonderful kindness* is what saves you." And Ephesians 2:8a, for example, reads "You were saved by faith in God, *who treats us much better than we deserve*" (emphasis added).

3. I will explore the "so what?" of the doctrine of grace later in the book. My purpose here is to give an example of why it is important not to discard theological terminology for language that is easier to understand.

4. 1 Pet 3:15, NRSV.

5. Immanuel Kant, *The Critique of Pure Reason,* trans. Norman Kemp Smith (Edinburgh: T&T Clark, 1929), 93.

6. Scholasticism spanned the twelfth through the seventeenth centuries, directly preceding the Enlightenment. Anselm lived 1033–1109 CE. Aquinas lived 1225–1274 CE.

7. See, for instance, Ps 139 and Matt 28.

8. Gen 32:22-32.

9. View this comic at http://www.gocomics.com/peanuts/1976/08/09.

10. Phil 2:5-8.

11. Matt 21:12-13.

12. Matt 15:21-28.

13. Mark 6:30-44.

14. Matt 16:16.

15. Matt 16:17-18.

16. Matt 16:23.

17. "Nones" is slang for "None of the above," as in: people who resist self-identifying as "True Believers" or as "Atheists" on religious surveys because they are neither of these two things. They are still searching to articulate what they believe. They are, in a word, curious.

18. Eric Weiner, *Man Seeks God: My Flirtations with the Divine* (New York: Hatchett, 2011).

19. Eric Weiner, "Americans: Undecided About God?" *The New York Times,* op-ed (December 11, 2011).

20. Anselm of Canterbury, "An Address (Proslogian)," in *Scholastic Miscellany: Anselm to Ockham,* ed. Eugene Fairweather, Library of Christian Classics (Louisville: Westminster John Knox, 1956), preface.

21. Weiner, "Americans: Undecided," Op-Ed.

22. John E. Rotelle, ed., *Sermons,* trans. Edmund Hill (Brooklyn: New City Press, 1990), Sermo 52, 6, 16: PL 38, 360 and Sermo 117, 3, 5: PL 38, 663.

23. Anselm of Canterbury, "An Address," 119.

24. Eph 3:20.

25. Edward Hallowell, *CrazyBusy: Overstretched, Overbooked, and About to Snap! Strategies for Handling Your Fast-Paced Life* (New York: Random House, 2007).

26. George Prochnik, "I'm Thinking. Please. Be Quiet," *New York Times Sunday Review*, op-ed (August 24, 2013).

27. A. A. Milne, *The Complete Tales of Winnie-the-Pooh* (New York: Penguin Books, 1994), 41.

28. See, for example, Scott Jaschik, "Disappearing Liberal Arts Colleges," Inside Higher Ed, last modified October 11, 2012, https://www.insidehighered.com/news/2012/10/11/study-finds-liberal-arts-colleges-are-disappearing.

29. Luke 1:38.

30. *Finding Nemo*, directed by Andrew Stanton and Lee Unkrich, Disney, 2003.

31. Luke 1:48.

32. I'm thinking, here, that the thief who derides Christ, hanging with him on the cross, might even be included. This is what Barth argues, in a sermon on Luke 23:33 titled "The Criminals with Him." See: Karl Barth, "The Criminals with Him," in *Deliverance to the Captives* (Portsmith, NH: Greenwood Publishing Group, 1979), 75–84.

33. Matt 17:20.

34. See, in particular, Mark 11:23, where the disciples are told they would have been able to heal a child of demonic possession if they had had more faith.

35. The Apostles' Creed is the earliest known Creed of the Christian church, dating back to the second century CE. It is confessed around the world, and by Christians of many denominations, still today. It can be accessed at: https://en.wikipedia.org/wiki/Apostles'_Creed.

36. 2 Tim 3:16.

37. See also John 5:39. The Scriptures have authority because they "testify to" the work of God in Jesus Christ. The subject of the authority of Scripture will be considered in greater detail in ch. 2.

38. Mark 11:22.

39. John 14:1, 18.

40. John 14:3.

41. Mark 9:21-24.

42. Martin Luther, *Lectures on Galatians*, eds. Jaroslav Pelican and William Hansen, Luther's Works, XXVI (Saint Louis: Concordia, 1963), 132 (Gal 2:16).

43. Barth, *CD* IV/2, §64.3, 245–46 (See also IV.1, §59.1, 201).

1. How Can We Speak of God?

1. Eph 3:20.

2. Eph 3:18.

3. C. S. Lewis, *Prince Caspian: The Return to Narnia* (New York: Collier Books, 1950), 141.

4. For some discussion on this, see Karl Tate, "How Quantum Entanglement Works (Infographic)," LiveScience, last modified April 8, 2013, http://www.livescience.com/28550-how-quantum-entanglement-works-infographic.html. This article reports that Einstein described the phenomenon of "quantum entanglement" as "spooky action from a distance."

5. This is, in my view, a stellar illustration of "postmodernity." If moderns think they can know everything there is to be known (given enough time, attention, and wherewithal), postmoderns know they can't know—and often take pride in "knowing" they don't know! David Harvey suggests that the tendency of postmoderns to "know they cannot know" is still a kind of knowing, claiming postmodernity, therefore, to be an extension of modernity. See, on this, David Harvey's, *Condition of Postmodernity* (Hoboken: Wiley/Blackwell, 1991).

6. This commonly held idea has more recently been de-bunked as a "myth." See, on this: Cate Matthews, "What Percentage of Our Brains Do We Actually Use? Popular Myth Debunked in TED-Ed Video," Huffpost Science, last modified February 4, 2014, http://www.huffingtonpost.com/2014/02/04/ted-ed-percentage-brain-richard-cytowic_n_4719173.html. This doesn't change the fact that we have been formed with the idea that we all have significant, untapped potential.

7. Kindly note that, if this reflection on films is not of interest to you, you can easily skip the next six paragraphs without losing the thread of the discussion.

8. *Lucy*, directed by Luc Besson, Universal Pictures, 2014.

9. *The Fifth Element*, directed by Luc Besson, Columbia Pictures, 1997.

10. Interesting that we could interpret the rules of religion in a similar way—the rule that would be broken in the Garden of Eden; the Ten Commandments.

11. See, for example, Isaac Asimov, *I, Robot*, reprint ed. (New York: Random House, 2008). First published in 1950.

12. *2001: A Space Odyssey*, directed by Stanley Kubrick, Metro-Goldwyn-Mayer, 1968.

13. *Close Encounters of the Third Kind*, directed by Steven Spielberg, Columbia Pictures, 1977.

14. *E. T. the Extra-Terrestrial*, directed by Steven Spielberg, Universal Studios, 1982.

15. *Contact*, directed by Robert Zemeckis, Warner Brothers, 1997. Based on Carl Sagan's 1985 novel by the same name.

16. I am referring to Skywalker's Jedi training, with Yoda.

17. *Star Wars: Episode IV*, directed by George Lucas, Lucasfilm, 1977.

18. The rule that says one culture should not meddle in the rules and traditions of another. *Star Trek: The Next Generation*, CBS, 1987–1994, created by Gene Roddenberry.

19. For example, copies of Harry's letter of admittance to Hogwarts—the school of wizardry to which Harry is admitted—keep on coming, in increasing numbers, impervious to the considerable efforts of Harry's mean and fearful aunt and uncle to deter them. J. K. Rowling, "The Letters from No One," in *Harry Potter and the Sorcerer's Stone* (New York: Scholastic, 1997).

20. *Monsters vs. Aliens*, directed by Conrad Vernon and Rob Letterman, produced by Dreamworks, Paramount Pictures, 2009.

21. Matt 4:19.

22. John 8:11.

23. John 4.

24. John 3.

25. Luke 14.

26. Matt 28.

27. Matt 17; Luke 9.

28. Luke 10.

29. John 15.

30. John E. Rotelle, ed., *Sermons*, trans. Edmund Hill (Brooklyn: New City Press, 1990), Sermo 52:6, Sermo 117:3.

31. Augustine, *Confessions*, trans. Henry Chadwick (Oxford: Oxford University Press, 1991).

32. Augustine, *Confessions*, 3.11.19.

33. Eph 3:20.

34. From the lyrics to Julie Gold's "From a Distance." "Julie Gold—From a Distance (Live) Lyrics," SongLyrics, http://www.songlyrics.com/julie-gold/from-a-distance-live-lyrics/.

35. Ps 139:8-10.

36. While the psalmists have generally been referred to as male, scholars have more recently hypothesized that there were probably female as well as male psalmists. John Eaton suggests, for example, that the presence and popularity of female singers in the temple argues that women may have written, as well as sung, a number of the psalms. Eaton points out, further, that women are identified both as professional mourners and as prophetesses, as in the case of Miriam. See John Eaton, *Psalms: An Historical and Spiritual Commentary with an Introduction and New Translation* (New York: Continuum, 2003), 8.

37. Ps 139:13, 16.

38. We will discuss in ch. 7 that this God who made us and is present with us also continues to make us. Not a deistic God, but a theistic/incarnational God.

39. And, in a sense, makes the God who has reached out to us both more knowable and, at the same time, more unknowable!

40. Ps 139:6.

41. Matt 10:29.

42. Isa 40:26.

43. Phil 2.

44. Luke 8.

45. Introduction to Varenne's anthology on Calvin. John F. Thornton and Susan B. Varenne, eds., *Steward of God's Covenant: Selected Writings/John Calvin* (New York: Picador, 2005), xvi. Robinson is the author of several novels as well as works of non-fiction, including the Pulitzer Prize–winning *Gilead* (New York: Picador, 2004).

46. Offering proofs for God's existence and other "apologetics" for God is, to be sure, a respectable enterprise—just not the approach I am taking here.

47. I am thinking, here, of the oft-spoken instruction of Jean-Luc Pickard in *Star Trek: The Next Generation* to the officers on the *Enterprise,* always spoken in face of impossible odds. As far as I know, the crew (like "the little engine that could") always beat the odds.

48. In *Star Trek*, for example, Spock put the odds that the mission would be successful at "less than 4.3 percent." *Star Trek*, directed by J. J. Abrams, Paramount, 2009.

49. Watty Piper, *Little Engine That Could* (New York: Platt and Munk, 1930).

50. Rev 3:20.

51. Book of Exodus, *passim.*

52. Ps 8:4.

53. Luke 1:34.

54. Book of Jonah, *passim.*

55. John 3:1-21; 7:50-51; 19:39-42.

56. See Luke 10:38-42.

57. A popular writer among evangelical Christians who value this approach is Josh McDowell. One of his most widely read books is *Evidence That Demands a Verdict* (San Bernadino: Thomas Nelson Publishers, 1999), 1 and 2; first published in 1972).

58. John 4:28.

59. See John 4, esp. vv. 39-42.

60. Acts 17:16-34.

61. 1 Cor 9:22.

62. Acts 17:22-23.

63. Philosophers and theologians have, for thousands of years, developed "proofs of God's existence." They have also argued about whether or not such proofs are effective for convincing people of the reality of God. Developing proofs for God is an "apologetical" approach to speaking about God rather than a "testimonial" approach.

64. Acts 17: 27-31.

65. This phrase was coined in a 2009 ad for the Apple iPhone 3G. It has made its way into common parlance and is used all over the Internet and by multiple advertisers. "iPhone 3g Commercial 'There's an App for That' 2009," video file, 00:30, YouTube, posted by CommercialKid, February 4, 2009, https://www.youtube.com/watch?v=szrsfeyLzyg.

66. Acts 17:27.

67. Acts 17:28.

68. Acts 17:27-28.

69. Acts 17:32 indicates that they scoffed specifically at the idea of the "resurrection of the dead."

70. Acts 17:34.

71. Acts 17:34.

72. Acts 17:28.

73. Acts 17:30.

74. Kurt Badenhausen, ed., "The World's Most Valuable Brands: #74 Red Bull," *Forbes*, last modified May 11, 2016, http://www.forbes.com/companies/red-bull/.

75. 1 Cor 13.

76. John 1:14.

77. This was in the context of deliberations on the doctrine of the Trinity, which will be considered in greater detail later in this book.

78. J. N. D. Kelly, *Early Christian Doctrines* (San Francisco: Harper and Row, 1978), 253–54.

79. *Forest Gump*, directed by Robert Zemeckis, Paramount Pictures, 1994.

80. See, for example, Alvin Kimel, "The God Who Likes His Name." In Alvin Kimel, ed., *Speaking the Christian God: The Holy Trinity and the Challenge of Feminism* (Grand Rapids: Eerdmans, 1992).

81. John Calvin, *Isaiah 33–66*, vol. VIII, Library of Christian Classics, Commentaries (Louisville: Westminster John Knox, 2006).

82. Elizabeth A. Johnson, *She Who Is: The Mystery of God in Feminist Theological Discourse* (New York: Crossroad, 1992), passim.

83. Barth, *CD* I/1, §10.1, 389.

84. Barth, *CD* IV/2, §64.2, 71.

85. Madeleine L'Engle, *Walking on Water: Reflections of Faith and Art* (New York: Crown Publishing Group, 2016), 13.

86. Annie Dillard, *Living by Fiction* (New York: Harper and Row, 1982), 144.

87. Dillard, *Living by Fiction*, 144.

88. Dillard, *Living by Fiction*, 144.

89. William C. Placher, *Triune God: An Essay in Postliberal Theology* (Louisville: Westminster John Knox, 2007), 23.

90. Here the doctrine of election is alluded to. This doctrine is controversial because, while it on the one hand emphasizes that God's grace is bestowed regardless of merit, it on the other hand seems unfairly to leave behind others even as it selects some.

91. See Gen 15:5.

92. See, for instance, Samuel P. Fowler, *Account of the Life, Character &c. of the Rev. Samuel Parris, of Salem Village* (Salem, MA: William Ives and George W. Pease, 1857) and John H. Van Evire, *Negroes and Negro Slavery: The First an Inferior Race; The Latter Its Natural Condition*, 3rd ed. (New York: Van Evrie, Norton & Co., 1863). For a broad treatment, see Jim Hill and Rand Cheadle, *The Bible Tells Me So: Uses and Abuses of Holy Scripture* (New York: Doubleday, 1996).

93. While the idea of "double predestination" is found in Calvin's thought, it is not nearly as prominent as stereotypes of him would lead us to suppose. And the

primary reason Calvin invokes it at all is because he understands it to be a logical extension of the idea that God is sovereign over all things, including every person's eternal destiny.

94. John 1:14.

95. We will discuss this in more detail in ch. 8.

96. See Col 3:12.

97. This is the "Master of Divinity" degree—the degree you commonly get when you are preparing to become a pastor.

98. See 1 Kings 19.

99. I Kings 19:15.

100. For more on this, see Christian Wiman, *My Bright Abyss* (New York: Farrar, Strauss and Giroux, 2014).

101. *My Bright Abyss* alludes to the psalmist's claim that God is somehow present in even the most desolate of places and circumstances. Psalm 139, for example, contains the exclamation that God is present even in the depths of "Sheol" (v. 8 NRSV).

2. Where Do We Find the Right Words to Say?

1. In the *Book of Confessions: The Constitution of the Presbyterian Church* (USA) (Louisville: Office of the General Assembly, 2016).

2. This name is fabricated.

3. I should note that my scientist student would likely object to my use of the term *slightly*. Which suggests 365.25 is "accurate enough" (my view) instead of just plain wrong (and lacking in authority).

4. This is a phrase that is habitually used not only by Christian communities, but by faith communities from the two other Abrahamic traditions—Judaism and Islam.

5. These include those who do work in the field of theology and science (including Wenzel van Huyssteen, Nancy Frankenberry, and Keith Ward, for example) as well as those who, in the field of biblical studies, resonate with the work of the Jesus Seminar.

6. The quadrilateral itself did not originate with Wesley. Albert Outler developed the concept as a way to remember and teach Wesley's theological method, as he

understood it, from Wesley's sermons and other pastoral writings. See Albert Outler, "The Wesleyan Quadrilateral in Wesley," *Wesleyan Theological Journal* 20, no. 1 (1985): 16–17.

7. Rom 1:19.

8. Rom 1:23.

9. Calvin, *Institutes of the Christian Religion* 2 vols., ed. John T. McNeill (Philadephia: Westminster Press, 1960), I.5.

10. This is an allusion to the first commandment, which condemns idolatry such as it is described in Romans 1: "You shall have no other gods before me."

11. "What else does this craving, and this helplessness, proclaim but that there was once in man a true happiness, of which all that now remains is the empty print and trace? This he tries in vain to fill with everything around him, seeking in things that are not there the help he cannot find in those that are, though none can help, since this infinite abyss can be filled only with an infinite and immutable object; in other words by God himself." Blaise Pascal, *Pensees* (New York; Penguin Books, 1966), 75.

12. Wesley, "On Working Out Our Own Salvation," John Wesley's *Sermons*, ed. Albert C. Outler (Nashville: Abingdon, 1991), 486–92, 488.

13. C. S. Lewis, "Hope," in *Mere Christianity* (New York: HarperCollins, 2001), III.

14. Calvin writes, for example: "Let those persons take note of this who are looking for miserable excuses to defend the execrable idolatry by which true religion has been overwhelmed and subverted" Calvin, *Institutes* I.11.9.

15. Paul Tillich, "Our Ultimate Concern," *Dynamics of Faith* (New York: Harper and Row, 1957), chap. 3.

16. See the story in Luke 10:38-42.

17. We will consider this further in ch. 7.

18. Paul Lehmann, *Forgiveness: A Decisive Issue in Protestant Thought* (Ann Arbor: University Microfilms, 1941).

19. Barth, *CD* I/1, §3, 55.

20. Gen 15:5.

21. Exod 3:1–4:17.

22. Gen 37:5-8.

23. Num 22:22-30.

24. Luke 1:26-28.

25. In order: 1 Kings 19:11-13; Ex 30:15; Matt 2:1-12; Luke 2:8-20; Gen 15:1; Gen 46:2; John 1:32; Ps 114:3; Heb 12:29; Gen 19:26; Judg 6:36-40.

26. James H. Evans, Jr., *We Have Been Believers* (Minneapolis: Fortress, 1992), 11, 12.

27. This program has been wildly successful in the United States in the last few years.

28. See the story in Matthew 19:16-22.

29. Matthew 19:21.

30. Ps 46:10, NRSV.

31. Calvin, *Institutes* III.2.1–43.

32. Calvin, *Institutes* I.7.1.

33. See, for example, Isa 63:7; and the Luke 19:1-10 story of Zacchaeus called by name by Jesus.

34. Psalm 104:33.

35. In Psalm 8:4.

36. "For just as eyes, when dimmed with age or weakness or by some other defect, unless aided by spectacles, discern nothing distinctly; so, such is our feebleness, unless Scripture guides us in seeking God, we are immediately confused." Calvin, *Institutes* I.14.1.

37. Calvin, *Institutes* 1.6.1

38. Col 3:3.

39. For more on this, see the introduction and ch. 1.

40. For example, Robert Lewis Dabney argues for the "righteousness" of slavery as it is apparent in the "common sense" reading of the Old and New Testaments. Robert Lewis Dabney, *Defence of Virginia and through Her, of the South, in Recent and*

Pending Contests against the Sectional Party (New York: E. J. Hale and Son, 1867), ch. 1.

41. George M. Marsden, *Fundamentalism and American Culture* (Oxford: Oxford University Press, 2006).

42. For more on this, see Harvey, *Condition of Postmodernity*.

43. The Synoptic Gospels are Matthew, Mark, and Luke.

44. See the story of God's creation in Gen 1.

45. The Montessori-based Godly Play method of children's Christian education is based on wondering. For more, see Elizabeth Caldwell, *I Wonder* (Nashville: Abingdon, 2016).

46. Described in Gen 22.

47. Søren Kierkegaard, *Fear and Trembling*, trans. Howard V. Hong and Maxine H. Hong (Princeton: Princeton University Press, 1983).

48. Karl Barth, *Word of God and the Word of Man* (Gloucester: Peter Smith, 1978), ch. 2.

49. See this story in Luke 10:25-37.

50. *Book of Confessions*, 5–7.

51. *Book of Confessions*, 299–306.

52. John 3:8.

53. See this much-discussed verse in 1 Timothy 2:12.

54. As we hear said in the traditional version of the Lord's Prayer.

55. Do see, if you are interested in reading a beautiful, expansive interpretation of 1 Timothy 2:13-15, Aída Bensaçon Spencer's *Beyond the Curse: Women Called to Ministry* (Edinburgh: Thomas Nelson, 1985).

56. Elizabeth Schüssler Fiorenza, *In Memory of Her: A Feminist Theological Reconstruction of Christian Origins* (New York: Crossroad Publishing, 1992), xiii. You can read this story in Luke 10:37-47. The same story is in all three other Gospels in a variation.

57. Barth, "Strange New World within the Bible," in Barth, *Word of God and the Word*, 42–43. I have made Barth's language inclusive with bracketed changes.

58. Karl Barth, *Göttingen Dogmatics: Instruction of the Christian Religion* (London: Bloomsbury Publishing, 1991), 213–14.

3. Where Does God Meet Us?

1. This last stanza is a verse I memorized when I was young and have carried around with me ever since. It is attributed to James Allan Francis, *One Solitary Life* (n.p.: 1963), 1–7.

2. From Cynthia L. Rigby, "More Than a Hero: The Practical Implications of the Incarnation in Ministry with Youth" (paper presented at Princeton Lectures on Youth, Church, and Culture, Princeton Theological Seminary, NJ, 1999). Published by the Institute for Youth Ministry: http://www.ptsem.edu/lectures/?action=tei&id=youth-1999-06. Used by permission.

3. "Westminster Catechism: The Shorter Catechism," in the *Book of Confessions*, 203–21 (7.001–7.110).

4. Matt 16:16.

5. To be fair, Calvin understands God's giving of Scripture itself to be a revelatory act, and Calvin sees Scripture confirming the attributes of God that he presents as true to who God is.

6. Calvin, *Institutes* I.13.1.

7. Calvin describes the attributes of God early on in the *Institutes.* He explains that because humanity has knowledge of God, we are able to recognize that God, "governs all things; and trusts that he is guide and protector, therefore giving itself over completely to trust in him." Calvin, *Institutes* I.2.2.

8. Calvin states, "Surely God does not have blood, does not suffer, cannot be touched with hands." Calvin, *Institutes* II.14.2.

9. Gen 6:5-7.

10. Gen 18:16-33.

11. John 11:35.

12. See Elizabeth A. Johnson, *She Who Is: The Mystery,* especially ch. 7, "Spirit-Sophia," and *Abounding in Kindness: Writings for the People of God* (Maryknoll, NY: Orbis, 2015), especially ch. 17, "Remembering the Holy Spirit: Love Poured Out."

13. This is interesting because Barth understood himself to be very much in Calvin's debt. Barth took very seriously the Reformation principle that the church is "Reformed and always reforming, according to the Word of God." That is why Barth was committed to correcting and improving upon Calvin's theology whenever he believed this was necessary. We, of course, should do the same with his.

14. See Daniel L. Migliore, *The Power of God and the Gods of Power* (Louisville: Westminster John Knox, 2008), *passim.*

15. Rom 8:22.

16. These ideas will be discussed further in chs. 7, 9, and 10.

17. Luke 1:35.

18. Miriam is the sister of Moses and Aaron in the Hebrew Scriptures.

19. Exod 15:1.

20. Luke 1:53.

21. Luke 2:11.

22. Q is translated literally as "what" in the German language, but in this context is understood to mean "source." This is a contested document among scholars; I have described but one way Q is understood to have functioned. For a description of this position, see Burton L. Mack, *Lost Gospel: The Book of Q and Christian Origins* (San Francisco: Harper, 1993). Other scholars posit that Luke used the material from Matthew and Mark, but did not include a document called Q. Marc Goodacre's work describes this opposite position. Marc Goodacre, *The Case against Q: Studies in Markan Priority and the Synoptic Problem* (Harrisburg, PA: Trinity Press International, 2002).

23. This is my imagined conversation John may have had with himself!

24. John 1:14, NRSV.

25. John 1:1

26. John 3:1-21; 4:7-30.

27. John 11:35.

28. John 20:27.

29. John 14:9-10.

30. You can read more about Athanasius in Kelly's "Early Christian Doctrines."

31. This is the noun form of *homoousios.* See Kelly, *Early Christian*, 255–58.

32. Kelly also describes Arius's view on the subject in *Early Christian*, 226–31.

33. From Athanasius, "Against Heresies (part 3)," in *Christological Controversy (Sources of Early Christian Thought),* ed. Richard A. Norris, William G. Rusch (Minneapolis: Fortress, 1980), 97.

34. Athanasius, "Chapter II: The Divine Dilemma and Its Solution in the Incarnation," in *On the Incarnation: The Treatise de Incarnatione Verbi Dei* (Crestwood, NY: St. Vladimir, 1998), 33–38.

35. This is how Karl Barth phrases the question, centuries later (Barth, *CD* IV/2, §64.4, 297).

36. Kelly, *Early Christian*, 151.

37. This was more the tendency of the "Alexandrian" school of thought, as represented at Chalcedon. At the heretical extreme of this side of the debate was Eutyches, who has been criticized by theologians for presenting Jesus Christ as though he is half human and half divine—almost a "third thing" (*tertium quid*). For more on this, see Kelly, *Early Christian*, 319–23.

38. This was the tendency of the "Antiochene" school of thought, as represented in the Chalcedonian debates. At the heretical extreme was Nestorius, who argued that Jesus Christ was the "two sons" of the Father—the divine one and the human one. For more on this, see Kelly, *Early Christian*, 301–9.

39. The emboldened words are my emphasis. For a complete version of the statement and a helpful recounting of how it was formulated, see Kelly, *Early Christian*, 151.

40. 1 Cor 13:1.

41. Matt 22:37, NRSV.

42. Matt 22:39, NRSV.

43. John 21:25.

44. This is an allusion to the *kenosis* ("self-emptying") hymn—especially the first half—in Philippians 2:6-8a.

45. For more on this, see Barth, "The Doctrine of Reconciliation," *CD* IV/1 and IV/2, *passim.*

46. See introduction for more on this.

47. Roberta Perry, “An Interview by Roberta Perry,” Eric Bazilian, last modified Spring 2003, http://www.ericbazilian.com/interview.html.

48. Mark 4:38-40.

49. John 11:35.

50. Matt 26:36-56.

51. Matt 27:46.

52. Matt 27:46, NRSV.

53. Col 3:3.

54. See 2 Cor 5:11-21, specifically v.18.

55. Sometimes I use the word “kin-dom” as a way of remembering that the Kingdom of God is not, in contrast to human kingdoms, a place framed by hierarchies and power differential. Rather, the Kingdom of God is a community in which all are “kin”; all are fully included; all are equally included, claimed, and gifted by the Spirit.

56. This is Barth’s way of framing “The Doctrine of Reconciliation” in *CD* IV/1 (“Jesus Christ: The Lord as Servant”) and IV/2 (“Jesus Christ: The Servant as Lord”).

57. This is a term commonly used by Karl Barth to name the way he thought people of faith should navigate truths that might at face value seem to contradict each other: acknowledge the tension between them and set them in ongoing dialogue. The truth is in the back and forth exchange, not in the winning of one over another.

58. Phil 2:12.

59. “Away in a Manger,” *Glory to God* (Louisville: Westminster John Knox, 2013), 114.

60. “Silent Night, Holy Night!” *Glory to God*, 122.

61. Or whatever height Jesus was. The point is not to pinpoint Jesus’s height, but to think about the implications of the fact that he was one height and not another.

62. “An *accidental property of an object* is one that it happens to have but that it could lack,” while an *essential property of an object* is a property that it must have, according to Teresa Robertson and Philip Atkins, “Essential vs. Accidental Properties,” *Stanford Encyclopedia of Philosophy Archive* (last modified April 29, 2008, https://plato.stanford.edu/archives/sum2016/entries/essential-accidental/).

63. Elizabeth A. Johnson, *Quest for the Living God: Mapping Frontiers in the Theology of God* (New York: Continuum, 2007), 160.

64. To read more about this historical controversy, see Kelly's *Early Christian Doctrines,* ch. XI.

65. This occurred at the Council of Constantinople in 381.

66. Gregory [Nazianzus], "Ep. CI.," in *Nicene and Post-Nicene Fathers: Cyril of Jerusalem, Gregory Nazianzen*, ed. Philip Schaff and Henry Wace, vol. 7, *Select Library of the Christian Church* (Peabody, MA: Hendrickson, 1999).

67. The conversation about how it is that Jesus saves us is sometimes described by theologians with the word *soteriology*, which we will address in a later chapter.

68. John Gray, *Men Are from Mars, Women Are from Venus: The Classic Guide to Understanding the Opposite Sex*, quill ed. (New York: HarperCollins Publishers, 2004).

69. Again, I am not meaning to say, here, that Jesus's gender is "an accident," but am using the word *accidents* in the Aristotelian sense.

70. This, by the way, immediately poses a challenge to the Roman Catholic teaching that priests must be male because they "represent Christ." If the Word assumes all humanity when he enters into the flesh, because the particularity of his male body was accidental to his essential humanity, then any human being equally qualifies to represent Jesus Christ in the Mass.

71. For more on this, see my "Scandalous Presence: Incarnation and Trinity," in *Feminist and Womanist Essays in Reformed Dogmatics*, ed. Amy Plantinga Pauw and Serene Jones, Columbia Series in Reformed Theology (Louisville: Westminster John Knox, 2006), 58–74.

72. As we recite in both the Apostles' and Nicene Creeds.

73. In other words, he would understand "seated at the right hand of God the Father Almighty" as a metaphor. Sometimes, I think Calvin would say, Jesus gets up and walks around!

74. This is the word Calvin uses to describe Jesus's human state as described in John 20:17. See: John Calvin, *Commentary on the Gospel According to John*, trans. William Pringle, 500th Anniversary ed., vol. II, *Commentaries* (Grand Rapids: Baker Books, 2009), 258–59.

75. Find this story in John 20:24-29.

76. Find this story in Luke 24:36-49.

77. Calvin, *Commentary on the Gospel*, 264.

78. This is the translation found in the King James Version of the Bible.

79. John Calvin, "Treatise on the Lord's Supper," in *Calvin: Theological Treatises*, ed. J. K. S. Reid (Nashville: Westminster, 1954), 142–66, 166.

80. Calvin, "Partaking of the Flesh and Blood," in *Calvin, "Treatise on the Lord's,"* 258–323, 275.

81. See the discussion of the mystery of God in the introduction.

82. See the discussion of Madeleine L'Engle's insight, in the introduction.

83. John 15:7.

84. 1 Cor 1:10.

85. Phil 2:12-13.

86. For more on this, see Barth, "Doctrine of Reconciliation," *CD* IV/2.

87. Rom 8:28.

88. Underlying these christological reflections is concern that the appeal to a transcendent God (manifested in the Chalcedonian commitment to Jesus Christ as "fully divine") is inherently damaging to human integrity and agency. Rita Nakashima Brock writes, along these lines, that "systems [that]... orient us to a transcendent, external power... encourage faintheartedness and make self-awareness and personal power difficult." See *Journeys by Heart: A Christology of Erotic Power* (New York: Crossroad, 1991), 16. In *Journeys* she develops an alternative christology that is "not centered in Jesus" but in relationship and community as the "whole-making, healing center of Christianity" (52).

89. This "hands and feet" is an allusion to Mother Teresa's insight that "God has no hands but ours."

90. Luke 1:53.

91. In order: Mark 6:1-6, Matt 15:21-28, John 11:30-36, Matt 27:45-46.

92. In order: Matt 13:14-21, Matt 14:22-33, Mark 1:22, Luke 7:36-50, Mark 16:1-8.

93. See Luke 4:18.

94. For a fuller exposition on the thinking underlying this idea, see my essay "Redeeming Words: Hypostatic Union and the Reading of Scripture," in *Reformed Theology: Identity and Ecumenicity II; Biblical Interpretation in the Reformed Tradition*, ed. Wallace M. Alston (Grand Rapids: Eerdmans, 2007), 331–48.

95. From the hymn "When I Survey the Wondrous Cross," *The Hymnbook* (Richmond, Virginia: Presbyterian Church in the USA, 1947).

96. 1 John 4:7-21. This is the insight of Daniel L. Migliore, who makes note of it in the chapter on "Trinity" in *Faith Seeking Understanding: An Introduction to Christian Theology*, third ed. (Grand Rapids: Eerdmans, 2014), 71.

4. In What Ways Does God Claim Us?

1. John 21:15-17.

2. Sandra Schneiders, "God Is More Than Two Men and a Bird," *U. S. Catholic*, May 1990, 20.

3. For more on the history of the development of the Apostles' Creed, see Williston Walker et al., *A History of the Christian Church* (New York: Simon and Schuster, 2014), 72–73.

4. One book containing several essays that illustrate this problem is Alvin Kimel, ed., *Speaking the Christian God: The Holy Trinity and the Challenge of Feminism* (Grand Rapids: Eerdmans, 1992) see, in particular, the essays by Kimel ("The God Who Likes His Name"), Achtemeier ("Exchanging God for 'No Gods'"), and Ziegler ("Christianity or Feminism?").

5. Barth uses this language to describe the relationship between men and women in "The Doctrine of Creation," Barth, *CD* III/4, §53, 48.

6. See, for example, Carol Gilligan's *In a Different Voice* (Boston: Harvard University Press, 2016) and Hayden White's *Fiction of Narrative: Essays on History, Literature, and Theory, 1957–2007*, ed. Robert Doran (Baltimore: Johns Hopkins University Press, 2010).

7. This is the language of Johnson in *She Who Is*. See, especially, "Equivalent Images of God Male and Female," in Elizabeth A. Johnson, *She Who Is: The Mystery of God in Feminist Theological Discourse* (New York: Crossroad, 1992), 54.

8. Calvin's comments through this paragraph can be found in his commentary on Isaiah 49:15 in John Calvin, Isaiah 33–66, vol. VIII, Library of Christian Classics, Commentaries (Louisville: Westminster John Knox, 2006).

9. Office of Theology and Worship, comp., *The Trinity: God's Love Overflowing* (Louisville: Presbyterian Church [USA], 2006).

10. Eph 3:20, NRSV.

11. Along these lines, in *The God of Life,* Gustavo Gutiérrez comments that "the mystery of the Trinity shows the fullness of life that is God" (Maryknoll, NY: Orbis, 1991), 2.

12. Catherine Mowry LaCugna, *God for Us: The Trinity and Christian Life* (San Francisco: HarperSanFrancisco, 1991), 1. Also LaCugna, "The Practical Trinity," *The Christian Century* 109, no. 22: 678–82.

13. Rom 8:31.

14. "Holy, Holy, Holy! Lord God Almighty!" *Glory to God*, 1.

15. I learned this helpful distinction between "mystery" and "mystification" from Catherine Keller, who writes that "mystery becomes mystification if it inhibits the struggle to understand, if it blocks the quest." Catherine Keller, *On the Mystery: Discerning Divinity in Process* (Minneapolis: Fortress, 2008), 19.

16. As quoted in Calvin's *Institutes* I.13.17.

17. I suppose this comment reflects my lack of understanding the beauty of numbers and is indicative of the fact that I am a "liberal arts" person. Apologies to my more mathematical friends and readers!

18. For further reading on the details of this fourth-century debate, see Kelly's *Early Christian Doctrines* and William G. Rusch, ed., *Trinitarian Controversy*, Sources of Early Christian Thought (Minneapolis: Fortress, 1980).

19. Epistemology is derived from the Greek *epistēmē* meaning "knowledge" and the suffix *-logia*, meaning "logical discourse" and also understood as "theory." In practical terms, this means that epistemology is our theory of knowledge, or how we come to know what we know.

20. See, for example, ch. 6 of Moltmann's *The Trinity and the Kingdom*, titled "The Kingdom of Freedom" (Minneapolis: Fortress, 1993), 191–222.

21. Ontology derives from the Greek *onto* meaning "being; that which is" and -logia "logical discourse" and also understood as "theory." In practical terms, this means that ontology is our theory of being, or how we understand what we "are."

22. See discussion on this topic in ch. 3.

23. See Kelly's *Early Christian Doctrines* to read more about the council of Alexandria.

24. "Visible unity" is a phrase commonly used in ecumenical conversations and conferences (e.g., those facilitated by the World Council of Churches and the World Alliance of Reformed Churches). It insists that it is not enough for Christians to *say* we are "one in the Spirit" or united in Christ. We must *show* it in the way we live, worship, and serve.

25. Walker et al., *A History*, 389–91.

26. Joseph F. Kelly, "Filioque," in *Early, Medieval, and Reformation Years*, ed. Roberto Benedetto, vol. 1, *Westminster Dictionary of Church History* (Louisville: Westminster John Knox, 2008), 245–56.

27. See, for example, Book IX, ch. 1 of *On the Trinity,* by Augustine of Hippo (New York: New City Press, 1999), 272–76.

28. You can read more about the events surrounding the adding of the *filioque* clause in Walker et al., *A History*, 231–60.

29. The Nicene Creed as approved by the Evangelical Lutheran Church of America is one instance.

30. See LaCugna, *God for Us: The Trinity*. See also LaCugna, "The Practical Trinity," 678–82.

31. "We Are One in the Spirit," *Glory to God*, 300.

32. Jürgen Moltmann, *The Way of Jesus Christ: Christology in Messianic Dimensions* (New York: Harper San Francisco, 1990), 73–77.

33. Moltmann, *Trinity and the Kingdom*, 220–22.

34. As referenced in Elizabeth A. Johnson's *Quest for the Living God.* Johnson, *Quest for the Living God: Mapping Frontiers in the Theology of God* (New York: Continuum, 2007), 203.

35. Isa 40:12.

36. Søren Kierkegaard, "C: The possibility of essential offense in relation to lowliness, that the one who passes himself off as God proves to be the lowly, poor, suffering, and finally powerless human being.," in *Practice in Christianity*, trans. Howard V. Hong and Edna H. Hong (Princeton: Princeton University Press, 1991), 102–4.

37. Scene in *The Sound of Music*, directed by Robert Wise, Twentieth Century Fox, 1965.

38. *Monty Python and the Holy Grail*, directed by Terry Gilliam and Terry Jones, EMI Films, 1975.

39. See 1 Cor 1:23-24.

40. Dietrich Bonhoeffer, *Letters and Papers from Prison*, vol. 8 (Minneapolis: Fortress, 2010), 479.

41. You can read the full statement in Henry Bettenson and Chris Maunder, eds., *Documents of the Christian Church*, 4th ed. (Oxford: Oxford, 2011), 54-5.

42. David Brown, "Trinitarian Personhood and Individuality," in *Trinity, Incarnation, and Atonement: Philosophical and Theological Essays*, ed. Ronald J. Feenstra and Cornelius Plantinga, Jr. (Notre Dame: University of Notre Dame Press, 1989), 48–78.

43. Kelly, *Early Christian*, 253–54.

44. Paul Tillich, *Courage to Be*, second ed. (New Haven: Yale University Press, 2000), 87–88. Also see "The Separation of Individualization from Participation" in Paul Tillich, *Systematic Theology* (Chicago: University of Chicago Press, 1957).

45. Malachi is the last book of the Old Testament and Matthew the first book of the New Testament. Christians believe the same God is borne witness to in both, even though the language of "Father, Son, and Holy Spirit" is found in the books of the New Testament and not the Old.

46. *Star Trek: First Contact*, directed by Jonathon Frakes, Paramount Pictures, 1996.

47. Col 3:3.

48. I am speaking, here, of my colleague and Professor of New Testament Lewis Donelson, who helped clarify the matter of the word's etymology as I worked on this chapter.

49. Again, I am borrowing these two terms from the theology of Paul Tillich, as well as his insight that they stand in tension with one another in a "fallen" world. Tillich articulates these ideas in volume 2 of his *Systematic Theology*. See, in particular, his subsection titled "Existence and the Christ."

50. This is true when they are mixed together subtractively, but not additively (when the three colors mixed together would yield white).

51. For more on this, see Barth's "Doctrine of Reconciliation" in *CD* IV.1–3.

52. See Luke 4:18.

53. See Ps 8, particularly v. 31.

54. In order: Rev 21:4, Isa 11:6, Matt 24:40-41.

55. Rom 8:29.

5. Who Did God Create Us to Be, and What Went Wrong?

1. Sometimes scholars refer to the creation "stories" (plural) in Genesis 1–2, since textual criticism shows there were two versions of the stories spliced together (Genesis 1–2:3 is the "priestly" version and Genesis 2:4-24 is the "Jahwistic" version). I am a theologian who thinks about the biblical narrative more in terms of the whole (see ch. 2). Therefore, I tend to read Genesis 1–2 as one story comprising two parts than as two conflicting stories (even though I well understand and appreciate that the one story we have now was composed of two stories that were "merged").

2. Eph 1:4.

3. Ps 139:13.

4. Ps 139:16.

5. *Pinocchio*, directed by Ben Sharpsteen, Walt Disney, 1940.

6. Margery Williams, *Velveteen Rabbit, Or, How Toys Become Real* (New York: Doubleday, 1991).

7. *Star Trek: The Next Generation*, "The Measure of a Man," episode 9, NBC, first broadcast February 1989, directed by Robert Scheerer, written by Melinda M. Snodgrass.

8. Martin Buber describes this encounter in his classic text *I and Thou* (first published in 1923). Martin Buber, *The Scribner Library. Philosophy/religion*, trans. Walter Arnold Kaufmann, vol. 243, *I and Thou* (New York: Charles Scribner, 1970).

9. The Word presses to become flesh.

10. *The Martian*, directed by Ridley Scott, 20th Century Fox, 2015.

11. From *The Martian.*

12. "Spirit of the Living God," *Glory to God*, 288.

13. See 2 Cor 5:17.

14. This phrase may be found in its context in 2 Cor 5:17.

15. For a poetic description of *Genesis ex nihilo*, see James Perkinson's exposition in Laurel C. Schneider and Stephen G. Ray, Jr, eds., *Awake to the Moment: An Introduction to Theology* (Louisville: Westminster John Knox, 2016), 121–27.

16. Calvin, *Institutes* II.1.10.

17. *Wonderment* is a word Calvin uses in his commentary on Genesis 15 (the story of Abraham being promised his descendants will be as numerous as the stars), Ps 145:5 (commenting on God's "wondrous works"), and in his *Institutes* I.5.9.

18. Ps 8:4.

19. See Ps 8:3, 7-8.

20. This is sometimes considered to be the most basic of all philosophical questions. See also: Roy Sorenson, "Nothingness," ed. Edward N. Zalta, *Stanford Encyclopedia of Philosophy,* last modified Summer 2015, https://plato.stanford.edu/entries/nothingness/.

21. See comments, in introduction, on "being enough of a person that God can find."

22. 1 Pet 3:15, NRSV. This is a theme developed at length in the introduction to this volume.

23. Especially in Kansas and Texas. See: Motoko Rich, "Creationists on Texas Panel for Biology Textbooks," *The New York Times*, September 28, 2013, Education. See also: Jodi Wilgoren, "Kansas Board Approves Challenges to Evolution," *The New York Times*, November 9, 2005, U.S.

24. Search the *Times* archive for John Tierney, "The Physics of Nothing," *New York Times*, June 12, 2009, for a short exposition on this topic. Or: Robert Adler's beautiful, "Why Is There Something Rather Than Nothing?" The Big Questions/Universe, last modified November 6, 2004, http://www.bbc.com/earth/story/20141106-why-does-anything-exist-at-all.

25. "Theology and science" is, in fact, a subfield of theology that focuses on interfaces such as this. For further reading see Nancy K. Frankenberry, *The Faith of Scientists: In Their Own Words* (Princeton: Princeton University Press, 2008); and John C. Polkinghorne, *Belief in God in an Age of Science* (New Haven: Yale University Press, 1998). For a discussion of the way in which it may be possible to carry faith in this secular age, see William Greenway, *A Reasonable Faith: Why God and Faith Make Sense* (Louisville: Westminster John Knox, 2015.

26. See Ps 8:3a.

27. See Ps 145:5b.

28. "All Things Bright and Beautiful," *Glory to God*, 20.

29. For more on this, see my "Mary and the Artistry of God" in *Blessed One: Protestant Perspectives on Mary*, ed. Cynthia Rigby and Beverly Roberts Gaventa (Louisville: Westminster John Knox, 2003), 145–58.

30. Calvin, *Institutes* I.14.1.

31. To see Moltmann expound on this topic, see "Jürgen Moltmann: How Does a Suffering God Give Us Hope?" video file, YouTube, posted by Benjamin Merritt, February 20, 2014, https://www.youtube.com/watch?v=XbqzbJkpm-w.

32. In the terms of the prior chapter on the Trinity, we might say that the problem comes when our instinct to survive, as individuals, overrides and interferes with living as interconnected, sharing members of the community.

33. L. W. King and Leonard W. King, *Enuma Elish (2 Volumes in One): The Seven Tablets of Creation; The Babylonian and Assyrian Legends Concerning the Creation of the World and of Mankind* (New York: Cosimo Classics, 2011).

34. For a wonderful reading of Genesis in conversation with the *Enuma Elish*, see William Greenway, *For the Love of All Creatures: The Story of Grace in Genesis* (Grand Rapids: Eerdmans, 2015).

35. Augustine, *Confessions*, 124–25.

36. This logic is reflected, again, in Augustine's argument in the *Confessions*.

37. This idea is supported, they thought, by the statement, found in the prologue to the Gospel of John, that "all things were made" through the Word who was with God "in the beginning." But it is also consistent with basic logic: hypothetically speaking, if there were something that exists that did *not* come from the God we know, it would have had to have come from elsewhere. But then, if there were another "source" from which the raw materials came, this would violate their conviction that there is only one God. To believe in one God meant, therefore, that all things that existed were made by this one.

38. Catherine Keller, *Face of the Deep: A Theology of Becoming* (London: Routledge, 2003).

39. Keller, *Face of the Deep*, and Thomas Oord, *Theologies of Creation:* Creatio Ex Nihilo *and Its New Rivals* (London: Routledge, 2015) and *The Nature of Love: A Theology* (St. Louis: Chalice Press, 2015).

40. See also William C. Placher, *The Domestication of Transcendence: How Modern Thinking about God Went Wrong* (Louisville: Westminster John Knox, 1996). Although Placher does not reject the doctrine of the creation *ex nihilo*, he does reject the idea that God is "impassible," or unaffected by creation. Placher offers an excellent

account of how this understanding of God is derived from Greek understandings of "perfection" that are inconsistent with the biblical witness.

41. For more on this, see Bonnie Miller-McLemore's *In the Midst of Chaos: Caring for Children as Spiritual Practice* (San Francisco: Jossey-Bass, 2007).

42. Process theology is a sub-field of theology that has these ideas at its center, meaning that understandings of all Christian doctrines are shaped around the idea that creation is a process with no beginning and no ending. The doctrine of Christian hope (eschatology), for example, does not emphasize that what God intends will inevitably come to fruition in the "end." Process theology holds, rather, that what happens in the future depends on what we (God and creatures) are creating today.

43. John 1:14.

44. Gen 2:23.

45. In Ps 139.

46. Dan 3:12-30.

47. Barth, *CD* III/4, §55.3, 552.

48. Jacquelyn Grant, *White Woman's Christ and Black Woman's Jesus: Feminist Christology and Womanist Response*, vol. 64, American Academy of Religion Academy Series (Atlanta: Scholars Press, 1989).

49. See, for example, his painting *The Persistence of Memory* (1931).

50. Chaim Potok, *My Name Is Asher Lev* (New York: Anchor Books, 2003, 1972).

51. "All Things Bright and Beautiful," *Glory to God*, 20.

52. See Gottfried Wilhelm Leibniz, *Theodicy: Essays on the Goodness of God, the Freedom of Man, and the Origin of Evil* (New York: Cosimo Classics, 2010), especially Part One (8) on page 128.

53. See Harold S. Kushner, ch. 5, in *When Bad Things Happen to Good People* (New York: Anchor Books, 2004, 1981).

54. See David R. Blumenthal, *Facing the Abusing God: A Theology of Protest* (Louisville: Westminster John Knox, 1993), *passim*, but especially 246–48.

55. See Augustine, *Confessions*, 3.7.

56. James H. Cone, *The Cross and the Lynching Tree* (Maryknoll, NY: Orbis Books, 2011), 178–80. Further attention to the matter of the relationship of institutional structures to sin and suffering will be given in the discussion of "systemic sin" included in ch. 6.

57. Cynthia L. Rigby, "Evil and the Principalities: Disarming the Demonic," in *Life amid the Principalities: Identifying, Understanding and Engaging Created, Fallen, and Disarmed Powers Today*, ed. Michael Root and James J. Buckley (Eugene, OR: Wipf and Stock, 2016).

6. Who Is God Making Us Into?

1. Rom 3:23.

2. Ps 8:5a, NRSV.

3. Rom 7:19, 24.

4. For a discussion on the question as to whether atonement is necessary for forgiveness, see: Cynthia L. Rigby, "Forgiveness," in *T&T Clark Companion to Atonement*, ed. Adam J. Johnson (New York: Bloomsbury, 2017), 493–97.

5. Phil 2:12, NRSV.

6. For a thorough exposition on this, see Clare Carlisle, *Kierkegaard's Philosophy of Becoming: Movements and Positions* (Albany: State University of New York Press, 2005).

7. I have been formed, in my thinking about this, by the work of Kierkegaard, especially in *The Concept of Anxiety* and *The Sickness Unto Death*. See: Søren Kierkegaard, *Concept of Anxiety: A Simple Psychologically Orienting Deliberation on the Dogmatic Issue of Hereditary Sin*, ed. Reidar Thomte, vol. VIII, *Keirkegaard's Writings* (Princeton: Princeton University Press, 1980); and Søren Kierkegaard, *Sickness Unto Death: A Christian Psychological Exposition for Upbuilding and Awakening*, ed. Howard V. Hong and Edna H. Hong, vol. XIX, *Kierkegaard's Writings* (Princeton: Princeton University Press, 1980).

8. Matt 23:27.

9. See John 8:7.

10. Matt 7:5.

11. For example, the language of "visible unity" is used at meetings of the National Council of Churches and the World Alliance of Reformed Churches.

12. "We Are One in the Spirit," *Glory to God*, 300.

13. Rom 8:19-23.

14. For a greater exposition on the connection between atonement theory and the Kingdom's presence, see: Cynthia L. Rigby, "Kingdom of God," in Johnson, *T&T Clark Companion to Atonement.*

15. For more on this, see Martin Luther's response to Erasmus, *Bondage of the Will*, trans. James I. Packer and O. R. Johnson (Revell, NJ: Revell, 2000).

16. See Augustine, *On the Free Choice of the Will, On Grace and Free Choice, and Other Writings*, Cambridge Texts in the History of Philosophy (Cambridge, UK: Cambridge University Press, 2010), especially ch. 33.

17. Reinhold Niebuhr's *Moral Man and Immoral Society* is an excellent theological study of these dynamics, emphasizing how "caught" all of us are. Reinhold Niebuhr, *Moral Man and Immoral Society: A Study in Ethics and Politics* (Louisville: Westminster John Knox, 2013).

18. Amos 5.

19. In Luke 4.

20. We will discuss the content of God's redemptive work in the section on "atonement theories," below.

21. Rom 14:11.

22. See John 10:10.

23. Barth, *CD* IV/2, §64.4, 297.

24. Barth, *CD* IV/2, §64.4, 303.

25. *Seinfeld*, "The Face Painter," episode 22, NBC, first broadcast May 11, 1995, directed by Andy Ackerman, written by Larry David and Fred Stoller.

26. Barth's language, as quoted above.

27. "We've Come This Far by Faith," *Glory to God*, 656.

28. See Paul Tillich, "Part III: Existence and the Christ," in *Systematic Theology* (Chicago: University of Chicago Press, 1957), 2. The "Ground of All Being" or "Being-Itself" is Tillich's way of referencing God.

29. *Cheers*, "I'm Okay, You're Defective," episode 11, NBC, first broadcast December 21, 1991, written by Dan Stanley and Rob Long, directed by James Burrows.

30. See above note referring to Tillich's *Systematic Theology* 2.

31. James Cone, *A Black Theology of Liberation* (Maryknoll, NY: Orbis, 2010), 18–19.

32. Marianne Williamson, *Return to Love: Reflections on the Principles of "A Course in Miracles,"* first Harper Perennial ed. (New York: Harper Perennial, 1993), 190–91.

33. Valerie Saiving, "The Human Situation: A Feminine View," in *Womanspirit Rising: A Feminist Reader in Religion*, ed. Carol P. Christ and Judith Plaskow (San Francisco: Harper and Row, 1979), 25–42.

34. Judith Plaskow, *Sex, Sin, and Grace: Women's Experience and the Theologies of Reinhold Niebuhr and Paul Tillich* (Washington, DC: University Press of America, 1980).

35. Biblically speaking, Mary in Luke 10 is "breaking out" of "feminine sin." Job, at the end of the book of Job, starts reverting to it when he tries to punt on speaking up and "answering" the God of the whirlwind. But God will not allow him to "melt"—calling him out and insisting that he speak. See Job 38–42.

36. Luke 22:42

37. Portions of this section originated in Spring 2000 of *Insights: The Faculty Journal of Austin Seminary.* Cynthia L. Rigby, "Are You Saved?," *Insights: The Faculty Journal of Austin Seminary* 115, no. 2 (Spring 2000): 3–18. Used by permission.

38. I am referring, in particular, to debates about "substitutionary atonement," which will be considered later in this chapter.

39. See, for example, JoAnne Carlson Brown and Rebecca Parker, "For God So Loved the World?" in *Christianity, Patriarchy, and Abuse*, ed. JoAnne Carlson Brown and Carole R. Brown (New York: Pilgrim Press, 1989); Rita Nakashima Brock and Rebecca Parker, *Proverbs of Ashes: Violence, Redemptive Suffering, and the Search for What Saves Us* (Boston: Beacon Press, 2001; and Harold Kushner, *How Good Do We Have to Be? A New Understanding of Guilt and Forgiveness* (Boston: Little, Brown, 1996).

40. Brock and Parker, *Proverbs of Ashes*, 195.

41. Eugene Fairweather, ed., *Scholastic Miscellany: Anselm to Ockham*, Library of Christian Classics (Louisville: Westminster John Knox, 1956).

42. Or, more inclusively, "victor."

43. Anselm of Canterbury, "Why God Became Man," in Fairweather, *Scholastic Miscellany*, 100–83.

44. David Bentley Hart, "A Gift Exceeding Every Debt: An Eastern Orthodox Appreciation of Anselm's *Cur Deus Homo*," *Pro Ecclesia* 7, no. 3 (Summer 1998): 333–49.

45. See, for instance, Brown and Bohn, *Christianity, Patriarchy, and Abuse.*

46. Peter Abélard, "Exposition of the Epistle to the Romans" (an excerpt from the second book). Fairweather, *Scholastic Miscellany*, 276–87, 282–83.

47. Cynthia L. Rigby, "Prodigal Cross," *Presbyterian Outlook*, March 31, 2014.

48. Calvin, *Institutes* II.16.2.

49. Dorothee Sölle, *Christ the Representative: An Essay in Theology after the "Death of God"* (Alva, Scotland: SCM Press, 1967).

50. Fairweather, *Scholastic Miscellany*, 278.

51. John 4:1-42 and Luke 15:11-42.

52. Matt 27:46.

53. Calvin, *Institutes* II.16.5.

54. This story references Matt 28. Elisabeth Schüssler Fiorenza discusses this point at some length in *Jesus: Miriam's Son, Sophia's Prophet* (New York: Continuum, 1994).

55. See Gustaf Aulén's *Christus Victor*. In this book, Aulén surveys the three major atonement theories, showing the weaknesses of the Anselmian and Abélardian approaches in favor of Christus Victor, which he argues is the "classic view," i.e., the view that is most consistent with the belief of the early church. Gustaf Aulén, *Christus Victor: An Historical Study of the Three Main Types of the Idea of Atonement*, trans. A.G. Herbert (Eugene, OR: Wipf and Stock, 2003).

56. See C. S. Lewis's *The Chronicles of Narnia*, 7 vols. (New York: Collier Books, 1950). In these mythological children's books, Aslan (the Christ figure) wages war with the White Witch (who represents Satan, the forces of darkness).

57. Irenaeus, "Against Heresies," *Apostolic Fathers with Justin Martyr and Irenaeus*, ed. Alexander Roberts and James Donaldson, vol. XXI, Anti-Nicene Fathers (Peabody, MA: Hendrickson, 1999), 548–50.

58. Thomas Finger, "Christus Victor and the Creeds: Some Historical Considerations," *Mennonite Quarterly Review* 72 (January 1998): 43.

59. Irenaeus, "Against Heresies," XXI.3.

60. Irenaeus, "Against Heresies," XXI.3.

61. "A Mighty Fortress Is Our God."

62. Gustavo Gutiérrez, *A Theology of Liberation* (Maryknoll, NY: Orbis, 1973), 172.

63. Gutierrez, *Theology of Liberation*, 172, 176.

64. Aulen, *Christus Victor*, 9–10.

65. *The United Methodist Hymnal* (Nashville: United Methodist Publishing House, 1989), 575.

66. Leanne Van Dyk, "Do Theories of Atonement Foster Abuse?" *Perspectives* 12 (1997): 13.

67. Thomas Torrance, "The Priesthood of Christ," unpublished manuscript cited by George Hunsinger in "The Politics of the Nonviolent God: Reflections on René Girard and Karl Barth," *Scottish Journal of Theology* 51, no 1 (1998), 75.

68. John 15.

69. Col 3:3.

70. Barth, *CD* II.1, *passim*.

71. John 15:15.

72. Barth, *CD* IV/1, §6.4, 234.

73. 1 Cor 12.

74. Phil 2.

75. Heb 12:1.

76. Rom 12:1.

7. Where Is Our Home?

1. John 3:8.

2. See Eph 5.

3. I recognize that this imagery, which is biblical, has been used to promote heterosexist paradigms. I would like to propose that it be used parabolically instead of paradigmatically (instead of avoided altogether) because it is a powerful analogy for the essential role of the church in relation to the work of God—the church is the partner of Christ who acknowledges its value and purpose.

4. "*Cheers* Intro," video file, 1:02, YouTube, posted by Tiktook, August 9, 2009, https://www.youtube.com/watch?v=7KtAgAMzaeg.

5. "Here Is the Church," video file, 0:34, YouTube, posted by MsRymetime, April 23, 2011, https://www.youtube.com/watch?v=-H3E33o4URc.

6. "If You Build It, They Will Come—*Field of Dreams* (1989)," YouTube, posted by Ruben Lopez, September 24, 2013, https://www.youtube.com/watch?v=o3c_pJ_CLJQ.

7. I'm thinking, for example, of lifechurch.tv and some of the churches that link to secondlife.com.

8. For example, the "1001 New Worshipping Communities" of the Presbyterian Church USA.

9. Calvin, *Institutes* IV.16.7.

10. Gustavo Gutiérrez, *A Theology of Liberation*, 264–65. For Gutiérrez's suggested corrective, see his "Denunciation and Annunciation" in the same text, 265–72.

11. For a discussion of how we may live our Christian lives in both of these two contexts, see Cynthia L. Rigby, "The Christian Life," in *Cambridge Companion to Reformed Theology*, ed. Paul T. Nimmo and David A. S. Fergusson (New York: Cambridge University Press, 2016).

12. History.com staff, Alexander Topence, "Alexander Topence, Pioneer (1923)," *A Treasury of Railroad Folklore: The Stories, Tall Tales, Traditions, Ballads, and Songs of the American Railroad Man*, Benjamin Albert Botkin (New York: Crown, 1953).

13. United Nations News Service, "Deputy UN Chief Calls for Urgent Action to Tackle Global Sanitation Crisis," UN News Centre, last modified March 21, 2013, http://www.un.org/apps/news/story.asp?NewsID=44452#.WkbqwTdG3IV.

14. See Deanna A. Thompson's book *The Virtual Body of Christ in a Suffering World* (Nashville: Abingdon, 2016).

15. A lively conversation is happening these days about the nature of ecclesiology in the face of a changing world. This conversation encompasses a range of voices, from evangelical to mainline, and includes many approaches. Some focus on technical fixes for the institutional church and its congregations, such as Lyle Schaller (Terry Mattingly, "Lyle Schaller, the Church Doctor in Changing Times," uExpress, last modified April 1, 2015, http://www.uexpress.com/on-religion/2015/4/1/lyle-schaller-the-church-doctor-in). Others consider the possibility of risking institutional death in favor of a search for the church's true vocation: see Michael Jinkins, *The Church Faces Death: Ecclesiology in a Post-Modern Context* (Oxford: Oxford University Press, 1999).

16. For an article on cleaning while conferencing, see Katie Hafner, "The Modern Meeting: Call In, Turn Off, Tune Out," *The New York Times*, December 4, 2015, Business Day, https://www.nytimes.com/2015/12/06/business/the-modern-meeting-call-in-turn-off-tune-out.html?_r=0. For a funny video illustrating how non-relational conference calls can be viewed, see: Fast Company staff, "This Hilarious Video Shows Why Conference Calls Are So, So Terrible," Fast Company, last modified February 3, 2014, https://www.fastcompany.com/3025791/this-hilarious-video-shows-why-conference-calls-are-so-so-terrible.

17. For a thoughtful discussion on this question, see Tim Hutchings, *Creating Church Online: Ritual, Community and New Media* (New York: Routledge, 2017).

18. For more on the resurrection, the ascension, and Jesus's risen body, see ch. 9.

19. Irenaeus put these words of Adam to Eve in the mouth of Jesus Christ to us.

20. John Koblin, "How Much Do We Love TV? Let Us Count the Ways," *The New York Times*, June 30, 2016, Media, https://www.nytimes.com/2016/07/01/business/media/nielsen-survey-media-viewing.html.

21. Americans, on average, give between 2 and 3 percent of their income to charity (see Urban Institute, "Charitable Giving in America: Some Facts and Figures," National Center for Charitable Statistics, http://nccs.urban.org/data-statistics/charitable-giving-america-some-facts-and-figures).

22. For a discussion on how we might recognize and reach out to skeptics among us, see: Cynthia L. Rigby, "Capacious Community: Recognizing Skeptics as Disciples" in *Essays on the New Worshiping Communities Movement*, ed. Mark D. Hinds (Louisville: Witherspoon Press, 2018).

23. Matt 15:21-8.

24. The baptism of infants highlights the fact that we are claimed by God through no choice of our own, before we even knew our name. Believers' baptism—generally, the baptism of older children, teenagers, or adults–includes a moment when the person being baptized offers a statement of faith. This way of baptizing highlights how important it is for us to subjectively appropriate the objective reality of grace.

25. The "marks" were added at Constantinople in 381.

26. Calvin, *Institutes* IV.1.8.

27. Luther, Calvin, and later Wesley all used the apostolic formula when they baptized infants or adults.

28. 2 Cor 5:17.

29. *Benefits* is a term Calvin frequently uses that is almost synonymous to "blessings."

30. Rom 12:2 KJV.

31. This is an allusion to the first of Calvin's three freedoms of the Christian. It is: "we are free from the law to obey it." The other two are: "we are free from things that don't matter" and "we are free to use God's gifts for God's purposes" (see *Institutes* III.19.1).

32. For further reflection of how God's law helps us imagine what God desires for our communal life, see Paul Louis Lehmann, *The Decalogue and a Human Future: The Meaning of the Commandments for Making and Keeping Human Life Human* (Grand Rapids: Eerdmans, 1995).

33. Barth talks about the Spirit "gathering," "building up," and "sending forth" the people of God in relation to Jesus Christ's work as priest, victor, and prophet in volumes IV/1–IV/3 of his *Church Dogmatics.* His thinking has formed the way I think about the work of the Holy Spirit in the church and is reflected in these chapters.

34. "Were You There," *Glory to God*, 228.

35. Ps 145:5 NRSV.

36. This is Calvin's metaphor.

37. 2 Cor 5:17.

38. The Lord's Prayer, too, also links God's forgiveness of us inextricably to our forgiveness of one another: "forgive us our debts, as we also have forgiven our debtors" it says (Matt 6:12 NRSV).

39. Matt 18:21-35.

40. Christians from *apophatic* traditions, which emphasize wordless approaches to worship, would likely choose another style of worship.

41. For more on this, see ch. 2.

42. Rom 8:14-17.

43. Calvin, *Institutes* III.20.1.

44. Rom 8:26.

45. John 13:14.

46. From the "Great Prayer of Thanksgiving" in the *Book of Common Worship* (Louisville: Westminster John Knox, 1993), 126.

47. World Food Programme, "Zero Hunger," wpf.org, http://www1.wfp.org/zero-hunger.

48. "The table of Holy Communion is Christ's table, not the table of The United Methodist Church or of the local congregation. The table is open to anyone who seeks to respond to Christ's love and to lead a new life of peace and love, as the invitation to the table says." See United Methodist Church, "FAQs: Communion," http://www.umc.org/what-we-believe/faqs-communion.

49. Luke 22:19.

50. These are words often said in the post-Communion prayer in Presbyterian churches.

51. Matt 25:21.

52. John 15:11.

53. Micah 6:8.

54. Karl Barth, *Karl Barth: Theologian of Freedom*, ed. Clifford Green (Minneapolis: Fortress, 1993), 234.

55. Matt 28:18-20 KJV.

8. What Does It Mean to Be God's Children?

1. Karl Barth, *Evangelical Theology: An Introduction* (Grand Rapids: Eerdmans, 1992), 83.

2. Barth, *Evangelical Theology*, 83.

3. Kathryn Tanner, *Jesus, Humanity, and the Trinity* (Minneapolis: Fortress, 2001), xiii.

4. Karl Barth, *Learning Jesus Christ through the Heidelberg Catechism* (Grand Rapids: Eerdmans, 1964), 104.

5. *The Heidelberg Catechism for Today*, trans. Shirley Guthrie (Richmond, VA: John Knox Press, 1964), 104.

6. Barth, *CD* IV/2, §64.1, 8.

7. Luke 15.

8. The preceding three paragraphs are adapted from Cynthia L. Rigby, "The Changing (Cyber)Face of Christian Community," in *Insights: The Faculty Journal of Austin Presbyterian Theological Seminary* 128, no. 2 (Spring 2013): 34–39.

9. Maybe because I was baptized, when I was fifteen, in the Babylon Town Pool in Babylon, NY!

10. John 3:4-10 NRSV.

11. John 3:6 NRSV.

12. As we sing in "Spirit of the Living God."

13. See Joel Osteen, *Your Best Life Now: 7 Steps to Living at Your Full Potential* (New York: Time Warner, 2004).

14. See John 3.

15. Søren Kierkegaard, "C: The possibility," 102–5.

16. Calvin, *Institutes* III.2.7.

17. Barth, *CD* III/4, 245–46.

18. Phil 2:12.

19. Col 3:3.

20. Luke 15:31.

21. John 3:16.

22. "When I Survey the Wondrous Cross," *Glory to God*, 223.

23. Ruth 1:16.

24. Attributed to evangelist Dwight Lyman Moody (1837–1899).

25. Rom 12:1.

26. Allusion to hymn, "Spirit of the Living God," cited earlier.

27. Ruth 1:4-14.

28. John 3:5.

29. Rom 8.

30. Rom 12:1 NRSV.

31. Rom 12:2.

32. Rom 12:2.

33. Barth, *CD* IV/1, §59.1, 234.

34. What Would Jesus Do?

35. Charles Sheldon, *In His Steps*, complete authorized ed. (New York: Grossett and Dunlap, 1935).

36. Although I would appreciate the opportunity to make such a case!

37. Dietrich Bonhoeffer, *The Cost of Discipleship* (New York: Touchstone, 1959).

38. This parable of Jesus can be found in Luke 15:11-32. Greenway, *A Reasonable Faith*, 129–32. William Greenway is both my spouse and my colleague, and I have heard him develop this interpretation of the parable over the course of many years. Bill's interpretation has profoundly affected the way I think about what it means to participate in grace, and how our participation in grace shapes the way we relate both to God and to one another.

39. Old Testament inheritance law indicates that the eldest son is entitled to a double portion of the estate upon his father's death, and that no son was entitled to any property prior. This is the dominant opinion among biblical scholars. Others argue differently. Richard H. Hiers looks carefully at various arguments in "Transfer of

Property by Inheritance and Bequest in Biblical Law and Tradition," *Journal of Law and Religion* 10, no. 1 (1993): 142–47, esp 146.

40. This language differentiating between the two "orders" comes from William Greenway (unpublished conversations).

41. This is how Luther is commonly paraphrased. In context he says: "God does not save those who are only imaginary sinners. Be a sinner, and let your sins be strong (sin boldly), but let your trust in Christ be stronger, and rejoice in Christ who is the victor over sin, death, and the world." Johann Georg Walsh, ed., *Dr. Martin Luther's Saemmtliche Schriften* (St. Louis: Concordia Publishing House, 1826), 15: cols. 2585–90; Letter 99, Paragraph 13.

42. This cannot mean that heinous sins are whisked away and forgotten. On the contrary, the cycle of confession, repentance, and restoration facilitates the remediation of injustices by insisting that abusive behaviors be named and changed and by creating a context conducive to the offering and receipt of remunerations that might contribute to the mending.

43. It is actually more true to the understanding of Karl Barth.

44. 1 Cor 5:21 NRSV.

45. Rigby, "Mary and the Artistry," 145–58.

46. This exchange between Jesus and a rich man may be found in the Gospel of Mark 10:17-31.

47. Phil 4:13

48. Luke 1:38.

49. Luke 1:46-55.

50. Eph 3:20.

51. Matt 25:31-46. I am profoundly influenced, in my interpretation of this parable, by William Greenway (See *A Reasonable Faith,* 151–52).

52. See John 21.

53. This is Calvin's third freedom of the Christian. *Institutes* III.19.8.

54. Bruce L. McCormack and Kimlyn J. Bender, eds., *Theology as Conversation: The Significance of Dialogue in Historical and Contemporary Theology; A Festschrift for Daniel Migliore* (Grand Rapids: Eerdmans, 2009), 105. The Barth quote within the passage is *CD* III/4, §55.3, 552.

55. Phil 1:9.

56. Gustavo Gutiérrez, "Remembering the Poor: An Interview with Gustavo Gutiérrez," by Daniel Hartnett, *America: The Jesuit Review*, February 3, 2003. https://www.americamagazine.org/issue/420/article/remembering-poor-interview-gustavo-gutierrez.

9. Where Are We Headed?

1. Phil 1:6.

2. Rom 8:22.

3. Even, at times and for some people, by way of the experience of losing hope.

4. Green, *Karl Barth*, 234.

5. See Isa 43:16-21.

6. These are comments made by Eric Weiner, the None with whom we were in conversation in the introduction, in "Americans Undecided About God?"

7. Phil 4:8 NRSV.

8. Karl Barth, "Look Up to Him!" in *Deliverance to the Captives* (Eugene, OR: Wipf and Stock, 2010), 43–50.

9. Isa 52:7 NAS. I have made the tense plural for the sake of inclusivity.

10. Jer 29:11.

11. Tim LaHaye and Jerry B. Jenkins, *Left Behind: A Novel of the Earth's Last Days* (Wheaton, IL: Tyndale House, 1995).

12. This promise is made again and again in Scripture. See, for example, Deut 31:8, Heb 13:5, and Matt 28:16-28.

13. See 1 Cor 15.

14. See John 14.

15. For more on this subject, see Cynthia Rigby, "Easter Focus: The Significance of the Resurrection," *Presbyterian Outlook* (March 21, 2005), http://pres-outlook.org/2005/03/easter-focus-the-significance-of-the-resurrection/; and Cynthia Rigby, "Chains Fall Off: The Resurrection of the Body and Our Healing from Shame," in

Shame, the Church and the Regulation of Female Sexuality, by Miryam Clough (New York: Routledge, 2017), 40–79.

16. Rom 8.

17. John 1:14.

18. Luke 4.

19. Tony Campolo, *It's Friday but Sunday's Comin'* (Nashville: Thomas Nelson, 1984).

20. Dante Alighieri, *The Divine Comedy*, vol. II: P*urgatory,* trans. Henry Wadsworth Longfellow (Digireads, 2017).

21. Aracely de Rocchietti, "Women and the People of God," *Women and the People of God,* ed. Elsa Tamez (Maryknoll, NY: Orbis, 1989), 96–117, 96.

22. Jürgen Moltmann, *Crucified God: The Cross of Christ as the Foundation and Criticism of Christian Theology* (Minneapolis: Fortress, 1974).

23. See Acts 1:1-11.

24. Gen 3:12.

25. John 14:1-3 NRSV.

26. Eph 5:27 NIV.

27. John 17:20-24 NRSV.

28. Luke 24:49.

29. Rom 7:19 NRSV. I have made Paul's words plural.

30. I am drawing from imagery, in this paragraph, from Isa 65:17-25.

31. Ps 139.

32. Ps 8:3-5.

33. Rev 21:6-8 NRSV.

34. I first told this story here: Cynthia L. Rigby, "Christianity and Culture: This Hour of Fire," *Insights: The Faculty Journal of Austin Presbyterian Theological Seminary*, 132, no. 2 (Spring 2017): 37–40. Used by permission.

10. What Are We Called to Do?

1. Barth, "Unto You Is Born This Day a Savior," *Deliverance to the Captives* (New York: Harper, 1961), 20–27, 25.

2. Barth, "Unto You Is Born," 25, citing Swiss novelist Jeremias Gotthelf (1797–1854); specific source unknown.

3. This is an allusion to Heb 12:1.

4. See, for example, suggestions made at https://www.randomactsofkindness.org/kindness-ideas.

5. Exod 4:10, Luke 1:26-33, Matt 4:18-22, and Luke 8:1-3.

6. See Phil 4:13.

7. See Rom 12:1-2.

8. See 2 Cor 5.

9. "The Rain, Rain, Rain Came Down, Down, Down," composed by Robert B. Sherman. Featured in "Winnie the Pooh and the Blustery Day," Walt Disney Productions (1968).

10. Eph 3:20.

11. From Calvin's Sermon #10 on 1 Corinthians, as quoted by William J. Bouwsma in *John Calvin: A Sixteenth Century Portrait* (New York: Oxford University Press, 1988), 134–35.

12. From Calvin's Commentary on Ps 104:31, as quoted by Bouwsma, *John Calvin*, 135.

13. Calvin, *Institutes* I.13.17, quoting Gregory of Nazianzus, *On Holy Baptism,* oration XL.41.

14. *Institutes* I.13.17.

15. I imagine, rather, that Calvin's stack includes a Bible, a copy of Augustine's *Confessions,* and the latest review of the imaginative theological statements developed at the great ecumenical councils (including, for example, the Chalcedonian Statement of 451, which invites us into full participation in God precisely by way of its creative insistence that Jesus Christ is *both* "fully human and fully divine").

16. Guillaume Farel, who insisted he come to Geneva.

17. For this reason, a large monument to Calvin and other religious figures who upheld religious liberties is the centerpiece of the town park in Geneva. To see a picture of this monument, go to: www.sacred-destinations.com/switzerland/geneva-reformation-monument.htm. For more on the complexities of Calvin's relationship to modern conceptions of religious freedom, see the Center for Public Justice's review of William Stevenson's *Sovereign Grace* at http://www.cpjustice.org/stories/.

18. It must be noted, at this point, that Calvin's support of the execution of Servetus was simply wrong. For a balanced discussion of this, including mention of Calvin's failed attempt to minimize Servetus's suffering, see Marilynne Robinson's "Marguerite de Navarre" in *The Death of Adam* (New York: Picador, 1998), 174–206, especially pp. 200–206.

19. See Luther D. Ivory, *The Rhythm of Discipleship* (Nashville: Geneva Press, 2008), ch. 5.

20. *Institutes* II.3.13.

21. John 4.

22. John 3.

23. Matt 14:13-21; Mark 6:30-42; Luke 9:12-17; John 6:1-14.

24. John 4:29.

25. John 4:42.

26. John 3.

27. John 7:45.

28. Mark 14:1-9.

29. Mark 6:30-44.

30. John 4:29.

31. See 4:29 and 4:39-42.

32. John 4:29b.

33. John 4:42.

34. See John 14.

35. A version of this story appears in my essay, "Evil and the Principalities: Disarming the Demonic," in *Life Amid the Principalities: Identifying, Understanding, and Engaging Created, Fallen, and Disarmed Powers Today* (Pro Ecclesia), ed. Michael Root and James J. Buckley (Eugene, OR: Cascade, 2016), 51–67.

36.This paragraph references Gen 1–2, Gen 15:5, 2 Kings 4:8-17, Luke 1:35, Mark 2:13-17, and Matt 27:32-50.

37. This is a paraphrase in an unpublished conversation I had with Dr. Boesak when he visited Austin Presbyterian Theological Seminary on October 1, 2012.

38. This comment of Russell's is unpublished, as far as I know. I heard Russell say it publicly at a conference held in Santa Fe, New Mexico, in 1996.

39. I reflect on the ways the church might imagine "deep thinking about God, made accessible enough that the world can see it" in "Knowing Our Limits and Laughing with Joy: Theology in Service to the Church Invisible," in *Theology in Service to the Church: Global and Ecumenical Perspectives*, ed. Allan Hugh Cole Jr. (Eugene, OR: Cascade Books, 2014).

40. Barth, *CD* IV/2, 244.

41. Barth, *CD* IV/2, 245.

42. Ps 46:10 NRSV.

43. Rom 12:2 KJV.

Reflection and Discussion Questions

Introduction: Transforming Theology

1. What do you think of when you think of *theology*? Do you agree with the author that every person who holds faith is a theologian? What does this mean to you?

2. People of faith are often accused, these days, of acting like know-it-alls. Do you agree that there is a problem with this? How is it possible to speak about God in ways that are both confident (e.g., about God's love for the world) and humble (i.e., honoring the divine mystery)?

3. Where, in your life, do you create "spaces" for theological reflection/thinking about God?

Chapter One: How Can We Speak of God? The Doctrine of Revelation

1. There is an exercise in the chapter that asks you to reflect on how you react and relate to mystery, connecting possible reactions to characters in movies. Was this exercise helpful, and why or why not?

2. What is the value of thinking of language for God as analogical as opposed to univocal or equivocal?

3. What do you think of the idea that theology is in the business of saying "something about everything"? Do you agree that this is what people want and need to hear?

4. What is the relationship between general and special revelation? Do you think it is important to distinguish between them? Why or why not?

Chapter Two: Where Do We Find the Right Words to Say? The Doctrine of Scripture

1. Complete the authority exercise that is included in the chapter. What understandings of authority came into play as you ranked the items on the list? Do you understand the Bible to be authoritative, and if so, in what sense?

2. John Wesley understood tradition, experience, and reason—along with Scripture—to come into play as we seek to find and form our words about God. Does this resonate with your own discerning processes? In what sense, if at all, do you think the Bible serves as the "norming norm" of all other sources about God?

3. Reflect on why Calvin used the analogy of "spectacles" for the Bible. What other analogies might be helpful?

Chapter Three: Where Does God Meet Us? The Doctrine of the Incarnation

1. How does each of the Gospel writers begin the story of Jesus differently, and how do where they begin shape their understanding of who Jesus is?

2. At the Council of Nicea in 325, what did our forebears decide about who Jesus Christ is in relation to the Father? Why does the *homoousion* matter to so many people who hold faith?

3. Why did our forebears (i.e., at Chalcedon in 451) think that to confess Jesus Christ as "fully human and fully divine" is "for our sake and the sake of our salvation"? How does *who* Jesus is save us?

4. What does the doctrine of the incarnation teach us about who God is? What does it teach us about who we are in relationship to God?

Chapter Four: In What Ways Does God Claim Us? The Doctrine of the Trinity

1. How do you experience God as *one*, and what is your experience of God as each of the three persons? Do you, in your spirituality, resonate more with one of the three persons of the Trinity than with the other two?

2. What are the pluses and minuses of using the traditional language of "Father, Son, and Holy Spirit" for God? Why might we want to supplement that language with more expansive language for God, such as maternal language?

3. What is the *filioque* debate all about, and why does it matter? Do you think that believing the Holy Spirit proceeds from the Father *and the Son* compromises on the full status of the Holy Spirit as equally God? What are the strengths and weaknesses of thinking of the Spirit as the "bond of love" between the Father (Lover) and Son (the Beloved), as Saint Augustine suggests?

4. What difference does it make to our lives of faith that we hold the "three-ness" of God in tension with the "oneness" and vice versa? Discuss the concept of *perichoresis*–is it helpful to you to think that God "dances" with Godself, and we with God, and we with one another in the context of Christian community?

Chapter Five: Who Did God Create Us to Be, and What Went Wrong? The Doctrine of Creation

1. If creation was made all good, and by a good God, where did evil come from? Why did Saint Augustine define evil as "the absence of good"? Why do some contemporary theologians (such as James Cone) question this definition?

2. What are thought to be the benefits of believing God created us *ex nihilo* (out of nothing)? Why do some theologians take issue with the idea?

3. Do you think human sinfulness is an aberration, meaning not true to who God made us to be? Or are we sinners, from our core, right from the start? Make a biblical/theological case for your position.

Chapter Six: Who Is God Making Us Into? The Doctrines of Sin and Salvation

1. How does Jesus save us, exactly? How did you answer that question before you read this chapter, and what questions about your understanding (if any) did the chapter provoke?

2. What is "salvation," exactly? What is it that Jesus saves us *from* and *for*? In what sense is salvation grounded in history, as James Evans insists?

3. Discuss the three main approaches to the atonement: Anselm's view (substitutionary atonement), Abélard's view (moral exemplar theory), and *christus victor*. What are the strengths and weaknesses of each?

4. What do you think of this idea of centering our understanding of salvation around the whole person and story of Jesus Christ, rather than solely around his death on the cross? What would we gain from doing that in our lives of faith? What would we lose?

Chapter Seven: Where Is Our Home? The Doctrine of the Church

1. How well does the metaphor of "home" work for understanding the church? What other metaphors might we use for understanding the blessing of the church?

2. How are the internet, social media, and other technologies changing the way we think about community? Can an avatar take Communion? Why or why not? What is the importance of flesh and blood bodies to life in community?

3. What is the relationship between the church visible and the church invisible (Calvin), between the *ekklesia* and the *koinonia* (Gutiérrez)?

4. The author lists a number of elements that "make" church in the second half of the chapter. What are they, and with which do you most resonate? What would you add?

Chapter Eight: What Does It Mean to Be God's Children? The Doctrine of the Christian Life

1. "How is it with your heart?" Reflect on this question and discuss with wise people whom you trust. Why is it important that every theologian consider this question, according to the chapter?

2. Why is it often challenging to hold faith?

3. According to the chapter, what is the *risk* of holding faith, jumping into the pool of grace? What is the *cost* of jumping in? What is the *promise* as we surface the water? And what does it look like to *practice* faith, to swim in the pool alongside others?

Chapter Nine: Where Are We Headed? The Doctrine of Christian Hope

1. What are your greatest hopes? What are your greatest fears? How is the doctrine of Christian hope related to these?

2. How is the cross a symbol of Christian hope?

3. What do the resurrection and the ascension lead us to hope for in the future but also in our present, day-to-day lives as people of faith?

4. How might exercising imagination help us share Christian hope with the world? What are the risks that come with being imaginative? How do we go about imagining what God desires rather than reducing Christian hope to our own wishful thinking?

Chapter Ten: What Are We Called to Do? The Doctrine of Christian Vocation

1. What does Karl Barth mean when he says we should not miss "the hour of fire" that is "right here and now"? What is the fire, and what are we in danger of missing?

2. How exactly do we go about imagining and participating in the music of God's Kingdom in such a way that we facilitate its coming to "earth as it is in heaven"? Is this, even, what we are called to do? Or should we leave this work up to God and focus, instead, on being patient? Should people who hold faith be patient or impatient in relation to the coming of God's Kingdom?

3. How do we know what it is God wants us to do exactly? Is Allan Boesak right that we always have to be ready, or we may miss opportunities that will affect the way the world looks tomorrow?

4. How does the ongoing study of theology contribute to the "renewal of our minds," readying us to do "the good, acceptable, and perfect will of God"? What are you taking away from this book that will support you in holding faith as you live, act, and shape this world God so loves?

Scripture Index

Old Testament

Genesis

Exodus

Numbers

Deuteronomy

Judges

Ruth

1 Samuel

2 Samuel

1 Kings

2 Kings

Job

Psalms

Proverbs

Ecclesiastes

Song of Solomon

Isaiah

Jeremiah

Daniel

Amos

Jonah

Micah

Malachi

New Testament

Matthew

Mark

Luke

John

Acts

Romans

Names and Topics Index

bold indicates definitions; *italics* indicates notes

CPSIA information can be obtained
at www.ICGtesting.com
Printed in the USA
LVHW02s1556140418
573434LV00002B/2/P

9 781426 758140